To Mike Barden at Intuit, Inc.
for his help, encouragement, and kind words

Contents At A Glance

Contents

Part III   Tracking Your Investments

Part V   Working with Quicken Data

Part VI   Saving Money and Achieving Your Goals

Acknowledgments

This book, like any other, is the end product of a lot of imagination and hard work by many people. I'd like to take a moment to thank the people who were involved with the creation of this book.

First, thanks to Joanne Cuthbertson at Osborne/McGraw-Hill, for developing the concept of this book way back when we did the first *Official Guide for Quicken*. Although Joanne has moved on to other work, she should be proud of the books in the Quicken Press series.

Next, thanks to Megg Bonar at Osborne/McGraw-Hill. Megg and I finally got a chance to work together, and I hope I didn't disappoint her—or make her too crazy with my flashpoint e-mail and voicemail messages. She did a great job keeping me on track, without too much nagging, even when we were getting close to the final push. (Now when are you going to come camping out at the Flying M Ranch North Forty?)

Next, many thanks to the folks at Intuit, starting with Mike Barden. Mike made sure I had everything I needed to write the book and then made sure everything I wrote was correct. I'd also like to thank the Quicken 2001 development team for somehow managing to improve Quicken yet again, and to the Quicken 2001 beta support team for giving me quick answers to quick questions when I had them.

More thanks go to the production and editorial folks at Osborne/McGraw-Hill, including Jenn Tust, the project editor; Nancy Crumpton, the copy editor; and Maureen Forys, who laid out pages and painstakingly positioned all those callouts and callout lines.

Another thanks to Cindy Wathen, the editorial assistant who managed the FedEx packages and e-mails between me, Megg, Mike, and Jenn. Cindy seemed to remain calm throughout the process, although I never once got a chance to speak to her on the phone.

Finally, a huge thanks to Jeremy Judson at Osborne/McGraw-Hill for suggesting me for the Quicken Press projects. The last two years were great; this year will be even better! (And I'm still waiting for you to come out here and go horseback riding with me.)

The last thanks goes to Mike (as usual) for putting up with my wild mood swings and deadline frenzies while working on this project. After 30 books, he knows the drill as well as I do.

Introduction

Choosing Quicken to organize your finances was a great decision. Quicken has all the tools you need to manage your personal finances. Its well-designed, intuitive interface makes it easy to use. And its online and automation features make entering transactions and paying bills a snap. But if that isn't enough, Quicken also offers features that can help you learn more about financial opportunities that can save you time and money—two things there never seems to be enough of.

Choosing this book to learn Quicken was also a good decision. As the Official Guide, it has Intuit's "seal of approval"—which means that Intuit, the developer of Quicken, was involved throughout the book's planning, writing, and production stages. The book was even reviewed for accuracy by the folks at Intuit's Technical Support Department.

This Introduction tells you a little about the book and a little about me—so you know what to expect in the chapters to come.

About This Book

Throughout this book, I tell you how to get the most out of Quicken. I start by explaining the basics—the common, everyday tasks that you need to know just to use the program. Then I go beyond the basics to show you how to use Quicken to save time, save money, and make smart financial decisions. Along the way, I show you all of Quicken's features, including a bunch that you probably didn't even know existed. You'll find yourself using Quicken far more than you ever dreamed you would.

Every book is based on certain assumptions, presents information in a certain order, and uses certain conventions to communicate information. This book is no different. Knowing the book's assumptions, organization, and conventions can help you understand how to use it as a learning tool.

Assumptions

In writing this book, I had to make a few assumptions about your knowledge of your computer, Windows, Quicken, and financial management. These assumptions give me a starting point, making it possible for me to skip over the things that I assume you already know.

What You Should Know About Your Computer and Windows

To use this book (or Quicken 2001, for that matter), you should have a general understanding of how to use your computer and Windows. You don't need to be an expert. As you'll see, Quicken uses many standard and intuitive interface elements, making it easy to use—even if you're a complete computer novice.

At a bare minimum, you should know how to turn your computer on and off and how to use your mouse. You should also know how to perform basic Windows tasks, such as opening and exiting programs, using menus and dialog boxes, and entering and editing text.

If you're not sure how to do these things, check the manual that came with your computer or try working through the Windows Tour. These two resources can provide all the information you need to get started.

What You Should Know About Quicken and Financial Management

You don't need to know much about either Quicken or financial management to get the most out of this book: I assume that both are new to you.

This doesn't mean that this book is just for raw beginners. I provide plenty of useful information for seasoned Quicken users—especially those of you who have used previous versions of Quicken—and for people who have been managing their finances with other tools, such as other software (welcome to Quicken!) or pencil and paper (welcome to the new millennium!).

Because I assume that all this is new to you, I make a special effort to explain Quicken procedures, as well as the financial concepts and terms on which they depend. New concepts and terms first appear in italic type. By understanding these things, not only can you better understand how to use Quicken, but you can also communicate more effectively with finance professionals such as bankers, stock brokers, and financial advisors.

Organization

This book is logically organized into six parts, each with at least two chapters. It starts with the most basic concepts and procedures, most of which involve specific

Quicken tasks, and then works its way up to more advanced topics, many of which are based on finance-related concepts that Quicken makes easy to master.

I want to stress one point here: It is not necessary to read this book from beginning to end. Skip around as desired. Although the book is organized for cover-to-cover reading, not all of the information may apply to you. For example, if you're not the least bit interested in investing, skip the chapters related to investing. It's as simple as that. When you're ready for the information that you have skipped, it'll be waiting for you.

Now here's a brief summary of the book's organization and contents.

Part I: Quicken Setup and Basics

This part of the book introduces Quicken's interface and features and helps you set up Quicken for managing your finances. It also provides the information you need to set up and test Quicken's online features. If you're brand-new to Quicken, I highly recommend reading at least the first two chapters in this part of the book.

Part I has three chapters:

- Chapter 1: Getting to Know Quicken
- Chapter 2: Setting Up Accounts and Categories
- Chapter 3: Going Online with Quicken and Quicken.com

Part II: Managing Your Bank and Credit Card Accounts

This part of the book is primarily how-to information about using Quicken to record financial transactions in bank and credit card accounts. One chapter concentrates on the basics, while the other chapter goes beyond the basics to discuss online features available within Quicken and on Quicken.com.

There are two chapters in Part II:

- Chapter 4: Recording Bank and Credit Card Transactions
- Chapter 5: Online Banking and Billing

Part III: Tracking Your Investments

This part of the book explains how you can use Quicken and Quicken.com to keep track of your investment portfolio and get information to help you make smart investment decisions. The first chapter covers the basics of Quicken's investment tracking features, while the other two chapters provide information about other tools within Quicken and on Quicken.com for entering investment transactions and researching investment opportunities.

There are three chapters in Part III:

- Chapter 6: Investment Tracking Basics
- Chapter 7: Tracking Investments Online
- Chapter 8: Maximizing Investment Returns

Part IV: Managing Your Household Finances

This part of the book concentrates on assets and liabilities, including your home, car, and related loans. It starts by explaining how you can track these items in Quicken, then goes on to explain how you can minimize expenses with research features on Quicken and Quicken.com.

There are two chapters in Part IV:

- Chapter 9: Monitoring Assets and Loans
- Chapter 10: Minimizing Home, Car, and Insurance Expenses

Part V: Working with Quicken Data

Once you've entered data into Quicken, you can use that information to manage and analyze your finances. That's what this part of the book is all about. It explains how to reconcile accounts and generate reports and graphs. But it starts with a useful topic for any Quicken user: automation.

There are three chapters in Part V:

- Chapter 11: Automating Your Quicken Transactions
- Chapter 12: Reconciling Accounts
- Chapter 13: Creating Reports and Graphs

Part VI: Saving Money and Achieving Your Goals

This part of the book helps you to save money by minimizing your income taxes and using Quicken's built-in and Web-based saving tools. This part also shows you how you can use Quicken to help achieve your goals through the use of Quicken's thorough and well thought-out planning features. Whether you want financial security in your retirement years or to save up for the down payment on a house or college education for your children, Quicken can help you.

Part VI has three chapters:

- Chapter 14: Minimizing Your Taxes with Quicken
- Chapter 15: Using Quicken to Plan for the Future
- Chapter 16: Saving Money with Quicken

Appendix

If 16 chapters of information aren't enough for you, there's more. The Appendix, Managing Quicken Files, explains how to back up, restore, and otherwise maintain Quicken files.

Conventions

All how-to books—especially computer books—have certain conventions for communicating information. The following sections outline the conventions I use throughout this book.

Menu Commands

Quicken, like most other Windows programs, makes commands accessible on the menu bar at the top of the application window. Throughout this book, I tell you which menu commands to choose to open a window or dialog box or to complete a task. I use the following format to indicate menu commands: Menu | Submenu (if applicable) | Command.

So, for example, if I wanted you to choose the One Step Update command under the Finance menu, I'd tell you to choose Finance | One Step Update. If I wanted you to choose the Balance My Checkbook command from the Banking Activities submenu under the Banking menu, I'd tell you to choose Banking | Banking Activities | Balance My Checkbook.

Keystrokes

Keystrokes are the keys you must press to complete a task. There are two kinds of keystrokes.

Keyboard Shortcuts   Keyboard shortcuts are combinations of keys you press to complete a task more quickly. For example, the shortcut for "clicking" a Cancel button may be to press the ESC key. When instructing you to press a key, I provide the name of the key in small caps, like this: ESC. If you must press two or more keys simultaneously, I separate them with a dash, like this: CTRL-P.

Literal Text   Literal text is text that you must type in exactly as it appears in the book. Although this book doesn't contain many instances of literal text, there are a few. I display literal text in bold type, like this: **Checking Acct**. If literal text includes a variable—text you must substitute when you type—I include the variable in bold italic type, like this: ***Payee Name.***

Icons

I use icons to indicate a wide variety of useful information.

Shortcut   *Like most other Windows programs, Quicken frequently offers more than one way to complete a task. The Shortcut icon identifies a method for completing a Quicken task more quickly than other methods.*

Tip   *A tip is a little something extra that you don't really need to know. Tips can help you get more out of Quicken when you're ready to go beyond the basics.*

Note   *A note is a relatively important piece of information that might help you better understand the way a Quicken feature works.*

Caution   *A caution is vitally important information that can protect you from data loss or other serious consequences. Don't skip the cautions!*

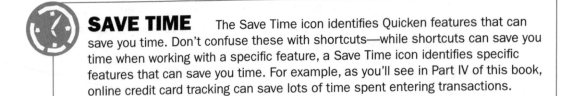

SAVE TIME   The Save Time icon identifies Quicken features that can save you time. Don't confuse these with shortcuts—while shortcuts can save you time when working with a specific feature, a Save Time icon identifies specific features that can save you time. For example, as you'll see in Part IV of this book, online credit card tracking can save lots of time spent entering transactions.

SAVE MONEY   The Save Money icon identifies Quicken features that can save you money.

GET SMARTER   The Get Smarter icon identifies Quicken features that can help you learn more about a concept. You'll find that the Get Smarter icons can help you make better, more informed decisions.

New in Quicken 2001　　In addition to interface changes, the folks at Intuit made changes to Quicken's feature set. The New in Quicken 2001 icon identifies many new features.

About the Author

Let me tell you a little bit about me.

I graduated from Hofstra University with a BBA in Accounting in—well, you don't really need to know *when*. I worked as an accountant, auditor, and financial analyst over the next eight years. Then I realized that I really didn't like what I was doing every day and took the necessary steps to change careers. I've written about 30 computer books since the change, many of which are about business and productivity software such as Word, Excel, and FileMaker Pro. In 1999, I wrote *Quicken 99: The Official Guide*, and I'm very pleased to be updating and revising it for each update of Quicken.

I use Quicken. I've been using it for years. I use it to manage five bank accounts and four credit card accounts, to track three mortgages, and to pay all my bills (online, of course). I also use its investment features to track my portfolio and research the companies in which I invest. While I don't use all Quicken features regularly, I've used them all at least once to save time, save money, make important financial decisions, or help me plan for my future.

Frankly, I can't imagine not using Quicken. And I'm glad to have the opportunity to show you why you should agree.

Quicken Setup and Basics

This part of the book introduces Quicken's interface and features. It begins by explaining how to install Quicken and showing you the elements of its user interface. It covers New User Setup, tells you all about Quicken's accounts and categories, and explains how you can modify the default setup to add your own accounts and categories. Finally, it tells you why you should be interested in online access and how you can set up your computer to access the Internet and Quicken.com. The chapters are:

Chapter 1: Getting to Know Quicken

Chapter 2: Setting Up Accounts and Categories

Chapter 3: Going Online with Quicken and Quicken.com

Getting to Know Quicken

In This Chapter:

- *An Overview of Quicken*

- *Installing Quicken*

- *Starting Quicken*

- *The Quicken Interface*

- *Customizing Quicken*

- *Onscreen Help*

If you're brand new to Quicken, get your relationship off to a good start by properly installing it and learning a little more about how you can interact with it.

In this chapter, I provide a brief overview of Quicken, explain how to install and start it, take you on a tour of its interface, and show you how to use its extensive onscreen Help features. Although the information I provide in this chapter is especially useful to new Quicken users, some of it also applies to users who are upgrading.

What Is Quicken?

On the surface, Quicken is a computerized checkbook. It enables you to balance your accounts and organize, manage, and generate reports for your finances. But as you explore Quicken, you'll learn that it's much more than just a computerized checkbook. It's a complete personal finance software package—a tool for taking control of your finances and making your money work harder for you.

What Quicken Can Help You Do

At the very least, Quicken can help you manage your bank and credit card accounts. You can enter transactions and have Quicken generate reports and graphs that show where your money went and how much is left.

Quicken can help you manage investment accounts. You can enter transactions and have Quicken tell you the market value of your investments. Quicken can also help you organize other data, such as the purchase price and current worth of your possessions, and vital information you may need in the event of an emergency.

With all your financial information stored in Quicken's data file, you can generate net worth reports to see where you stand today. You can also use a variety of financial planners to make financial decisions for the future. And Quicken's Deduction Finder helps you find deductible expenses for tax time.

With Quicken's online features, you can automate much of your data entry. Online banking enables you to keep track of bank account transactions and balances and to pay bills without writing checks or sticking on stamps. You can also explore a whole world of up-to-date information that you can use to shop for the best bank accounts, credit card accounts, loans, and insurance. You can read news and information about investment opportunities and advice offered by financial experts. You can get in touch with other Quicken users to see how they use Quicken to manage their money.

Now tell me, can the paper check register that came with your checks do all that?

Save Time, Save Money, Get Smarter

This book has an underlying theme: save time, save money, and make informed financial decisions. You'll see plenty of examples of how Quicken can do this throughout this book, but here are a few simple examples to whet your appetite:

 SAVE TIME   Entering transactions into registers can be tedious. But Quicken offers several features for speeding up this process, including memorized transactions, QuickFill, and the ability to download transactions from a financial institution or brokerage firm.

 SAVE MONEY   Many of the organizations you pay every month—credit card companies, banks, and utilities—charge a late fee when payment is received after the due date. Quicken's reminders help you remember when payments are due. Its online payments and scheduling features can work together to automatically pay bills when they are due. Making timely payments saves money.

 GET SMARTER   Buying a home is a big purchase decision that is based on many smaller decisions. How much can you afford to spend on a home? How much is your current home worth? What are the interest rates and other loan terms? What will your monthly payments be? Which loan is right for you? Quicken can help answer all of these questions by providing access to up-to-date information via QuickenLoans and a variety of planning tools, such as the Loan Planner.

These are just a few examples. Quicken is full of smart features like these. It takes the drudgery out of organizing and managing your finances and rewards you by helping you make the most of your money.

Quicken Basic Versus Quicken Deluxe

Intuit offers two versions of Quicken for managing personal finances: Basic and Deluxe.

Quicken Basic is an entry-level product designed for people who are new to personal finance software. As its name suggests, it includes basic features to track bank accounts, credit cards, investments, budgets, and loans. It also enables you to use online account access and payment, shop for insurance and mortgages, and download investment information for a brokerage account.

Quicken Deluxe is more robust. Designed for people who want to take a more active role in financial management, investments, and planning, it includes all the features in Quicken Basic plus the financial alerts feature, money-saving features for tax time and debt reduction, free access to investment information, and the Emergency Records Organizer and Home Inventory features.

Tip   *Intuit also offers a special version of Quicken for small business owners: Quicken Home & Business. This one program can handle all your personal and basic business financial needs.*

This book covers Quicken Deluxe. Although much of its information also applies to Quicken Basic, this book covers features that are not included in the Basic version. If you're a Quicken Basic user, consider upgrading to Quicken Deluxe so you can take advantage of the powerful features it has to offer.

Getting Started

Ready to get started? In this section, I explain how to install, open, and register Quicken. I also explain how to prepare a data file. If you're upgrading from a previous version of Quicken, be sure to consult the section "Upgrading from a Previous Version," later in this chapter.

Installing Quicken

Quicken uses a basic Windows setup program that should be familiar to you if you've installed other Windows programs.

First-Time Installation

Insert the Quicken 2001 CD into your CD-ROM drive. A dialog box that offers to install Quicken 2001 on your hard disk should appear. Click Yes to start the Quicken 2001 installer.

If this dialog box does not automatically appear, you can start the installer by following these steps:

1. Click the Start button on the Windows task bar.
2. Click Settings.
3. Click Control Panel.
4. Double-click Add/Remove Programs.
5. Click Install.
6. Click Next.
7. Click Finish.

The installer displays a series of dialog boxes with information and options for installing Quicken. Read the information in each dialog box carefully and click the Next or Yes button to continue. You'll be asked to agree to a license agreement, to choose a destination location for Quicken files, and to select a type and version of installation. (If you don't agree to the license agreement, the installation process will cancel.) If you're not sure what to select in any of these dialog boxes, use the default options—those are the same options used throughout this book.

Finally, the installer will display a Check Settings dialog box like the one shown next. If everything is correct, click Start Copying. Otherwise, you can click the Back button to return to and change previously selected options.

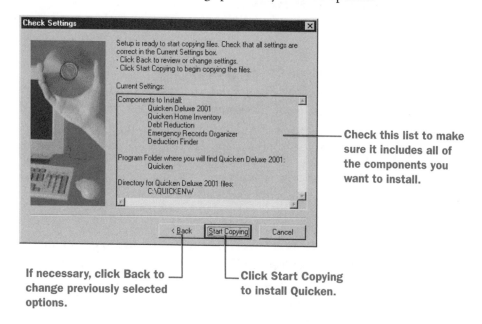

Check this list to make sure it includes all of the components you want to install.

If necessary, click Back to change previously selected options.

Click Start Copying to install Quicken.

Wait while Quicken copies files to your hard disk. When it's done, it may display dialog boxes with information about other products. Click Next when you've finished reading each of them. In the Setup Complete dialog box, select the Yes option button and click Finish to exit the installer and restart your computer.

Upgrading from a Previous Version

To upgrade from a previous version of Quicken, begin following the instructions in the previous section, "First-Time Installation." The message that appears when you insert the CD-ROM disk tells you that an older version of Quicken is already installed and offers to install the new version. Click Yes.

Later in the installation process, after choosing a location for Quicken, a dialog box may appear, asking if you want to uninstall the previous copy of Quicken. Click Yes. You will then be prompted to confirm that you want to remove the previous version of Quicken. Click Yes again. Only the Quicken program files are deleted; your data files remain intact and can be used with Quicken 2001.

Follow the prompts in the Uninstaller dialog boxes that appear to remove the previous version of Quicken from your computer. When the Uninstaller is finished, click OK. Then continue following the instructions in the section "First-Time Installation."

Running Quicken

You can run Quicken several different ways. Here are the two most common methods.

Opening a Quicken Shortcut

An Express installation of Quicken places one or two shortcuts on your Windows desktop, depending on the components of Quicken you have installed:

Quicken Deluxe 2001   Double-clicking this shortcut opens Quicken Deluxe.

QuickEntry 2001   Double-clicking this shortcut opens QuickEntry, a program that enables you to enter transactions into Quicken without opening Quicken itself. I tell you more about QuickEntry in Chapter 4.

Opening Quicken from the Task Bar

You can also use the Windows task bar's Start button to open Quicken and other Quicken components, such as QuickEntry (if installed). Choose Start | Programs | Quicken | Quicken Deluxe 2001 to open Quicken.

Registering Quicken

The first time you open Quicken after setting up a Quicken data file, the Product Registration dialog box appears. It tells you about the benefits of registering Quicken. Because some Quicken features will not work unless you register, it's a good idea to register right away. Click the Register button and follow the instructions that appear onscreen to register online or by telephone. It takes only a few minutes and doesn't cost a thing.

If you register online, part of the registration process prompts you to set up a Quicken.com member name. Doing so enables you to customize certain features of Quicken.com so they show your data. I tell you more about the features of Quicken.com in Chapter 3 and elsewhere throughout this book.

Preparing a Data File

Quicken stores all of your financial information in a Quicken data file. Before you can use Quicken, you must either create a data file with New User Setup or convert an existing data file for use with Quicken 2001.

New User Setup

If you're a brand-new Quicken user, the Quicken New User Setup dialog box, which is shown next, appears the first time you run Quicken. It offers a quick way to set up Quicken so you can get right to work. I explain how to use Quicken New User Setup in Chapter 2.

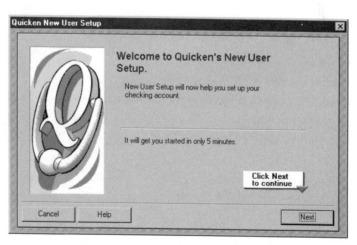

Converting Existing Data

If you upgraded from a previous version of Quicken, when you first start Quicken 2001, it displays a dialog box like the one shown next, telling you that it needs to upgrade your data. Click OK.

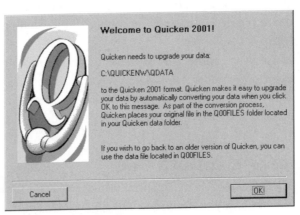

Quicken saves a copy of the data in C:\Quickenw\Q00files\—this makes it possible to go back to the previous version of Quicken if necessary. It then converts the data file for use with Quicken 2001, and the default My Finances window appears (see Figure 1-1). I tell you more about Center windows like this one a little later in this chapter and throughout this book.

The Quicken Interface

Quicken's interface is designed to be intuitive and easy to use. It puts the tools you need to manage your finances right within mouse-pointer reach. You never have to dig through multiple dialog boxes and menus to get to the commands you need most.

In this section, I tell you about the components of the Quicken interface and explain how you can use them to make your work with Quicken easy.

Windows

Quicken displays information in windows. It has different types of windows for the different types of information it displays. Quicken allows you to have up to 30 windows open at once. You move from one window to another with QuickTabs.

Financial Activity Centers

Financial Activity Centers, such as the My Finances window shown in Figure 1-1, provide information about your financial status. They also offer clickable links to access-related Quicken and Quicken.com features.

There is a Financial Activity Center for each major area of Quicken:

- **My Finances** (see Figure 1-1) provides an overview of your finances, including account balances, alerts, and scheduled transactions. You can customize the My Finances window's view or create new views to show the things that interest you most. I tell you how later in this chapter.

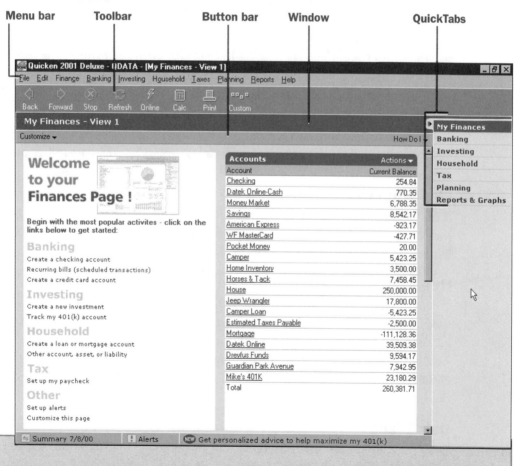

Figure 1-1 • The My Finances window is one of several Financial Activity Center windows

- **Banking Center** provides information about your cash, bank, and credit card accounts, as well as income and expenses. I discuss the Banking Center and its options in detail in Chapters 4 and 5.
- **Investing Center** provides information about your investment accounts and individual investments. I cover investing and the Investing Center in Chapters 6 through 8.
- **Household Center** provides information about asset and liability accounts, including your home, car, and related loans. I discuss the Household Center and related features in Chapters 9 and 10.
- **Tax Center** provides information related to your taxes, including a tax calendar and your year-to-date income. I cover Quicken's tax features and the Tax Center in Chapter 14.
- **Planning Center** gives you access to Quicken's financial planners, as well as the assumptions you need to set up to use the planners effectively. I discuss Quicken's financial planners and the Planning Center in Chapters 15 and 16.
- **Reports and Graphs Center** enables you to create reports and graphs based on information in your Quicken data file. I tell you how you can use the Reports and Graphs Center to keep track of your Quicken data in Chapter 13.

List Windows

A list window (see Figure 1-2) shows a list of information about related things, such as accounts, categories, classes, or scheduled transactions. You can use a list window to perform tasks with items in the list.

Register Windows

You use a register window (see Figure 1-3) to enter and edit transactions for a specific account. Each account has its own register. A pop-up menu beside the account name makes it easy to switch from one account register to another. Account tabs at the bottom of the window enable you to switch from the register entries to account information. I tell you more about using registers throughout this book.

QuickTabs

QuickTabs are navigation buttons you can click to quickly switch from one open window to another. They appear on the right side of the screen and are organized by Center, with open windows for a specific Center indented below the Center

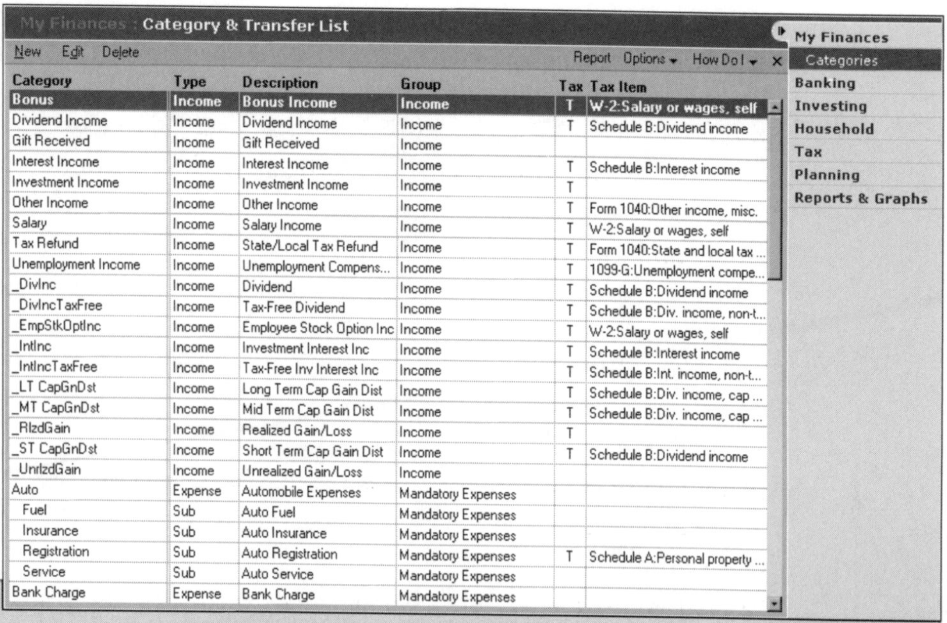

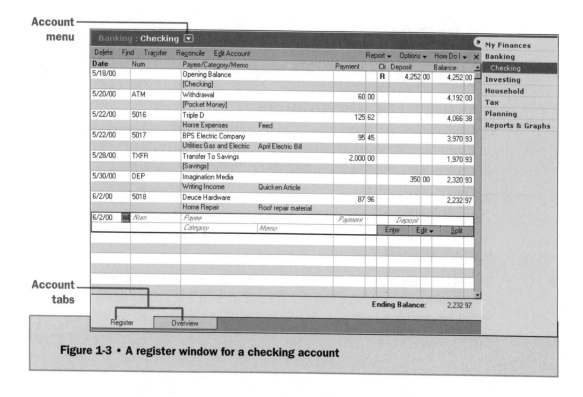

Figure 1-2 • The Category & Transfer List window displays a list of category and transfer accounts

Account menu

Account tabs

Figure 1-3 • A register window for a checking account

name, as shown next. This window grouping is further emphasized by color; the QuickTab button for an active window matches the background color of the window's title area.

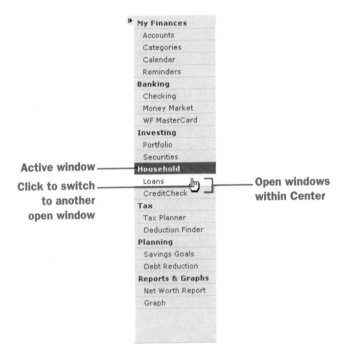

Features and Commands

Quicken offers a number of ways to access its features and commands, including standard Microsoft Windows elements such as menus and dialog boxes, and Quicken elements such as the toolbar and button bar.

Menus

Like all other Windows programs, Quicken displays a number of menus in a menu bar at the top of the screen (see Figure 1-1). You can choose commands from the menus in three ways:

- Click the menu name to display the menu. If necessary, click the name of the submenu you want (see Figure 1-4), and then click the name of the command that you want.

- Press ALT to activate the menu bar and press the keyboard key for the underlined letter in the menu that you want to open. If necessary, press the key for the underlined letter in the submenu that you want to open and then press the key for the underlined letter in the command that you want.

- Press the shortcut key combination for the menu command that you want. A command's shortcut key, if it has one, is displayed to the right of the command name on the menu (see Figure 1-4 on the next page).

Shortcut Menus

Shortcut menus (which are sometimes referred to as *contextual* or *context-sensitive* menus) can be displayed throughout Quicken. Point to the item for which you want to display a shortcut menu and click the right mouse button. The menu, which includes only those commands applicable to the item, appears at the mouse pointer:

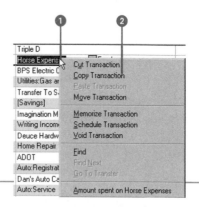

❶ Click with the right mouse button to display a shortcut menu.

❷ Click with the left mouse button to choose a menu command.

Toolbar

The *toolbar* is a row of buttons along the top of the application window (see Figure 1-1) that gives you access to other navigation techniques and features. The toolbar is customizable—I explain how to customize it later in this chapter. Here's a quick look at the buttons that appear by default, before you customize the toolbar.

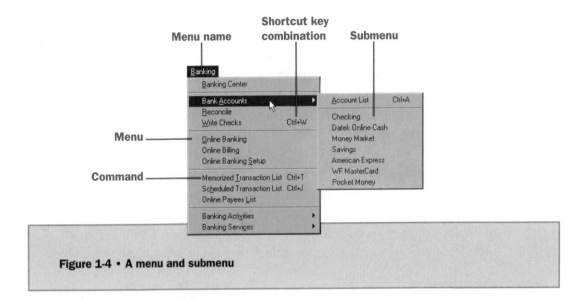

Figure 1-4 • A menu and submenu

Web browser buttons   The first four buttons should be familiar to you if you've used a Web browser to "surf the Web." Although they're designed to work with Web content within the Quicken window, the first two buttons also work with other windows.

- **Back** displays the previous open window.
- **Forward** displays the window that was open before you clicked the Back button.
- **Stop** stops loading information into the current window.
- **Refresh** reloads the content of the current window.

Other Buttons   Four other buttons offer access to additional Quicken features:

- **Online** opens the One Step Update window so you can connect to the Internet and update all your online information at once.
- **Calc** opens the Quicken Calc dialog box, so you can make quick calculations.
- **Print** prints the contents of the active window.
- **Custom** opens the Customize Toolbar dialog box so you can customize the toolbar.

Button Bar

The button bar is a row of textual buttons and menus that appears near the top of many windows (see Figure 1-1). Most items on the button bar, which vary from window to window, are buttons; simply click one to access its option. The items with triangles beside their names are menus that work just like the menu bar menus.

Tip   *If you're not sure what a toolbar button, button bar button, or button bar menu does, point to it. A box containing a brief description appears:*

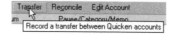

Dialog Boxes

Like other Windows applications, Quicken uses dialog boxes to communicate with you. Some dialog boxes display a simple message, while others include text boxes, option buttons, check boxes, and drop-down lists you can use to enter information. Many dialog boxes also include a Help button that you can use to get additional information about dialog box options.

Customizing Quicken's Interface

Quicken offers a number of ways to customize its interface to best meet your needs. In this part of the chapter, I explain how to customize the My Finances window, toolbar, and various settings that affect the entire Quicken program.

Tip   *I explain how to customize many other feature-specific options throughout this book.*

Customizing the My Finances Window

You can customize the My Finances window by creating or modifying views. This makes it possible to include only the information you think is important in the window.

Modifying the Current View

In the My Finances window, choose Customize This View from the Customize menu on the button bar. The Customize View dialog box appears:

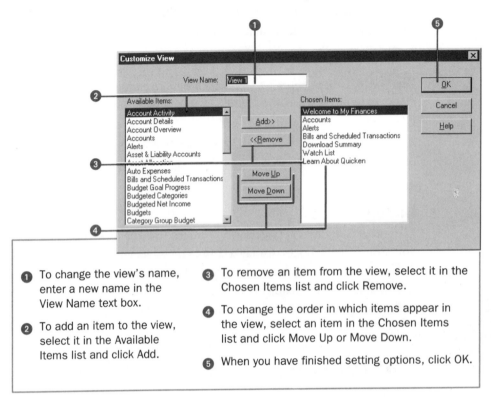

1 To change the view's name, enter a new name in the View Name text box.

2 To add an item to the view, select it in the Available Items list and click Add.

3 To remove an item from the view, select it in the Chosen Items list and click Remove.

4 To change the order in which items appear in the view, select an item in the Chosen Items list and click Move Up or Move Down.

5 When you have finished setting options, click OK.

To add an item, select it in the Available Items list and click Add. Its name appears in the Chosen Items list. You can include up to 15 items in the My Finances window. You can rearrange the order of items in the Chosen Items list by selecting an item and clicking the Move Up or Move Down button. To remove an item from the My Finances window, select it in the Chosen Items list and click Remove. When you've finished making changes, click OK. The My Finances window is redrawn to reflect your changes.

Creating a New View

If desired, you can create multiple views. This makes it possible to make several versions of the My Finances window, each with a specific set of information. You can then switch from one view to another to quickly see the information you want.

In the My Finances window, choose Create A New View from the Customize menu on the button bar. The Customize View dialog box, previously illustrated, appears. This time, the Chosen Items list is empty.

Enter a name for the view in the View Name text box. Then add items to the Chosen Items list as previously instructed. When you've finished, click OK. The new My Finances window view is created to your specifications and appears onscreen.

Switching from One View to Another

If you have created more than one view for the My Finances window, each view is listed at the bottom of the Customize menu, as shown next. To switch from one view to another, simply select it from the menu.

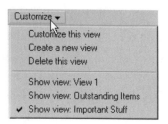

Deleting a View

To delete a view, begin by switching to the view you want to delete. Then choose Delete This View from the Customize menu on the button bar. Click OK in the confirmation dialog box that appears. The view is deleted, and another view takes its place.

Tip   *You cannot delete a view if it is the only one that exists for the My Finances window.*

Customizing the Toolbar

You can customize the toolbar by adding, removing, or rearranging buttons or changing the display options for toolbar buttons. You can do all this with the Customize Toolbar dialog box:

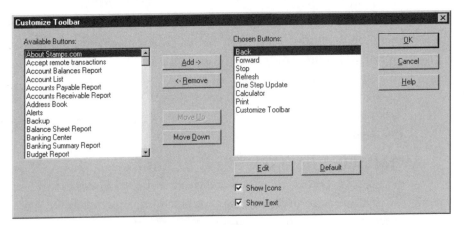

There are two ways to open this dialog box:

- Click the Custom button on the toolbar (if you haven't already removed it).
- Choose Edit | Options | Customize Toolbar.

Adding, Removing, and Rearranging Buttons

To add a button, select it in the Available Buttons list and click Add. Its name appears in the Chosen Buttons list. Similarly, to remove a button, select it in the Chosen Buttons list and click Remove. Its name is removed from the Chosen Buttons list.

Tip *You can include as many buttons as you like on the toolbar. If the toolbar includes more buttons than can fit within the Quicken application window, tiny scroll bars appear at either end so you can scroll through the buttons to find the one you want.*

You can rearrange the order of buttons in the toolbar by changing their order in the Chosen Buttons list. Simply select a button that you want to move and click the Move Up or Move Down button to change its position in the list.

When you've finished making changes, click OK. The toolbar is redrawn to reflect your changes.

Changing the Toolbar Display Options

There are several ways you can use the Customize Toolbar dialog box to change the way toolbar buttons are displayed:

- Turn the Show Icons check box on or off to toggle the display of toolbar button icons.

- Turn the Show Text check box on or off to toggle the display of toolbar text.

Tip   *Turning both the Show Icons and Show Text check boxes off removes the toolbar from view.*

- Click the Edit button to display the Edit Toolbar Button dialog box, which is shown next. Then change the label or shortcut key for the toolbar button's command. Click OK to save your changes.

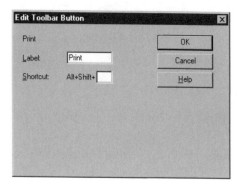

Restoring the Default Toolbar

To restore the toolbar back to its "factory settings," click the Default button in the Customize Toolbar dialog box. Then click OK in the confirmation dialog box that appears. The buttons return to the way they appear throughout this book.

Setting Quicken Program Options

You can use options in the General Options dialog box to change the appearance and functionality of other elements of Quicken's interface. Choose Edit | Options |

Quicken Program to display the dialog box. Then click the tab at the top of the dialog box for the category of option you want to change.

Setting QuickTabs and Color Scheme Options

In the General Options dialog box, click the QuickTabs tab to display its options. The default settings look like this:

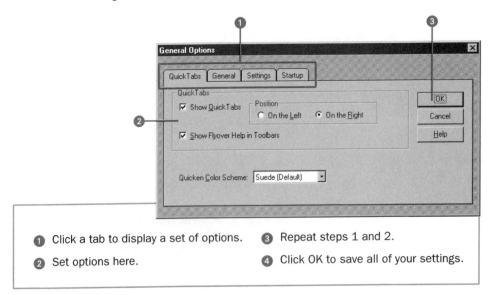

1 Click a tab to display a set of options.   3 Repeat steps 1 and 2.

2 Set options here.   4 Click OK to save all of your settings.

- **Show QuickTabs** controls the display of QuickTabs (see Figure 1-1). If you do not use QuickTabs, you may want to turn off this check box so you don't have to see them. (Frankly, I think Quicken's QuickTabs is one of the best interface features.)
- **Position** enables you to select the position for the QuickTabs. The default position is on the right, but you can move them to the left if desired.
- **Show Flyover Help In Toolbars** controls the display of brief descriptions when you point to a button. This useful feature helps you identify buttons, but if you find it annoying, you can always disable this check box.
- **Quicken Color Scheme** enables you to select a predefined color scheme for Quicken's windows and other interface elements. This is a matter of personal preference; check out some of the color schemes to see which one you like best.

Setting General Options

In the General Options dialog box, click the General tab to display its options. The default settings are:

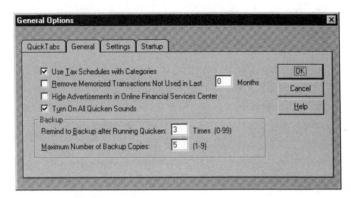

- **Use Tax Schedules With Categories** enables you to assign tax forms or schedules to categories. This feature can save you time at tax time, but if you prefer not to use it, you can turn it off here. I tell you more about this feature in Chapter 14.

- **Remove Memorized Transactions Not Used In Last ___ Months** tells Quicken to remove memorized transactions that have not been used within the number of months you specify. By default, this feature is turned off; as a result, Quicken remembers the first 2,000 transactions you enter and then stops remembering transactions. By turning on this check box and entering a value of 6 (for example), Quicken memorizes only the transactions you entered in the past six months, thus keeping the memorized transactions list manageable. Using this feature with a lower value (for example, 3) can weed one-time transactions out of the memorized transaction list. Changing this option does not affect transactions that have already been entered. I discuss memorized transactions in Chapter 11.

- **Hide Advertisements In Online Financial Services Center** tells Quicken not to display financial institution advertisements in the Online Financial Services Center window. (Other ads cannot be turned off.) This can help remove unnecessary information from your screen, but it also prevents you from viewing the Marketplace (Financial Institution News) tab. I cover the Online Financial Services Center later in this book.

- **Turn On All Quicken Sounds** enables Quicken sound effects. You may want to turn this check box off if you use Quicken in an environment where its sounds might annoy the people around you.

- **Remind to Back Up Quicken After Running ___ Times** enables you to specify how often you should be reminded to back up your Quicken data file. The lower the value in this text box, the more often Quicken reminds you to back up. Keep the value low if you don't regularly back up Quicken data with other files. I tell you how to back up your data in Appendix A.

- **Maximum Number of Backup Copies** is the number of backup copies Quicken should keep. The higher the value in this text box, the more backup copies of your Quicken data are saved. This enables you to go back further if you discover a problem with your current Quicken data file. I tell you more about backing up data in Appendix A.

Setting Keyboard, Calendar, and Currency Options

In the General Options dialog box, click the Settings tab to display its options. The default settings are:

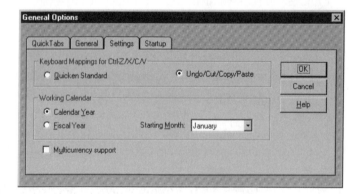

Keyboard Mappings   In most Windows programs, the CTRL-Z, CTRL-X, CTRL-C, and CTRL-V shortcut keys perform commands on the Edit menu. Because these commands have limited use within Quicken, you can map several Quicken-specific commands to these keys. Select the option button as shown in Table 1-1 for the mapping you want.

Keystroke	Quicken Standard	Undo/Cut/Copy/Paste (Windows Standard)
CTRL-Z	QuickZoom a report amount	Edit | Undo
CTRL-X	Edit | Transaction | Go to Matching Transfer	Edit | Cut
CTRL-C	Finance | Category & Transfer List	Edit | Copy
CTRL-V	Edit | Transaction | Void	Edit | Paste

Table 1-1 • Keyboard Mapping Options

Working Calendar   The folks at Intuit realize that not everyone manages their finances on a calendar year basis. You can use the Working Calendar options to set up your fiscal year.

- **Calendar Year** is a 12-month year beginning with January.
- **Fiscal Year** is a 12-month year beginning with the month you choose in the drop-down list.

Multicurrency Support   If your finances require that you account for transactions and investments in more than one currency, turn on the Multicurrency Support option. This feature assigns a "home" currency to all of your current data, placing a currency symbol beside every amount. You can then enter amounts in other currencies by entering the appropriate currency symbol. You can confirm the default currency in the Windows Regional Settings control panel. It is not necessary to set this option unless you plan to work with multiple currencies in one Quicken data file.

Setting Startup Options

In the General Options dialog box, click the Startup tab to display its options. The default settings are:

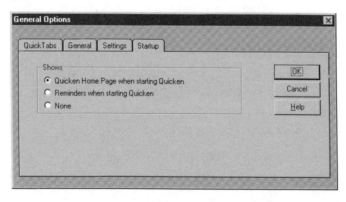

These options determine which window is displayed when you start up Quicken. Choose one of the three option buttons:

- **Quicken Home Page When starting Quicken** displays the My Finances or "Home Page" window when you first start Quicken. You may want to select this option if you want to see an overview of your finances before you start working with Quicken data.
- **Reminders When Starting Quicken** displays current reminders when you first start Quicken. You may find this option useful if you make extensive use of Quicken's reminder feature. I cover reminders in Chapter 11.
- **None** displays the window that was active when you last exited Quicken. You may find this useful if you like to resume work where you left off.

Onscreen Help

In addition to the How Do I menu in the button bar of Quicken windows, and the Help button in dialog boxes, Quicken includes an extensive Onscreen Help system to provide more information about using Quicken while you work. You can access most Help options from the Help menu:

Here's a brief summary of some of the components of Quicken's Onscreen Help system.

Quicken Help

Quicken's Onscreen Help uses the same Help engine as most Windows programs. You can use it to browse or search Help topics or display Help information about a specific window.

Show Me Videos

Show Me Videos provide narrated movies that show you exactly how to complete a specific task with Quicken. Choose Help | Show Me Videos to display the Show Me window. Then click one of the topics on the left side of the window. Movie controls and a movie "screen" appear beside the topic list. Watch the movie to learn about the topic you clicked.

Note   *You'll need an Internet connection to watch most of the movies that are part of this feature. To see the Quicken 2001 Tour movie, insert your Quicken CD.*

Product Support

The Product Support command on the Help menu opens the Product Support dialog box, which offers buttons you can click to explore support options:

- **Troubleshoot** displays a Help topic window full of common troubleshooting questions. Click a question to get the answer.
- **Go To Web** takes you to the Quicken Support Network page on Intuit's Web site. (An Internet connection is required to use this feature.)
- **Call For Support** displays technical support phone numbers.
- **System Info** opens a Tech Help window full of information about your computer's configuration. This information can be valuable to a technical support staff member if you ever need to call for support.

Exiting Quicken

When you're finished using Quicken, choose File | Exit. This saves your data file and closes the Quicken application.

Tip   *Sometimes, when you exit Quicken, you'll be asked if you want to back up your Quicken data file. I tell you about data files, including how to back them up, in Appendix A.*

Setting Up Accounts and Categories

In This Chapter:

Chapter 2

To make the most of Quicken, you must properly set it up for your particular financial situation. There are two parts to the setup process:

1. Use Quicken New User Setup to quickly create a primary checking account and a basic set of categories. This takes about five minutes and must be completed when you first set up Quicken.

2. Add accounts and categories as necessary to meet your specific needs. This takes only a minute or two for each account or category. You'll probably want to do this when you first start using Quicken, but you can do it any time you like.

In this chapter, I explain how to set up the Quicken accounts and categories you'll use to organize your finances.

Before You Begin

Before you start the setup process, it's a good idea to have an understanding of how data files, accounts, and categories work. You should also gather together a few documents to help you properly set up your accounts.

Data Files

All of the transactions you record with Quicken are stored in a *data file* on your hard disk. This file includes all the components—accounts, categories, and transactions—that make up your Quicken accounting system.

Although it's possible to have more than one Quicken data file, it isn't usually necessary. One file can hold all of your transactions. In fact, it's difficult (if not downright impossible) to use more than one Quicken file to track a single account, like a checking or credit card account. And splitting your financial records among multiple data files makes it impossible to generate reports that consolidate all of the information.

When would you want more than one data file? Well, you could use two data files if you wanted to use Quicken to organize your personal finances and the finances of your business, which has entirely separate bank, credit, and asset accounts, or if you're using Quicken to track the separate finances of multiple individuals.

Note   *I tell you more about working with Quicken data files in Appendix A.*

Accounts and Categories

There are two primary components to every transaction you record in Quicken: account and category.

An *account* is a record of what you either own or owe. For example, your checking account is a record of cash on deposit in the bank that is available for writing checks. A credit card account is a record of money you owe to the credit card company or bank for the use of your credit card. All transactions either increase or decrease the balance in one or more accounts.

A *category* is a record of where your money comes from or goes to. For example, salary is an income category for recording the money you earn from your job. Dining is an expense category you might use to record the cost of eating out. Categories make it possible to track how you earn and spend money.

If you know anything about accounting, these concepts should sound familiar, even if the names don't match what you learned in school or on the job. Accounts are what you'd find on a *balance sheet*; categories are what you'd find on an *income statement*. Quicken can produce reports like these; I tell you how in Chapter 13.

What You Need

To properly set up accounts, you should have balance information for the accounts that you want to monitor with Quicken. You can get this information from your most recent bank, investment, and credit card statements. It's a good idea to gather these documents before you start the setup process so they're on hand when you need them.

If you plan to use Quicken to replace an existing accounting system—whether it's paper based or prepared with a different computer program—you may also find it helpful to have a *chart of accounts* (a list of account names) or a recent income statement. This way, when you set up Quicken accounts and categories, you can use familiar names.

Creating a Quicken Data File

To use Quicken, you must have at least one data file. In this section, I explain how new Quicken users can create a data file with Quicken New User Setup and how any Quicken user can create additional Quicken data files when needed.

Quicken New User Setup

The Quicken New User Setup main dialog box, which is shown next, appears when you start Quicken for the first time as a new user. Click the Next button to begin the setup process and create a new data file.

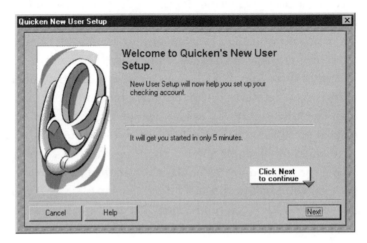

The Quicken New User Setup dialog boxes walk you through the creation of a checking account—the primary account you'll use to enter transactions. It does this by asking questions that determine your category needs and prompting you for information about your checking account. The process is relatively straightforward, so you shouldn't have any trouble understanding exactly what Quicken wants, but here are a few tips in case you get stuck:

- If your bank isn't on the drop-down list of financial institutions Quicken displays, don't panic. Just type the name of your bank into the text box. The drop-down list includes the financial institutions that support online financial services.

- If you don't have your bank statement handy, Quicken can create the account with a balance of $0.00 as of the current date.

- The balance information you enter is your starting point for recording checking account transactions with Quicken. You will not need to enter transactions that cleared the bank before the balance date. Later, you'll enter only those transactions that have not yet cleared the bank—including those that you make in the future.

When the setup process is complete, Quicken New User Setup displays a summary dialog box:

Check the information in this dialog box and click Done. Quicken creates a data file named Qdata and displays the account register for your checking account (see Figure 2-1).

You're now ready to start using Quicken.

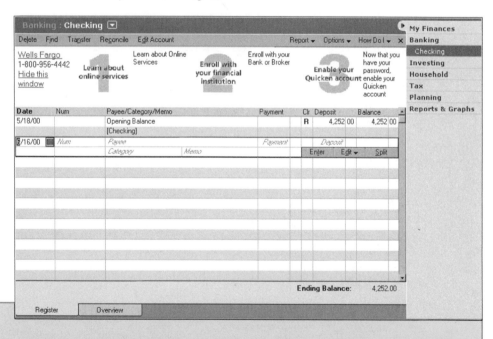

Figure 2-1 • The account register for a new checking account. The large numbers near the top of the window appear only if your bank supports Quicken's online banking feature

Creating Another Data File

Chances are, you won't need more than one Quicken data file. But, just in case you do, here's how you can create another one.

Start by choosing File | New. A dialog box appears, asking whether you want to create a New Quicken File or a New Quicken Account. (Some users confuse the two and try to use the File menu's New command to create a new account. I tell you the correct way to create an account later in this chapter.) Select New Quicken File and click the OK button.

A Create Quicken File dialog box, like the one shown next, appears. Use it to enter a name for the data file. Although you can also change the default directory location, it's easier to find the data file if it's in the Quickenw directory with other Quicken data files.

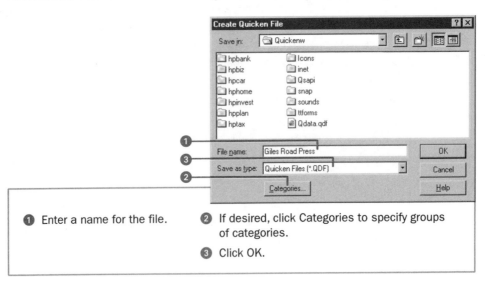

① Enter a name for the file.

② If desired, click Categories to specify groups of categories.

③ Click OK.

To specify what categories should be included in the data file, click the Categories button. The Quicken Categories dialog box appears. Use it to turn on check boxes for the category groups you expect to use in your new account:

- Standard categories
- Categories for married people
- Categories for those with children
- Categories for homeowners
- Categories for use with a small business

When you have finished selecting category groups, click OK to return to the Create Quicken File dialog box. Then click OK to create the new file.

Next, Quicken displays the Create New Account dialog box, which is shown in the section "Setting Up Accounts," later in this chapter. Use it to create a checking account for the new data file. When you have finished, you can begin working with the new Quicken data file.

Tip *If you have more than one Quicken data file, you can see which one is open by looking at the filename in the application window's title bar (see Figure 2-1). To open a different data file, choose File | Open and use the dialog box that appears to select and open a different file. Only one Quicken data file can be open at a time.*

Customizing Your Data File

When you create a data file with Quicken New User Setup or the File menu's New command, Quicken performs the bare minimum setup: one account (checking) and a collection of categories based on options you selected. But in many cases, you'll want to customize the data file to add accounts and add or remove categories. The rest of this chapter tells you more about accounts and categories and explains how you can customize the data file.

Accounts

While the majority of your expenditures may come from your checking account, you probably have more than one account that Quicken can track for you. By setting up all of your accounts in Quicken, you can keep track of balances and activity to get a full picture of what you own and what you owe.

Types of Accounts

Quicken Deluxe offers different kinds of accounts for tracking what you own and what you owe:

What You Own

In accounting jargon, what you own are *assets*. In Quicken, an asset is one type of account, but there are several others, most of which have subtypes:

Bank Bank accounts are for tracking money in the bank. When you set up an account, Quicken distinguishes between three different types of bank accounts: Checking, Savings, and Money Market.

Cash Cash is for tracking cash inflows and expenditures—pocket money, so to speak.

Asset   Asset accounts are for tracking items that you own. Quicken distinguishes between three different types of asset accounts: House, Vehicle, and Asset. When you set up a House or Vehicle account, Quicken knows that a loan may be related to the account and enables you to set up a Mortgage or Vehicle Loan at the same time.

Investment   Investment accounts are for tracking the stocks, bonds, and mutual funds in your portfolio. Quicken distinguishes between five different types of investment accounts: Brokerage, IRA or Keogh, 401(k), Dividend Reinvestment Plan, and Other Investment.

What You Owe

The accounting term for what you owe is *liabilities*. Quicken offers two kinds of accounts for amounts you owe:

Credit   Credit is for tracking credit card transactions and balances.

Liability   Liability is for tracking loans and other liabilities. When you set up an account, Quicken distinguishes between three types of liability accounts: Mortgage, Vehicle Loan, and Liability. You can set up a Mortgage or Vehicle Loan when you set up a House or Vehicle account, or at another time.

Setting Up Accounts

You create new accounts with the Account Setup dialog box. No matter what type of account you create, Quicken steps you through the process, prompting you to enter information about the account, such as its name and balance. In this section, I explain how to use the Account Setup dialog box to set up new accounts and tell you what kind of information you'll have to enter for each account type.

Getting Started

Begin by opening the Create New Account dialog box. There are several ways to do this; here are three of them:

- Click the New Account link in the Activities area of the Banking Center window.
- Choose Banking | Banking Activities | Create New Account.
- Choose Finance | Account List (or press CTRL-A) to display the Account List window (see Figure 2-2 later in this chapter). Then click the New button in the button bar.

The Create New Account dialog box, which is shown next, appears. Select the option button for the type of account you want to create. Then click Next to continue.

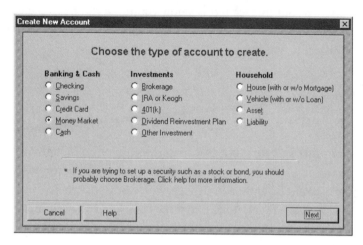

The Account Setup dialog box appears. The exact title and appearance of this dialog box varies depending on the type of account you are creating. In the following illustration, I've begun creating a money market account.

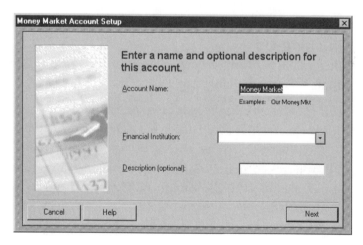

Entering Account Information

The Account Setup dialog boxes all work very much the same, no matter what they are titled or what options they include. Use the Next button to walk through the account creation process. You can click the Back button at any time to go back and change information. You know you're finished when the Next button is replaced with a Done button; click it to save the account information.

The rest of this section is a quick summary of the basic information you'll have to provide for every account. I provide details for creating specific types of accounts throughout this book:

- Bank, cash, and credit accounts are covered in Chapter 4.
- Investment accounts are covered in Chapter 6.
- Asset and liability accounts are covered in Chapter 9.

Account Information   Account information includes the account name, financial institution, an optional description, the account balance, and the date of the account balance. Almost every type of Quicken account requires this information. If you don't know the balance of an account, you may set it to $0.00 and make adjustments later, either when you get a statement or when you reconcile the account.

Tax Information   When you click the Tax button in the Account Setup dialog box, a Tax Schedule Information dialog box appears. It enables you to associate an account with a specific tax return form or schedule. I tell you about using this feature in Chapter 14.

Finishing Up

When you've finished entering information for a new account, click the Done button. One of two things happens:

- If you created a bank, cash, asset, or liability account, the account is created, and the Account Setup dialog box disappears. You can begin using the account immediately.
- If you created an investment account, you may be prompted to enter additional information about the investment. Consult Chapter 6 for instructions on how to proceed.

Working with the Account List

You can view a list of all of your accounts at any time. Choose Finance | Account List or press CTRL-A. The Account List appears (see Figure 2-2). For each account, it displays the account name, type, description, number of transactions, current and ending balances, and number of checks.

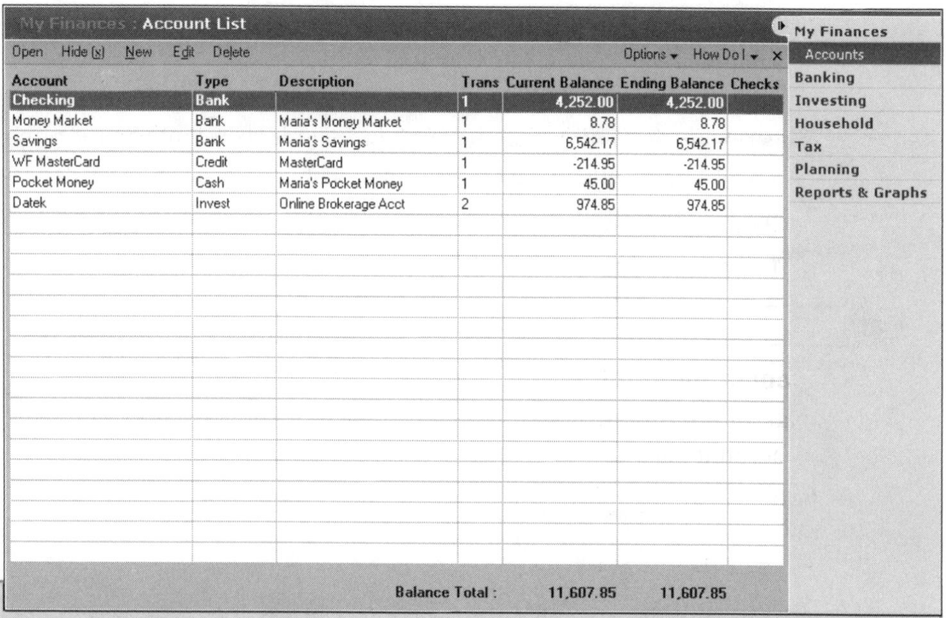

Figure 2-2 • The Account List window gives you access to all of your accounts

The Account List offers a quick and easy way to maintain all of your accounts. Click an account to select it, and then click one of the buttons or choose a menu command on the button bar to perform a task.

- **Open** opens the register for the selected account. Figure 2-1 shows the account register for a brand-new checking account. I explain how to use the various types of account registers throughout this book.

Shortcut | *You can also open an account by double-clicking its name in the Account List window.*

- **Hide(x)** removes the account from view so it does not appear in lists, cannot be used in transactions, and does not appear in reports. This is a good way to get an inactive account out of the way without deleting it and its transactions.

Tip | *To redisplay a hidden account, choose Options | View Hidden Accounts on the button bar. When hidden accounts are viewed, a hand appears beside the name of each account that is normally hidden. To unhide an account, select it and click the Hide button on the button bar again.*

- **New** displays the Create New Account dialog box, shown earlier in this chapter, so you can create a new account.
- **Edit** displays the Overview tab of the register window for the selected account. As shown in Figure 2-3, this window includes basic information about the account, as well as detailed information about the account's balance and status. You can use this window to modify account attributes; just click the item you want to change and make the change.

Tip   *Use the Account Attribute area in the Overview tab (see Figure 2-3) for a Quicken account to store additional information about the account, such as your account number and the financial institution's contact information. By consistently storing this information for all of your accounts, it'll be easy to find when you need it.*

Change account
attributes here.

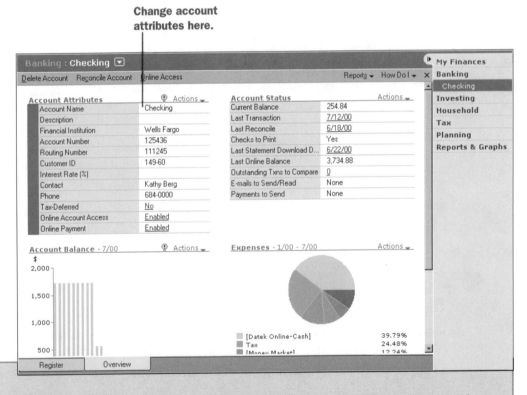

Figure 2-3 • The Overview tab of the register window for an account displays a variety of information about the account

- **Delete** enables you to delete the selected account. It displays a dialog box you can use to confirm that you want to delete the account. You must type **yes** into the dialog box and click OK to delete the account.

Caution   *When you delete an account, you permanently remove all of its transactions from your Quicken data file. To get the account out of sight without actually deleting it and its data, consider hiding it instead.*

- **Options** offers additional commands for working with the Account List window:

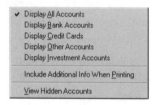

- **How Do I** offers commands that display Help windows for a variety of common Account List window tasks.

Categories

When you create a data file, Quicken automatically creates dozens of commonly used categories based on options you set. Although these categories might completely meet your needs, there may be times when you'll want to add, remove, or modify a category to fine-tune Quicken for your use.

Types of Categories

There are basically two types of categories: income and expense.

Income   *Income* is incoming money. It includes things such as your salary, commissions, interest income, dividend income, child support, gifts received, and tips.

Expense   An *expense* is outgoing money. It includes things such as insurance, groceries, rent, interest expense, bank fees, finance charges, charitable donations, and clothing.

Subcategories

A *subcategory* is a subset or part of a category. It must be the same type of category as its primary category. For example, the Auto category may be used to track expenses to operate your car. Within that category, however, you may want subcategories to record specific expenses, such as auto insurance, fuel, and repairs. Subcategories make it easy to keep income and expenses organized into manageable categories, while providing the transaction detail you might want or need.

Displaying the Category & Transfer List

You can view a list of all of your categories at any time. Choose Finance | Category & Transfer List. The Category & Transfer List appears (see Figure 2-4). For each category, it displays the category name, type, description, group, and tax status. (I tell you about groups, which are used primarily for budgeting, in Chapter 16, and about setting tax options in Chapter 14.) You can use the Category & Transfer List to create, edit, and delete categories.

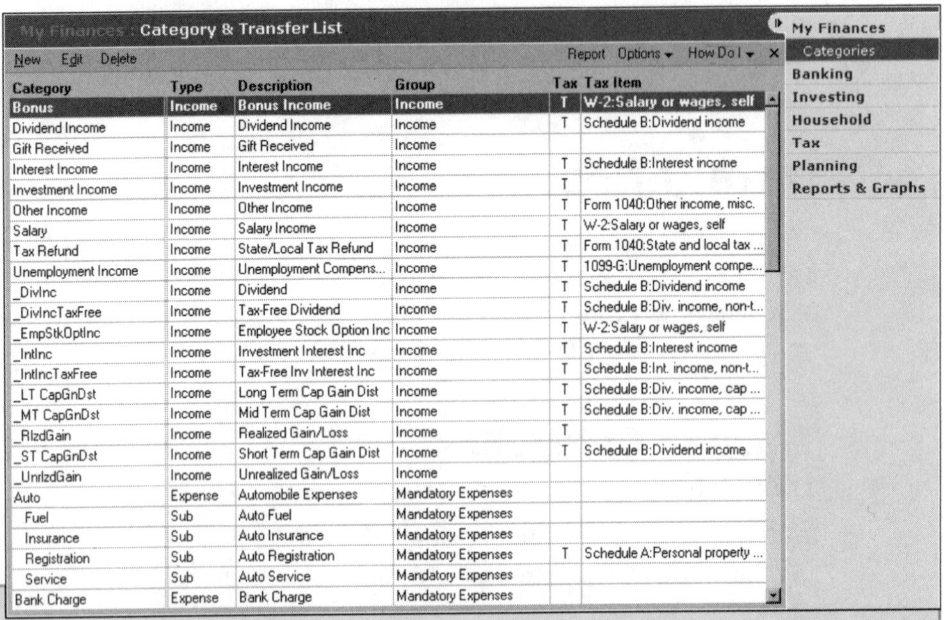

Figure 2-4 • The Category & Transfer List, with categories automatically created by Quicken

Creating a New Category

To create a new category, start by displaying the Category & Transfer List window (see Figure 2-4). Then click the New button on the button bar. The Set Up Category dialog box appears. Enter information about the category and click OK:

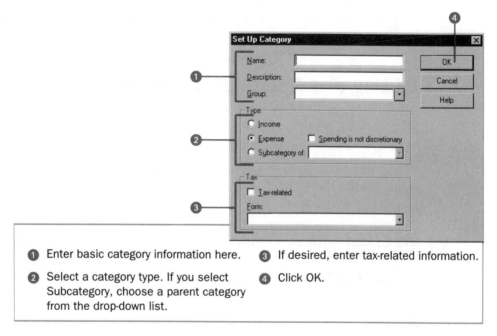

❶ Enter basic category information here.

❷ Select a category type. If you select Subcategory, choose a parent category from the drop-down list.

❸ If desired, enter tax-related information.

❹ Click OK.

Here's a quick summary of the kind of information you should provide for each category:

Category Information   The basic category information includes the category name, which is required, and the description and group, which are optional. Groups are used primarily for budgeting, so I discuss them in Chapter 16. For now, you can either leave the Group box empty or choose an existing group from the drop-down list.

Type   Use options in the Type area to select the type of category: Income, Expense, or Subcategory. In addition to properly classifying income and expense items, the type of category you specify will determine where the category appears in reports and graphs. For example, income categories always appear before expense categories and subcategories appear immediately below their parent categories. If you select Subcategory, you must choose a category from the drop-down list beside it. If you do not have complete control over spending for an expense category, you can turn on the Spending Is Not Discretionary check box. This option, which is also used primarily for budgeting, applies to required fixed expenditures such as rent, car insurance, and child care.

Tax   You can use the tax area options to specify whether a category is tax related and, if so, what tax form it appears on. This can be a real time-saver at tax time by enabling you to organize your income and expenditures as they are on tax forms. I tell you more about using Quicken at tax time in Chapter 14. You are not required to enter anything in this area.

When you've finished entering information in the Set Up Category dialog box, click OK. The category is added to the list.

Editing and Deleting Categories

You can also use the Category & Transfer List window to edit or delete a category. Select the name of the category you want to edit or delete, and then click the Edit or Delete button on the button bar.

Edit   The Edit button displays the Edit Category dialog box, which looks and works just like the Set Up Category dialog box. You can use this to make just about any change to a category.

Tip   *You can "promote" a subcategory to a category by changing its type.*

Delete   The Delete button displays different dialog boxes depending on the category that is selected:

- If you selected a category with no subcategories, the Delete Category dialog box, which is shown next, appears. You can use this dialog box to delete the selected category or replace it with another throughout your data file.

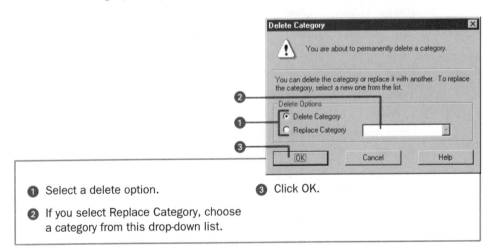

1 Select a delete option.

2 If you select Replace Category, choose a category from this drop-down list.

3 Click OK.

- If you selected a category with subcategories, a dialog box tells you that you can't delete a category with subcategories.
- If you selected a subcategory, a dialog box offers to merge the subcategory with its parent category. Click Yes to merge the category and subcategory; click No to delete the subcategory without merging it.

Caution   *When you delete a category without replacing it with another category, or delete a subcategory without merging it with its parent category, you permanently remove the category or subcategory from all of the transactions that referenced it, resulting in uncategorized transactions.*

Other Category & Transfer List Options

Options on the right end of the Category & Transfer List window's button bar (see Figure 2-4) enable you to perform other tasks with list contents.

Report   The Report button creates a report of the transactions for the selected category. I tell you more about creating reports in Chapter 13.

Options   The Options menu offers additional options for working with the Category & Transfer List window:

Tip   *You can use the Add Categories command on the button bar's Options menu to add a group of predefined categories all at once. For example, suppose you just got married (congratulations!) and want to add categories for married people to your Quicken data file. Choose the Add Categories command to display the Add Categories dialog box, then use options within the dialog box to add multiple categories with just a few clicks of your mouse.*

How Do I   The How Do I menu includes commands that display Help windows for a variety of common Category & Transfer List window tasks.

Going Online with Quicken and Quicken.com

In This Chapter:

- *Benefits of Going Online with Quicken*

- *What You Need to Connect to the Internet*

- *Setting Up an Internet Connection*

- *Testing and Troubleshooting Your Connection*

- *An Introduction to Web Surfing*

- *Accessing Quicken.com*

- *Quicken Financial Partners*

Many of Quicken's features work seamlessly with the Internet. If you have access to the Internet, either through a connection to an Internet Service Provider (ISP) or through a connection to an online service such as America Online or CompuServe, you can take advantage of these online features to get up-to-date information, automate data entry, pay bills, and obtain Quicken maintenance updates automatically.

In this chapter, I tell you why you might want to take advantage of Quicken's online features. Then I explain how to set up Quicken to go online. Finally, I tell you a little about surfing the Web and introduce you to Quicken.com, Intuit's excellent financial information Web site.

Tip *If you don't already have access to the Internet but think you may want to get it, be sure to read this chapter. It will convince you that now's the time to go online.*

Going Online

If you're already using your computer to access the features of the Internet or online services such as America Online, you probably already know a lot about it. In this part of the chapter, I fill in any gaps in your knowledge by telling you about the benefits of going online with Quicken and addressing any security concerns you might have. Finally, for the folks who aren't already online, I explain what you need to connect to the Internet to use Quicken's online features.

Why Go Online?

Before I go any further, I want to remind you that you don't *have* to go online to use Quicken. Quicken is a good financial management software package, even without its online features. But Quicken's online features make it a *great* financial management software package. As you'll see in this section and throughout this book, Quicken 2001 uses the Internet to help you make better financial decisions. How? By providing you with information and resources that are relevant to your personal financial situation.

The best way to explain the benefits of going online is to list a few of the features online users can take advantage of.

If You Have a Bank Account, You Can Benefit

Throughout the month, you write checks and mail them to individuals and organizations. You enter these transactions in your checking account register. At month's end, you reconcile the account. You can do all this without going online. I tell you how in Chapters 4 and 12.

But if you register for online account access with your bank, you can download all bank account activity on a daily basis so you know exactly when the transactions hit your account—even the ATM and debit card transactions you always forget to enter. If you register for online payment, you can pay your bills without licking another envelope or pasting on another stamp. I explain how all this works in Chapter 5.

If You Have Credit Cards, You Can Benefit

Do you have credit cards? Then you may take advantage of Quicken's credit card tracking features, which I cover in Chapter 4, to keep track of your charges, payments, and balances. You don't need to go online.

But if you sign up for online account access, all your credit card charges can be downloaded directly into Quicken, eliminating the need for time-consuming data entry, while giving you an up-to-date summary of your debt and how you spent your money. Online account access can even tell you when your bills are due and prepare the transactions for payment. I tell you more about this in Chapter 5.

If You Invest, You Can Benefit

Quicken can keep track of your investments, whether they are 401(k) accounts, mutual funds, or stocks. You can enter share, price, and transaction information into Quicken, and it will summarize portfolio value, gains, and losses. It'll even keep track of securities by lot. You don't need to go online to track your investments. I explain how in Chapter 6.

But with online investment tracking, Quicken can automatically obtain quotes on all the securities in your portfolio and update your portfolio's market value. Depending on your brokerage firm, you may also be able to download transactions, account balances, and holdings. Quicken can also alert you about news stories that affect your investments and automatically download the headlines so you can learn more with just a click. I tell you about all this in Chapter 7.

 GET SMARTER   But wait, there's more! You can also get valuable up-to-date research information about securities that interest you. This helps you make informed investment decisions. You can learn more in Chapter 8.

If You Want to Save Money, You Can Benefit

Car insurance. Mortgages. Car loans. Bank accounts. All of these things have one thing in common: Their rates vary from one provider to another. Shopping for the best deal can be a lot of time-consuming work—wading through newspaper and magazine ads, making calls, visiting banks. Quicken can help you understand the basics of insurance, loans, and banking. Its planners can help you evaluate the deals you learn about, and all without going online.

But with the help of Quicken's built-in Internet links, you can shop for the best deal online, without leaving the comfort of your desk, getting newspaper ink all over your hands, or spending an afternoon listening to music while on hold. Up-to-date rates are only a mouse click away with an Internet connection and Quicken to guide you. I tell you more in Chapter 10.

Enough Already!

If all this doesn't convince you that going online with Quicken can help you save time, save money, and get smarter, stop reading and skip ahead to Chapter 4. You'll probably never be convinced. I will say one more thing, however: After using Quicken's online features for more than four years now, I can't imagine using Quicken any other way.

Security Features

Perhaps you're already convinced that the online features can benefit you. Maybe you're worried about security, concerned that a stranger will be able to access your accounts or steal your credit card numbers.

You can stop worrying. The folks at Intuit and the participating banks, credit card companies, and brokerage firms have done all the worrying for you. They've come up with a secure system that protects your information and accounts.

PINs

A *PIN*, or *personal identification number*, is a secret password you must use to access your accounts online. If you have an ATM card or cash advance capabilities through your credit card, you probably already have at least one PIN, so the idea shouldn't be new to you. It simply prevents anyone from accessing the account for any reason without first entering the correct PIN.

An account's PIN is initially assigned by the bank, credit card company, or brokerage firm. Some companies, like American Express, require that your PIN consist of a mixture of letters and numbers for additional security. You can change your PINs to make them easier to remember—just don't use something obvious like your birthday or telephone number. And don't write it on a sticky note and attach it to your monitor! If you think someone might have guessed your PIN, you can change it.

> **Tip**   It's a good idea to regularly change all your PINs and passwords—not just the ones you use in Quicken.

Encryption

Once you've correctly entered your PIN, the instructions that flow from your computer to the bank, credit card company, or brokerage firm are encrypted. This means they are encoded in such a way that anyone able to "tap in" to the transactions would "hear" only gibberish. Quicken does the encryption using, at a minimum, the 56-bit single Data Encryption Standard (DES). Quicken is also capable of encrypting data with stronger methods, including the 128-bit RC4 or 168-bit triple DES. Once the encrypted information reaches the computer at the bank, credit card company, or brokerage firm, it is unencrypted and then validated and processed.

Encryption makes it virtually impossible for any unauthorized party to "listen in" to your transaction. It also makes it impossible for someone to alter a transaction between the moment it leaves your computer and the moment it arrives at your bank, credit card company, or brokerage firm for processing.

Other Security Methods

Quicken also takes advantage of other security methods for online communications, including Secure Sockets Layer (SSL) encryption, digital signatures, and digital certificates. Together, all of these security methods make online financial transactions secure—even more secure than telephone banking, which you may already use!

What You Need

To take advantage of Quicken's online features, you need a connection to the Internet. There are different ways to connect and different organizations that can provide the connection. In this section I explain your options.

> **Tip**   If you already have a connection to the Internet or online service, you may already have everything you need. Read on to make sure.

Internet Service Provider (ISP)

An *ISP* is an organization that provides access to the Internet, usually for a monthly fee. These days, literally thousands of ISPs can provide the access you need for Quicken's online features.

> **Tip**   America Online (AOL), CompuServe, and Prodigy are ISPs that provide an Internet connection as well as additional information and online services.

If you don't already have an account with an ISP, you must set one up before you can configure Quicken to use its online features. Consult the information that came with your copy of Quicken for special deals on Internet accounts through Quicken-preferred ISPs. Or check your local phone book to find an ISP near you.

Internet Connection Methods

You can connect to the Internet in either of two ways: with a direct connection or a dial-up connection.

Direct Connection   A *direct* or *network* connection directly connects your computer to the ISP, usually via a network. This is common in office environments these days, but it is still uncommon for households because it's expensive and can be difficult to set up.

Dial-Up Connection   A *dial-up* or *modem* connection uses a modem to connect to an ISP via a telephone line. The modem dials a telephone number, connects to your ISP's computer, exchanges some ID and protocol information, and connects to the Internet. This is the most common connection method for households because it's inexpensive and easy to set up.

Keep two things in mind if you use a dial-up connection:

- If you have only one phone line, that phone line will be in use while you are accessing Quicken's online features (or any other Internet feature). That means you can't accept incoming calls. And if someone picks up an extension while you're online, there's a good chance you'll be disconnected. If you spend a lot of time online, whether using Quicken or just "surfing the Net," you might want to consider adding a second line to your house. It's not as expensive as you might think. Just don't let the phone company talk you into a special data phone line for modem connections. You don't need a special line, and you certainly don't need to pay for one.

- If you have call-waiting, you must disable it when you connect to the Internet. Otherwise, the call-waiting tone that sounds when there's an incoming call can disconnect you. You can automatically disable call-waiting by entering specific digits—usually *70—before dialing the phone. If you have call-waiting, check with the phone company to see what the codes in your area are.

More About Modems

If you know that modem stands for *mod*ulator/*dem*odulator, I'm impressed! But do you *need* to know that? No. Modem connections are so easy to set up and use that you don't need to know the geeky terminology for the things that make it work.

Anyway, a dial-up connection requires a modem. Here are some things to consider when shopping for a modem:

- If you have a 9,600 bps modem lying around, give it away (if you can find someone to take it). Although it will be fast enough to exchange data for online account access, online payment, and online quotes, you'll fall asleep if you try to use it to view Web pages. A 28.8 Kbps modem is (barely) okay; a 33.6 Kbps modem is better. If you buy a new modem, don't buy anything slower than 56 Kbps if you expect it to last more than a few years. These numbers, in case you haven't caught on, refer to speeds; the higher the number the better.

- Modem prices are way down these days—you should be able to get a good 56 Kbps fax-modem for well under $200. And yes, I did say fax-modem. That means you can use it to send and receive faxes, too. (It isn't worth buying a modem that can't handle faxes, even if you could find one.)

- Modems can be internal or external. If internal, the modem plugs into a slot on your computer's main circuit board. That means you (or your friendly neighborhood computer guru) must open the computer's case and install it. If external, the modem plugs into your computer's serial port. That means you must have an available serial port.

Modems really are easy to set up. Read the manual that comes with yours. It'll tell you everything you need to know—and more.

Fringe Benefits

One more thought I'd like to share with you here: If you set up an Internet account, you can use it for a wide variety of things—not just Quicken. Use it to exchange e-mail with friends and family members. Use it to search the Internet for information about your hobbies and interests, your next vacation, or the local weather. Shop online. Chat. Download shareware, freeware, or the latest updates to commercial software products.

Heck, if you have it, you may as well use it. Just remember to turn off your computer and go outside once in a while.

Setting Up and Testing an Internet Connection

To use Quicken's online features, you need to set up Quicken for your Internet connection. This part of the chapter explains how to set up Quicken for your Internet connection, then test the connection and troubleshoot any problems you might have.

Internet Connection Setup

You set up Quicken for an Internet connection with Internet Connection Setup. In this section, I provide step-by-step instructions for setting up a connection.

Getting Started

Choose Edit | Internet Connection Setup. The Intuit Internet Connection Profile Manager dialog box appears:

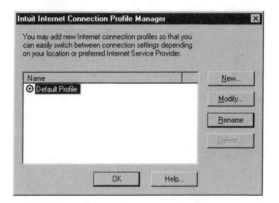

This new feature of Quicken enables you to set up multiple Internet connection profiles. You can then switch from one to another as desired. For example, say you use Quicken on a laptop computer that you use at home, the office, and on the road. You may access the Internet via AOL or another ISP when at home or on the road and via a network connection when at the office. This feature makes it quick and easy to switch setups.

The first time you set up Quicken's Internet connection, you should modify the Default Profile. Select Default Profile and click the Modify button. The Internet Connection Setup dialog box appears. Select the option that best describes your Internet connection situation:

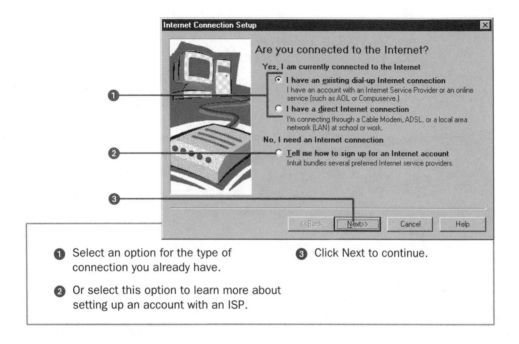

❶ Select an option for the type of connection you already have.

❷ Or select this option to learn more about setting up an account with an ISP.

❸ Click Next to continue.

Setting Up an Existing Connection

If you selected the first option in the Internet Connection Setup dialog box, when you click Next, Quicken scans your Windows setup, looking for Internet connection configurations. It lists all of them in a dialog box like the one shown next. Select the one you want to use and click Next.

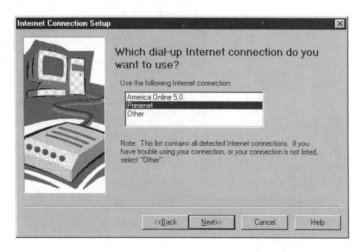

If you choose Other, the Internet Connection Setup dialog box displays a message with instructions. It tells you to complete the setup, connect to your ISP in the usual way, and then access the desired Quicken online feature. Be aware that you may have to do this each time you want to use an online feature.

No matter what kind of connection you have, a message with information about the Web browser appears next. It tells you that although you can use any Web browser you like with Quicken, some features require Microsoft Internet Explorer version 4.0 or later. Because Internet Explorer version 5.0 can be installed with Quicken, it's a good idea to select that as the browser for use with Quicken. This will enable you to display Web pages for Quicken features right within Quicken. You can still use other browsers outside of Quicken.

Tip *If you decide not to use Internet Explorer, Quicken will automatically launch your browser when it needs to display a Web page.*

Click Next to display a dialog box with a list of installed browsers. Select the one you want to use with Quicken and then click Next.

If you have a direct connection to the Internet, a dialog box appears, prompting you to enter Proxy Server information. If you're not sure what to enter, ask your system administrator.

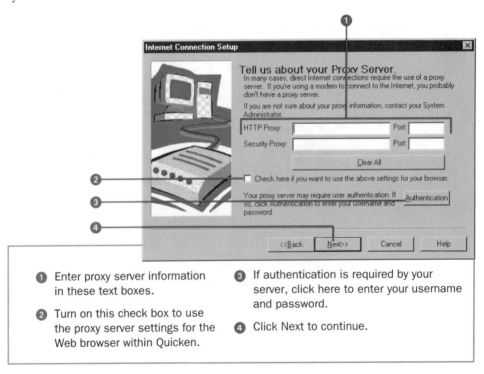

❶ Enter proxy server information in these text boxes.

❷ Turn on this check box to use the proxy server settings for the Web browser within Quicken.

❸ If authentication is required by your server, click here to enter your username and password.

❹ Click Next to continue.

The next dialog box offers you the option of sending diagnostic data to Intuit during your Internet sessions. The data you send—which is completely transparent to you—helps Intuit improve Internet access for its software products. The dialog box that appears explains all this. Select an option and click Next to continue.

The last Internet Connection Setup dialog box (shown next) summarizes your setup options. Check to make sure they're correct. You can click the Back button to return to previous screens and make changes if necessary. When you're satisfied that everything is correct, click Finish.

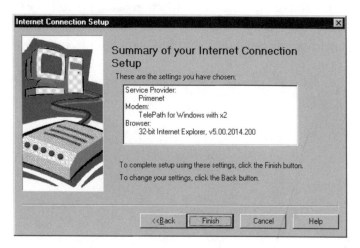

The Connection tab of the Customize Quicken 2001 Download dialog box may appear next. Use it to set your preferences for the Internet connection. I tell you more about this dialog box in the section "Setting Internet Connection Options" later in this chapter. Skip ahead to that section now.

Tip *You can change these options at any time. Just follow the preceding instructions again.*

Setting Up a New Internet Account

If you don't already have an Internet account, you'll have to set one up. Your Quicken software package includes information about special deals for Intuit-preferred ISPs. Be sure to check them out.

Of course, you don't have to use any of the ISPs listed with Quicken literature or in this book. You can use any ISP you like. Shop around and find the ISP that best meets your needs. (If you live in a remote area, as I do, you may find only one or two within your local calling area.)

Contact the ISP and set up an account. The ISP should provide all the instructions you need. (If it doesn't, find another ISP—one that can provide technical support when it's needed.) Then, when your computer is set up to access the Internet, return to the Internet Connection Setup dialog box, choose one of the first two options, and follow the instructions appropriate to setting up Quicken for your connection.

Setting Internet Connection Options

At the end of the Internet Connection Setup process, the Connection tab of the Customize Quicken Download dialog box may appear. If it doesn't, you can open it by choosing Edit | Options | Internet Options. It looks like this:

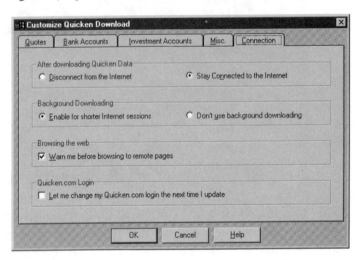

Here's a quick rundown of the Internet connection options you can set.

Connection Options

The After Downloading Quicken Data section of the dialog box offers two options for your Internet connection once Quicken has finished obtaining the data it needs:

- **Disconnect From The Internet** tells Quicken to sever your Internet connection. You might find this option especially useful if you don't use many online features, or if you have a dial-up connection with only one telephone line that you don't want to tie up.
- **Stay Connected To The Internet** tells Quicken to maintain your Internet connection. You might find this option useful if you use many online features

or use Quicken's online features as part of a daily online routine. Because I have a dedicated phone line for my dial-up connection and tend to do all my online work at once—e-mail, Web browsing, and online financial work with Quicken—I use this option. Keep in mind, however, that if you use this option with a dial-up connection, you eventually have to manually disconnect from the Internet to free up your phone line.

Background Downloading Options

The Background Downloading section of the dialog box offers two options to set the way Quicken downloads or retrieves information from the Internet:

- **Enable For Shorter Internet Sessions** enables the Quicken Download Manager, which will run automatically whenever you start your computer. This feature uses an Internet connection to download information such as program patches, even if Quicken isn't running. Because this feature works in the background, you probably won't even notice it. When the Download Manager is active, however, a Q appears on the far right side of the task bar at the bottom of your screen.

Tip *You can disable the Download Manager for the current session by right-clicking the Q when it appears in the task bar.*

- **Don't Use Background Downloading** disables the Quicken Download Manager. This means you will only receive Quicken patches and other information when you specifically request them.

Browsing the Web Option

The Warn Me Before Browsing To Remote Pages check box tells Quicken to display a warning dialog box when you choose a menu command or click a link that displays a Web page on the Internet. You may want to keep this check box turned on if you have a dial-up connection to the Internet and want to be warned before Quicken makes a connection.

Quicken.com Login Option

The Let Me Change My Quicken.com Login The Next Time I Update check box instructs Quicken to display the Quicken.com login screen when you connect to Quicken.com. With this option turned off, Quicken can automatically enter your saved login information if, when you registered with Excite or Quicken.com, you selected the option to save your login information and are connecting with the same computer. This check box is disabled until you set up a Quicken.com login by registering your copy of Quicken online. (I tell you about registering Quicken in Chapter 2.)

Note   *Some of these options are not available for a setup with a direct Internet connection.*

Testing Your Connection

Once you've set up Quicken for an Internet connection, you're ready to test it. Here are two simple tasks to get you started.

Visiting Quicken.com

A good connection test is a visit to Quicken.com, Intuit's feature-packed financial Web site for Quicken users and other visitors. I tell you more about Quicken.com later in this chapter and throughout this book. For now, let's just connect to it to make sure your Internet connection works.

Choose Finance | Quicken On The Web | Quicken.com. Quicken attempts to connect to the Internet using the ISP you selected in the Internet Connection Setup dialog box.

What you see during the connection process will vary depending on your ISP. If you use an online service such as America Online, CompuServe, or Prodigy, the service's access software may start automatically to make the connection. You may be prompted to enter a username or password. Other dialog boxes may appear. It may be necessary to switch from connection software back to Quicken by clicking the Quicken button on the Windows task bar.

When the connection is complete, Quicken requests the Quicken.com home page. It appears in an Internet window (see Figure 3-1).

Tip   *If you were already connected to the Internet when you accessed one of Quicken's online features or you have a direct connection to the Internet, you won't see the connection happening. Instead, the Quicken.com page will simply appear in an Internet window.*

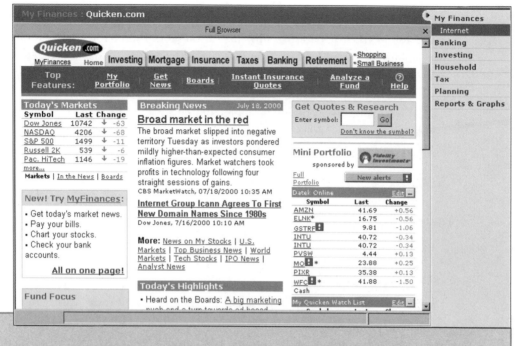

Figure 3-1 • Quicken.com's home page changes daily to offer new information and features

Disconnecting from the Internet

To manually disconnect from the Internet when you have finished using Quicken's online features, choose File | Disconnect. One of two things will happen:

- If you are connected via an online service such as America Online, CompuServe, or Prodigy, Quicken may tell you that it cannot disconnect from the Internet. Switch to the online service's access software by clicking its name in the task bar, and then use that software to disconnect from the Internet.

- If you are connected via another ISP, Quicken may display a dialog box offering to disconnect from the Internet. Click Yes to disconnect.

Tip Once you have successfully completed the Internet connection setup process, Quicken reminds you to disconnect from the Internet each time you exit the program. The dialog box that appears even offers to disconnect for you.

Troubleshooting Connection Problems

If you follow the instructions I provided throughout this chapter, you shouldn't have any trouble connecting to the Internet with Quicken. But things aren't always as easy as they should be. Sometimes even the tiniest problems can prevent you from successfully connecting and exchanging data.

In this section, I provide some troubleshooting advice to help you with connection problems you may experience. Check this section before you start pulling out your hair and cursing the day computers were invented.

Setup Problems

To determine whether the problem is a Quicken setup problem or a general Internet setup problem, exit Quicken and try connecting to the Internet from another program, such as your regular Web browser or e-mail program.

- If you can connect to the Internet from another program but not from Quicken, the problem may be with Quicken's Internet connection setup. Go back to the section "Setting Up an Internet Connection" earlier in this chapter, and repeat the setup process.

- If you can't connect to the Internet from any other program or with dial-up networking (for dial-up connections), the problem is with your Internet setup for Windows, your modem (for dial-up connections), or your network (for direct connections). You must fix any problem you find before you can successfully set up and connect with Quicken.

Modem Problems

Problems with a dial-up connection may be related to your modem. Try each of the following, attempting a connection after each one:

- Check all cables between your computer and your modem (if you have an external modem), and between your modem and the telephone outlet.

- Check the telephone line to make sure it has a dial tone and that it is not being used by someone else or another program.

- Turn off your modem and then turn it back on. Or, if you have an internal modem, restart your computer. This resets the modem and may resolve the problem.

If you can connect but have trouble staying connected, try the following:

- Make sure no one is picking up an extension of the phone line while you are online.

- Make sure call-waiting is disabled by entering the appropriate codes for the dial-up connection.
- Have the phone company check the line for noise. If noise is detected, ask the phone company to fix the problem. (It shouldn't cost you anything if the line noise is the result of a problem outside your premises.)

Network Problems

Problems with a direct connection may be related to your network. Try these things, attempting a connection after each one:

- Check all cables between your computer and the network hub or router.
- Check to make sure the correct Proxy Server information was entered into Quicken's Internet Connection Setup dialog box, which I discuss earlier in this chapter.
- Restart your computer. Sometimes resetting your computer's system software can clear network problems.
- Ask your system administrator to check your network setup.

Exploring Quicken.com

The World Wide Web has had a greater impact on the distribution of information than any innovation since the invention of movable type hundreds of years ago. The Web makes it possible to publish information almost instantly, as it becomes available. Accessible by anyone with a computer, an Internet connection, and Web browsing software, it gives individuals and organizations the power to reach millions of people worldwide without the delays and costs of traditional print and broadcast media.

While this power to publish has flooded the Internet with plenty of useless and trivial information, it has also given birth to exceptional Web sites, full of useful, timely, and accurate information that can make a difference in your life. Quicken.com, Intuit's site, is one of the best financial information sites around.

In this part of the chapter, I'll lead you on a short tour of Quicken.com and other Quicken features on the Web. My goal is to introduce you to what's out there so you can explore the areas that interest you most.

Tip   *If you haven't already completed Quicken's online setup process, go back and do that now so you can follow along.*

Keep one thing in mind as you read through this chapter: Quicken.com is an incredibly dynamic Web site that changes frequently. The screen illustrations and features I tell you about will probably appear differently when you connect. In addition, brand-new features might be added after the publication of this book. That's why I won't go into too much detail. The best way to learn about all the online features of Quicken and Quicken.com when you're ready for them is to check them out for yourself.

Tip   *This part of the chapter assumes you have set up Internet Explorer 4.0 or later as the Web browser for use with Quicken. If you are using another browser, Quicken will launch that browser and display Web pages in its windows, rather than in the Quicken Internet window.*

An Introduction to Web Surfing

Before I start my overview of Quicken on the Web, let me take a moment to explain exactly what you're doing when you connect to Quicken.com and the other Quicken features on the Web. If you're brand new to Web surfing—that is, exploring Web sites—be sure to read this section. But if you're a seasoned surfer, you probably already know all this stuff and can skip it.

One more thing: This section is not designed to explain everything you'll ever need to know about browsing the World Wide Web. It just provides the basic information you need to use the Web to get the information you need.

Going Online

When you access Quicken's online features, you do so by connecting to the Internet through your ISP. It doesn't matter whether you connect via a modem or a network, or whether your ISP is America Online or Joe's Dial-up Internet Service. The main thing is having a connection or a conduit for information.

Think of an Internet connection as some PVC piping running from your computer to your ISP's, with a valve to control the flow of information. Once the valve is open (you're connected), any information can flow through the pipe in either direction. You can even exchange information through that pipe in both directions at the same time. This makes it possible to download (or retrieve) a Web page with your Web browser while you upload (or send) e-mail with your e-mail program.

Quicken's online features use the pipe (or connection) in two ways:

- The integrated Web browser enables you to request and receive the information you want. It's live and interactive—click a link, and a moment later your information starts to appear. Quicken displays Web pages in its Internet window (see Figure 3-2).

- The online account access and payment features work in the background to communicate with financial institutions with which you have accounts. Quicken sends information you prepared in advance and retrieves the information the financial institution has waiting for you.

This chapter concentrates on Web browsing with Quicken—using Quicken's integrated Web browser to access interactive features on Quicken.com. But it also provides some information to help you find financial institutions that work with Quicken for the online account access and payment features.

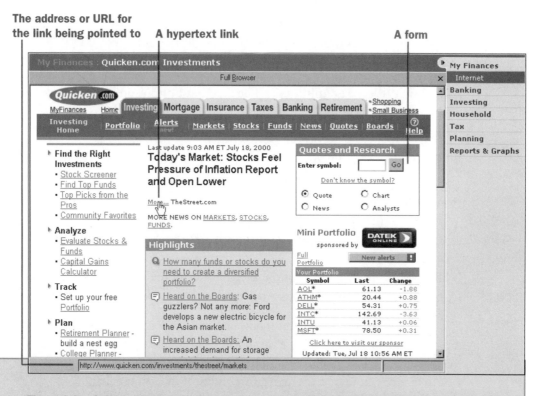

Figure 3-2 • Quicken displays Web pages in a window like this one, which shows the Investing channel home page on Quicken.com

Navigating

The main thing to remember about the Web is that it's interactive. Every time a Web page appears on your screen, it'll offer a number of options for viewing other information. This is known as navigating the Web.

Hyperlinks and Forms   You can move from page to page on the Web in two ways (both of which are illustrated in Figure 3-2):

- **Hyperlinks** (or links) are text or graphics that, when clicked, display another page. Hypertext links are usually underlined, colored text. Graphic links sometimes have a colored border around them. You can always identify a link by pointing to it—your mouse pointer will turn into a hand with a pointing finger.
- **Forms** offer options for going to another page or searching for information. Options can appear in pop-up menus, text boxes that you fill in, check boxes that you turn on, or option buttons that you select. There often are multiple options. You enter or select the options you want and click a button to send your request to the Web site. The information you requested appears a moment later.

Other Navigation Techniques   The first four buttons on Quicken's toolbar are navigation buttons:

- **Back** displays the previously viewed page.
- **Forward** displays the page you viewed after the current page. This button is only available after you have used the Back button.
- **Stop** stops the loading of the current page. This may result in incomplete pages or error messages on the page. You might use this button if you click a link and then realize that you don't really want to view the information you requested.
- **Refresh** loads a new copy of the Web page from the Web site's server. This button is handy for updating stock quotes or news that appears on a page.

In addition, the button bar for many Internet windows includes a Full Browser button (see Figure 3-2). Clicking this button starts and switches to your default Web browser. Quicken continues to run in the background, and you can switch back to it at any time by clicking its icon on the Windows task bar.

Working Offline

When you've finished working with online features and if you have a dial-up connection, you may want to disconnect. This frees up your telephone line for incoming calls. You can continue working offline with features that don't require Internet access.

To work offline, choose File | Disconnect. Quicken displays a dialog box offering to disconnect you from the Internet. Click Yes.

Tip *If you're connected via a direct network connection, the Disconnect command will not be available because you can't disconnect.*

Accessing Quicken on the Web

You can access Quicken's online features using commands on its Finance menu. One of these commands, Quicken On The Web, is really a submenu full of options for Quicken Web features. I tell you more about some of these options next.

Quicken.com

Quicken.com is Intuit's financial Web site. Although designed to be of most use to Quicken users, most of its features are accessible to anyone. Tell your friends about it.

Quicken.com is divided into different *channels*. You can go to a channel by clicking its tab or link near the top of the Quicken.com home page (refer to Figure 3-1). Here's a brief look at what each channel offers.

Investing   The Investing channel (see Figure 3-2) has information of interest to investors, including news, quotes, and research tools. There's specific information about stocks, mutual funds, and bonds. If you're new to investing, you'll find plenty of basic information about investing, written in plain English.

Mortgage   The Mortgage channel (Quicken Loans) should be your first stop if you're looking for a home or shopping for the right mortgage. In addition to current information about national mortgage rates, you'll find interactive tools to help you find out what kinds of loans you qualify for and how much you can afford. Even if you're not shopping for a home, this channel might help you decide whether now is the right time to refinance your current home.

Insurance   The Insurance channel provides a wide range of tools for evaluating your insurance needs. A number of links offer information about insurance basics so you know what your agent is talking about when he or she throws around words like *annuity* and *rider*. You can even shop for insurance online.

Taxes   The Taxes channel provides information you can use to prepare and file your tax returns, including federal and state tax forms and IRS publications. News, articles, and advice offer additional insight into the world of taxation, to help you understand and minimize your tax burden. There are even links to the TurboTax home page, where you can learn about and download Intuit's TurboTax package.

Banking   The Banking channel offers a wealth of up-to-date information about current interest rates on savings and loans, as well as banking-related news stories. This is where you can follow links to find a bank account, get your credit report, and shop for a credit card. If you don't know much about banking or credit, this is the place to come to learn.

Retirement   It's never too early to plan for your retirement. (In fact, the earlier you start planning, the better off you'll be.) The Retirement channel is a great place to research options for funding your retirement years. Learn about 401(k) and 403(b) plans, and all kinds of IRAs. There's even information about social security, pension plans, mutual funds, and stocks. News, articles, and advice provide expert insight to put you on the right path.

Shopping   Like to save money on purchases? Like to shop online? If so, the Shopping channel can help. It offers information about finding the best deals, shopping online, and helping to control your teens' spending. The Product Reviews area offers dozens of reviews on products and services you buy, including autos, computers, electronics, books, and travel. You'll even find links to the interactive Web versions of several Quicken features, such as the Loan Calculator and Savings Calculator. The Quicken Shopper software, which is available as a free download from the Shopping channel's home page, enables you to get price comparisons while shopping online.

Small Business   The Small Business channel is a great Web destination for small business owners and self-employed individuals. You'll find links to information about taxes, accounting, payroll, benefits, retirement, legal issues, and your industry. Research tools help you shop for the best deals in office supplies, hardware, and software. And, of course, there are timely articles about the issues facing small business owners today.

Quicken FAQs

The Quicken FAQs command takes you to the Quicken Technical Support page. This is where you can find answers to frequently asked questions, information about solving problems with Quicken, and program updates. Use this command when you can't find the information you need in this book or with Quicken's Onscreen Help feature.

Quicken Store

The Quicken Store is Intuit's online shopping center, where you can buy Quicken software and supplies for personal finance, tax preparation, and small business. Stop by once in a while to check out its special offers and new products.

Internet Search

Internet Search brings you to the Excite.com home page. You can use Excite's powerful Internet searching features to find information on the Web. There are dozens of links on this page, too—making it a perfect starting point for browsing the Web for a wide variety of topics that interest you.

Quicken Financial Partners

If you're interested in keeping track of your finances with the least amount of data entry, you should be considering Quicken's online features for account access and payment, credit card account access, and investment tracking. I explain the benefits of these features near the beginning of this chapter. Chapters 5 and 7 tell you how to use them. But you can't use them until you've set up an account with a Quicken financial partner and have applied for the online financial services you want to use.

Finding a Quicken Partner

Finding a Quicken financial partner is easy. Choose Finance | Online Financial Institutions List. The Apply For Online Financial Services window appears (see Figure 3-3). This page, which is updated each time a new partner comes on board, offers links with information about each of the partner institutions.

Tip *If you have not set up Quicken for your Internet connection or registered the Quicken software, a dialog box may appear, telling you that you need to do one or both of these things to continue. Follow the prompts within the dialog box as necessary. Eventually, the Apply For Online Financial Services window (see Figure 3-3) will appear.*

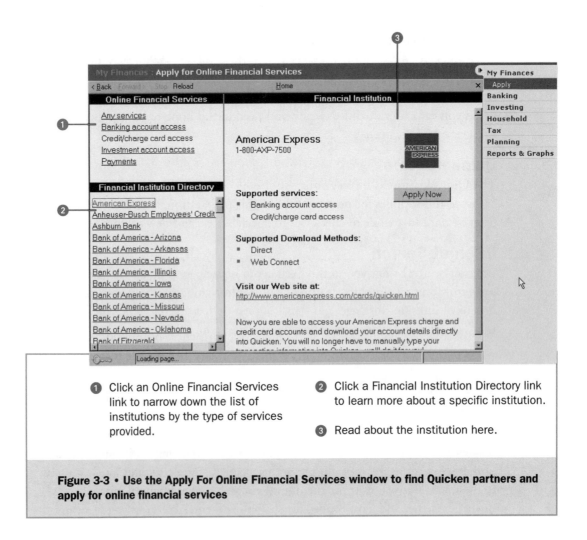

① Click an Online Financial Services link to narrow down the list of institutions by the type of services provided.

② Click a Financial Institution Directory link to learn more about a specific institution.

③ Read about the institution here.

Figure 3-3 • Use the Apply For Online Financial Services window to find Quicken partners and apply for online financial services

Quicken partner institutions offer four types of services:

- **Banking Account Access** enables you to download bank account transactions directly into your Quicken data file.

- **Credit/Charge Card Access** enables you to download credit or charge card transactions directly into your Quicken data file.

- **Investment Account Access** enables you to download brokerage and other investment account transactions directly into your Quicken data file.

- **Payments** enables you to send payment instructions from within Quicken. This makes it possible to pay bills and send payments to anyone without writing a check.

If your bank, credit card company, or brokerage firm is not on the list, you have four options:

Change financial institutions.   I know it sounds harsh, but if your bank or credit card company doesn't support Online Account Access with Quicken and you really want to use this feature, you can find a financial institution that does support it and open an account there.

Wait until your financial institution appears on the list.   The list of partner institutions is updated quite often. If your bank or credit card company doesn't appear there today, it may appear next month. Or next year. You can hurry things along by asking your financial institution to become a Quicken partner institution. If enough customers ask for it, they might add this feature.

Check to see if your financial institution supports Quicken Web Connection.   This feature enables you to download transactions from your financial institution in a specially formatted, Quicken-compatible .QFX file. You can then import the transactions into your Quicken data file. This method limits your online activities to online account access; payment is not supported. Contact your financial institution for details and step-by-step instructions for using this feature.

Use Intuit Online Payment.   If all you're interested in is the Online Payment feature, you can use Intuit Online Payment. This enables you to process online payments via CheckFree Corporation, which can prepare checks from your existing bank accounts. And, there's no need to change banks or wait until your bank signs on as a Quicken partner. You can learn more about Intuit Online Payment in the Financial Institution Directory window, where the other financial institutions are listed.

Applying for Online Financial Services

The information pane of the window for the financial institution you selected (see Figure 3-3) provides information about how you can apply for online account access. In most cases, you'll either click the Apply Now button to apply or learn more, or call the toll-free number that appears onscreen and speak to a company representative. This gets the wheels turning to put you online. It may take a few days to get the necessary access information, so apply as soon as you're sure you want to take advantage of the online financial services features.

Managing Your Bank and Credit Card Accounts

This part of the book explains how to use Quicken to keep track of your bank and credit card accounts. It starts by explaining the basics of manually recording bank and credit card transactions, then goes on to tell you how you can take advantage of Quicken's online account access, payment, and billing features to automate much of the data entry. This part has two chapters:

Chapter 4: *Recording Your Bank and Credit Card Transactions*

Chapter 5: *Online Banking and Billing*

Recording Bank and Credit Card Transactions

In This Chapter:

- *Entering Payments and Other Transactions*

- *Writing and Printing Checks*

- *Entering Credit Card Transactions*

- *Transferring Money*

- *Working with Existing Transactions*

- *Using Splits and Classes*

- *Using QuickEntry*

- *Setting Check and Register Options*

A t Quicken's core is its ability to manage your bank accounts. This is probably Quicken's most used feature. You enter the transactions and Quicken keeps track of account balances and the source and destination of the money you spend. You can even have Quicken print checks for you.

Using similar transaction entry techniques, Quicken can also keep track of credit card accounts. You enter transactions as you make them or at month's end when you receive your statement and pay your bill. Quicken keeps track of balances and offers you an easy way to monitor what you used your credit card to buy. It also enables you to keep an eye on how much your credit cards cost you in terms of finance charges and other fees.

Tip *Quicken's Online Account Access and Online Payment features can save you time and money. Once you understand the basics of entering transactions as discussed in this chapter, be sure to consult Chapter 5 to see how Quicken's online features can make transaction entry quicker and easier.*

Quicken Banking Overview

Quicken groups all of its banking-related commands and features in two separate places: the Banking menu and the Banking Center window. Here's a quick look at each.

Tip *As you may have already realized, Quicken offers numerous ways to access each of its features and commands. Rather than include them all in the book, I'll concentrate on the quickest and easiest ways.*

The Banking Menu

Quicken's Banking menu, which is shown next, includes a variety of commands you can use to access Quicken's banking features, including its online banking features. I cover most of these features in this chapter and Chapter 5.

You might find a few commands especially useful as you work with Quicken's banking features:

- **Bank Accounts** displays a submenu that lists all of your bank accounts. This offers a quick and easy way to open the register for a specific account; simply choose its name from the menu.
- **Write Checks** opens the Write Checks window, which you can use to enter payment transactions into your checking account. I discuss the Write Checks feature later in this chapter.
- **Banking Activities** displays a submenu of banking-related tasks that aren't used as often as those on the main Banking menu. These include tasks such as balancing your checkbook, entering transactions into the active account register, and creating a new account. I cover all of these tasks in this chapter, Chapter 5, and elsewhere in this book.
- **Banking Services** displays a submenu of banking-related services available from Quicken, Quicken.com, and other providers. This is where you'll find commands for ordering checks and supplies, automating your daily file backup, and applying for a Quicken MasterCard.

The Banking Center Window

The Banking Center window (see Figure 4-1) is full of information about your banking accounts, as well as links to banking-related Quicken and Quicken.com features and services. To open the Banking Center window, click its QuickTab on the right side of the screen.

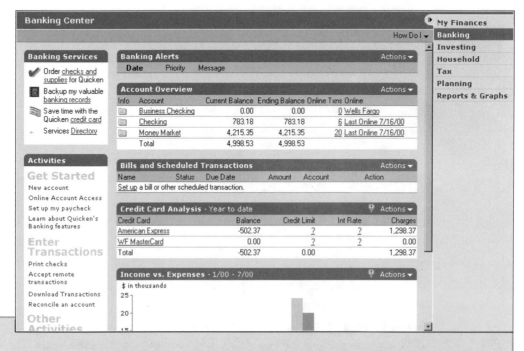

Figure 4-1 • The Banking Center window is a great place to access information about your bank and credit card accounts, as well as Quicken's banking-related features

The Banking Center window is separated into three main parts: Banking Services, Activities, and banking snapshots.

Banking Services   The Banking Services area lists a few of the most commonly used services available for Quicken users. Click an underlined link to access that service. For a complete list of services, click the Directory link in the Banking Services area.

Activities   The Activities area offers clickable links to Quicken features. These are separated into Activities and Questions:

- **Activities** are the same commands available under the Banking menu, reworded to make them less cryptic than a menu command. For example, Reconcile An Account is the same as the Banking menu's Reconcile command.

- **Questions** are banking-related questions that Quicken can answer for you, such as How Can I Save More?

Banking Snapshots The Banking Center snapshots fill most of the Banking Center window. They include information about your bank and credit card accounts. The Actions menu for each snapshot offers commands that apply to the snapshot or information it contains. The following snapshots appear in this window:

- **Banking Alerts** displays alerts related to your bank and credit card accounts. I tell you about alerts in Chapter 11.

- **Account Overview** lists all of your bank accounts, along with their current and ending balances. (You'll see why those two numbers can be different for an account later in this chapter.) You can click the name of an account to open its account register.

- **Bills And Scheduled Transactions** lists outstanding bills and transactions you have scheduled for the near future. I tell you how to use Quicken's scheduling feature in Chapter 11.

- **Credit Card Analysis** provides some basic information about your credit card accounts, including balance, limit, interest rate, and monthly charges. You can click the name of the account to open its register. If an interest rate does not appear, you can click the question mark that appears in its place to enter rate information.

- **Income Versus Expenses** displays a year-to-date column chart of your monthly income and expenses. You can click a column to display a box that tells you the exact amount the column represents.

Getting Started

Before you can use Quicken to track bank and credit card transactions, you should prepare by creating the necessary accounts and having a good idea of how recording transactions works. In this section, I provide an overview of the account types, along with examples of transactions you might make. I also provide some detailed information about the information you should provide when creating specific types of accounts.

Overview of Accounts and Transactions

Most of the transactions you track with Quicken will involve one or more of its banking and cash accounts. Here's a closer look at each account type, along with some transaction examples. As you read about these accounts, imagine how they might apply to your financial situation.

Bank Accounts

Quicken offers three types of accounts that you can use to track the money you have in a bank:

- **Checking** accounts include check-writing privileges. These accounts usually have a lot of activity, with deposits to increase the account balance and checks that decrease the account balance.
- **Savings** accounts are for your savings. These accounts usually don't have as much activity as checking accounts. You can use a savings account to track the balance in a certificate of deposit (CD), holiday savings club, or similar savings account.
- **Money market** accounts are similar to savings accounts, but, as I discuss in Chapter 8, they are not guaranteed by the FDIC. That makes them a kind of cross between a bank savings account and an investment account.

Generally speaking, bank account transactions can be broken down into three broad categories: payments, deposits, and transfers.

Payments   *Payments* are cash outflows. Here are some examples:

- You write a check to pay your electric bill.
- You withdraw money from your savings account to buy a gift for your mother.
- You use your ATM card to withdraw spending money from a bank account.
- You use your debit card to buy groceries.
- You pay a monthly checking account fee.

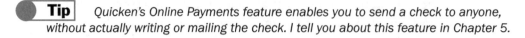

Tip   *Quicken's Online Payments feature enables you to send a check to anyone, without actually writing or mailing the check. I tell you about this feature in Chapter 5.*

Deposits   *Deposits* are cash inflows. Here are some examples:

- You deposit your paycheck in your checking account.
- You sell your old computer and deposit the proceeds in your savings account.
- Your paycheck or social security check is deposited into your bank account as a direct deposit.
- You earn interest on your savings account.

Transfers   A *transfer* is a movement of funds from one account to another. Here are some examples:

- You transfer money from an interest-bearing savings account to your checking account when you're ready to pay your bills.
- You transfer money from a money market account to your home equity line of credit account to reduce its balance.

Credit Card Accounts

Credit card accounts track money you owe, not money you own. Some credit cards, such as MasterCard, Visa, American Express, and Discover, can be used in most stores that accept credit cards. Other credit cards, such as Macy's, Dillards, and Texaco, can only be used in certain stores. But they all have one thing in common: If there's a balance, it's usually because you owe the credit card company money.

Credit card account transactions can also be broken down into two categories: charges and payments.

Charges   *Charges* result when you use your credit card to buy something or the credit card company charges a fee for services. Here are some examples:

- You use your Visa card to buy a new computer.
- You use your Discover card to pay for a hotel stay.
- You use your Texaco card to fill the gas tank on your boat at the marina.
- A finance charge based on your account balance is added to your Macy's bill at month's end.
- A late fee is added to your MasterCard bill because you didn't pay the previous month's bill on time.
- A fee is added to your American Express bill for annual membership dues.

The opposite of a charge is a *credit*. Think of it as a negative charge; don't confuse it with a payment. Here are two examples:

- You return the sweater you bought with your American Express card to the store you bought it from.
- In reviewing your MasterCard bill, you discover that a merchant charged you in error, and you arrange to have the incorrect charge removed.

Payments   *Payments* are amounts you send to a credit card company to reduce your balance. Here are three examples:

- You pay the minimum amount due on your Visa card.
- You pay $150 toward the balance on your Macy's card.
- You pay the balance on your American Express card.

Cash Accounts

Quicken also offers cash accounts for tracking cash expenditures. For example, you might create an account called My Wallet or Spending Money and use it to keep track of the cash you have on hand. Cash accounts are like bank accounts, but there's no bank. The money is in your wallet, your pocket, or the old coffee can on the windowsill.

Cash accounts have two types of transactions: receive and spend.

Receive   When you *receive* cash, you increase the amount of cash you have on hand. Here are some examples:

- You withdraw cash from the bank for weekly spending money.
- You sell your *National Geographic* magazine collection for cash at a garage sale.
- You get a 20-dollar bill in a birthday card from your grandmother.

Spend   When you *spend* cash, you reduce your cash balance. Here are some examples:

- You buy coffee and a newspaper and pay a bridge toll on your way to work.
- You give your son his allowance.
- You put a 20-dollar bill in the birthday card you send to your granddaughter.

> **Tip**   *Tracking every penny you spend, from the cup of coffee you buy at work in the morning to the quart of milk you pick up on your way home that evening, isn't for everyone. You may prefer to track only large cash inflows or outflows and record the rest as Miscellaneous expenses.*

Creating Bank, Credit Card, and Cash Accounts

In Chapter 2, I explain how to use the Account Setup dialog box to create new Quicken accounts. Here are two additional things you should keep in mind when creating bank, credit card, and cash accounts.

Account Names   Give each account a name that clearly identifies it. For example, if you have two checking accounts, don't name them "Checking 1" and "Checking 2." Instead, include the bank name (such as "USA Bank Checking") or account purpose (such as "Business Checking") in the account name. This prevents you from accidentally entering a transaction in the wrong account register.

Balance Information   For bank and credit card accounts, get the balance date and amount from your most recent statement. Then be careful not to enter transactions that already appear on that statement or in previous statements.

Entering Transactions

To make the most of Quicken, you must be willing to spend a little time entering transactions for the accounts you want to track. There are different ways to enter transactions, based on the type of transaction you want to enter:

- Use *registers* to record virtually any type of transaction, including manual checks, bank account payments and deposits, credit card charges and payments, and cash receipts and spending.
- Use the *Write Checks window* to record checks to be printed by Quicken.
- Enter *transfers* to transfer money from one account to another.
- Use *QuickEntry* to enter transactions without opening the full Quicken program.

In this section, I cover all of these techniques.

Using Account Registers

Quicken's account registers offer a standard way to enter all kinds of transactions. As the name suggests, these electronic account registers are very similar to the paper checking account register that comes with your checks.

To open a register, choose its name from the Bank Accounts submenu under the Banking menu (shown earlier) or click its name in the Banking Center window (refer back to Figure 4-1). The account's register window appears (see Figure 4-2). Use it to enter and record transactions.

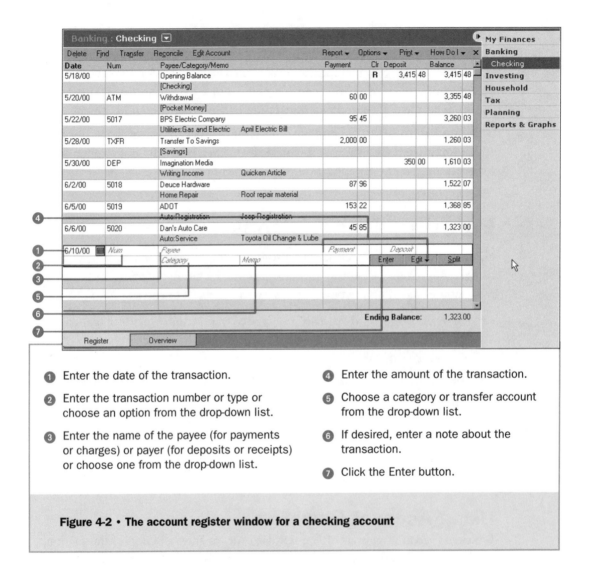

1. Enter the date of the transaction.

2. Enter the transaction number or type or choose an option from the drop-down list.

3. Enter the name of the payee (for payments or charges) or payer (for deposits or receipts) or choose one from the drop-down list.

4. Enter the amount of the transaction.

5. Choose a category or transfer account from the drop-down list.

6. If desired, enter a note about the transaction.

7. Click the Enter button.

Figure 4-2 • The account register window for a checking account

Basic Entry Techniques

Figure 4-2 provides basic step-by-step instructions for using the account register window. Here are a few additional things to consider when entering transactions.

Advancing from Field to Field   To move from one text box to another when entering transactions, you can either click in the text box or press the TAB key. Pressing TAB is usually quicker.

Using Buttons   Buttons appear when certain text boxes are active:

- When the Date text box is active, a calendar icon appears. You can click it to display a calendar and then click calendar buttons to view and enter a date.
- When the Payment or Deposit text box is active, a calculator icon appears. You can click it to use a calculator and enter calculated results.

Using the Num Field   The Num field is where you enter a transaction number or type. You can enter any number you like or use the drop-down list to display a list of standard entries; click an option to enter it for the transaction:

- **Next Check Num** automatically increments the most recently entered check number and enters the resulting number in the Num field.
- **ATM** is for ATM withdrawals.
- **Deposit** is for deposits.
- **Print Check** is for transactions for which you want Quicken to print a check. Quicken automatically records the check number when the check is printed.
- **Send Online Payment** is for online payments. This option only appears when online payment is enabled for the account. I tell you about paying bills online in Chapter 5.
- **Online Transfer** is for online transfers of funds from one account to another. This option only appears when online banking is enabled for the account. I tell you about online banking in Chapter 5.
- **Transfer** is for a transfer of funds from one account to another.
- **EFT**, which stands for Electronic Funds Transfer, is for direct deposits and similar transactions.

Tip   *You can press the + or – key on the keyboard to increment or decrement the check number while the Num field is active.*

QuickFill   As you start to enter the name of a payee or payer that is already in Quicken's data file, Quicken may fill in the entire name and most recent transaction for you. This is Quicken's QuickFill feature, which I tell you more about in Chapter 11.

Entering New Categories   If you enter a category that does not exist in the Category & Transfer List, Quicken displays a dialog box, like the one shown next, that offers to create the category for you. Click Yes to create a new category or click No to return to the register and enter a different category. I explain how to create categories in Chapter 2.

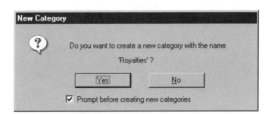

Tip   _You can instruct Quicken to automatically create new categories for you. Simply turn off the Prompt Before Creating New Categories check box in the New Category dialog box. From that point forward, Quicken will automatically display the Set Up category dialog box every time you enter a category that does not exist in the Category & Transfer List._

Entering Multiple Categories   To enter more than one category for a transaction, click the Split button. I tell you about splits next.

Using Splits

A _split_ is a transaction with more than one category. For example, suppose you pay one utility bill for two categories of utilities—electricity and water. If you want to track each of these two expenses separately, you can use a split to record each category's portion of the payment you make. This enables you to keep good records without writing multiple checks to the same payee.

To record a transaction with a split, click the Split button in the account register or Write Checks window when entering the transaction. The Split Transaction window appears; it enables you to enter as many categories as you like:

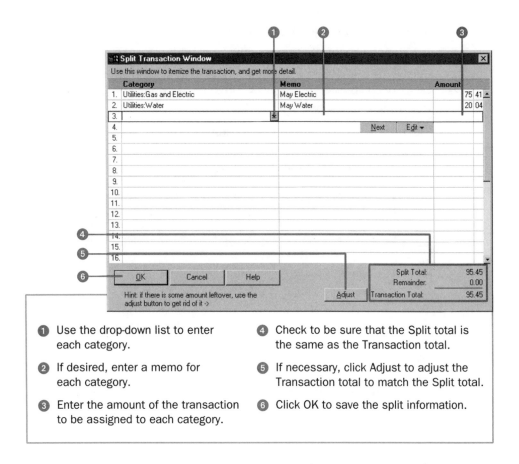

① Use the drop-down list to enter each category.

② If desired, enter a memo for each category.

③ Enter the amount of the transaction to be assigned to each category.

④ Check to be sure that the Split total is the same as the Transaction total.

⑤ If necessary, click Adjust to adjust the Transaction total to match the Split total.

⑥ Click OK to save the split information.

When you complete the split, the word *Split* appears in the Category field of the transaction. Here's what it looks like in the account register window:

Click here to view and edit the split.

Click here to clear all lines from the split.

 Caution | *Clearing all lines from a split permanently removes them.*

Using Classes

A *class* is an optional identifier for specifying what a transaction applies to. For example, if you have two cars for which you track expenses, you can create a class for each car—for example, "Jeep" and "Toyota." Then, when you record a transaction for one of the cars, you can include the appropriate class with the category for the transaction. Because Quicken can produce reports based on categories, classes, or both, classes offer an additional dimension for tracking and reporting information.

Working with the Class List Window   Quicken maintains a list of all the classes you create. You can display the Class List by choosing Finance | Class List, or by pressing CTRL-L. Here's an example with some classes I created:

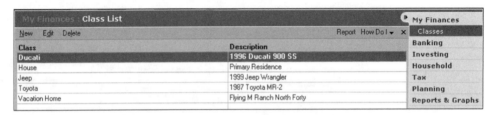

You can use three buttons in the button bar near the top of the Class List window to work with the class list or a selected class:

- **New** enables you to create a new class.
- **Edit** enables you to modify the currently selected class name or other information.
- **Delete** enables you to delete the currently selected class.

Creating a New Class   Click the New button on the button bar in the Class List window. The Set Up Class dialog box appears; use it to enter information about the class:

Only one piece of information is really necessary: the class name. You may want to make it short so it's easy to remember and enter. The description can be used to provide additional information on what the class is used for. The copy number enables you to associate different classes with different but similar activities. For example, if you have two separate businesses for which you report activity on two Schedule Cs, you can assign Copy 1 to one business's classes and Copy 2 to the other business's classes.

Including a Class in a Transaction   To include a class in a transaction, enter a slash (/) followed by the class name after the category. Here's an example in the register window:

6/6/00	5020	Dan's Auto Care		45 85	*Deposit*	1,418 45
		Auto:Service/Toyota	Oil Change & Lube		Enter Edit ▾ Split	

Tip   *If you enter a class name that is not on the Class List, Quicken displays the Set Up Class window so you can create the class on the fly.*

Credit Card Tracking Techniques

You can use either of two techniques for paying credit card bills and monitoring credit card balances:

- Use your checking account register or the Write Checks window to record amounts paid to each credit card company. Although this does track the amounts you pay, it doesn't track how much you owe or the individual charges.

- Use a credit card account register to record credit card expenditures and payments. This takes a bit more effort on your part, but it tracks how much you owe and what you bought.

Tip   *Knowing how much you owe on your credit cards helps you maintain a clear picture of your financial situation. In my opinion, it's worth the extra effort to track your credit card expenditures and balances in individual credit card accounts.*

You can use two strategies to record transactions in credit card accounts. Choosing the strategy that's right for you makes the job easier to handle.

Enter As You Spend   One strategy is to enter transactions as you spend. To do this, you must collect all the credit card receipts that are handed to you when you use your credit cards—which might be something you already do. Don't forget to jot down the totals for any telephone and online shopping you do. Then, every day or every few days, sit down with Quicken or QuickEntry and enter the transactions.

While this strategy requires you to stay on top of things, it offers two main benefits:

- Your Quicken credit card registers always indicate what you owe to credit card companies. This prevents unpleasant surprises at month's end or at the checkout counter when you're told you've reached your limit. It also enables you to use the alerts feature to track credit card balances; I tell you about that in Chapter 11.
- At month's end, you don't have to spend a lot of time entering big batches of transactions. All (or at least most) of them should already be entered.

I'll be the first to admit that I never was able to use this strategy. I just don't like holding onto all those pieces of paper. (Of course, since signing up for Online Account Access, all this information is entered regularly for me.)

Enter When You Pay   The other strategy, which you may find better for you, is to enter transactions when you get your monthly statement. With this strategy, when you open your credit card statement, you'll spend some time sitting in front of your computer with Quicken to enter each and every transaction. If there aren't many, this isn't a big deal. But it could take some time if there are many transactions.

Of course, the main benefit of this strategy is that you don't have to collect credit card receipts and spend time throughout the month entering your transactions. But you still have to enter them! This is the method I use for the one credit card I have that I cannot access online yet.

Entering Credit Card Transactions

Once you select a strategy, you're ready to enter the transactions. Here are a few tips; Figure 4-3 illustrates some examples.

Entering Individual Charges   Open the account register for the credit card account. Then enter the charge transaction, using the name of the merchant that accepted the charge as the payee name. You can leave the Ref text box empty.

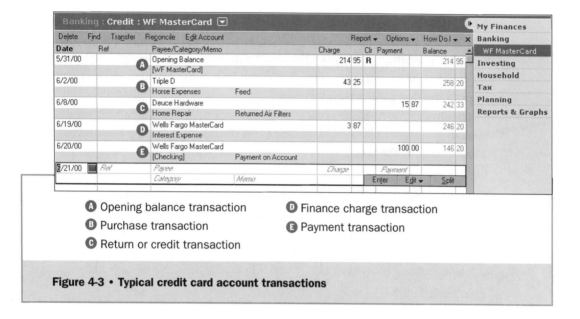

- **Ⓐ** Opening balance transaction
- **Ⓑ** Purchase transaction
- **Ⓒ** Return or credit transaction
- **Ⓓ** Finance charge transaction
- **Ⓔ** Payment transaction

Figure 4-3 • Typical credit card account transactions

Entering Credits   Enter the transaction just as if it were a charge, but put the amount of the credit in the Payment text box. This subtracts it from your account balance.

Entering Finance Charges   In the credit card account register, enter the name of the credit card company as the payee and the amount of the finance charge as a charge.

Entering Payments   In the account register for your checking account or in the Write Checks window, enter a payment transaction with the credit card company name in the Payee text box. Enter the credit card account name in the Category text box; you should find it as a transfer account at the bottom of the Category drop-down list that appears when you activate the field. The checking account register transaction should look like the one shown next; Figure 4-3 shows what this transaction looks like in the credit card account register.

| 6/20/00 | 5021 | Wells Fargo MasterCard | | 100 00 | | 5,438 12 |
| | | [WF MasterCard] | Payment on Account | | | |

Tip   *You can also enter a payment transaction for your credit card account at the end of the credit card account reconciliation process, which I discuss in Chapter 12.*

Entering Cash Transactions

Although Quicken enables you to keep track of cash transactions through the use of a cash account, not everyone does this. The reason: Most people make many small cash transactions every day. Is it worth tracking every penny you spend? That's something you need to decide.

Personally, I don't track all cash transactions. I only track expenditures that are large or tax deductible. You may want to do the same. If so, you still need to set up a cash account, but you don't need to record every transaction. That's what I do; Figure 4-4 shows an example.

Cash Receipts   Cash receipts may come from using your ATM card, cashing a check, or getting cash from some other source. If the cash comes from one of your other accounts through an ATM or check transaction, when you record that transaction, use your Cash account as the transfer in the Category check box. That increases your cash balance. Here's what the transaction might look like in your checking account:

5/20/00	ATM	Withdrawal	60	00		3,355	48
		[Pocket Money]					

Important Cash Expenditures   In your cash account, record large, tax-deductible, or other important cash expenditures like any other transaction. Be sure to assign the correct category.

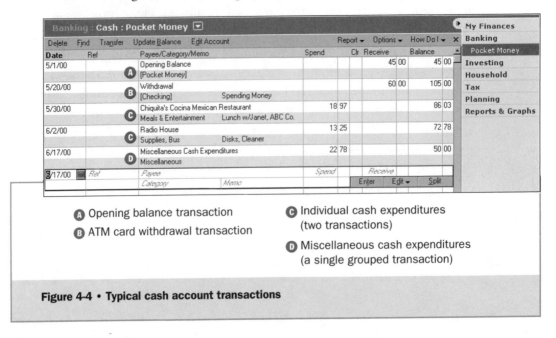

Ⓐ Opening balance transaction

Ⓑ ATM card withdrawal transaction

Ⓒ Individual cash expenditures (two transactions)

Ⓓ Miscellaneous cash expenditures (a single grouped transaction)

Figure 4-4 • Typical cash account transactions

Other Cash Expenditures   Throughout the week, you may spend 50 cents for a newspaper, a dollar for a cup of coffee, and about seven dollars for lunch at your favorite sushi restaurant. Recording transactions like these can be tedious, so don't bother if you don't want to. Instead, at the end of the week, compare your cash on hand to the balance in your cash account register. Then enter a transaction to record the difference as an expenditure. You can use a Miscellaneous category and put anything you like in the Payee text box.

Writing Checks

Quicken's Write Checks window uses a basic checklike interface to record checks. You enter the same information that you would write on an actual check. You then tell Quicken to print the check based on the information you entered.

Tip   *To print the checks you write in Quicken, you must order compatible check stock from Intuit or another check printer. I tell you how and explain how to print checks later in this chapter.*

To open the Write Checks window, choose Banking | Write Checks, press CTRL-W, or click the Write A Check link in the Banking Center window. The Write Checks window, which is shown in Figure 4-5, appears. If necessary, choose the name of the account for which you want to write checks from the pop-up menu in the document window's title bar. Then enter the necessary information for a check and record the transaction.

Figure 4-5 provides basic step-by-step instructions for using the Write Checks window. As you can imagine, it works a lot like the account register window discussed earlier in this chapter—consult that section for more information. Here are a few additional things to consider when entering transactions in the Write Checks window.

Addresses on Checks   If you enter an address on the check, you can mail the check using a window envelope. The address is automatically added to the Quicken Address Book. You can click the Address button in the Write Checks window to display the Edit Address Book Record dialog box, which you can use to modify an address in the Address Book.

Check Memos   If you enter a note on the memo line of a check, it might be visible if you mail the check in a window envelope.

Online Payments   An Online Payment check box appears in the Write Check window if online payment is enabled for the account for which you are writing a check. I tell you about online payments in Chapter 5.

Transferring Money

You can also record the transfer of funds from one account to another. You might find this feature especially useful for recording telephone or ATM transfers.

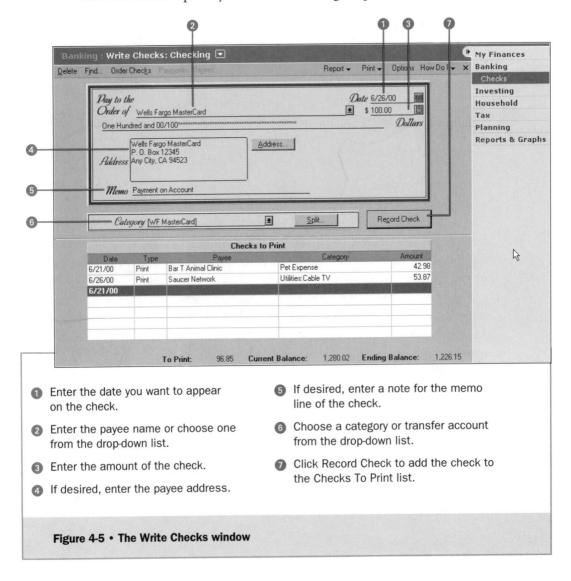

Figure 4-5 • The Write Checks window

1. Enter the date you want to appear on the check.

2. Enter the payee name or choose one from the drop-down list.

3. Enter the amount of the check.

4. If desired, enter the payee address.

5. If desired, enter a note for the memo line of the check.

6. Choose a category or transfer account from the drop-down list.

7. Click Record Check to add the check to the Checks To Print list.

SAVE TIME   Online Account Access enables you to transfer money from one account to another by simply entering the transaction and sending its instructions to the bank via an Internet connection. There's no need to call or visit your bank or submit any paper forms.

Using the Transfer Dialog Box

One way to record a transfer is with the Transfer dialog box. Open the account register window for one of the accounts involved in the transfer transaction and click the Transfer button on the button bar. The Transfer dialog box appears; use it to enter information about the transfer and click OK:

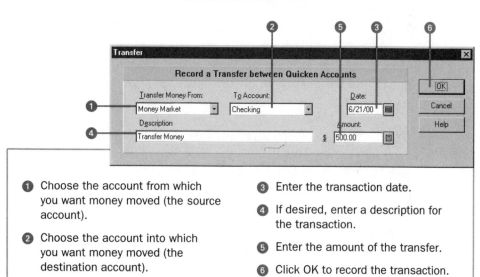

❶ Choose the account from which you want money moved (the source account).

❷ Choose the account into which you want money moved (the destination account).

❸ Enter the transaction date.

❹ If desired, enter a description for the transaction.

❺ Enter the amount of the transfer.

❻ Click OK to record the transaction.

Recording a Transfer in the Account Register Window

The Transfer dialog box isn't the only way to record a transfer. You can also record a transfer in the account register window of either the source or destination account. When you choose Transfer (TXFR) from the Num drop-down list, the Category drop-down list displays only transfer accounts. Choose the other transfer account from the list and complete the transaction.

The following illustrations show a transfer from a money market account to a checking account. Here's what the money market account transaction looks like:

6/21/00	TXFR	Transfer Money	500	00			7,508	78
		[Checking]						

And here's what the corresponding checking account transaction looks like:

6/21/00		Transfer Money					500	00	1,823	00
		[Money Market]								

Using QuickEntry

Quicken Deluxe users can also enter transactions with QuickEntry. This program, which works just like the account register feature of Quicken, makes it possible to enter transaction information without opening Quicken. Then, the next time you open Quicken, you can review and either accept or reject the QuickEntry transactions.

Tip   *You might find QuickEntry useful if both you and your spouse want to track payments and deposits, but only you know how to use Quicken. This prevents your spouse from accidentally changing the financial records, while enabling him or her to help you enter transactions.*

Opening QuickEntry

To use QuickEntry, open it by double-clicking its icon on the desktop or choosing it from the Quicken submenu in the Programs folder on the Start menu of the Windows task bar. As shown in Figure 4-6, QuickEntry looks and works very much like the account register shown in Figure 4-2.

Note   *You cannot run QuickEntry if Quicken is running. Be sure to exit Quicken before trying to run QuickEntry.*

When you've finished entering information in QuickEntry, choose File | Exit. The transactions you entered are automatically saved for review the next time you use Quicken.

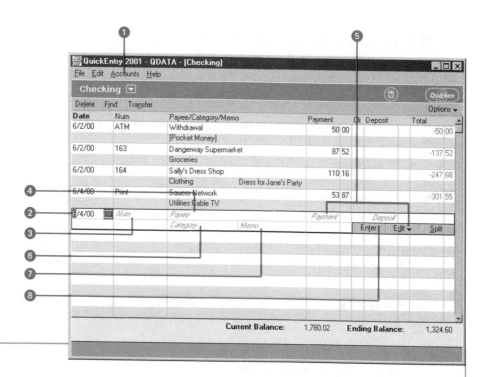

1 Choose the account for which you want to enter transactions.

2 Enter the date of the transaction.

3 Enter the transaction number or Num code.

4 Enter the name of the payee (for a payment or charge) or payer (for a deposit or cash receipt).

5 Enter the transaction amount.

6 Choose a category from the drop-down list.

7 If desired, enter a note for the transaction.

8 Click Enter to record the transaction.

Figure 4-6 • The QuickEntry window

Reviewing QuickEntry Transactions

When you use QuickEntry to enter one or more transactions, the transactions are stored in your Quicken data file—but they are not automatically recorded in the appropriate account. It's your job to review the transactions, make corrections if necessary, and record them.

Tip *You can easily see whether transactions are waiting to be recorded in an account by looking at the account's QuickTab. A lightning bolt appears beside the name of the account (see Figure 4-7).*

New in 2001

Open the register for an account for which QuickEntry transactions exist. The window is split and shows transactions to be reviewed and entered in the bottom half (see Figure 4-7).

Select a transaction to view it or begin entering it in the account register.

Enter or edit transactions in this area.

If necessary, choose QuickEntry from this drop-down menu.

Use these buttons to work with QuickEntry transactions.

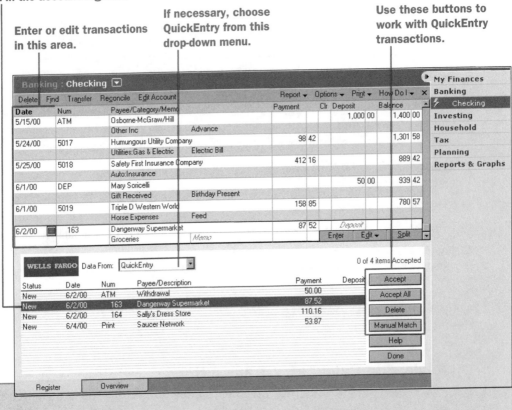

Figure 4-7 • **Transactions waiting to be entered appear in the bottom half of an account's register window**

Note *The process of reviewing and accepting QuickEntry transactions is very similar to the process of reviewing and accepting transactions downloaded from online sources, including your bank, credit card company, investment firm, QIF Import, WebConnect file, and WebEntry. Read this section carefully if you plan to use any of these other features, which are discussed throughout the remainder of this book. The techniques you learn here will apply over and over again with Quicken's online features.*

The Status column in the bottom half of the window identifies three types of transactions:

- **Match** identifies transactions that match those in the register. This will happen if the transaction has already been entered in the Quicken register.
- **New** identifies transactions that do not appear to be in the register.
- **Accepted** identifies matched transactions that you have accepted.

Accepting a Matched Transaction   If a transaction matches one in the register, you can accept it by selecting it in the list at the bottom of the window and clicking the Accept button. (When accepting downloaded transactions, a small *c* appears in the Clr column of the register to indicate that the item has cleared the bank but has not yet been reconciled.)

Entering and Accepting a New Transaction   To enter and accept a new transaction, select the transaction in the bottom half of the window. Quicken begins preparing a register transaction entry for it as you can see in Figure 4-7. Fill in the missing details, including the payee, category, and memo. Then click Enter. Quicken enters and accepts the transaction.

Tip *When you click the Accept or Accept All button, you may be prompted to enter additional information, such as the transaction category, for transactions identified as New.*

Matching a New Transaction   If a downloaded transaction identified as New should match one in the register, you can modify the information in the register to match the information in the downloaded transaction. When you click the Enter button for the register transaction, the word *Match* should appear beside the downloaded transaction. You can then accept it.

Manually Matching a Transaction   If a single transaction corresponds to multiple transactions in your account register, you can manually match them up. Select the transaction that you want to manually match, and click Manual Match to display the Manually Match Transactions dialog box, which is shown next. Turn on the check boxes for each transaction you want to include in the match. The Difference noted near the bottom of the dialog box should equal zero; if it does not, Quicken includes the difference in the transaction but does not categorize it. When you click Accept, Quicken creates an entry for the transaction that includes each of the register transactions (and any differences) on a separate split line. You can click the Split button for the transaction to edit it as desired.

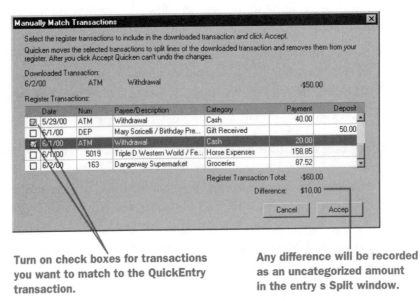

Turn on check boxes for transactions you want to match to the QuickEntry transaction.

Any difference will be recorded as an uncategorized amount in the entry s Split window.

Unmatching a Matched Transaction   If a matched transaction really shouldn't be matched, select it in the bottom half of the window and click the Unmatch button. (This button appears where the Delete button is when a matched transaction is selected.) You can then treat it as a new transaction.

Deleting a New Transaction   To delete a new transaction, select the transaction in the bottom half of the window and click the Delete button. The transaction is removed from the transaction list.

Tip   *This option is especially useful the first time you download transactions from your financial institution, as discussed in Chapters 5 and 7. You may download transactions that have already been reconciled. Use the Unmatch button to unmatch them as necessary, and then use the Delete button to delete them from the transaction list.*

Finishing Up   When you've finished comparing transactions to register transactions, click the Done button. If you failed to accept all of the transactions, Quicken displays a dialog box offering to finish now or later. If you click the Finish Later button, the unaccepted transactions are saved for the next time you compare transactions.

Caution   *Downloaded transactions that have not been accepted may not be entered in your account register. Thus, your register balance may be misstated until you accept all downloaded transactions.*

Working with Existing Transactions

So far, this chapter has concentrated on entering transactions. What do you do when you need to modify a transaction you already recorded? That's what this section is all about.

Searching for Transactions

Quicken includes three primary commands to help you locate and work with transactions:

- **Find** enables you to search for transactions in the active account based on any field.
- **Find/Replace** enables you to find transactions based on any field and replace any field of the found transactions.
- **Recategorize** enables you to find transactions for a specific category and replace the category.

Tip   *You might also find it helpful to use the Sort options (under the Options menu in the account register window's button bar) to change the sort order of transactions. For example, sorting by check number groups the transactions by the Num field, making it easy to find transactions by type. You can quickly move to a specific date or transaction number by dragging the scroll box; the QuickScroll feature displays the date and number of the transaction that will appear when you release the scroll box.*

The following sections take a closer look at each of these commands.

Using the Find Command

To use the Find command, begin by opening the account register or Write Checks window for the account that you want to search. Then choose Edit | Find & Replace | Find, click the Find button on the window's button bar, or press CTRL-F. The Quicken Find dialog box appears; use it to search for transactions that match the criteria you enter:

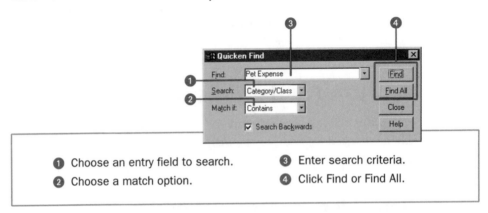

1. Choose an entry field to search.   3. Enter search criteria.
2. Choose a match option.   4. Click Find or Find All.

After setting up the search, if you click the Find button, Quicken selects the first match found in the window. You can then click the Find button again to find the next match. If you click the Find All button, Quicken displays the Quicken Find window, which lists all the matches it found. You can double-click a match to view it in the account register window.

Tip *Quicken remembers a Find setup throughout the Quicken session. Later, to conduct the same search, you can choose Edit | Find & Replace | Find Next, or press SHIFT-CTRL-F.*

Using the Find/Replace Command

The Find/Replace command works throughout Quicken—not just with the active account register or Write Checks window. To use it, choose Edit | Find & Replace | Find/Replace. The Find and Replace dialog box appears. The top part of the dialog box looks and works very much like the Quicken Find dialog box. Once you set up the search and click the Find All button, a list of matches appears in the bottom half of the dialog box; you can then enter replacement options:

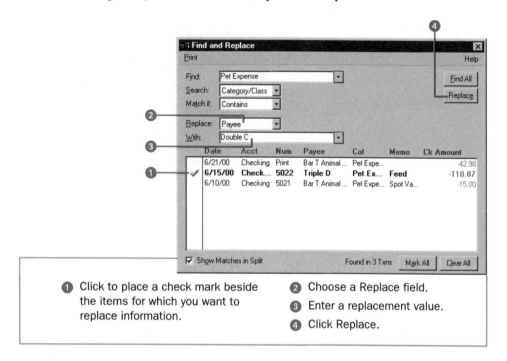

① Click to place a check mark beside the items for which you want to replace information.

② Choose a Replace field.

③ Enter a replacement value.

④ Click Replace.

Using the Recategorize Command

The Recategorize command works like the Find/Replace command, but it finds and replaces only categories. For example, suppose you are using the Miscellaneous category a little more often than you should, and you know that some transactions could be recategorized. You can use the Recategorize command to find transactions with the Miscellaneous category and then change some or all of them to a more appropriate category.

Choose Edit | Find & Replace | Recategorize to display the Recategorize dialog box. Start by using the Find menu on the dialog box's button bar to choose the type of transaction you want to find: Transactions (entered transactions), Memorized Transactions, or Scheduled Transactions. Then choose a category from the Search Category drop-down list and click Find All. A list of matches appears in the

Recategorize dialog box. Select the transactions for which you want to change the category, choose a new category, and replace the categories for selected transactions all at once:

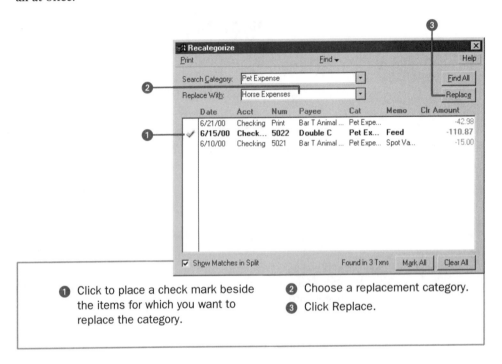

① Click to place a check mark beside the items for which you want to replace the category.

② Choose a replacement category.

③ Click Replace.

Changing Transactions

Quicken enables you to change a transaction at any time—even after it has been cleared. This makes it possible to correct errors in any transaction you have entered.

If all you want to do is change one of the fields in the transaction—such as the category, date, or number—simply find the transaction in the appropriate account register, make changes as desired, and click the Enter button to record them.

The Edit drop-down menu that appears in the account register window offers other options for working with a selected transaction:

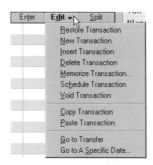

- **Restore Transaction** enables you to change a transaction back to the way it was before you started changing it. This option is only available if you have made changes to the selected transaction.
- **New Transaction** enables you to create a new transaction for the account. This does not affect the currently selected transaction.
- **Insert Transaction** enables you to insert a transaction before the selected transaction in the account register. This does not affect the currently selected transaction.
- **Delete Transaction** deletes the selected transaction. This is the same as clicking the Delete button in the button bar.

Caution   *Deleting a transaction removes the transaction from the Quicken data file, thus changing the account balance and category activity.*

- **Memorize Transaction** tells Quicken to add the selected transaction to its list of memorized transactions.
- **Schedule Transaction** enables you to schedule the transaction for a future date or to set up the transaction as a recurring transaction. I tell you more about scheduling transactions in Chapter 11.
- **Void Transaction** marks the selected transaction as void. This reverses the effect of the transaction on the account balance and category activity without actually deleting the transaction.
- **Copy Transaction** copies the selected transaction.
- **Paste Transaction** pastes the last-copied transaction into the current account register. This option is only available after a transaction has been copied.

Tip   *You might want to copy a transaction to paste it into another register if you realize that you entered it in the wrong register. You can then go back and delete the original transaction.*

- **Go To Transfer** displays the selected transaction in the account register for the other part of a transfer. For example, if the selected transaction involves the checking and savings accounts and you are viewing it in the checking account register, choosing the Go To Transfer command displays the same transaction in the savings account register. This command is only available if the selected transaction includes a transfer.
- **Go To A Specific Date** enables you to move to a different date within the register. This does not affect the currently selected transaction.

Printing Checks

Quicken's ability to print checks enables you to create accurate, legible, professional-looking checks without picking up a pen (or a typewriter). In this section, I explain how to print the checks you enter in the Write Checks window discussed earlier in this chapter.

Getting the Right Checks

Before you can print checks from Quicken, you must obtain compatible check stock. Quicken supports checks in a number of different styles:

- **Voucher** checks pair each check with a similarly sized voucher form. When you print on a voucher check, the transaction category information, including splits and classes, can be printed on the voucher part.
- **Wallet** checks pair each check with a stub. When you print on a wallet check, the transaction information is printed on the stub.
- **Standard** checks print just checks. There's no voucher or stub.

In addition to these styles, you can get the checks in two different formats for your printer:

- **Sheet-fed** or **page-oriented** checks are for laser and inkjet printers.
- **Continuous** checks are for pin-feed printers.

A catalog and order form for checks came with your copy of Quicken. You can use it to order checks. If you have an Internet connection, you can order checks online from within Quicken by choosing Banking | Banking Services | Order

Checks & Supplies, or by clicking the Order Checks button in the button bar of the Write Checks window.

Setting Up

Quicken must also be set up to print the kind of checks you purchased. You do this once, and Quicken remembers the settings.

Choose File | Printer Setup | For Printing Checks to display the Check Printer Setup dialog box shown next. Use the drop-down lists and option buttons to specify settings for your printer and check stock. Here are a few things to keep in mind when making settings in this dialog box.

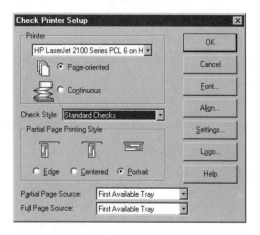

Partial Page Printing Options

If you select the Page-Oriented option and either Standard or Wallet checks in the Check Printer Setup dialog box, you can also set options for Partial Page Printing Style. This enables you to set up the printer for situations when you're not printing an entire page of checks.

- **Edge** is for inserting the page against one side of the feeder. The left or right edge of the checks enters the feeder first.
- **Centered** is for centering the page in the feeder. The left or right edge of the checks enters the feeder first.
- **Portrait** is also for centering the page in the feeder, but in this case, the top edge of each check enters the feeder first.

If your printer supports multiple feed trays, you can also set the source tray for partial and full pages by choosing options from the Partial Page Source and Full Page Source drop-down lists.

Continuous Printing Options

If you select the Continuous option and either Standard or Wallet checks in the Check Printer Setup dialog box, the dialog box changes to offer two Continuous options:

- **Bypass The Driver** should be turned on for a continuous printer that skips checks or prints nothing.
- **Use Low Starting Position** should be turned on for a continuous printer that cuts the date or logo off your checks.

Checking the Settings for Page-Oriented Checks

If you're using page-oriented checks, you can check your settings by printing a sample page on plain paper. Here's how:

1. Click the Align button in the Check Printer Setup dialog box.
2. In the Align Checks dialog box that appears, click the Full Page of Checks button.
3. In the Fine Alignment dialog box, click the Print Sample button.
4. When the sample emerges from your printer, hold it up to the light with a sheet of check stock behind it. The sample should line up with the check.
5. If the sample does not line up properly with the check stock, set Vertical and/or Horizontal adjustment values in the Fine Alignment dialog box. Then repeat steps 3 through 5 until the alignment is correct.
6. Click OK in each dialog box to accept your settings and close it.

Printing Checks

Once setup is complete, you're ready to print checks. Insert the check stock in your printer. Then choose File | Print Checks, or click the Print button in the Write Checks window. The Select Checks To Print dialog box appears. Enter the number of the first check that will be printed in the First Check Number box. Then use the drop-down lists and option buttons to set other options:

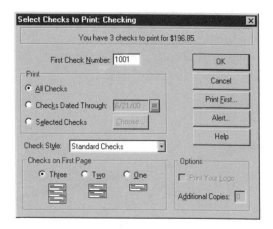

Tip   *If you select the Selected Checks option in the Select Checks To Print dialog box, you can click the Choose button to display a list of checks and check off the ones you want to print. Click Done in that window to return to the Select Checks To Print dialog box.*

When you click Print First or OK, Quicken sends the print job to your printer. It then displays a dialog box asking if the checks printed correctly. You have two options:

- If all checks printed fine, just click OK.
- If there was a problem printing the checks, enter the number of the first check that was misprinted and then click OK. You can then go back to the Select Checks To Print dialog box and try again.

Setting Register and Check Options

The Register Options and Check Options dialog boxes enable you to fine-tune the way the account register and Write Checks windows work. This makes it possible for you to customize these windows so they work the way you want them to. The options are similar in both dialog boxes, so I'll discuss them together.

To Set Register Options

To set Register options, begin by opening the Register Options dialog box. Choose Edit | Options | Register, or choose Register Options from the Options menu on the button bar in the account register window.

There are three categories of options: Display, Miscellaneous, and QuickFill. Each set of options can be found on its own tab in the Register Options dialog box. Here's what the Display and Miscellaneous options can do for you; I explain the QuickFill options in Chapter 11.

Display Options

Display options affect the way the transactions you enter appear in the account register window:

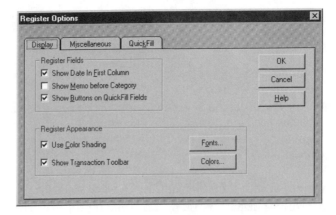

- **Show Date In First Column** displays the transaction date in the first column of the register. This option is turned on by default.
- **Show Memo Before Category** displays the Memo field above the Category field.
- **Show Buttons On QuickFill Fields** displays drop-down list buttons on fields for which you can use QuickFill. This option is turned on by default. I tell you about QuickFill in Chapter 11.
- **Use Color Shading** displays each type of register with a different background color. This option is turned on by default.
- **Show Transaction Toolbar** adds the Enter, Edit, and Split buttons to the currently selected transaction. This option is turned on by default.
- **Fonts** displays a dialog box in which you can select the font for register windows.
- **Colors** displays a dialog box in which you can select the background colors for the various types of register windows.

Miscellaneous Options

Miscellaneous options affect the way you are notified about problems when you
enter transactions in the register and the way transactions are entered:

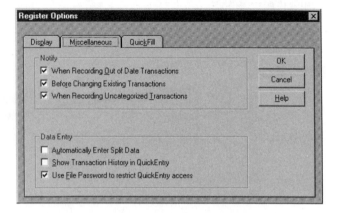

- **When Recording Out Of Date Transactions** warns you when you try to
  record a transaction with a date after the current date. This option is turned on
  by default.
- **Before Changing Existing Transactions** warns you when you try to modify a
  previously entered transaction. This option is turned on by default.
- **When Recording Uncategorized Transactions** warns you when you try to
  record a transaction without assigning a category to it. This option is turned
  on by default.
- **Automatically Enter Split Data** turns the OK button in the Split Transaction
  window into an Enter button for entering the transaction.
- **Show Transaction History In QuickEntry** displays all transactions—
  including transactions already entered into Quicken—in the account register
  within QuickEntry's window. This feature is only available in Quicken Deluxe.
- **Use File Password To Restrict QuickEntry Access** extends your Quicken
  password to protect QuickEntry as well. This feature is only available in
  Quicken Deluxe. I tell you about file passwords in Appendix A.

To Set Check Options

To set Check options, begin by opening the Check Options dialog box. Choose
Edit | Options | Write Checks or click Options on the button bar in the Write
Checks window.

There are three categories of options: Checks, Miscellaneous, and QuickFill. Each set of options can be found on its own tab in the Check Options dialog box. Here's what the Checks and Miscellaneous options are all about; I explain the QuickFill options in Chapter 11.

Check Options

Checks options affect the way the checks you enter with the Write Checks window appear when printed:

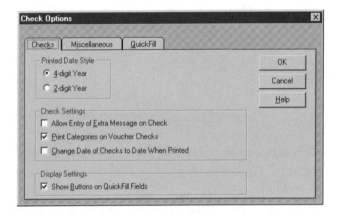

- **Printed Date Style** enables you to select a four-digit or two-digit date style. The four-digit style is selected by default.
- **Allow Entry Of Extra Message On Check** displays an additional text box for a message in the Write Checks window. The message you enter is printed on the check in a place where it cannot be seen if the check is mailed in a window envelope:

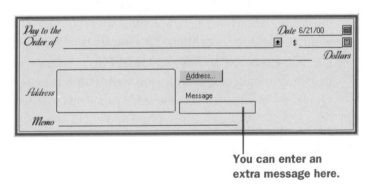

You can enter an extra message here.

- **Print Categories On Voucher Checks** prints category information, including splits and classes, on the voucher part of voucher checks. This option only affects voucher-style checks. This option is turned on by default.
- **Change Date Of Checks To Date When Printed** automatically prints the print date, rather than the transaction date, on each check.
- **Show Buttons On QuickFill Fields** displays drop-down list buttons on fields for which you can use QuickFill. This option is turned on by default. I tell you about QuickFill in Chapter 11.

Miscellaneous Options

Miscellaneous options affect the way you are notified about problems when you enter transactions in the Write Checks window. All of these options are turned on by default:

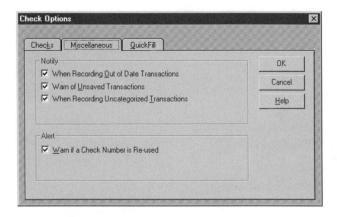

- **When Recording Out Of Date Transactions** warns you when you try to record a transaction with a date after the current date.
- **Warn Of Unsaved Transactions** warns you when you try to leave a transaction before you have clicked Enter to save it.
- **When Recording Uncategorized Transactions** warns you when you try to record a transaction without assigning a category to it.
- **Warn If A Check Number Is Re-Used** warns you if you assign a check number that was already assigned in another transaction.

Online Banking and Billing

In This Chapter:

- *Benefits and Costs of Online Banking*

- *Setting Up Online Banking*

- *Downloading and Comparing Transactions*

- *Importing QIF and WebConnect Files*

- *Setting Up Payees*

- *Processing Online Payments and Transfers*

- *Entering Transactions on the Web*

- *Synchronizing Your Bank Accounts*

Quicken's Online Account Access and Online Payment features enable you to do most (if not all) of your banking from the comfort of your own home. These two individual features, which are supported by dozens of banks and credit card companies, can be used separately or together:

- **Online Account Access** enables you to download bank and credit card account activity and transfer money online between accounts.
- **Online Payment** enables you to pay bills online, without manually writing or mailing a check.

In addition, two banking-related features work in conjunction with Quicken.com:

- **WebEntry** enables you to enter Quicken transactions on the Web. This makes it possible to record Quicken transactions from anywhere in the world.
- **Bank Account Synchronization** enables you to export your account balances to Quicken.com so you can view them from any computer with Internet access. This is a brand-new feature of Quicken 2001.

In this chapter, I explain how these features work and how you can use them to save time and money.

Note   *The instructions in this chapter assume that you have already configured your computer for an Internet connection. If you have not done so, do it now. Chapter 3 provides the instructions you need to set up and test an Internet connection. This chapter also assumes that you understand the topics and procedures discussed in Chapters 2 and 4. This chapter builds on many of the basic concepts discussed in those chapters.*

Why Do Your Banking Online?

Consider the following scenario: Every week (or two), you go to the bank to deposit your paycheck. (If you're lucky, you can use an ATM or drive-up window where you don't have to wait in line.) Throughout the month, you stop at ATMs and withdraw cash. You use your debit card at the pharmacy. You write checks for groceries, dentist visits, and car repairs. Periodically, you sit down to pay your bills. You write checks, insert them with statement stubs in window envelopes, put your return address on the envelopes, and stick on stamps. Once in a while, you call your bank to transfer money from one account to another. At month's end, you get a bank statement full of surprises: ATM withdrawals, debit card transactions, and checks you neglected to enter. Your bank balance may be dangerously close to zero because of these omissions. Or maybe you even bounced a few checks. And what about late payments (and fees) for the bills that lay on a table by the door, waiting for days to be mailed?

Sound familiar? At least some of it should. Life can be pretty hectic sometimes—too hectic to keep track of your bank accounts, pay bills before they're overdue, and buy stamps. But with Online Account Access and Online Payment, banking can be a lot less of a chore.

Benefits

The benefits of online financial services vary depending on the services you use. I've been doing my banking online for years. Here are some of the benefits I've seen.

Online Account Access

Quicken's Online Account Access feature can perform three tasks.

Download Transactions That Have Cleared Your Account   Bank account transaction downloads include all deposits, checks, interest payments, bank fees, transfers, ATM transactions, and debit card transactions. Credit card transaction downloads include all charges, credits (for returns), payments, fees, and finance charges. Quicken displays all the transactions, including the ones you have not yet entered in your account register, as well as the current balance of the account. A few clicks and keystrokes is all it takes to enter the transactions you missed. This feature makes it virtually impossible to omit entries, while telling you exactly how much money is available in a bank account or how much money you owe on your credit card account. No more surprises in that monthly statement.

Transfer Money Between Accounts   If you have more than one bank account at the same financial institution, you can use Online Account Access to transfer money between accounts. Although many banks offer this feature by phone, it usually requires dialing a phone number and entering an account number and PIN while navigating through voice prompts. Even if you get a real person on the phone, you still have to provide the same information every time you call. With Online Account Access, you merely enter a transfer transaction and let Quicken do the rest.

Send E-Mail Messages to Your Financial Institution   Ever call the customer service center at your bank or credit card company to ask a question? If you're lucky, real people are waiting to answer the phone. But if you're like most people, your financial institution uses a call routing system that requires you to listen to voice prompts and press telephone keypad keys to communicate with a machine. Either way, when a real person gets on the line, you have to provide all kinds of information about yourself just to prove that you are who you say you are. Then you can ask your question.

The e-mail feature that's part of Online Account Access enables you to exchange e-mail messages with your bank or credit card company's customer service department. You normally get a response within one business day.

Online Payment

Online Payment enables you to send a check to anyone without physically writing, printing, or mailing a check. You enter and store information about the payee within Quicken. You then create a transaction for the payee that includes the payment date and amount. You can enter the transaction weeks or months in advance if desired—the payee receives payment on the date you specify.

Online Payment is one of the least understood Quicken features. Many folks think it can only be used to pay big companies like the phone company or credit card companies. That just isn't true. You can use Online Payment to pay any bill, fund your IRA, donate money to a charity, or send your sister a housewarming gift.

How It Works   Suppose you use Quicken to send Online Payment instructions to pay your monthly bill at Joe's Hardware Store. You've already set up Joe as a payee by entering the name, address, and phone number of his store, as well as your account number there. Quicken sends your payment instructions to your bank, which stores it in its computer with a bunch of other Online Payment instructions. When the payment date nears, the bank's computer looks through its big database of payees that it can pay by wire transfer. It sees phone companies and credit card companies and other banks. But because Joe's store is small, it's probably not one of the wire transfer payees. So the bank's computer prepares a check using all the information you provided. It mails the check along with thousands of others due to be paid that day.

Joe's wife, who does the accounting for the store (with Quicken Home & Business, in case you're wondering), gets the check a few days later. It looks a little weird, but when she deposits it with the other checks she gets that day, it clears just like any other check. The amount of the check is deducted from your bank account and your account balance at Joe's. If you use Online Account Access, the check appears as a transaction. It also appears on your bank statement. If your bank returns canceled checks to you, you'll get the check along with all your others.

> **Tip**   *If your bank doesn't return canceled checks, you can see for yourself what an Online Payment check looks like. Just use the Online Payment feature to write a check to yourself. It'll arrive in the mail on or before the date you specified. Although the check looks different, it works like any other check.*

When the Money Leaves Your Account   The date the money is actually withdrawn from your account to cover the payment varies depending on your bank. There are four possibilities:

- One to four days before the payment is processed for delivery
- The day the payment is processed for delivery
- The day the payment is delivered
- The day the paper check or electronic funds transfer clears your bank

You can find out when funds are withdrawn from your account for online payments by contacting your bank.

The Benefits of Online Payment   Online Payment can benefit you in several ways. You can pay your bills as they arrive, without paying them early—the payee never receives payment before the payment date you specify. You don't have to buy stamps, and the bank never forgets to mail the checks.

Costs

The cost of Online Account Access and Online Payment varies from bank to bank. Check with your bank to see what the exact fees are. Here's what you can expect:

- Online Account Access is often free to all customers or to customers who maintain a certain minimum account balance. Otherwise, you could pay up to $5 for this service. My bank claims it charges $3, but I haven't been billed once. (Don't tell anyone.)
- Online Payment is sometimes free, but more often it costs from $5 to $10 per month for 20 to 25 payments per month. Each additional payment usually costs 40¢ to 60¢. Again, some banks waive this fee if you maintain a certain minimum balance. My bank, for example, requires a $5,000 minimum account balance to waive the fee.

If you think this sounds expensive, do the math for your bank's deal. Here's an example. I get 25 payments per month for $5. If I had to mail 25 checks, it would cost me $8.25. So I'd actually save $3.25 per month if I made 25 online payments. Although I don't make 25 payments a month—it's more like 20 for me—I also don't have to stuff envelopes, apply return address labels, or stick on stamps. My bills get paid right on time, I earn more interest income, and I haven't bounced a check in over five years.

Does it sound like I'm sold on this feature? You bet I am!

Security

If you're worried about security, you must have skipped over the security information in Chapter 3. Go back and read that now. It explains how Quicken and financial institution security works to make Online Account Access and Online Payment safe.

Setting Up Online Banking

To use either Online Account Access or Online Payment, you must configure the appropriate Quicken accounts. This requires that you enter information about your financial institution and the account with which you want to use these online banking features.

Applying for Online Account Access and Online Payment

Before you can use Online Account Access or Online Payment, you must apply for it. I tell you how at the end of Chapter 3. Normally, all it takes is a phone call, although some banks and credit card companies do allow you to apply online. The process usually takes a week but may take less. You'll know that you're ready to go online when you get a letter with setup information.

Tip *If your bank does not directly support Quicken's online banking features, you may be able to use Quicken's QIF or WebConnect file import feature to download transaction data from your bank's Web site and Intuit Online Payment service to handle online payments. I tell you more about QIF and WebConnect files later in this chapter. Intuit Online Payment works just like the Online Payment feature for regular banks.*

The setup information your financial institution sends usually consists of the following:

A PIN (or personal identification number)   You'll have to enter this code into Quicken when you access your account online. This is a security feature, so don't write down your PIN on a sticky note and attach it to your computer screen. There is a chance that your bank may send this information separately for additional security.

A customer ID number   This is often your social security number or taxpayer identification number.

The bank routing number   This information tells Quicken which bank your account is with. You may not get this information for a credit card account.

Account number for each online-access-enabled account   This tells your financial institution which account you want to work with.

Setting Up

With a PIN, a routing number, and account numbers in hand, you're ready to set up your account(s) for online banking features. There are a number of ways to set up; rather than cover them all, I'll cover the most straightforward method.

Choose Banking | Online Banking Setup to display the Online Account Setup dialog box, which is shown next. How you proceed depends on whether you want to set up an existing account or a new account for online banking.

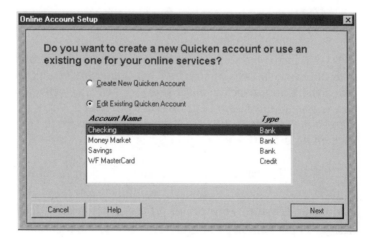

Tip   *These instructions assume you are setting up a checking, savings, or money market account. If you are setting up a credit card account, different dialog boxes may appear near the end of the setup process. If you have all the information provided to you by your financial institution, you should have no trouble entering the proper information to complete the setup.*

Setting Up an Existing Account

To set up online banking for an existing Quicken account, select the Edit Existing Quicken Account option in the Online Account Setup dialog box. Then select the name of the account for which you want to set up online banking and click Next. The account register window for the account, which is shown next, appears. Online setup steps appear in the top of the window. At this point, you should have already completed steps 1 and 2 of the online setup process. (If you haven't, click the links in the setup area to complete them. Then wait until you get the information you need from your financial institution to complete the setup process.)

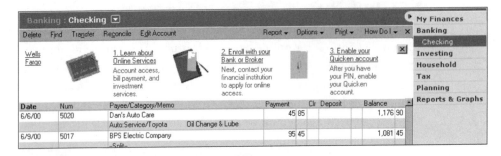

Tip   *If the online setup steps do not appear at the top of the window as illustrated here, choose View Online Setup from the Options menu on the window's button bar. If that doesn't work, check to make sure your financial institution is listed in the Online Financial Institutions List; I explain how in Chapter 3. If it is, make sure you have entered the correct bank or credit card company name in the Attributes area of the account register's Overview tab; I discuss the Overview tab in Chapter 2.*

Click the link labeled "3. Enable Your Quicken Account." Quicken may connect to the Internet to update the information it has about your financial institution. Do not interrupt this process. It also might display a dialog box asking where you got your copy of Quicken. Provide the requested information and click Continue.

The next dialog box asks you to select the services you are going to use. The options vary depending on the type of account and financial institution. Select the Yes option beside each service you want to use. Then click Next.

Next, you're prompted to enter the information your financial institution sent you: the routing number, account number, account type, and customer ID. Here's what this dialog box looks like, completed for a checking account; other account types may request less information:

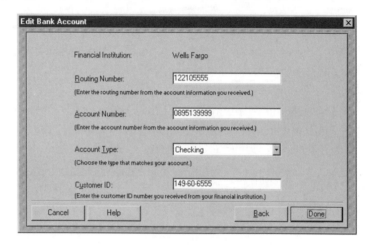

Skip ahead to the section "Completing the Setup Process."

Setting Up a New Account

To set up online banking for an account that you have not yet created in Quicken, select the Create New Quicken Account option in the Online Account Setup dialog box and click Next. This displays the Create New Account dialog box. Follow the prompts in the dialog boxes that appear to create a new Quicken account. (Consult Chapter 2 if you need help.) When you're finished and the account has been created, go back to the previous section ("Setting Up an Existing Account") and follow the instructions there.

Completing the Setup Process

Click Done. A little Service Agreement Information dialog box may appear next. It tells you that online financial services are provided by your financial institution and not Intuit. (I think the lawyers at Intuit whipped this one up.) Read the contents of the dialog box and click OK.

There are at least two ways you can tell whether an account is set up for online banking:

- In the Account List window, a lightning bolt appears in the type column for each account that has online banking enabled:

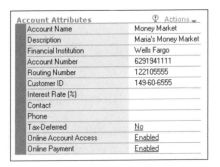

- The Account Attributes area of the Overview tab for the account's register window displays the online access information for the account and indicates which services are enabled:

The Online Center

When you enable Online Account Access and/or Online Payment, you can use the Online Center to work with Quicken's online features. This window gives you access to all the lists and commands you need to download transactions, create payments, transfer money, and exchange e-mail with your bank.

Using the Online Center Window

To open the Online Center window, choose Banking | Online Banking. Figure 5-1 shows what this window looks like for my setup.

Click to select an account for the current financial institution.

Choose a financial institution from the drop-down list.

Click a tab to move from one activity to another.

Downloaded transactions appear here.

Click Update/Send to exchange information with your financial institution.

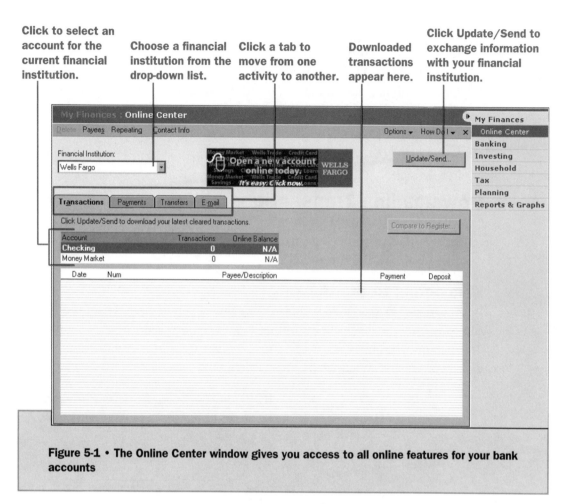

Figure 5-1 • The Online Center window gives you access to all online features for your bank accounts

A number of button bar buttons and menus enable you to work with the window's contents:

- **Delete** removes the selected transaction.
- **Payees** displays the Online Payee List window, which I discuss later in this chapter.
- **Repeating** displays the Repeating tab of the Scheduled Transaction List window, along with the Create Repeating Online Payment dialog box. I tell you more about both of these features later in this chapter.
- **Contact Info** displays the Contact Information dialog box for the currently selected financial institution. You can use the information in the dialog box to contact the bank or credit card company by phone, Web site, or e-mail.

- **PIN Vault** (not shown) gives you access to Quicken's PIN Vault feature, which I discuss later in this chapter. (This option only appears if you have online banking features enabled for accounts at more than one financial institution.)
- **Options** displays a menu of commands for working with the current account or window.
- **How Do I** provides additional instructions for working with the Online Center window.

Downloading Transactions

One of the main features of Online Account Access is the ability to download transactions directly from your financial institution into Quicken. Here's how you can take advantage of this feature.

Connecting to the Bank

In the Online Center window, choose the name of your bank or credit card company from the Financial Institution drop-down list. If necessary, click the Transactions tab. Then click the Update/Send button. The Instructions to Send dialog box appears. Enter your PIN and click Send.

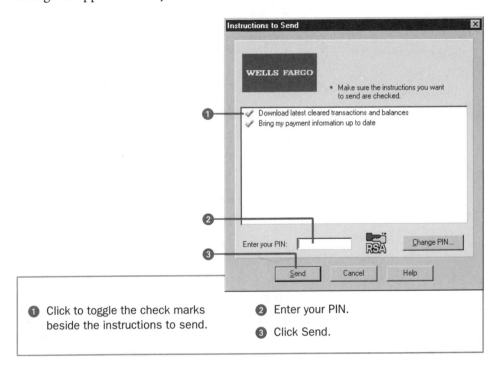

1. Click to toggle the check marks beside the instructions to send.
2. Enter your PIN.
3. Click Send.

Tip   *The first time you communicate with your bank, the Instructions to Send dialog box may not include a text box for your PIN, as shown in the preceding illustration. Instead, when you click Send, a Change Assigned PIN dialog box may appear. Enter the PIN the bank assigned to you in the top text box. Then enter a preferred PIN code in the bottom two text boxes. None of the characters you enter will appear onscreen. Instead, you'll just see asterisks (*). Click OK.*

Wait while Quicken connects to your bank. A status dialog box appears while it works. When it has finished exchanging information, the dialog box disappears.

Reviewing Transactions

When the connection is complete, an Online Transmission Summary window appears to summarize the activity that took place while you waited. Here's what it might look like:

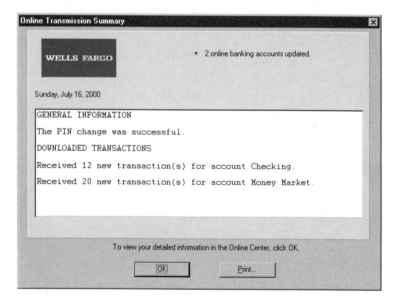

The transactions you downloaded appear in the Transactions tab of the Online Center window, as shown in Figure 5-2. As you can see, not much information is provided for checks because the bank's computer doesn't record payee names or Quicken categories.

Note   *The first time you connect, the bank sends all transactions from the past 60 days. After that, only new transactions will be downloaded.*

Click Compare To
Register to compare
downloaded transactions
to transactions in your
account register.

A lightning bolt appears
beside accounts with
downloaded transactions
that have not yet been
reviewed and accepted.

Downloaded
transactions
appear here.

Select the account
you want to view.

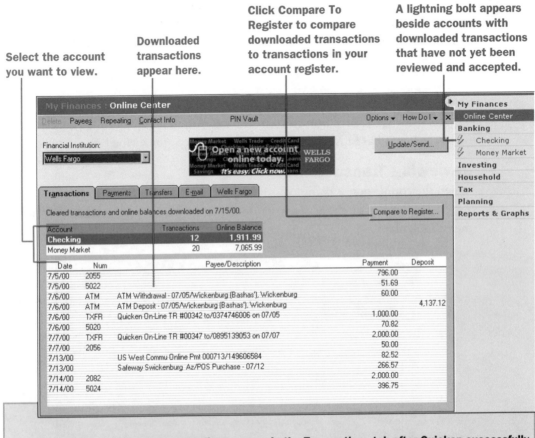

Figure 5-2 • Downloaded transactions appear in the Transactions tab after Quicken successfully
downloads transactions from the Internet

Comparing Downloaded Transactions to Register Transactions

Once the information has been downloaded, you can compare the transactions to
the transactions already entered in your account register. This enables you to
identify transactions that you neglected to enter or that you entered incorrectly.

Click the Compare To Register button. The Register window opens, with the
downloaded transaction list in the bottom half of its window. Figure 5-3 shows
what the window might look like with one transaction already accepted. This

window looks and works exactly like the split window that appears when you accept QuickEntry transactions into Quicken; consult the section "Reviewing QuickEntry Transactions" in Chapter 4 for details.

 SAVE TIME Because Quicken will automatically enter a date, transaction number, and amount—and in the case of a debit card transaction, the payee and category (based on previously memorized transactions)—using this method to enter a transaction can be much faster than entering it manually in the account register window.

Enter or edit transactions as necessary here.

Click a transaction to view it or to begin entering it in the account register.

Use these buttons to work with a selected transaction or accept all downloaded transactions.

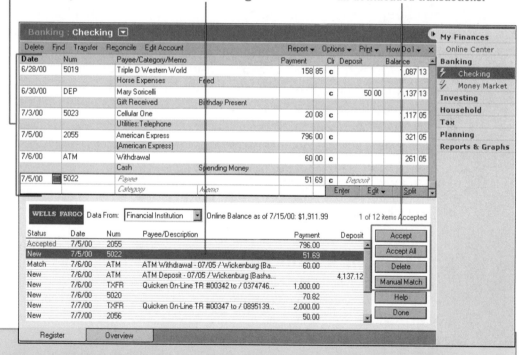

Figure 5-3 • Use this window to compare the transactions in your account register to the transactions you downloaded

Other Ways to Download Transaction Data

If your financial institution is not a Quicken partner, it may offer other methods to download data from its Web site for importing into Quicken. The two most commonly available Quicken-compatible methods are:

- **QIF files** are specially formatted text files that contain transaction data. You download a QIF file from your financial institution to your hard disk. Then you choose File | Import | QIF and use the dialog box that appears to import the file into Quicken. Many banks offer this format.

- **WebConnect files** are specially formatted files that have additional instructions for working with Quicken. When you download a WebConnect file from your financial institution, it is automatically imported into Quicken. Quicken can automatically check WebConnect files and discard transactions that are not new to Quicken. American Express offers this format, which it refers to as Direct Access Download or OFX files.

No matter which type of file you import into Quicken, the downloaded transactions appear in the bottom of the register window (see Figure 5-3) just as if they'd been downloaded using the Online Center window discussed earlier in this chapter. This is the next best thing to Quicken's built-in Online Account Access feature.

To get started using QIF or WebConnect, call your financial institution to see which options are available. It can provide complete instructions for taking advantage of the feature it offers. But remember, neither of these features are as convenient as Quicken's built-in Online Account Access, so always look for that option first.

Tip *If you do use WebConnect, be sure to check out the options you can set in the WebConnect Options dialog box. Choose Edit | Options | WebConnect to check them out for yourself.*

Paying Your Credit Card Bill

If payment on your credit card bill is due, you're notified in the Online Transmission Summary window when you successfully download transactions. When you've finished reviewing, comparing, and accepting downloaded transactions, you can use Quicken to review your bill and enter a payment transaction.

Click the Payment Information button in the Online Center window. A dialog box appears, providing information about the statement date, minimum payment due, and account balance:

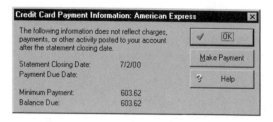

If you click the Make Payment button, the Make Credit Card Payment dialog box appears; use this dialog box to set up a payment transaction for the credit card account:

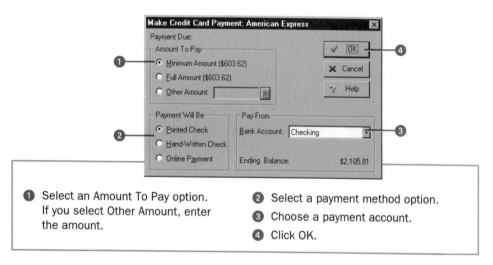

① Select an Amount To Pay option. If you select Other Amount, enter the amount.

② Select a payment method option.

③ Choose a payment account.

④ Click OK.

The option you select in the Payment Will Be area determines what happens when you click OK:

- **Printed Check** displays the Write Checks window, with the payment transaction already filled in. Edit the transaction as necessary and click the Record Check button to complete it. The check can be printed the next time you use the Print Checks command.

- **Hand-Written Check** displays the account register window, with the payment transaction already filled in. Edit the transaction as necessary and click the Enter button to complete it. You must then write the check by hand.

- **Online Payment** displays the Payments tab of the Online Center window with the payment transaction already filled in. Edit the transaction as necessary and click the Enter button to complete it. The payment instruction will be sent to your bank the next time you click the Update/Send button. I tell you more about making online payments in the next section.

> **Tip**   To use the Online Payment option, one of your bank accounts must be set up for Online Payment through your bank or Intuit Online Payment. In addition, the credit card company must be set up as an online payee.

Making Payments

The Payments tab of the Online Center window enables you to enter payment instructions for accounts for which you have enabled the Online Payment feature. Figure 5-4 shows what it looks like.

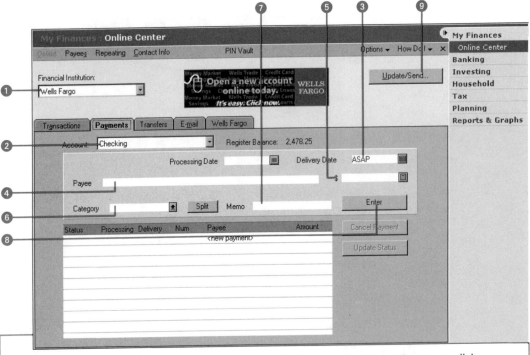

① Choose the financial institution with which you want to work.

② Select an account from which you want to send a payment.

③ Enter the date you want the payment delivered.

④ Enter or choose a payee name.

⑤ Enter the payment amount.

⑥ Enter or choose a category, or click the Split button to enter multiple categories.

⑦ If desired, enter a note for the transaction.

⑧ Click Enter to complete the entry.

⑨ When you're finished entering instructions, click Update/Send to send them to the financial institution.

Figure 5-4 • Use the Payments tab of the Online Center window to make online payments

In the rest of this section, I explain how to set up online payees, enter payment information for one-time and repeating payments, and work with payment instructions.

Entering Online Payee Information

To send payments from your account, your bank must know who and where each payee is. To ensure that your account with the payee is properly credited, you must also provide account information. You do this by setting up online payees.

Click the Payees button in the Online Center window or choose Banking | Online Payee List. The Online Payee List window shown here lists all the individuals and organizations you pay using Quicken's Online Payment feature:

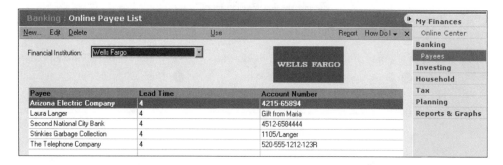

You can use options on the button bar to work with items in the window:

- **New** enables you to create a new online payee.
- **Edit** enables you to modify the information for the selected online payee.
- **Delete** removes the selected online payee.

> **Tip**   *Deleting a payee simply deletes the payee's information from the Online Payee List. It does not change any transactions for a payee. You cannot delete a payee for which unsent payment instructions exist in the Online Center window.*

- **Use** switches you back to the Payments tab of the Online Center window (see Figure 5-4) and inserts the selected payee into the payment form.
- **Report** displays a report of all payments made to the selected online payee.
- **How Do I** provides instructions for performing specific tasks with the Online Payee List window.

To create a new online payee, click the New button. Then fill in the text boxes in the Set Up Online Payee dialog box:

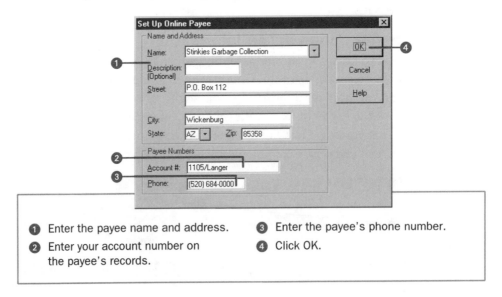

① Enter the payee name and address.

② Enter your account number on the payee's records.

③ Enter the payee's phone number.

④ Click OK.

When you click OK, a dialog box containing the information you just entered appears. Check the information in this box and click OK. The payee is added to the list with a default lead time of four days. I explain what lead time is all about later in this chapter.

Caution   *Check the payee information carefully! If there is an error, your payment might not reach the payee, or it might not be properly credited to your account. Remember, your bank will not be sending a billing stub with the payment—just the check.*

Entering Payment Instructions

If necessary, switch back to the Payments tab of the Online Center window (see Figure 5-4). Then fill in the fields in the middle of the window with the payment information:

- **Delivery Date** is the date you want the payee to receive payment. This is the date the bank will either write on the check or make the electronic funds transfer. The check may be received before that date, depending on the mail. The date you enter, however, must be at least the same number of business days in advance as the lead time for the payee—usually four days. That means if you want to pay a bill on Wednesday, June 30, you must enter and send its instructions to your bank on or before Friday, June 25. Quicken will adjust the date for you if necessary. To process payment as soon as possible, just enter **ASAP**. Quicken will enter the date for you.

> **Tip**   *Whenever possible, I give the bank an extra two days. So, in the previous example, if the bill is due on June 30, I'd instruct the bank to pay on June 28. This isn't because I don't have confidence in Quicken or my bank. It's because I have less confidence in the postal service.*

- **Payee** is the online payee to receive payment. Quicken's QuickFill feature fills in the payee's name as you type it. If desired, you can choose it from the drop-down list of online payees. If you enter a payee that is not in the Online Payee List, Quicken displays the Set Up Online Payee dialog box so you can add the new payee's information. This enables you to create online payees as you enter payment instructions.
- **$** is the amount of the payment.
- **Category** is the category to which the payment should be associated. You can either enter a category, choose one from the drop-down list, or click the Split button to enter multiple categories.
- **Memo**, which is optional, is for entering a note about the transaction.

When you've finished entering information for the transaction, click Enter. The transaction appears in the list in the bottom half of the window. You can repeat this process for as many payments as you want to make.

Scheduling Repeating Online Payments

Some payments are exactly the same every month, such as your rent, a car loan, or your monthly cable television bill. You can set these payments up as repeating online payments.

Here's how it works. You schedule the online payment once, indicating the payee, amount, and frequency. Quicken sends the instructions to your bank. Thirty days before the payment is due, your bank creates a new postdated payment based on your instructions. It notifies you that it has created the payment. Quicken automatically enters the payment information in your account register with the appropriate payment date. The payment is delivered on the payment date. This happens regularly, at the interval you specify, until you tell it to stop.

> **Tip**   *Using this feature to pay an amortized loan such as a mortgage works a little differently. I tell you about it later in this chapter.*

In the Online Center window, click the Repeating button. The Repeating Online tab of the Scheduled Transaction List window appears (see Figure 5-5). You can use button bar options to work with items listed in this window:

- **Pay** processes the payment transaction immediately. This button is grayed out for repeating online payments because it does not apply.
- **New** enables you to create a new repeating online payment.
- **Edit** enables you to modify the selected repeating online payment.
- **Delete** removes the repeating online payment from the list, thus canceling future payments.
- **Options** offers commands for changing the sort order of payments in the list.
- **How Do I** provides instructions for completing tasks with the Scheduled Transaction List.

The Create Repeating Online Payment dialog box (shown next) may appear automatically; if it does not, click the New button on the button bar. Use this dialog box to enter information about the repeating payment. When you click Authorize, the payment appears in the Scheduled Transaction List window (see Figure 5-5).

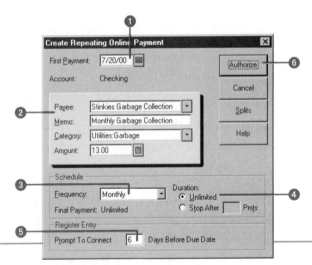

① Enter the date that the first payment should be made.

② Enter payee and payment information. You can click the Splits button to enter more than one category for the transaction.

③ Choose a payment frequency.

④ Select a payment duration. If you select Stop After, also enter the total number of payments that should be made.

⑤ If desired, enter the number of days before the payment date that Quicken should prompt you to connect to receive payment confirmation.

⑥ Click Authorize.

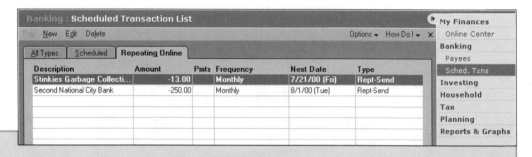

Figure 5-5 • **The Repeating Online tab of the Scheduled Transaction List window displays all repeating online payments**

SAVE TIME *The best part of the Repeating Online Payment feature is that once a payment instruction is sent, you don't have to do a thing to continue paying regularly. The more payments you make with this feature, the more time you save.*

Linking a Repeating Online Payment to an Amortized Loan

Repeating online payments are perfect for paying off loans. After all, loan payments are the same every month and must be paid by a certain date. You can set up a repeating online payment instruction, send it to your financial institution, and let Quicken and your bank make the payments automatically every month for you.

Set up the repeating online payment instruction for the loan payment as instructed in the earlier section "Scheduling Repeating Online Payments." Don't worry about all the categories that are part of a loan payment transaction. Just choose the loan account as the category. You don't even have to get the date or amount right. When you link the transaction to the loan, Quicken will make the necessary adjustments. Be sure to click Authorize to save the payment instruction.

Choose Household | Loans to display the Loans window. If necessary, choose the loan account's name from the Choose Loan menu in the button bar to display the information for the loan for which you want to use the payment instruction.

Click the Edit Payment button to display the Edit Loan Payment dialog box. Click the Payment Method button. In the Select Payment Method dialog box, select Repeating Online Payment. Then choose the repeating online payment instruction you created from the Repeating Payment drop-down list. It might look something like this:

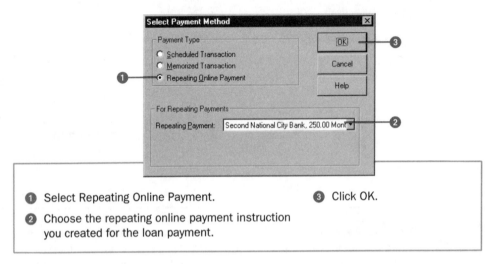

① Select Repeating Online Payment.
② Choose the repeating online payment instruction you created for the loan payment.
③ Click OK.

Click OK in each dialog box to dismiss it. Quicken links the loan payment to the repeating online payment instruction. It makes changes to the payment instruction, if necessary, to match the payment categories and split information. The next time you connect to your financial institution, the instruction will be sent, and payments will begin.

Sending Payment Instructions

Remember the bills I told you about? The ones waiting on a table by the door to be mailed? Payment instructions that have not yet been sent to the bank are just like those stamped envelopes. They're ready to go, but they won't get where they're going without your help.

Once your payment instructions have been completed, you must connect to your bank to send the instructions. In the Online Center window, click the Update/Send button. Quicken displays the Instructions To Send window, which lists all of the payment instructions, including any repeating payment instructions. Enter your PIN and click the Send button.

Wait while Quicken establishes an Internet connection with your bank and sends your payment (or payment cancellation) instructions. When it has finished, it displays the Online Transmission Summary window. Review the information in this window to make sure all instructions were sent and no errors occurred.

When you've finished, click OK to return to the Payments tab of the Online Center window. The word *Sent* appears in the Status column beside the payment instructions that have been sent to your bank.

Canceling a Payment

Occasionally, you may change your mind about making a payment. Perhaps you found out that your spouse already sent a check. Or that you set up the payment for the wrong amount. For whatever reason, you can cancel an online payment that you have sent to your bank—as long as there's enough time to cancel it.

Here's how it works. When you send a payment instruction to your bank, it waits in the bank's computer. When the processing date (determined by the number of days in the payee's lead time and the payment date) arrives, the bank makes the payment. Before the processing date, however, the payment instructions can be canceled. If you send a cancel payment instruction to the bank before the processing date, the bank removes the instruction from its computer without sending payment to the payee. Quicken won't let you cancel a payment if the processing date has already passed. If you wait too long, the only way to cancel the payment is to call the bank directly and stop the check.

Tip   *Canceling a payment instruction isn't the same as stopping a check. If you send the cancel payment instruction in time, the bank should not charge a fee for stopping the payment.*

Canceling a Regular Online Payment   In the Online Center window, select the payment that you want to cancel and click the Cancel Payment button. Click Yes in the confirmation dialog box that appears. The word *Cancel* appears in the Status column beside the payment. Use the Update/Send button to send the cancel payment instruction.

Stopping a Single Repeating Online Payment   In the Online Center window, select the payment you want to stop, and click the Cancel Payment button. Click Yes in the confirmation dialog box that appears. The word *Cancel* appears in the Status column beside the payment. Use the Update/Send button to send the cancel payment instruction.

Stopping All Future Payments for a Repeating Online Payment   In the Scheduled Transaction List window, select the payment you want to stop and click Delete. Click Yes in the confirmation dialog box that appears. The transaction is removed from the list. Then use the Update/Send button in the Online Center window to send the cancel payment instruction.

Caution   *You must send the cancel payment instruction to your bank to cancel a payment. Be sure to click the Update/Send button in the Online Center window after canceling any payment. If you fail to do this, the cancel payment instruction may not reach your bank in time to cancel the payment.*

Transferring Money Between Accounts

If you have more than one account enabled for Online Account Access at the same financial institution, you can use the Transfers tab of the Online Center window, shown in Figure 5-6, to transfer money from one account to another.

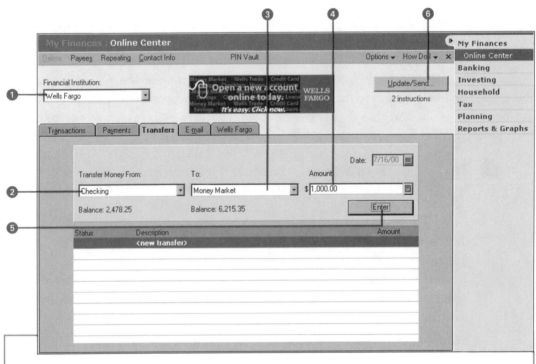

1. Choose the financial institution with which you want to work.

2. Choose the account from which you want to transfer money (the source account).

3. Choose the account to which you want to transfer money (the destination account).

4. Enter the amount of the transfer.

5. Click Enter.

6. When you're finished entering transactions, click Update/Send to send them to your bank.

Figure 5-6 • Use the Transfers tab of the Online Center window to transfer funds from one account to another at the same financial institution

Enter the transfer information in the fields in the middle of the window. When you click Enter, the information is added to the list of transfers at the bottom of the window.

Like payment instructions, you must send transfer instructions to your bank in order for the transaction to take place. Click the Update/Send button to display the Instructions To Send window, which includes the transfer instructions to be sent. Enter your PIN and click the Send button. Then wait while Quicken establishes an Internet connection with your bank and sends the instructions.

When Quicken has finished, it displays the Online Transmission Summary window. Review the information in this window and click OK. The word *Sent* appears in the Status column beside the transfer instructions that have been sent to your bank.

Exchanging E-Mail with Your Financial Institution

You can use the E-mail tab of the Online Financial Services Center window (see Figure 5-7) to exchange e-mail messages with financial institutions for which you have enabled Online Account Access.

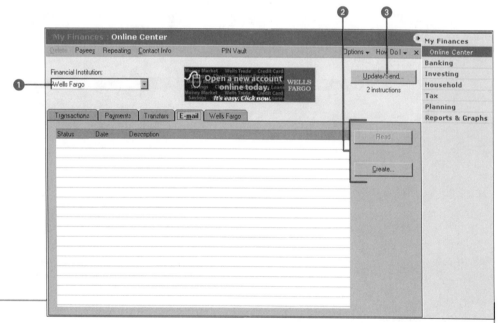

1   Choose the financial institution with which you want to exchange e-mail.

2   Click Read to read a selected message, or click Create to create a new message.

3   When you're finished creating messages, click Update/Send to send them to your financial institution

Figure 5-7 • The E-mail tab of the Online Center window is where you can exchange e-mail with your financial institution

Creating an E-Mail Message

In the Online Center window, click Create. The Create dialog box appears, as shown next. Use it to set general options for your e-mail message. If your message is about an online payment, choose the account from the Account drop-down list and select the payment from the Payments scrolling list.

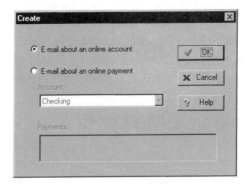

When you click OK, a message window appears. Use it to compose your e-mail message. Here's what the Message window looks like for a message about an account; it appears differently for a message about a payment:

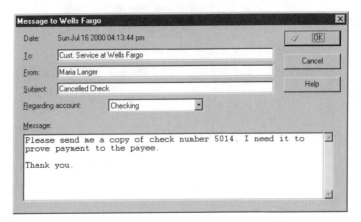

When you click OK, the message is saved. It appears in the bottom half of the E-mail tab of the Online Center window (see Figure 5-7), ready to be sent to your financial institution.

Exchanging E-Mail Messages

Using e-mail is a lot like having a box at the post office. When you write a letter, you have to get it to the post office to send it to the recipient. When you receive a letter, you have to go to the post office and check your box to retrieve it. E-mail works the same way. Connecting is a lot like going to the post office to send and retrieve messages.

In the Online Center window, click the Update/Send button. Quicken displays the Instructions To Send window, which includes any e-mail messages you may have created that need to be sent. Enter your PIN and click the Send button. Then wait while Quicken establishes an Internet connection with your bank and exchanges e-mail.

When Quicken has finished, it displays the Online Transmission Summary window. Review the information in this window and click OK. The word *Sent* appears in the Status column beside the e-mail messages that have been sent to your bank.

Reading an E-Mail Message

When your bank sends you an e-mail message, it appears in the E-mail tab of the Online Center window (see Figure 5-7). To read the message, select it and click Read. The message appears in a Message window. If desired, you can click the Print button to print the message for future reference.

WebEntry

Quicken's WebEntry feature enables you to enter transactions for your Quicken accounts via the Web. You use a Web browser to navigate to a specific Web page on the Quicken.com site, enter your user ID and password if prompted, and enter transactions. Then, when you're back at your desk with Quicken running, you can use the One Step Update command to download transactions stored on the Web into your Quicken data file.

Tip   *This feature is especially useful if you're away for an extended period of time. By entering transactions periodically via the Web, you won't have to enter them all at once when you return.*

Note   *You must register Quicken before you use this feature. Registering Quicken sets up a Quicken.com account for you to store your transaction information.*

Entering and Reviewing Transactions

Use a Web browser to navigate to the Quicken.com home page at
http://www.quicken.com/. Scroll down and click the Quicken WebEntry link—
you'll find it at the bottom of the page. The WebEntry page appears. Figure 5-8
shows an example of what it looks like with a transaction ready to be entered.

Note   If the WebEntry window includes a link prompting you to log in to
Quicken.com, click the link to log in to your Quicken.com account. You must do this
before you can enter transactions with WebEntry.

Enter transaction information into the form and click Enter Transaction to enter
the transaction into the Web database. Repeat this process for as many transactions as
you like. Don't worry if you don't know the exact name of an account or category;
you can correct any errors when you download the transactions into Quicken.

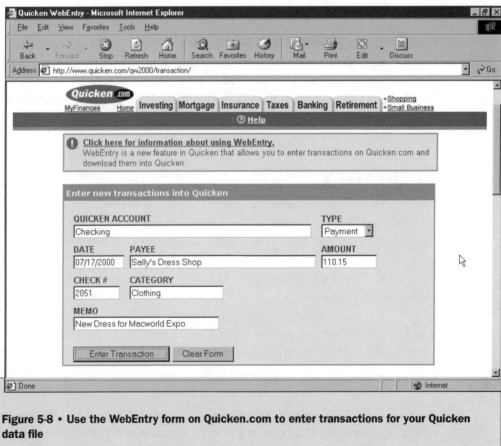

**Figure 5-8 • Use the WebEntry form on Quicken.com to enter transactions for your Quicken
data file**

You can review the transactions you enter by scrolling down in the window after entering any transaction. The Review WebEntry Transactions area lists each transaction stored in the database on Quicken.com:

Review WebEntry transactions				
07/17/2000	Money Market	Osborne-McGraw Hill		$1,000.00
		Other Income	Advance Check	Deposit
STATUS:	Not Downloaded	Delete Edit		
07/17/2000	Checking	Sally's Dress Shop		$110.15
	2051	Clothing	New Dress for Macworld Expo	Payment
STATUS:	Not Downloaded	Delete Edit		

Enabling WebEntry Downloads in Quicken

Next, you have to tell Quicken that you plan to download WebEntry transactions. You do this in the Misc tab of the Customize Quicken Download dialog box, which is shown next. To display it, choose Edit | Options | Internet Connection and click the Misc tab in the dialog box that appears.

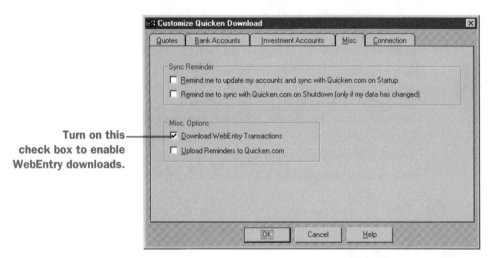

Turn on this check box to enable WebEntry downloads.

Turn on the Download WebEntry Transactions check box and click OK. Quicken is now ready to download the transactions you entered on the Web.

Downloading Transactions into Quicken

Click the Online button on Quicken's toolbar. The One Step Update Download Selection dialog box, which I tell you more about throughout this book, appears. Make sure the check mark beside Update WebEntry is turned on, as shown next. Then click Update Now. If a Quicken.com Login dialog box appears, enter your username and password in the appropriate text boxes and click OK.

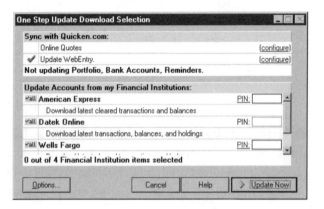

Quicken establishes a connection to the Internet and displays a status dialog box while it updates information. When it's finished, it displays the Download Summary dialog box, which informs you that your Web transactions were downloaded.

Accepting Transactions

You're not done yet. The downloaded transactions must be accepted into the Quicken accounts. Open the account register for an account for which you have downloaded a WebEntry transaction. The window appears with a split with the downloaded transactions in the bottom half, as shown in Figure 5-9.

Tip   *If you have downloaded transactions from other sources such as QuickEntry or Online Account Access, you may need to choose WebEntry from the Data From drop-down list in the bottom half of the window to view WebEntry transactions.*

Does this window look familiar? It should! It's almost identical to the one in Figures 4-7 and 5-3. It works the same, too. You can learn more in the section "Reviewing QuickEntry Transactions" in Chapter 4 for details.

Select a transaction to view it or begin entering it in the register.

If necessary, choose WebEntry from this drop-down list.

Use these buttons to work with the selected transaction or accept all downloaded transactions.

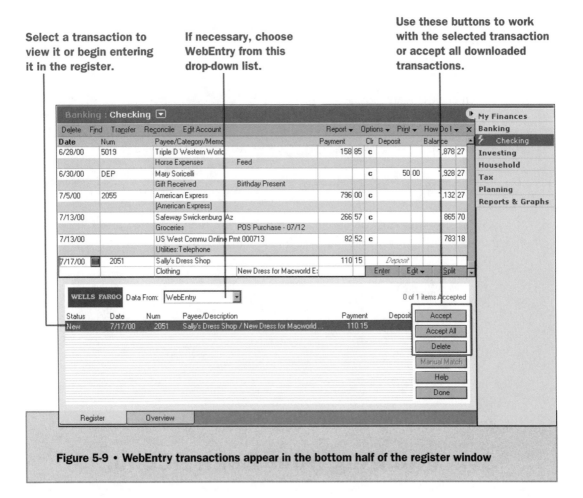

Figure 5-9 • **WebEntry transactions appear in the bottom half of the register window**

Using WebEntry Again

The next time you use WebEntry, you should notice two things:

- Drop-down lists appear for the Quicken Account and Category fields, as shown next. These drop-down lists are updated each time you download WebEntry transactions. This makes it easier to accurately enter transactions in the future.

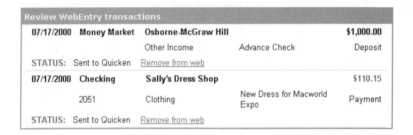

- The transactions you entered on the Web and then imported into Quicken have the status *Sent to Quicken*. These transactions will not be sent again.

Review WebEntry transactions				
07/17/2000	Money Market	Osborne-McGraw Hill		$1,000.00
		Other Income	Advance Check	Deposit
STATUS:	Sent to Quicken	Remove from web		
07/17/2000	Checking	Sally's Dress Shop		$110.15
	2051	Clothing	New Dress for Macworld Expo	Payment
STATUS:	Sent to Quicken	Remove from web		

Synchronizing Your Bank Accounts

Quicken 2001 now enables you to download your account balances to Quicken.com, where you can view them from any computer in the world.

Why would you want to do that? Well suppose you're traveling for business and one of the local shops has an incredible, hand-woven Navajo rug that you really want to buy. You're not sure how much money is in your checking account, and you don't want to write a check for the purchase unless you know for sure that you can cover it. So while you're at work checking your portfolio on Quicken.com (as discussed in Chapter 7), you take a peek at your account balance, which your spouse has been updating with Quicken while you're away. Fortunately, you have enough, and you can make the purchase. You can even use WebEntry to enter that big check in your account (as discussed in the previous section).

Think this might be helpful? Here's how you set it up and make it happen.

Setting Up the Sync

Choose Edit | Options | Internet Options to display the Customize Quicken Download dialog box. Click the Bank Accounts tab to display its options, shown here:

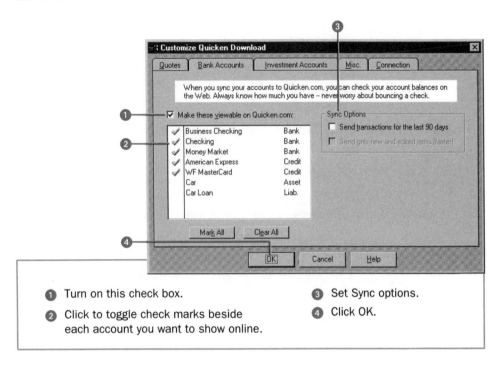

1. Turn on this check box.
2. Click to toggle check marks beside each account you want to show online.
3. Set Sync options.
4. Click OK.

Begin by turning on the check box labeled Make These Viewable On Quicken.com. This enables the Bank Account Synchronization feature. Then click to toggle the check marks beside the accounts you want to view online. Finally, turn on the check boxes in the Sync Options area for the transactions you want to download (if any). Click OK to save your settings and dismiss the dialog box.

Synchronizing Account Information

Click the Online button in the button bar to display the One Step Update Download Selection dialog box shown earlier in this chapter. An Update Bank Accounts option should appear in the dialog box; click to turn on the check mark beside it. Then click Update Now. Wait while Quicken connects to the Internet and sends your data. (You may have to log in to Quicken.com; if so, a dialog box will appear.) Click Done in the Quicken Download Summary dialog box that appears. You're done.

Checking Account Balances on Quicken.com

You can view your account balances on Quicken.com by using a Web browser to visit **http://www.quicken.com/myaccounts/**. Figure 5-10 shows what this page might look like; as you can see, it includes not only your bank accounts, but Portfolio Export information as well. I tell you more about Portfolio Export in Chapter 7.

Note *You must be logged in to Quicken.com for your account information to appear. If you are not logged in, Quicken will prompt you to log in.*

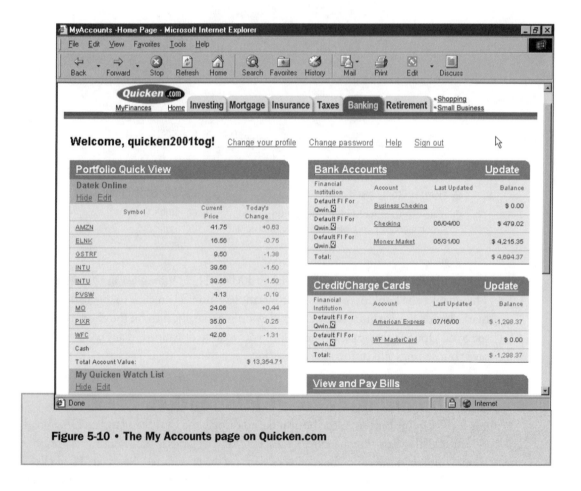

Figure 5-10 • The My Accounts page on Quicken.com

Tracking Your Investments

This part of the book explains how you can use Quicken to track your investments. It begins by explaining the basics of tracking investments in Quicken, then goes on to explain how you can use Quicken's online investment tracking features to download investment information from your brokerage firm and from Quicken's databases. Finally, it provides a wealth of information you can use to invest wisely and maximize your investment returns.

This part has three chapters:

Chapter 6: Investment Tracking Basics

Chapter 7: Tracking Investments Online

Chapter 8: Maximizing Investment Returns

Investment Tracking Basics

In This Chapter:

- *Investment Basics*

- *Setting Up Investment Accounts*

- *Viewing Investment Information*

- *Adding and Editing Securities*

- *Recording Investment Transactions*

- *Tracking the Market Value of Investments*

Investments offer individuals a way to make their money grow. Although more risky than deposits made to an FDIC-insured bank, stocks, bonds, mutual funds, and other types of investments have the potential to earn more. That's why many people build investment portfolios as a way to save for future goals or retirement.

In this chapter, I tell you a little about investments and portfolio management and then explain how you can use Quicken to keep track of the money you invest.

Quicken Investment Basics

Quicken enables you to record your investment transactions and track your portfolio value. With the information about your investments that you enter into Quicken, you can see how various investments perform, generate reports for tax time, and get a clear picture of what your investments are worth.

Before learning how to use Quicken to track your investments, here's a review of what investments and portfolios are.

Types of Investments

An *investment* is a security or asset that you expect to increase in value and/or generate income. There are many types of investments:

- **A certificate of deposit, or CD,** is an account with a bank or other financial institution. It earns a fixed rate of return and has a predetermined maturity date. Withdrawals before the maturity date normally result in penalty fees, which can exceed earned interest. CDs on deposit with a bank are normally FDIC-insured against loss.

- **A money market fund** is an account with a bank or other financial institution that earns interest based on short-term cash values. Money market funds are not FDIC-insured against loss.

- **Stocks** represent part ownership of an organization. Stock investments can earn you money by paying dividends or appreciating in value.

- **Bonds** represent loans to an organization. Bonds can earn you money by paying interest either during the bond's term or at its maturity date.

- **Treasury bills** represent loans to the U.S. government. They are issued at a discount and redeemed at face value; the difference between the two prices are the earnings.

- **Mutual funds** consist of multiple investments owned by many people. When you buy into a mutual fund, you pool your money with other investors to buy stocks, bonds, or other securities. Mutual funds can earn you money by paying dividends and interest and appreciating in value.
- **Annuities** are regularly funded accounts that earn interest or dividends paid in the future.
- **401(k)** and **403(b) plans** are employer-funded retirement investments. They can consist of stocks, bonds, mutual funds, or any other type of investment.
- **IRAs, SEPs,** and **Keogh accounts** are employee-funded retirement investments. They have special tax implications and rules for funding. They can consist of stocks, bonds, mutual funds, or any other type of investment.
- **Real estate** is land or buildings. Real estate investments can earn money from rental or lease income and by appreciating in value.

Most investments can also earn you money if you sell them for more than you paid for them. I provide details about investment types in Chapter 8.

Your Quicken Portfolio

The term *portfolio* refers to the total of all of your investments. For example, if you have shares of one company's stock, shares in two mutual funds, and a 401(k) plan account, these are the items that make up your portfolio.

Types of Investment Accounts

Your Quicken portfolio can include five types of investment accounts: Brokerage, IRA or Keogh, 401(k), Dividend Reinvestment Plan, and Other Investment. You can have as many investment accounts as you need to properly represent the investments that make up your portfolio.

Brokerage   A brokerage account is for tracking a wide variety of investments handled through a brokerage firm, including stocks, bonds, mutual funds, and annuities. There are two types of brokerage accounts:

- **A multi-investment or brokerage account** is for tracking one or more securities or mutual funds. Similar to the account at your brokerage firm, it can track income, capital gains, performance, market values, shares, and cash balances.
- **A single mutual fund investment or brokerage account** is for tracking a single mutual fund. It can track the share balance, market value, income, capital gains, and performance of the fund. It can't, however, track interest, cash balances, or miscellaneous income or expenses.

> **Tip**   *Although you can always convert a single mutual fund investment account to a multi-investment account, you can't convert a regular investment account to a single mutual fund investment account.*

IRA or Keogh   An IRA or a Keogh account is for tracking a variety of retirement accounts, including standard IRA, Roth IRA, Education IRA, Keogh Plan, and SEP IRA.

401(k)   A 401(k) account is for tracking 401(k) or 403(b) accounts. It can track performance, market value, and distribution among investment choices. If you (and your spouse) have more than one 401(k) plan, you should set up a separate account for each.

Dividend Reinvestment Plan   A dividend reinvestment plan (or DRIP) account is for tracking the securities in a company's dividend reinvestment plan. These plans, which are offered by many blue chip corporations, automatically reinvest dividends to buy additional shares of the security. Like the brokerage account, a dividend reinvestment plan account can account for multiple securities or a single security.

Other Investment   The other investment account is for an investment that doesn't fall into any of the other investment categories. Examples might include bonds (including U.S. Savings Bonds), Treasury bills, and commodities.

Choosing the Right Type of Account

Sometimes it's not clear which kind of account is best for a specific kind of investment. Table 6-1 offers some guidance.

> **Tip**   *When trying to decide between an investment account and an asset account, consider the investment. Does its value change regularly? If so, you should use an investment account, which offers better tools for tracking changing values. If the value does not change regularly or you cannot obtain accurate estimates of changing values, an asset account may be better. You can always update the asset value when an accurate market value is available.*

This chapter concentrates on investment accounts tracked in brokerage, IRA or Keogh, 401(k), dividend reinvestment plan, and other investment accounts.

Type of Investment	Type of Account
CD	Savings account, other investment account, or asset account
Money market fund	Money market account
Stocks in your possession	Brokerage account (either one per security or one for all securities)
Brokerage account with one or more securities, with or without an associated cash, checking, or interest-earning account	Regular brokerage account with or without linked checking account
Bonds, including U.S. Savings Bonds	Other investment account
Treasury bills	Other investment account or asset account
Mutual fund with no cash balance	Single mutual fund brokerage account (one per mutual fund)
Variable annuities	Other investment account
Fixed annuities	Other investment account or asset account
401(k) or 403(b) plan	401(k) account
IRA, SEP, or Keogh account	IRA or Keogh account
Real estate	Asset account
Real estate investment trusts (REITs) or partnerships	Other investment account

Table 6-1 • Quicken Accounts for Various Investment Types

The Importance of Portfolio Management

At this point, you may be wondering why you should bother including investment information in your Quicken data file. After all, you may already get quarterly (or even monthly) statements from your broker or investment firm. What you may not realize, however, is how you can benefit from keeping a close eye on your investments. Take a look at what portfolio management with Quicken can do for you.

Centralizing Your Investment Records

Unless you have only one brokerage account for all your investments, you probably get multiple statements for the stocks, bonds, mutual funds, and other investments in your portfolio. No single statement can provide a complete picture of your portfolio's worth. Quicken can, however. By entering the transactions and values on each statement within Quicken, you can see the details of your entire portfolio in one place.

Knowing the Value of Your Portfolio on Any Day

Brokerage statements can tell you the value of your investments on the statement's ending date, but not what they're worth today. Or what they were worth on June 26, 2000. Quicken, however, can tell you what your portfolio is worth on any day for which you have entered security prices, and it can estimate values for dates without exact pricing information.

 SAVE TIME   If you like to keep your portfolio's value up to date with the latest security prices, retrieve prices online. I show you how to take advantage of this feature in Chapter 7.

Keeping Track of Performance History

Manually compiling a complete pricing and performance history for an investment is no small task, especially for periods spanning multiple statements. If you consistently enter investment information in your Quicken data file, however, preparing performance charts and reports is as easy as choosing a menu command or clicking a button.

Calculating Your Return on Investment

Return on investment varies from one investment to another. Quicken enables you to see the return on investment for each security you hold—all in one place!

 GET SMARTER   Use this feature to make better financial decisions. When you're ready to invest more money in your portfolio, it's easy to see which holding is best—and may deserve more funding.

Calculating Capital Gains Quickly and Easily

Calculating the gain on the sale of an investment isn't always easy. Considerations include not only the purchase and selling prices, but commissions, fees, stock splits, and purchase lots. Quicken can take all the work out of calculating capital gains—even if you're just considering the sale and want to know what its impact will be. This is extremely helpful at tax time, as I discuss in Chapter 14.

Quicken Investing Overview

Quicken groups all of its banking-related commands and features in two separate places: the Investing menu and the Investing Center window. Here's a quick look at each.

The Investing Menu

Quicken's Investing menu, which is shown next, includes a variety of commands you can use to access Quicken's investing features, including its online investing features. I cover most of these features in this chapter and the following two chapters.

There are a few commands that you might find especially useful as you work with Quicken's investing features:

- **Investing Accounts** displays a submenu that lists all of your investment accounts. This offers a quick and easy way to open the register for a specific account; simply choose its name from the menu.

- **Investing Activities** displays a submenu of investment-related tasks that aren't used as often as those on the main Investing menu. These include tasks such as creating a new investment, tracking your 401(k), updating a cash or share balance, and reconciling an investment account. I cover these tasks in this chapter and the following two chapters.

- **Investing Services** displays a submenu of investment-related services available from Quicken, Quicken.com, and other providers. This is where you'll find commands for getting real-time quotes, maximizing your 401(k), and automating your daily file backup.

The Investing Center Window

The Investing Center window (see Figure 6-1) is full of information about your investment accounts, as well as links to investment-related Quicken and Quicken.com features and services. To open the Investing Center window, click its QuickTab on the right side of the screen.

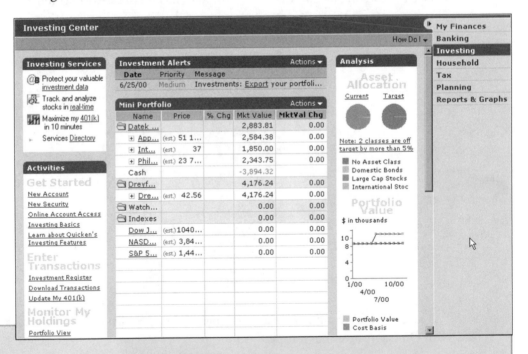

Figure 6-1 • The Investing Center window is a great place to access information about your investments, as well as Quicken's investment-related features

The Investing Center window is separated into three main parts: Investing Services, Activities, and investment snapshots.

Investing Services   The Investing Services area lists a few of the most commonly used services available for Quicken users. Click an underlined link to access that service. For a complete list of services, click the Directory link in the Investing Services area.

Activities   The Activities area offers clickable links to Quicken features. These are separated into a number of categories:

- **Get Started** includes links for setting up accounts and securities, as well as information for learning more about investing and Quicken's investment-related features.

- **Enter Transactions** offers links for entering transactions, both manually and via download.

- **Monitor My Holdings** provides links to switch to various security information views, including Portfolio View and Security Detail View. It also offers links for updating prices, charting, and exporting portfolio data.

- **Before You Buy** provides links to Quicken.com for getting more information about investments. These are valuable research and evaluation tools you should use before you invest in a specific security.

- **Before You Sell** provides links to Quicken and Quicken.com tools, such as the Capital Gains Estimator, to evaluate a selling decision.

- **Optimize My Investments** offers links for learning more about asset allocation and 401(k) accounts.

- **Evaluate** offers links you can use to evaluate your investments, including reports and graphs.

Investing Snapshots   Investing snapshots fill most of the Investing Center window. They include information about your investment accounts and securities. The Actions menu for each snapshot offers commands that apply to the snapshot or information it contains. The following snapshots appear in this window:

- **Investment Alerts** displays alerts related to your investments and investment accounts. I tell you about alerts in Chapter 11.

- **Mini Portfolio** lists all of your investment accounts, along with the securities they contain and the most recent price and market value information. You can click the folder icon in front of an account name to hide or display the securities it contains. You can click the plus or minus sign in front of a security name to display or hide purchase lot information for that security. The Mini Portfolio also includes your Watch List and a number of investment Indexes, including the Dow Jones Industrial Average and the Standard and Poor's 500.

- **Analysis** shows charts for three different areas: Asset Allocation, Portfolio Value, and Investment Returns. These charts can help you better understand your investments and their performance.

Setting Up Accounts

Ready to start tracking your investments with Quicken? The first thing to do is set up the accounts you'll need to do it right. I provide basic information about setting up accounts in Chapter 2. In this section, I provide the specifics for working with investment accounts.

Creating Brokerage, IRA or Keogh, DRIP, and Other Investment Accounts

Creating a brokerage, IRA or Keogh, dividend reinvestment plan, or other investment account is a multiple-step process:

1. Enter general information about the account.
2. Use the Set Up A New Security or Set Up Mutual Fund Security dialog box to enter information about the security.
3. If the account has a linked checking account, you may have to adjust the balance in the account.
4. If you create an account with a single mutual fund, you may want to provide beginning balance information for the account.

In this section, I explain how to complete these steps.

Entering Account Information

When you create a brokerage, IRA or Keogh, dividend reinvestment plan, or other investment account, Quicken displays the Investment Account Setup dialog box, which you can use to enter general information for the account.

Account Name   Give each account a name that clearly identifies it. For example, if you have stock certificates in a safe deposit box and a brokerage account that contains more stock, don't name the two accounts *Stock 1* and *Stock 2* (or *Stock* and *More Stock*). Instead, give them names like *Stock on Hand* and *Joe's Discount Brokerage*.

Type of IRA   When you create an IRA or Keogh account, Quicken asks what type of IRA you will be tracking. Select the appropriate option: Standard IRA, Roth IRA, Education IRA, Keogh Plan, or SEP IRA.

Check Writing/Debit Card Privileges   If you indicate that the account includes check writing or debit card privileges, Quicken links a checking account to the investment account. This enables you to track cash balances separately. You can let Quicken create a new checking account for you or link the investment account to an existing checking account. If the account includes cash balances but the cash is not easily accessible, be sure to say No when asked if you can write checks or use a debit card.

Type of Securities   As part of the account setup process, Quicken asks if the account will track Stocks, Bonds, Or Several Mutual Funds, or One Mutual Fund. Select the appropriate option. If the account will also track cash balances, be sure to select Stocks, Bonds, Or Several Mutual Funds.

Tax Status   When you create a brokerage, dividend reinvestment plan, or other investment account, Quicken asks if it is tax-deferred or tax-exempt. (It doesn't ask this for IRA or Keogh accounts because they are, by definition, tax-deferred.) Select the appropriate option. I explain how to include tax information for investment and other accounts in Chapter 14.

Cash Balance Information   Quicken may ask for cash balance information for the account (or a linked cash account). Whenever possible, get the balance information for the account from the most recent account statement. Then be sure that you don't enter cash transactions that appear on that statement or previous statements.

Online Services   If your brokerage or investment firm offers online services, Quicken will tell you and let you indicate whether you want to use online services with the account. For now, choose the I'm Not Interested At This Time Option. I explain how to set up investment accounts to take advantage of Quicken's online account access features in Chapter 7.

Entering Security Information

When you create any investment account other than a 401(k) account or single mutual fund brokerage account, Quicken automatically displays the first screen of the Set Up A New Security dialog box, which you can use to enter information about the securities you already own. I explain how to use this dialog box in the section "Adding a New Security," later in this chapter.

> **Tip** *At the end of the security setup process, Quicken asks if you want to set up another security. If you select Yes, the whole process starts all over again. If you say No and you entered ticker symbols for stock, Quicken offers to go online to download asset classes and historical prices. If you have an Internet connection, you can take advantage of this feature by selecting Yes and clicking Done; I tell you more about downloading investment information in Chapter 7.*

Entering Single Mutual Fund Information

When you create a single mutual fund brokerage account, Quicken automatically displays the Set Up Mutual Fund Security dialog box shown next, which you can use to enter information about the mutual fund in the account. Enter basic information about the mutual fund in this dialog box's fields and click OK. I provide more details on using this dialog box, which works a lot like the Edit Security dialog box, in the section "Editing a Security," later in this chapter.

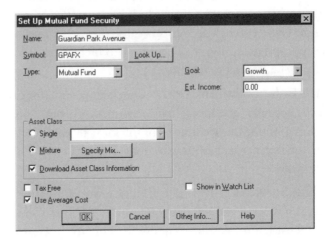

Next, Quicken displays the Create Opening Share Balance dialog box (see the next illustration), which you can use to enter opening balance information for the single mutual fund. Enter balance date, shares, and price per share information from your most recent account statement. That will become the beginning balance for the account, and all performance tracking will begin from that date.

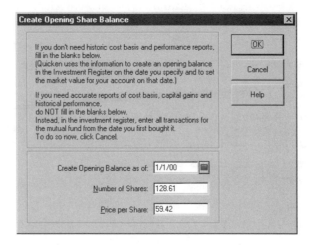

Viewing Your New Account

When you're all finished setting up securities for a new investment account, Quicken displays the account's Investment Register window. Figure 6-2 shows an example. The account (and any linked checking account) also appears in the Account List window, as shown in Figure 6-3.

Adjusting the Balance of a Linked Account

When you enter securities in an investment account, the cost of those securities may be deducted from a linked bank account, thus reducing the value of the linked account. You can see this in the Account List window (see Figure 6-3 for an example).

You can correct the balance in the linked account by entering an adjustment transaction in the misstated account, as shown next. Just be sure to use the same account name as a transfer account in the Category field. When you click Enter, Quicken warns you that you are recording a transfer back into the same account. Click Yes to accept the transaction and correct the account balance. (I explain how to use account registers in Chapter 4.)

6/1/00	Adj	Adjustment				4,379 97	485 65
		[Datek Online-Cash]	Adjust Opening Balance				

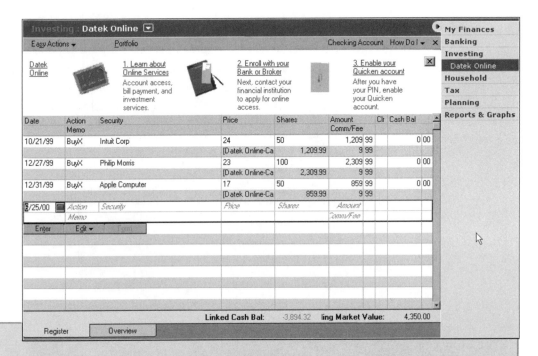

Figure 6-2 • The Investment Register window for a new brokerage account shows initial stock purchases and other transactions you entered while creating the account

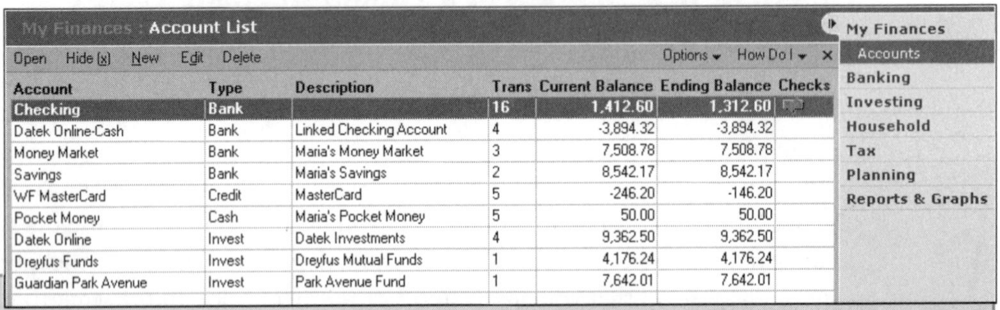

Figure 6-3 • The Account List window lists all accounts, including investment accounts and their linked checking accounts

Creating a 401(k) Account

When you create a 401(k) account, Quicken displays the 401(k) Setup dialog box, which you can use to enter information for the account and any loans you might have taken on it. This dialog box has been completely revised for Quicken 2001 to gather more information. It uses Quicken's EasyStep approach to walk you through the process of entering information, then summarizes the information at the end of the setup process. Here's what the Summary tab of the 401(k) Set Up dialog box looks like with a two-security account set up:

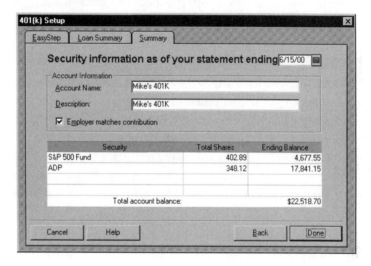

> **Note** *You can also set up a 401(k) account after using the Paycheck Wizard to set up a paycheck with 401(k) deductions. You'll see the same dialog boxes that appear in this section.*

Entering Information

Before you begin, grab a copy of your most recent 401(k) statement. You'll need it to enter accurate information about the account's securities. In the sections that follow, I discuss the pieces of information you'll have to enter.

Account Name, Description, and Financial Institution Use these fields to enter an identifying name and description for the 401(k) plan. This is especially important if you track more than one—yours and your spouse's—in your Quicken data file. Include the name of the financial institution that holds account funds.

Additional Information   The Additional information screen asks a few other questions about the account. Enter the name of the employer and whether it is a current or previous employer. Then indicate whether the account is yours or your spouse's. If the employer contributes to the account, say so and enter the vested percentage. You should have all of this information on your account statement or the paperwork you got when you started the account. Finally, to link the account to a paycheck transaction, turn on the Set Up A Withdrawal From My Paycheck For This Account check box. If you turn on this check box, the next screen will ask whether you have set up your paycheck in Quicken and, if so, which paycheck it is. If you haven't set up your paycheck in Quicken, Quicken will display the Paycheck Wizard when you're finished entering 401(k) information. I explain how to use the Paycheck Wizard in Chapter 11.

Loans   If you have any loans against the account, be sure to say so and indicate how many. Quicken will then prompt you for information about each loan, including a description, the current balance, and the original loan amount. Check boxes enable you to specify whether you want Quicken to set up a loan account to track the loan balance as you make payments. I tell you how to track loans in Chapter 9. If your paycheck has been set up in Quicken, you can also tell Quicken to set up a paycheck withdrawal for loan payments and indicate the amount of the payment.

Statement Information   Provide the statement date and number of securities (not number of shares) for the 401(k) account. You'll also have to indicate whether your statement includes details about the number of shares held.

Security Information   For each security held in the 401(k) account, Quicken prompts you for information about the security name, the number of shares held, and the ending balance. You should find all of this information on your most recent 401(k) statement. If you enter the name of a security that has not yet been created in Quicken, the Set Up Security dialog box appears. I explain how to use this dialog box later in this chapter.

Viewing 401(k) Account Information

When you're finished setting up your 401(k) account, the Overview tab of the account window appears (see Figure 6-4). It lists all the information about the account and includes links you can click to get more information. Like you can with any other account, you can click items in the Account Attributes area to change them.

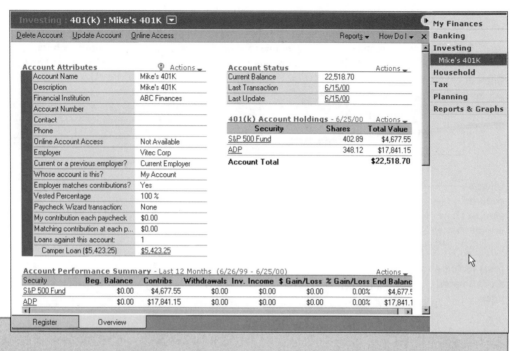

Figure 6-4 • **The Overview tab of a 401(k) account window shows all kinds of information about the account**

Viewing Your Investments

In addition to the Investing Center window (see Figure 6-1), Quicken offers a number of other ways to view your investment information. Each method also offers options to add transactions or edit securities. Here's an overview of each method so you know their options, benefits, and drawbacks.

Portfolio View

The Portfolio View window (see Figure 6-5) displays all of your investments in one place. Information can be viewed in a wide variety of ways to show you exactly what you need to see to understand the performance, value, or components of your portfolio.

To open the Portfolio View window, choose Investing | Portfolio View, press CTRL-U, or click the Portfolio button in the button bar of the Investment Register window (see Figure 6-2) or Security Detail View window (see Figure 6-6 later in the chapter).

Click the name
of a security to
view commands
for working with it.

Click the newspaper icon
beside a security to view
and link to recent news
headlines for it.

Use options here
to change the view.

Click an
account folder
to collapse
or expand it.

Click a
security +/—
sign to show
or hide lots.

(est) indicates
an estimated
price.

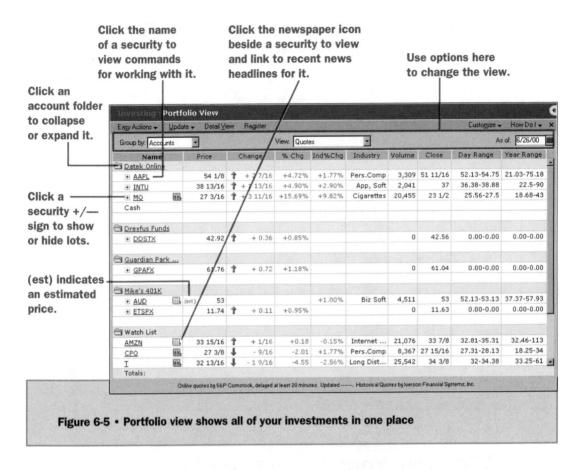

Figure 6-5 • Portfolio view shows all of your investments in one place

The real strength of Portfolio view is its flexibility. It includes many commands
and options for working with and viewing your portfolio.

Using Button Bar Options

The button bar in Portfolio view offers several options to change the view of your
portfolio:

- **Easy Actions** is a menu full of common transaction types for investment
  accounts. Choosing an option displays a form for entering the transaction. I
  tell you how to enter transactions using Easy Actions later in this chapter.

- **Update** is a menu full of options for using an Internet connection to update
  current and historical price information for securities you own or watch. These
  options can be real time-savers, as I discuss in Chapter 7.

- **Detail View** opens the Security Detail View window (see Figure 6-6) for the currently selected security. I tell you about the Security Detail View window later in this chapter.

- **Register** opens the Investment Register window (see Figure 6-2) for the currently selected investment account. If no account is selected, a dialog box asks which account you want to view. I tell you about the Investment Register later in this chapter.

- **Customize** offers options for customizing the window's display. The Edit Current View command displays the Customize View dialog box. You can use it to change the name of the view and the information that appears in it. This dialog box has been improved and expanded in Quicken 2001:

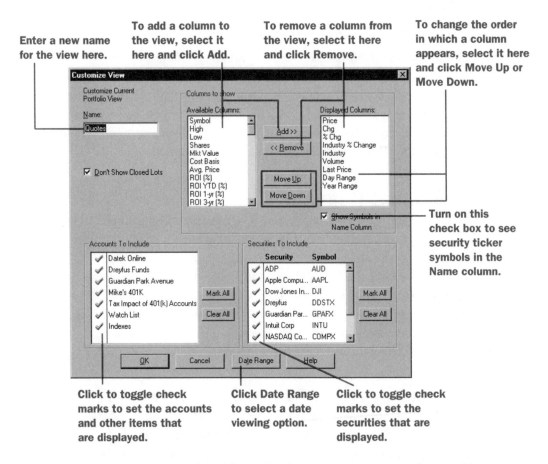

Enter a new name for the view here.

To add a column to the view, select it here and click Add.

To remove a column from the view, select it here and click Remove.

To change the order in which a column appears, select it here and click Move Up or Move Down.

Turn on this check box to see security ticker symbols in the Name column.

Click to toggle check marks to set the accounts and other items that are displayed.

Click Date Range to select a date viewing option.

Click to toggle check marks to set the securities that are displayed.

- **How Do I** provides additional information about using the Portfolio View window and its options.

Using Portfolio View Options

You can further customize Portfolio view by using the Group By, View, and As Of options. There are many view combinations—far too many to illustrate in this book. Here's a brief discussion of options that you can use to explore Portfolio view options on your own.

Using the Group By Options   The Group By options enable you to select the order in which securities appear. The drop-down list offers seven options: Accounts, Industry, Security, Security Type, Investment Goal, Asset Class, and Sector. I explain all of these options later in this chapter.

Using the View Options   The View drop-down list enables you to specify the view that should be used to display the information. Each of the eight predefined views can be customized with the Customize View dialog box shown earlier. There are also nine "custom" views that you can customize to make your own views of the data.

Setting the Portfolio Date   You can use the As Of box to set the date for which you want to view the portfolio. For example, suppose you want to see what your portfolio looked like a month ago, before a particularly volatile market period. Enter that date in the text box. Or click the calendar button beside the text box to display a calendar of dates, and then click the date you want to display. The view changes to show your portfolio as of the date you specified.

Investment Register

The Investment Register window, shown in Figure 6-2, looks similar to the Account Register window. It enables you to view, enter, and edit transactions for an investment account.

To open the Investment Register window, click the name of an account in the Investing Center window or click the Register button in the Portfolio View window (see Figure 6-5) or Security Detail View window (see Figure 6-6). To switch from one account to another, use the pop-up menu in the window's title bar.

The button bar buttons in the Investment Register window enable you to enter investments and work with the register:

- **Easy Actions** is a menu full of common transaction types for investment accounts. Choosing an option displays a form for entering the transaction. I tell you how to enter transactions using Easy Actions later in this chapter.
- **Portfolio** opens the Portfolio View window (see Figure 6-5), which I discuss earlier in this chapter.

- **Checking Account** opens the account register for a linked checking account (if one exists).
- **How Do I** provides additional information about using the Investment Register window and its options.

Security Detail View

The Security Detail View window (see Figure 6-6) provides a wealth of information about a specific security, including value and performance information, transactions, and price or market value history. You can use this window to enter transactions, update prices, edit a security, or open the Portfolio View or Investment Register windows.

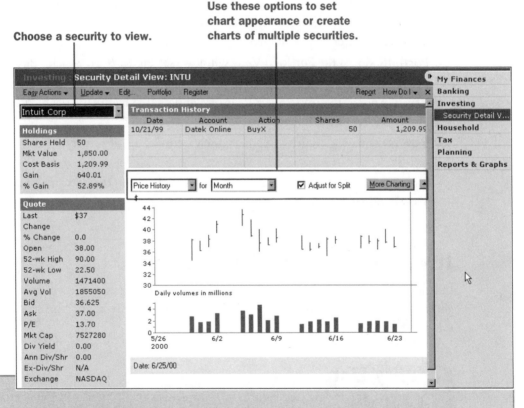

Choose a security to view.

Use these options to set chart appearance or create charts of multiple securities.

Figure 6-6 • The Security Detail View window displays all kinds of information about a security you own or watch

To open the Security Detail View window, choose Investing | Security Detail View or click the Detail View button in the Portfolio View window (see Figure 6-5). To switch from one security to another, use the drop-down list in the upper-left corner of the window.

The button bar buttons in the Security Detail View window enable you to enter investments and switch to other views:

- **Easy Actions** is a menu full of common transaction options for investment accounts. Choosing an option displays a form for entering the transaction. I tell you how to enter transactions using Easy Actions later in this chapter.

- **Update** is a menu full of options for using an Internet connection to update current and historical price information for securities you own or watch. These options can be a real time-saver, as I discuss in Chapter 7.

- **Edit** displays the Edit Security dialog box, which you can use to change information about the security. I tell you more about editing security information later in this chapter.

- **Portfolio** opens the Portfolio View window (see Figure 6-5), which I discuss earlier in this chapter.

- **Register** opens the Investment Register window (see Figure 6-2), which I discuss earlier in this chapter.

- **Report** displays a Security Report, which summarizes all activity for the security.

- **How Do I** provides additional information about using the Security Detail View window and its options.

Investment List Windows

Quicken also offers windows that list securities, security types, and investment goals. You can use these lists to view, add, edit, or remove list items. This section explains how.

Security List

The Security List window (see Figure 6-7) simply lists the securities in Quicken's data file. You can use this window to add, edit, delete, or hide securities, including Watch List securities—securities you don't own but want to monitor. To open this window, choose Investing | Security List or press CTRL-Y.

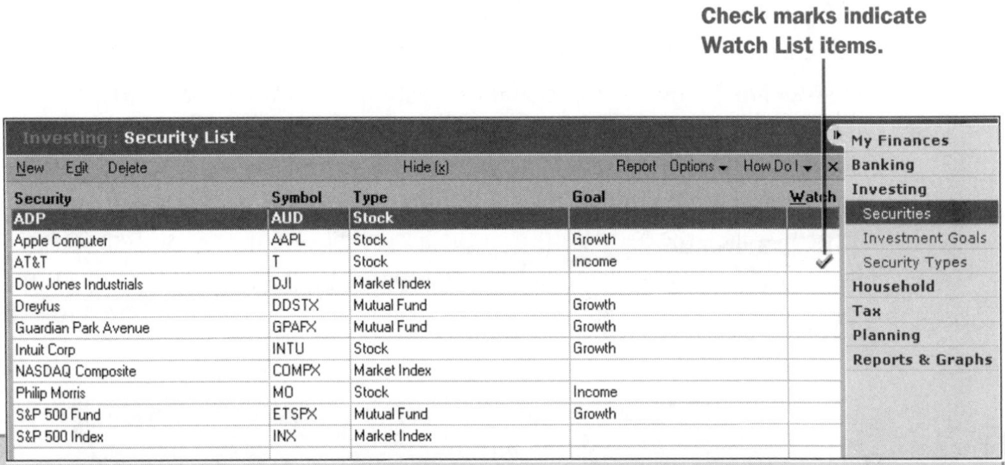

Check marks indicate
Watch List items.

Figure 6-7 • Use the Security List window to view, add, edit, or remove securities that you own or watch

Using the Button Bar

Button bar options enable you to work with the list's items:

- **New** enables you to create a new security.
- **Edit** enables you to modify the currently selected security.
- **Delete** removes the currently selected security.

Caution *Do not delete a security for which you want to maintain historical information, even if you no longer own it. Deleting a security removes all record of the security from your Quicken data file. If you want to keep the information but don't want to see the security in lists, hide the security instead.*

- **Hide** removes the currently selected security from all lists without actually deleting it.

Tip *To view a hidden security, choose View Hidden Securities from the Options menu on the button bar. To unhide a security, view and select it, and then click the Hide button on the button bar.*

- **Report** displays a Security Report for the selected security.

- **Options** displays a menu that enables you to toggle the view of hidden securities.
- **How Do I** provides additional instructions for using the Security List window.

Adding a New Security

To add a new security to your Quicken data file—either as a holding or a Watch List item—click the New button in the Security List window (see Figure 6-7). The Set Up A New Security dialog box appears. (This is the same dialog box that appears when you first set up an investment account and are prompted to add new securities to it.)

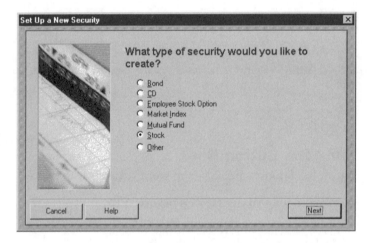

The Set Up A New Security dialog box displays screens that prompt you for information about a security. The process is pretty straightforward, so I won't spend too much time providing detailed instructions. Instead, I'll explain what some of the less obvious options are all about.

Type of Security   The first thing you're prompted for is the type of security. There are seven options: Bond, CD, Employee Stock Option, Market Index, Mutual Find, Stock, and Other. Select the appropriate option.

Tip   *Market Index enables you to track popular market indexes, such as the Dow Jones Industrial Average or the S&P 500.*

Security Name   In most cases, Quicken prompts you for two pieces of information: the name of the security and the ticker symbol. Provide the full name of the security or a shorter name you use to refer to it. The ticker symbol is required if you want to use Quicken's online features to download security values; I tell you more about that in Chapter 7. (If you have an Internet connection, you can use the Lookup button to look up the ticker symbol for securities.)

Employee Stock Options   If you are creating an employee stock option, you can create a new security or select a security that you already track. Each screen in the Set Up A New Security dialog box prompts you for information about the stock option—such as the date it was granted, grant number, number of shares, exercise price, vesting schedule, and expiration date—so you may want to have the related paperwork handy to consult to ensure that your entries are correct. Once set up, Quicken will track the value of the stock and its option and automatically enter necessary vesting transactions in your account register.

Market Indexes   If you selected Market Index as the type of security, Quicken displays a dialog box like the one that follows, asking which market indexes you want to track. Place a check mark beside the desired indexes. Quicken will add them to your watch list, which I discuss later in this chapter.

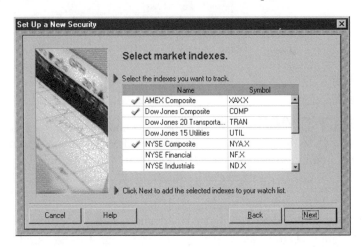

Asset Class   Asset class information works with Quicken's Asset Allocation feature to help you diversify your portfolio so it best meets your investment goals. There are eight asset class options: Domestic Bonds, Global Bonds, Large Cap Stocks, Small Cap Stocks, International Stocks, Cash, Other, and Unclassified. If you know which asset class the security belongs to, select it. Because mutual funds are usually a mixture of asset classes, Quicken supports class mixtures; use a dialog box to specify the exact mixture:

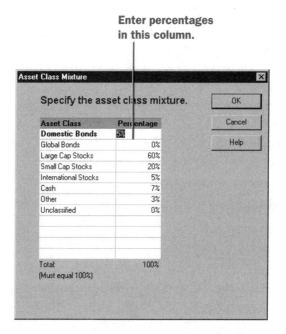

Enter percentages
in this column.

Asset Class Mixture			

Specify the asset class mixture.

Asset Class	Percentage
Domestic Bonds	5%
Global Bonds	0%
Large Cap Stocks	60%
Small Cap Stocks	20%
International Stocks	5%
Cash	7%
Other	3%
Unclassified	0%

OK
Cancel
Help

Total: 100%
(Must equal 100%)

GET SMARTER   If you don't know a security's asset class and have access to the Internet, you can have Quicken automatically download asset class information when you connect. I tell you how in Chapter 7.

Investment Goal   An investment goal is how the security fits into your investment scheme. There are six predefined options: None, College Fund, Growth, High Risk, Income, and Low Risk. Specifying an investment goal enables you to group securities by goal onscreen and in printed reports.

Tip   *You can modify the list of investment goals. I explain how a little later in this chapter.*

Cost Basis　　Quicken supports two methods of tracking the cost of your securities:

- **Lot Identification** enables you to track the cost of each security by its purchase lot. This is the most accurate way to track investment costs and performance. It also enables you to control capital gains timing by allowing you to choose the lots you sell.
- **Average Cost** enables you to average the cost of all the purchases of a security. This method is commonly used for mutual funds reporting and has less bookkeeping requirements for tax purposes.

Tip　　*Although you can switch methods at any time, the IRS requires that you stick to a method for a security once you have reported your first capital gain.*

Holdings Versus Watch List Securities　　Quicken enables you to track the securities you own as well as the ones you want to watch. The securities you own are referred to as your *holdings*. The securities you don't own but want to watch are referred to as *watch list securities*. If you own shares of the security you are setting up, be sure to select the Track My Holdings option.

Tip　　*Although the Watch List feature does not require Internet access, it's a heck of a lot more useful if you regularly download stock prices using the Online Quotes feature of Quicken. I tell you about Online Quotes in Chapter 7.*

Tracking Start Date　　There are three options for setting the start date for tracking a security:

- **Today** begins tracking an investment as of the current date. This is the quickest option.
- **The end of last year** begins tracking an investment as of the last day of the previous year. This enables you to generate accurate reports for the current year and the future.
- **The date you purchased this security** begins tracking an investment from the date you enter. Although this option may require a bit more work on your part, you should select it if you are using lot identification and want to generate accurate reports—including capital gain/loss tax reports—for all years.

Holdings Information   As illustrated next, for each security, Quicken prompts you to enter the number of shares, cost per share, and commission or fee for the purchase transaction. You can enter fractions for per share prices. For example, if a stock sells for $10^3/_4$, you can enter either **10 3/4**—with a space between the 0 and the 3—or **10.75**. Quicken converts fractions to decimal equivalents. Quicken will automatically calculate the total cost and display it in the window:

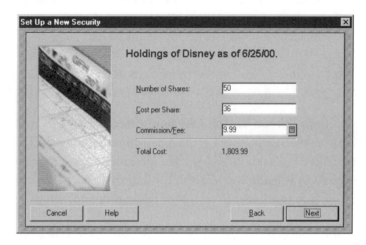

Caution   *If you're interested in tracking stocks by lot, you must enter each purchase of a security separately. For example, suppose you purchased 50 shares of Intuit on January 16, 1999; 50 more shares on June 20, 1999; and 100 more shares on May 1, 2000. Don't enter 200 shares with an average purchase price and total fee. Instead, enter the first purchase in the Set Up a New Security dialog box, and then enter each subsequent purchase lot separately in the investment account register to properly track each acquisition date and price. This makes it possible to take advantage of Quicken's Capital Gains Estimator feature, which I tell you about in Chapter 8.*

Editing a Security

You can edit a security to correct or clarify information you previously entered for it. Select the security's name in the Security List window (Figure 6-7) and click the

Edit button on the button bar. The Edit Security dialog box appears. Enter or edit information in the dialog box and click OK to save your changes:

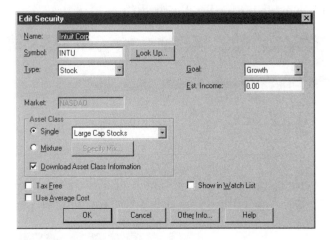

As you can see, this dialog box offers the same basic options as the Set Up A New Security dialog box discussed earlier. It does, however, offer additional options that you might find useful.

Est. Income   Estimated Income is the amount you expect to earn per year per share of the security. Normally, this field is used for expected annual dividends per share.

Tax Free   Turn on the Tax Free check box if income from this security is not taxable. An example would be a tax-free municipal bond.

Use Average Cost   If you don't want to track the security by lot, turn on the Use Average Cost check box. As discussed earlier in this chapter, this affects the way Quicken calculates the cost of securities.

Show in Watch List   Turning on the Show In Watch List check box adds the security to your Watch List so you can track its prices even if you don't own it.

Other Info   Clicking the Other Info button displays a dialog box you can use to enter additional information about the security, such as the broker name and phone number, security rating, and comments.

Security Type List

The Security Type List displays a list of security types. You can use button bar buttons to modify the list if desired:

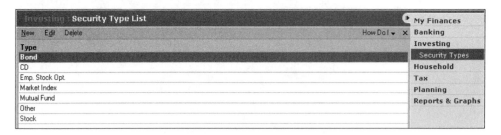

- **New** enables you to create a new security type. Clicking this button displays the Set Up Security Type dialog box; use it to enter security type information:

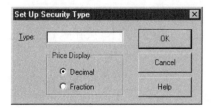

- **Edit** enables you to modify the currently selected security type. Clicking this button displays the Edit Security Type dialog box, which looks and works just like the Set Up Security Type dialog box.
- **Delete** enables you to remove the currently selected security type from the list.
- **How Do I** provides instructions for working with the Security Type List window.

Tip   Adding or removing security types does not affect the first screen of the Set Up A New Security dialog box, which lists standard security types.

Investment Goal List

As illustrated next, the Investment Goal List window displays a list of all investment goals. You may find investment goals useful for organizing your investments based on what you expect them to do for you.

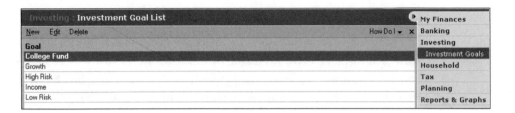

You can use button bar buttons to modify the list if desired:

- **New** enables you to create a new investment goal. Clicking this button displays the Set Up Investment Goal dialog box. Use it to enter a name for the goal.
- **Edit** enables you to modify the currently selected investment goal. Clicking this button displays the Edit Investment Goal dialog box, which you can use to modify the name of the goal.
- **Delete** enables you to remove the currently selected investment goal from the list.
- **How Do I** provides instructions for working with the Security Type List window.

Recording Investment Transactions

The most important part of properly tracking investments is recording all investment transactions. This includes purchases, sales, dividends, and other activity affecting your portfolio's value.

In this section, I provide instructions for entering most common investment transactions using Quicken's Easy Actions feature.

Before You Start

Before you enter a transaction, you must have all of its details. In most cases, you can find the information you need on a confirmation form or receipt you receive from your broker or investment firm. The information varies depending on the transaction, but it generally should include the security name, transaction date, number of shares, price per share, and commissions or fees.

You can enter most security transactions within the Investment Register window (see Figure 6-2) for the account that the transaction affects, or the Security Detail View window (see Figure 6-6) for the security that is affected. Switch to one of those windows when you're ready to enter the transaction.

Using Easy Actions

The easiest way to enter an investment transaction is with Easy Actions, a Quicken feature that displays a custom dialog box or form for virtually every kind of investment transaction. You can open an Easy Actions dialog box by choosing the transaction type from the Easy Actions menu in the button bar:

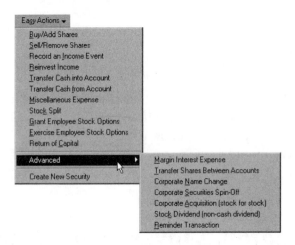

Shortcut *Experienced Quicken users may prefer to enter transactions directly into the Investment Register for an account. A drop-down list in the transaction's entry area offers appropriate transaction codes for all kinds of transactions. Explore this feature on your own once you're accustomed to entering investment transactions with Easy Actions.*

- **Buy/Add Shares** adds shares to an investment account. Shares are normally purchased, but they can also be added as a result of a gift or inheritance.
- **Sell/Remove Shares** removes shares from an investment account. Shares are normally sold, but they can also be given as a gift or written off when a company folds.
- **Record An Income Event** enables you to record income from interest and dividends.
- **Reinvest Income** enables you to account for investment income (such as dividends) that are reinvested in the security. This is common with dividend reinvestment plans and mutual funds.

- **Transfer Cash Into Account** enables you to transfer cash into the account from another account.
- **Transfer Cash From Account** enables you to transfer cash from the account into another account.
- **Miscellaneous Expense** enables you to record investment expenses other than commissions.
- **Stock Split** enables you to record additional shares received as a result of a stock split.
- **Grant Employee Stock Options** enables you to record the receipt of an employee stock option.
- **Exercise Employee Stock Options** enables you to use a stock option to buy stock.
- **Return Of Capital** enables you to record the return of part of your investment capital.
- **Create New Security** displays the Set Up New Security dialog box so you can add a new security to your Quicken data file.
- **Margin Interest Expense** enables you to record the amount of interest paid as a result of purchasing securities on margin.
- **Transfer Shares Between Accounts** enables you to move shares from one Quicken investment account to another.
- **Corporate Name Change** enables you to record the change of the name of a company for which you own stock. This preserves the old name information; simply editing the security name in the Edit Security dialog box does not.
- **Corporate Securities Spin-Off** enables you to record securities obtained through a spin-off of a smaller company from one of the companies in which you own securities.
- **Corporate Acquisition** enables you to record securities obtained in exchange for other securities you own, normally as a result of a corporate acquisition.
- **Stock Dividend** enables you to add shares of a security paid as a dividend.
- **Reminder Transaction** enables you to enter an investment reminder that will appear each time you start Quicken. You may find this option useful if you want to conduct a transaction at a future date and are worried that you may forget to do it.

Note *The options that appear vary depending on the window in which the Easy Actions menu appears.*

Easy Actions dialog boxes and forms are generally self-explanatory and easy to use. Here are a few common transactions to illustrate how they work.

Purchases

A security purchase normally involves the exchange of cash for security shares. In some cases, you may already own shares of the security or have it listed on your Watch List. In other cases, the security may not already exist in your Quicken data file, so you'll need to set up the security when you make the purchase.

Start by choosing Easy Actions | Buy/Add Shares. The EasyStep tab of the Buy/Add Shares window appears. Follow its prompts to enter information about the shares you want to add. Here's some additional information to help you out.

Security Name or Investment Account Name   If the Investment Register window was active when you used the Easy Actions command, the first piece of information you'll have to provide is the security name. How you proceed depends on whether you already own shares in the security:

- To add shares for a new security, enter the security name in the text box. When you click Next, the Set Up Security dialog box appears. Enter information about the security and click OK to add it to the Security List.
- To add shares for a known security, select its name from the drop-down list.

If the Security Detail View window was active when you used the Easy Actions command, Quicken asks which account the transaction should be recorded in. Choose the appropriate account from the drop-down list.

Source of Funds   Quicken offers two options for the source of funds for the purchase:

- **Yes, From The Following Account** enables you to select a Quicken account from which money should be deducted for the purchase of the shares.
- **No, Deposit The Shares Without Affecting Any Cash Balance** adds the shares to your investment account without deducting cash from any other account. You might use this option to add shares omitted when you initially set up the account.

Transaction Details   Transaction details include the number of shares, price per share, date of the transaction, and amount of commission. All of this information should be available on your transaction receipt or brokerage statement.

Finishing Up   When you've finished stepping through the entry process, the information you entered appears in the Summary tab of the Buy/Add Shares window. It might look something like this:

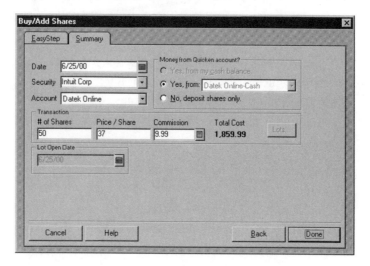

When you click Done, the entry is added to the account register:

6/25/00	BuyX	Intuit Corp	37	50	1,859	99	0	00
			[Datek Online-Ca	1,859.99	9	99		

Sales

A security sale also involves the exchange of cash for security shares. Normally, you dispose of shares you already own, but in some instances, you may sell shares you don't own. This is called *selling short,* and it is a risky investment technique sometimes used by experienced investors.

Start by choosing Easy Actions | Sell/Remove Shares. The EasyStep tab of the Sell/Remove Shares window appears. Follow its prompts to enter information about the shares you want to add. Here's some additional information to guide you.

Security Name or Investment Account Name   If the Investment Register window was active when you used the Easy Actions command, the first thing Quicken wants to know is what security you are selling. You have two options:

- To remove shares of a security you own or watch, select its name from the drop-down list.
- To remove shares of a security that you do not own or watch, enter the security name in the text box. When you click Next, the Set Up Security dialog box appears. Enter information about the security and click OK to add it to the Security List.

If the Security Detail View window was active when you used the Easy Actions command, Quicken asks which account the transaction should be recorded in. Choose the appropriate account from the drop-down list.

Destination of Funds   There are two options for recording proceeds from the sale:

- **Yes, Transfer To The Following Account** enables you to select a Quicken account to which money should be added from the sale of the shares.
- **No, Withdraw The Shares Without Affecting Any Cash Balance** removes the shares from your Investment Register account without adding cash to any other account. You might use this option to record the disposal of shares given as a gift.

Transaction Details   Transaction details include the number of shares, sale price per share, date of the transaction, and amount of commission. All this information should be available on your transaction receipt or brokerage statement. It also includes two cost-basis method options that are important if the shares you are selling were purchased in more than one lot:

- **Average Cost** calculates the average cost of the shares you are selling based on the average cost of all purchase lots.
- **Lot Identification** calculates the exact cost of the shares you are selling based on purchase lots. You can use this option for additional control over capital gains. For example, if you want to take advantage of long-term capital gains tax breaks, you could sell shares that have been in your possession for more than 12 months. If you want to record a loss, you could sell shares that cost more than the selling price. Obviously, your options will vary depending on the lots, their acquisition prices, and your selling price. If you select this option, click the Specify Lots button to display a dialog box; use it to select the lots you are selling and click OK:

When the Shares to
Sell equals the Total
Selected, click OK.

Enter the number of shares
to sell in this column for one
or more lots...

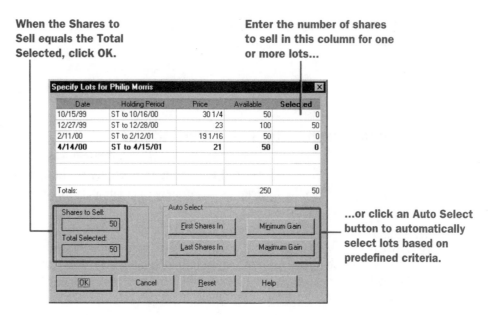

...or click an Auto Select
button to automatically
select lots based on
predefined criteria.

 SAVE MONEY   By controlling the term and amount of capital gains,
you can minimize your tax bill. Use the Capital Gains Estimator, which I discuss in
Chapter 8, to help you select lots before you sell investments.

When you've finished entering information about the sale in the EasyStep tab
windows, the Summary tab of the Sell/Remove Shares window appears. It might
look something like this:

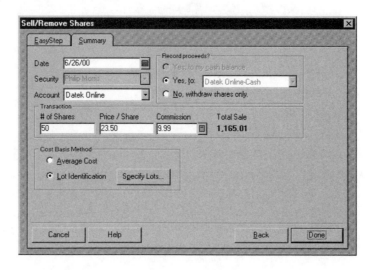

When you click Done to save the transaction, the entry is added to the account register:

| 6/25/00 | SellX | Philip Morris | 23 1/2 | 50 | 1,165 01 | 0 00 |
| | | [Datek Online-Ca | | 1,165.01 | 9 99 | |

Dividend Payments and Other Income

Many investments pay dividends, interest, or other income in cash. (That's why they're so attractive to an investor!) Recording this activity in the appropriate account register enables Quicken to accurately calculate performance, while keeping account balances up to date.

Caution   *Many mutual funds are set up to reinvest income, rather than pay it in cash. Do not use the steps in this section to record a reinvestment of income. Instead, choose Easy Actions | Reinvest Income and use the Reinvest Income dialog box that appears to enter transaction information.*

Choose Easy Actions | Record An Income Event. The Record Income dialog box appears. Use it to enter information about a cash payment on an investment:

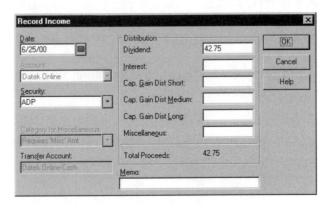

When you click OK to record the transaction, it appears in the Investment Register window for the account:

| 6/25/00 | DivX | ADP | | | 42 75 | 0 00 |
| | | | | [Datek Online-Ca | | |

Other Transactions

Other transactions are just as easy to enter as purchases, sales, and dividends. Simply choose the appropriate option from the Easy Actions menu or submenu, and then enter the transaction information in the window or dialog box that appears. If you have the transaction confirmation or brokerage statement in front of you when you enter the transaction, you have all the information you need to enter it.

Tip *If you need additional guidance while entering a transaction, click the Help button in the transaction window or dialog box to learn more about the options that must be entered.*

Editing Transactions

You can also use Easy Actions forms to edit transactions. In the Investment Register window, select the transaction and click the Form button beneath it. Edit the transaction in the form dialog box that appears and click Done or OK to save your changes.

Adjusting Balances

Occasionally, you may need to adjust the cash balance or number of shares in an investment account or update the balance in a 401(k) account. Here's how.

Updating an Account's Cash Balance   You can adjust the balance in a linked cash account, an investment account with a cash balance, or an asset account used to track investments and cash. Open the register window for the account you want to adjust and choose Investing | Investing Activities | Update My Cash Balance. Then enter the adjustment date and correct balance in the dialog box that appears. When you click OK, Quicken creates an adjusting entry.

Update Share Balance   You can adjust the number of shares in an investment account. Open the Investment Register window for the account you want to adjust and choose Investing | Investing Activities | Update My Share Balance. Enter the adjustment date, security, and correct number of shares in the dialog box that appears. When you click OK, Quicken creates an adjusting entry.

Updating 401(k) Balances   401(k) account balances change every time you make a contribution through your paycheck. To adjust the balance, choose Investing | Investing Activities | Track My 401(k). In the dialog box that appears, specify that you want to update an existing 401(k) account and then choose the

401(k) account that you want to update. Follow the prompts in the EasyStep tab of the Update 401(k) Account dialog box that appears to update the information. The statement information screen is shown next. When you've finished, check your entries in the Summary tab and click Done.

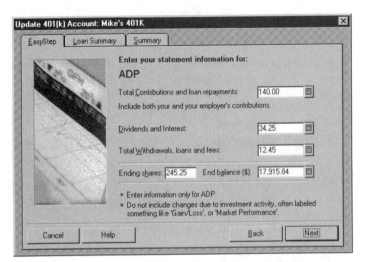

SAVE TIME Don't manually adjust your 401(k) balance every payday. Instead, use Quicken's Paycheck Wizard to record 401(k) account transactions as part of your regular paycheck. I explain how in Chapter 11.

Tracking Security Values

Quicken can automatically do all the math to tell you what your investments are worth—if you take the time to enter the per share prices of each of your securities. When you record transactions, Quicken automatically records the security price. It uses the most recently entered price as an estimate to calculate the current value of the investment. You can see this in the Portfolio View window (see Figure 6-5)—those black **(est)** characters indicate that the price is an estimate. The **(est)** characters appear if the current date is on a weekend or holiday or you haven't entered or downloaded the current day's prices. Of course, Portfolio view is a lot more valuable with up-to-date security price information and a history of prices.

You can enter price information two ways: manually (the hard way) and automatically (the easy way). I show you how to manually enter security prices in this chapter; to learn how to automatically enter prices via Internet download, skip ahead to Chapter 7.

SAVE TIME   If you track more than one or two securities and want to update price information more often than once a week, stop reading now. You don't want to enter security prices manually. Trust me. It's an extremely tedious task. Quicken's ability to download stock prices directly from the Internet—even five-year price histories—can save you tons of time and prevent data-entry errors. And best of all, it's free. All you need is an Internet connection. Learn about setting up an Internet connection in Chapter 3 and about downloading quotes in Chapter 7.

Entering Security Prices

Manually entering security prices isn't really hard. It's just time consuming. And the more securities you track, the more time-consuming it is. But without an Internet connection, this may be the only way you can enter prices into Quicken.

Start by choosing Investing | Security Detail View to display the Security Detail View window (see Figure 6-6). Use the drop-down list within the window to display the security for which you want to enter price information. Then choose Edit Price History from the Update menu on the button bar. The Price History window for the security appears. It shows all the price information stored within the Quicken data file for the security. You can use buttons on the window's button bar to add, edit, delete, and print the price history:

Date	Price	High	Low	Volume
6/26/00	23 1/2			
6/25/00	23 1/2			
12/27/99	23			

Price History for: Philip Morris

New   Edit   Delete   Print   Close

When you click the New button, the New Price dialog box appears, which is shown next. Use it to enter the date and closing price for the security. Optionally, you can even enter the daily high, low, and volume.

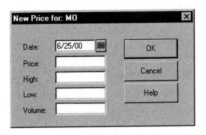

The Edit Price dialog box looks and works much the same way.

Viewing Market Values and Performance

Once you've entered price information for your securities, you can view their market value and performance information in the Portfolio View window (see Figure 6-5) and Security Detail View window (see Figure 6-6). Use options within the windows to modify the information that is displayed. I explain how earlier in this chapter.

Tracking Investments Online

In This Chapter:

- *Benefits and Costs of Online Investment Tracking*

- *Downloading Transactions*

- *Comparing Downloaded Transactions to Register Transactions*

- *Reviewing Account Balance Details*

- *Comparing Downloaded Holdings to Recorded Holdings*

- *Downloading Stock Quotes and News Headlines*

- *Synchronizing Your Portfolio with Quicken.com*

Chapter 7

Quicken offers three separate features for tracking investments online:

- **Online Investment Tracking** enables you to download transactions and balances for your investment accounts. This helps automate the entry of investment transactions and keeps your Quicken records in sync with your brokerage firm's records.
- **Online Quotes and Info** enables you to obtain current and historical quotes, asset allocation information, and news headlines about individual stocks, mutual funds, and other investments. This automates the tracking of market values and provides valuable information you can use to make better investment decisions.
- **Web Portfolio Export** enables you to put a copy of your investment portfolio on the Quicken.com Web site, where you can track its value from any computer connected to the Internet—without Quicken.

In this chapter, I tell you about each of these features and explain how they can help you save time and stay informed about your investments.

Tip *The instructions in this chapter assume that you have already configured your computer for an Internet connection. If you have not done so, do it now. Chapter 3 provides the instructions you need to set up and test an Internet connection. This chapter also assumes that you understand the topics and procedures discussed in Chapters 2 and 6, and builds on many of the basic concepts discussed in those chapters.*

Online Investment Tracking

Online Investment Tracking enables you to download transactions, balance details, and holding information directly from the financial institutions with which you maintain investment accounts. Each transaction can then be entered into your Quicken investment account with the click of a mouse button. You can also review downloaded account balance details and compare downloaded holdings information to the information recorded in your portfolio.

Note *To use Online Investment Tracking, your brokerage or investment firm must be a Quicken partner listed in the Apply For Online Financial Services window. Choose Finance | Online Financial Institutions List to view this list. You can learn more about Quicken partners in Chapter 3.*

Setting Up Online Investment Tracking

To use Online Investment Tracking, you must configure the appropriate Quicken accounts. This requires that you enter information about your financial institution and the account(s) you want to track.

Setting up Online Investment Tracking is virtually identical to setting up Online Account Access for a bank account or credit card account. Just start by choosing Investing | Online Investing Setup to display the Online Account Setup dialog box. I provide step-by-step instructions for setting up an account for online account access in Chapter 5, so I won't repeat them here. Consult that chapter for details. Keep in mind that you won't need to enter a routing number.

Using the Online Center Window

When you enable Online Investment Tracking, you can use the Online Center to download account information, compare it to data in your Quicken file, and enter new transactions and adjustments. Choose Investing | Online Investing. Figure 7-1 shows what this window looks like for a Datek Online investment account.

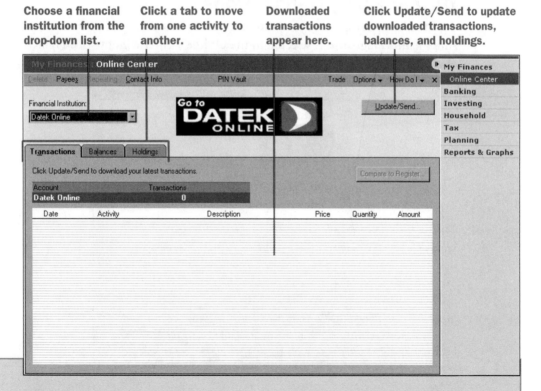

Figure 7-1 • Use the Online Center window to work with Online Investment Tracking options.

The button bar offers a number of options you can use for investment tracking:

- **Payees** displays the Online Payee List window, which I discussed in Chapter 5.
- **Contact Info** displays the Contact Information dialog box for the currently selected financial institution. You can use the information in the dialog box to contact the bank or credit card company by phone, Web site, or e-mail.
- **PIN Vault** gives you access to Quicken's PIN Vault feature, which I discuss later in this chapter. (This option only appears if you have online banking features enabled for accounts at more than one financial institution.)
- **Trade** uses Quicken's built-in Web browser to connect to your brokerage firm so you can log on and enter trade information.
- **Options** displays a menu of commands for working with the current account or window.
- **How Do I** provides additional instructions for working with the Online Center window.

Downloading Transactions

To download transactions, you must connect to your financial institution. Make sure the brokerage firm is selected in the Online Center window (see Figure 7-1) and click the Update/Send button. The Instructions To Send dialog box appears:

Enter your PIN and click Send. Wait while Quicken connects to your financial institution. A status window appears during the connection.

Reviewing Transactions

When Quicken is finished exchanging information, the status window disappears, and an Online Transmission Summary window appears to summarize the activity that took place while you waited.

Reviewing a List of Downloaded Transactions

The transactions you download appear in the Transactions tab of the Online Center window. Because your investment firm knows exactly what you bought and sold, all transaction details appear in the window:

Click Compare To Register to compare downloaded transactions to transactions in your account register.

Review downloaded transactions here.

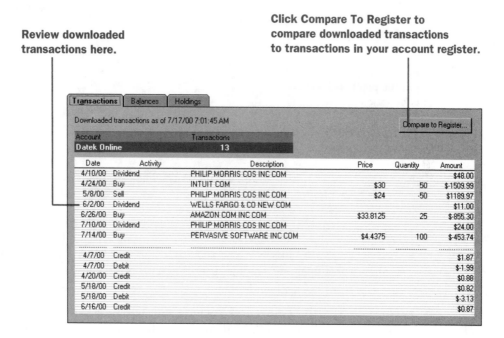

Date	Activity	Description	Price	Quantity	Amount
4/10/00	Dividend	PHILIP MORRIS COS INC COM			$48.00
4/24/00	Buy	INTUIT COM	$30	50	$-1509.99
5/8/00	Sell	PHILIP MORRIS COS INC COM	$24	-50	$1189.97
6/2/00	Dividend	WELLS FARGO & CO NEW COM			$11.00
6/26/00	Buy	AMAZON COM INC COM	$33.8125	25	$-855.30
7/10/00	Dividend	PHILIP MORRIS COS INC COM			$24.00
7/14/00	Buy	PERVASIVE SOFTWARE INC COM	$4.4375	100	$-453.74
4/7/00	Credit				$1.87
4/7/00	Debit				$-1.99
4/20/00	Credit				$0.88
5/18/00	Credit				$0.82
5/18/00	Debit				$-3.13
6/16/00	Credit				$0.87

Downloaded transactions as of 7/17/00 7:01:45 AM — Compare to Register...

Account: Datek Online — Transactions: 13

Tip *The first time you connect, your financial institution sends all transactions from the past 60 days (or more). After that, only new transactions will be downloaded.*

Comparing Downloaded Transactions to Register Transactions

You can also compare downloaded transactions to the transactions already entered in your account register. This enables you to identify transactions you neglected to enter or entered incorrectly.

Click the Compare To Register button in the Transactions tab of the Online Center window. Quicken attempts to match securities in the downloaded Transaction List to securities in the Security List within Quicken. It displays the Matching Security dialog box for each security it doesn't recognize:

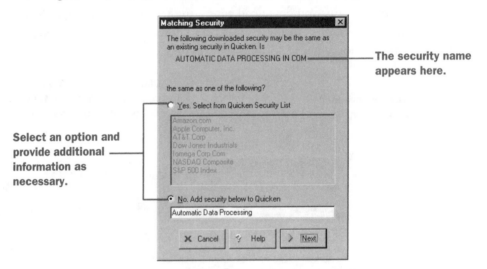

Choose an option for the security:

- **Yes. Select From Quicken Security List.** This tells Quicken that the security is already in Quicken's data file. If you select this option, you must select a security from the list below it.

- **No. Add Security Below To Quicken.** This tells Quicken that the security is new to the Quicken data file. If you select this option, you must enter a name for the security in the text box below it.

Click Next to move to the next security. When you've finished matching or entering securities, the account register window opens with the downloaded Transaction List in the bottom half of its window. Figure 7-2 shows what the window might look like with one transaction matched and another already accepted.

Enter or edit transactions
as necessary here.

Click a transaction to
view it or begin entering
it in the account register.

Use these buttons to work
with a selected transaction
or accept all transactions.

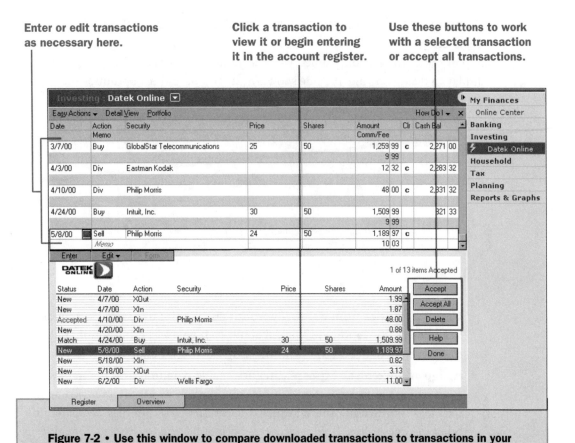

Figure 7-2 • Use this window to compare downloaded transactions to transactions in your
account register

Accepting Transactions　The split register window in Figure 7-2 looks and
works very much like the split window that appears when you accept QuickEntry
and downloaded transactions into Quicken; consult the section "Reviewing
QuickEntry Transactions" in Chapter 4 for details. In most cases, you'll simply
select a new or matched transaction and click the Accept button to accept it or
enter and accept it.

SAVE TIME　Because Quicken will automatically enter most transaction
information, using this method to enter an investment transaction can be much
faster than entering it manually in the account register window.

Entering and Accepting a Transfer In or Transfer Out Transaction

Transactions that display *XIn* or *XOut* in the action column are for cash transfers into or out of the account. When you select one of these transactions, Quicken displays a dialog box like the one shown next. You have three options:

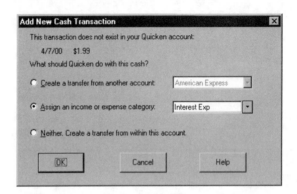

- **Create a transfer from another account** enables you to record the transaction as a transfer from another Quicken account. If you select this option, be sure to choose the right account from the drop-down list beside it.
- **Assign an income or expense category** enables you to record the transaction as an income or expense item. This is commonly used for interest income (a transfer in) or margin interest expense (a transfer out), but may be related to other income or fees. If you select this option, be sure to choose a category from the drop-down list beside it.
- **Neither. Create a transfer from within this account.** This option enables you to record the transfer in or out without affecting any other Quicken accounts or categories. You might use this option to record a transfer that occurred before you began recording transactions with Quicken.

Caution   *Downloaded transactions that have not been accepted may not be entered in your investment register. Thus, your register and portfolio balances may be misstated until you accept all downloaded transactions.*

Note   *If your Quicken portfolio and brokerage portfolio don't match, Quicken displays a dialog box to tell you. Click Yes in that dialog box to display the window in Figure 7-3 and compare the portfolios. I explain how to use this window in the section "When Holdings Don't Match" a little later in this chapter.*

Reviewing Balances

When you download transactions from your financial institution, you also receive detailed account balance information. To review this information, click the Balances tab in the Online Center window. Here's what it looks like for a brokerage account:

Balance	Amount	Description
Cash	$0.00	Available Cash
Margin	$0.00	Margin Balance
Short	$0.00	Market Value of Securities Held Short
Real Cash Balance	$-1062.57	Real Cash Balance
Available Cash Balance	$13653.73	Available Cash Balance
Current Buying Power	$27307.46	Current Buying Power
Account Value	$13167.43	Account Value

Balances at Datek Online as of 7/17/00 9:32:14 AM

Reviewing Holdings

The financial institution also sends you information about your individual holdings. You can review this information in the Online Center window and compare it to the information in your portfolio.

To review holdings, click the Holdings tab in the Online Center window. Here's the Holdings tab for the same account shown in the previous illustration:

Holdings at Datek Online as of 7/17/00 9:32:14 AM

Description	Ticker	Units	Unit price	Market value	Account type
Amazon.com	AMZN	25.0000	$41 1/8	$1028.13	MARGIN
Earthlink Network	ELNK	80.0000	$17 5/16	$1385.00	MARGIN
GlobalStar Telecommunications	GSTRF	50.0000	$10 7/8	$543.75	MARGIN
Intuit, Inc.	INTU	100.0000	$41 1/16	$4106.25	MARGIN
Pervasive Software	PVSW	100.0000	$4 1/4	$425.00	MARGIN
Philip Morris	MO	50.0000	$23 1/2	$1175.00	MARGIN
Pixar	PIXR	100.0000	$35 1/4	$3525.00	MARGIN
Wells Fargo	WFC	50.0000	$43 3/8	$2168.75	MARGIN

To compare downloaded holdings to holdings in your portfolio, click the Compare To Portfolio button. Quicken compares the holdings information. What happens next depends on whether the holdings information matches.

When Holdings Match

When downloaded holdings match the holdings recorded in your portfolio, Quicken displays a dialog box telling you that your Quicken account and your Brokerage Holdings are in agreement. Click OK to dismiss it and continue working with Quicken.

When Holdings Don't Match

When downloaded holdings don't match the holdings recorded in your portfolio, the investment register window for the account appears. A list of discrepancies between the downloaded and recorded holdings is included in the bottom half of the window, as shown in Figure 7-3.

When you select a discrepancy item and click the Add Adjustment button, a set of Easy Action dialog boxes to record the transaction appears. (I tell you how to use these dialog boxes in Chapter 6.) Use the dialog box to provide details for the adjusting entry. Do this for each discrepancy listed in the bottom half of the investment account register. When you have finished, Quicken displays a dialog box confirming that the information matches. Click OK to dismiss the dialog box and continue working with Quicken.

Online Quotes and Info

Quicken's Online Quotes feature enables you to download up-to-date stock quotes and news headlines for the securities in your portfolio and on your Watch List. You set it up once and then update the information as often as desired. You can even download historical price information so you can review price trends for a security that only recently caught your eye. I tell you about all these features next.

Tip *Because Online Quotes and Info is a built-in Quicken Deluxe feature, it doesn't rely on your brokerage firm for information. That means you can take advantage of Online Quotes and Info even if your brokerage firm doesn't offer Online Investment Tracking. All you need is Internet access.*

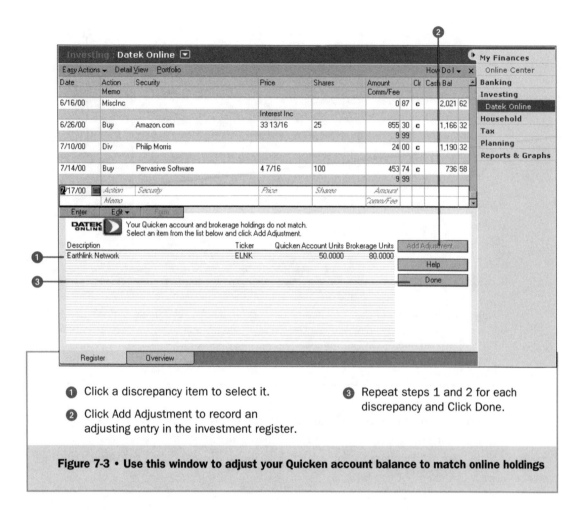

① Click a discrepancy item to select it.

② Click Add Adjustment to record an adjusting entry in the investment register.

③ Repeat steps 1 and 2 for each discrepancy and Click Done.

Figure 7-3 • Use this window to adjust your Quicken account balance to match online holdings

Setting Up Online Quotes and Info

Before you can get quotes online, you must set up the feature. Choose Investing | Investing Activities | Set Up My Quotes Download. The Quotes tab of the Customize Quicken Download dialog box appears. Use it to specify the securities for which you want to download quotes and click OK:

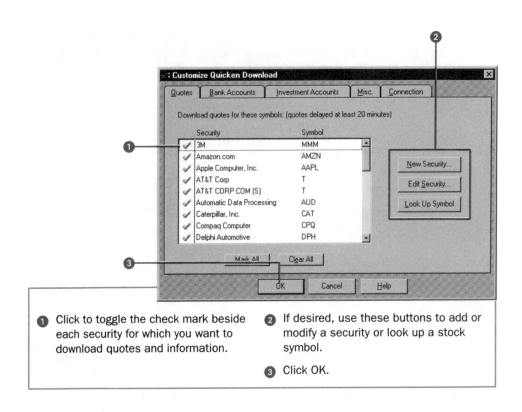

❶ Click to toggle the check mark beside each security for which you want to download quotes and information.

❷ If desired, use these buttons to add or modify a security or look up a stock symbol.

❸ Click OK.

Quicken may immediately connect to the Internet to update quotes. When it's finished, it displays the Quicken Download Summary dialog box, which I discuss a little later in this chapter. You can click Done to dismiss it and continue working with Quicken.

Updating Quotes

You can update quotes and information any time you like. Choose Investing | Security Detail View to display the Security Detail View window, which I discuss in detail in Chapter 6. Then choose Get Online Quotes from the Update menu on the button bar. The One Step Update Download Selection dialog box appears:

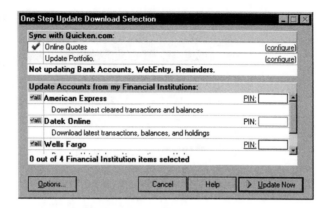

Shortcut *Clicking the Online button at the top-right corner of any window also displays this dialog box. Use it to update all your online information at once. I tell you more about One Step Update in Chapter 11.*

Make sure a check mark appears beside Online Quotes in the list. Then click the Update Now button. Quicken connects to the Internet and begins downloading information. While it works, a Download Status dialog box shows you what's going on. When it has finished, Quicken displays the Quicken Download Summary dialog box, which tells you how many securities were updated and how many headlines were received. Click Done to dismiss it.

Viewing Downloaded Quotes and News

You can view quotes and news headlines for a security in the Portfolio View window. Choose Investing | Portfolio View to display the window, then choose Quotes from the View drop-down list near the top of the window. It might look something like Figure 7-4.

Viewing Stock Quotes

The downloaded stock quote appears right in the Portfolio View window beside the security name or ticker symbol. You can see this in Figure 7-4. Quotes are delayed 20 minutes during the trading day.

You can also view stock quotes by selecting the security in the window and choosing Edit Price History from the Update menu on the button bar. This displays the Price History window, which displays all of the recorded stock quotes for the security:

Date	Price	High	Low	Volume
7/17/00	41 1/16	42 1/8	40 3/8	1,688,300
7/14/00	42 1/4	43 15/16	41 3/4	1,908,100
7/13/00	42 11/16	43 7/8	41 1/4	2,497,700
7/12/00	42 7/16	45	41 1/8	2,518,100
7/11/00	43 3/4	46 1/8	43 7/16	3,127,500
7/10/00	44 3/4	46 3/16	43 1/4	1,619,100
4/24/00	30			
12/31/99	24			

A newspaper icon indicates that news stories for the security are available.

Choose Quotes from this drop-down list.

Name	Price		Change	% Chg	Ind%Chg	Industry	Volume	Close	Open	Day Range	Year R
Datek Online											
AMZN	41 1/8	↓	- 1 3/8	-3.24%	+1.42%	Internet Soft	6,526	42 1/2	42.875	40.25-43.94	32.46-1
ELNK	17 5/16	↑	+ 1 1/2	+9.49%	+4.77%	Internet Serv	2,045	15 13/16	16.00	15.75-17.50	10.56-
GSTRF	10 7/8	↑	+ 5/16	+2.96%	-0.51%	Foreign Tele...	5,208	10 9/16	10.9375	10.44-12.25	5.81-
INTU	41 1/16	↓	- 1 3/16	-2.81%	0.35%	App, Soft	1,688	42 1/4	42.0625	40.38-42.13	22.50-
MO	23 1/2	↓	- 1	-4.08%	-2.94%	Cigarettes	14,722	24 1/2	24.4375	23.25-24.56	18.68-
PIXR	35 1/4	↓	- 3/4	-2.08%	+4.85%	Multimedia	102	36	35.75	34.50-35.84	32.20-
PVSW	4 5/16	↓	- 3/8	-8.0%	0.35%	App, Soft	245	4 11/16	4.25	4.25-4.63	4.00-
WFC	43 3/8	↓	- 5/16	-0.72%	-0.81%	Natl. Bank	2,408	43 11/16	43.875	43.00-44.00	31.37-
Cash											
Indexes											
COMPX	4,274...	↑	+ 28....	+0.67			0	4,246.10	4243.5498	4215.86-42...	0.00
DJI	10804...	↓	- 8.5498	-0.08			0	10812.75	10812.4...	10749.40-1...	0.00
INX	1,510...	↑	+ 0.5...	+0.03			0	1,509.98	1509.92...	1505.26-15...	0.00

Totals:

Online quotes by S&P Comstock, delayed at least 20 minutes. Updated 7/17/00 at 14:19 local time.

Figure 7-4 • You can view quotes in the Portfolio View window

Viewing News Headlines

To view news headlines for a security, click the newspaper icon that appears beside the ticker symbol for any security with news stories. A window pops up with links to recent news stories. When you click a link, Quicken launches your Web browser, connects to the Internet, and displays the news story in the browser window (see Figure 7-5).

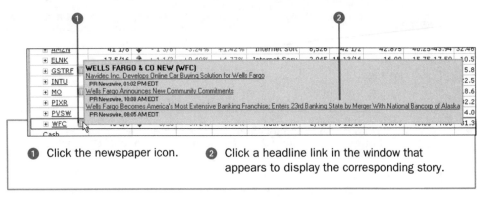

❶ Click the newspaper icon.

❷ Click a headline link in the window that appears to display the corresponding story.

Downloading Historical Quote Information

You can also download historical price information from within the Security Detail View or Portfolio View window. Choose Get Historical Prices from the Update menu on the button bar. Quicken displays the Get Historical Prices dialog box:

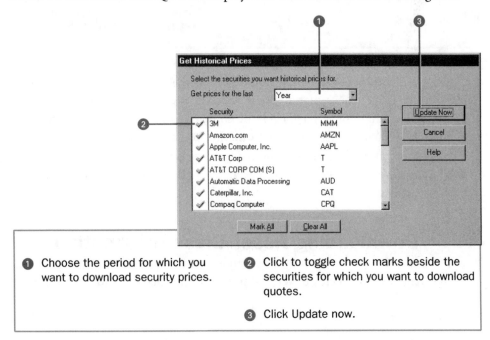

❶ Choose the period for which you want to download security prices.

❷ Click to toggle check marks beside the securities for which you want to download quotes.

❸ Click Update now.

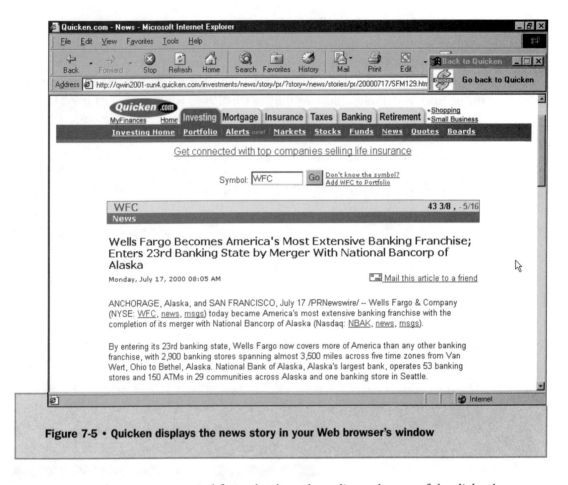

Figure 7-5 • Quicken displays the news story in your Web browser's window

Choose a time period from the drop-down list at the top of the dialog box. Make sure check marks appear beside all securities for which you want to get historical quotes. Then click the Update Now button. Quicken connects to the Internet and retrieves the information you requested. When it is done, it displays the Quicken Download Summary dialog box. Click Done to dismiss the dialog box. You can review the quotes that were downloaded in the Security Detail View window.

Downloading Asset Class Information

For each security you own or watch, you can include asset class information. This enables you to create accurate asset allocation reports and graphs. I explain how to manually enter asset class information in Chapter 6 and how you can use this information to diversify your portfolio to best meet your investment goals in Chapter 8.

The trouble is, most mutual funds consist of many investments in a variety of asset classes. Manually looking up and entering this information is time consuming and tedious. Fortunately, Quicken can download this information from the Internet and enter it for you.

Choose Get Asset Classes from the Update menu on the button bar of the Security Detail View window. Quicken displays the Download Security Asset Classes dialog box, which looks and works very much like the Get Historical Prices dialog box shown in the previous illustration. Make sure check marks appear beside all securities for which you want to download asset class information, and then click the Update Now button. Quicken connects to the Internet and retrieves the information you requested. When it is done, it displays the Quicken Download Summary dialog box. Click Done to dismiss the dialog box. The asset classes are automatically entered for each security.

Web Portfolio Export

The Web Portfolio Export feature enables you to track your portfolio's value on the Web. Although you can do this without Quicken by manually customizing and updating the default portfolio Web page at Quicken.com, it's a lot easier to have Quicken automatically send updated portfolio information to Quicken.com for you.

Note   *To use this feature, you must register Quicken. (Quicken will remind you if you haven't completed this step.) The registration process sets up a private Quicken.com account for you to store your portfolio data.*

Exporting Your Portfolio

In Quicken, choose Investing | Investing Activities | Export my portfolio to Quicken.com. The Investment Accounts tab of the Customize Quicken Download dialog box appears:

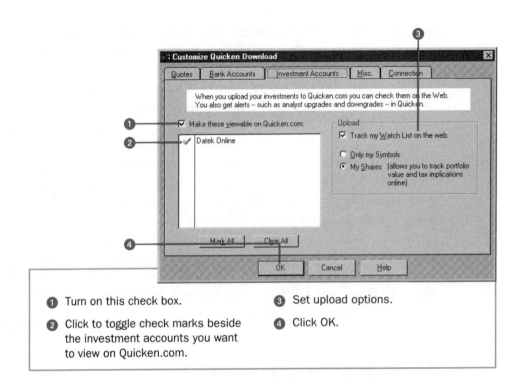

1. Turn on this check box.

2. Click to toggle check marks beside the investment accounts you want to view on Quicken.com.

3. Set upload options.

4. Click OK.

Begin by turning on the Make These Viewable On Quicken.com check box to enable the Web Export feature. Then click to toggle the check marks beside each account that you want to track on the Web. If you also want to track Watch List items on the Web, turn on the Track My Online Quotes List On The Web check box. Finally, select one of the upload options:

- **Only My Symbols** exports just the ticker symbols for your portfolio. This enables you to track prices but not portfolio values.

- **My Shares** exports the ticker symbols and the number of shares of each security you own for your portfolio. This enables you to track both prices and portfolio values.

When you're finished, click OK to save your settings and dismiss the dialog box.

Next, choose Portfolio Export from the Update menu on the button bar in the Portfolio View (refer to Figure 7-4) or Security Detail View window. The One Step Update Download Selection dialog box shown earlier appears. Make sure the check mark beside Update Portfolio is turned on, then click Update Now.

A Quicken.com Login dialog box may appear. Use it to log on to Quicken.com and click the Update Now button. Quicken establishes a connection to the

Internet, and displays a status dialog box while it updates information. When it's finished, it displays the Download Summary dialog box. Click done to dismiss it.

Tip   *If the Quicken.com Login dialog box did not appear, you probably instructed Quicken to remember your login information. You can force this dialog box to appear (so you can change your password, if desired) by turning on the Let Me Change My Quicken.com Login The Next Time I Update check box in the Connection tab of the Customize Quicken Download dialog box. I tell you more about connection options in Chapter 3.*

Checking Your Portfolio on the Web

Once your portfolio has been updated, you can view it at any time from any computer with Web access. Use a Web browser to navigate to **http:// www. quicken.com/investments/portfolio/**. (Or simply click the Your Portfolio link on the Quicken.com home page, **http://www.quicken.com/**.) The contents of your portfolio appear on the page. Figure 7-6 shows an example.

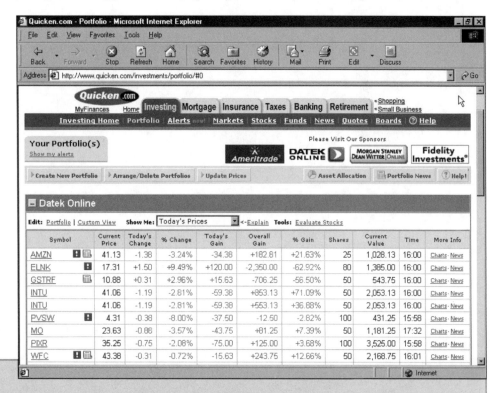

Figure 7-6 • Once your portfolio has been exported, it can be viewed on the Web from any computer

Tip *If your computer is set to save your Quicken.com login information or you have manually logged on to Quicken.com, an abbreviated version of your portfolio (called a Mini Portfolio) appears right on the Quicken.com home page, in place of the default portfolio.*

Maximizing Investment Returns

Chapter 8

I f you're good at managing your finances, you probably have a little left over every month. If you're concerned about risk and don't mind relatively low returns, the savings accounts and certificates of deposit offered by your local bank may be just the place for your money. But if you don't mind a little risk for the possibility of greater financial rewards, there's a good chance you've discovered Wall Street and investing.

In this chapter, I provide some basic information about investing, as well as what you can do to get started. I also tell you about the tools within Quicken and on Quicken.com that can help you research your investments to make smart financial decisions.

Tip   *If you think Wall Street and its risks are just for high rollers, skip this chapter for now and move ahead to Chapter 16. That's where I tell you about savings and the types of low-risk accounts you can open with your local bank.*

Investment Basics

An investment is a security you purchase with the hope that it rises in value, pays you interest or a dividend, or both. Investments differ from savings in several ways:

- An investment is somewhat more difficult to redeem for cash, thus making it less liquid.
- An investment's value varies depending on the market—what another investor is willing to pay for it—thus giving it the potential to be worth far more (or less) than you paid for it.
- An investment is not insured against loss, thus making it more risky.

In this section, I provide the information you need to understand what investments are available, what you need to know before deciding on a specific investment type, and the things you can do to get started as an investor.

Types of Investments

There are many types of investments, and each one has its pros and cons. Following is a summary of the most common types of investments.

Money Market Funds

A *money market fund* or *account* is an investment in short-term debt instruments such as certificates of deposit, commercial paper, banker's acceptances, Treasury bills, and discount notes. Although you can open a money market account with your local bank, it is not insured by the FDIC (Federal Deposit Insurance Corporation) as are most other bank accounts. The rate of return and value is not guaranteed. Money market funds earn income for investors by paying dividends.

Treasury Bills

A *Treasury bill* (or *T-bill*) is a short-term government security, sold through the Federal Reserve Bank by competitive bidding. T-bills are the most widely used of all government debt securities. They are backed by the full faith and credit of the U.S. government. T-bills earn money for investors by paying interest.

Stocks

A *stock* is part ownership of a corporation. Sold as shares through stock exchanges throughout the world (as well as privately, in the case of private corporations), their market values fluctuate daily. Thousands or millions of shares of any given stock can change hands each day. Stocks earn money for investors by paying dividends or rising in value.

Bonds

A *bond* is essentially a loan made by the investor to a company or government entity. Bonds earn money for investors by paying interest. The actual interest rate paid often depends on the stated interest rate and the purchase price of the bond.

Mutual Funds

A *mutual fund* is a group of securities held by a group of investors. When you invest in a mutual fund, your investment dollars are pooled with other investors. A fund manager buys and sells securities to maximize the fund's return. Mutual funds earn money for investors by paying dividends (which can often be automatically reinvested in the fund) or rising in value. In return for his or her services, the fund manager is paid a fee. Other fees may include *loads,* which can be applied when you invest or sell mutual fund shares.

There are thousands of mutual funds, each with its own "mix" of investment types. Investors—especially novice investors—find mutual funds attractive because an investment professional can make decisions for them.

Investment Considerations

When evaluating an investment, you should consider several important factors: return, risk, goal, and taxability.

Return

An investment's *return* is what it earns for the investor. Most investments earn money by paying interest, paying dividends, or rising in value.

Interest   *Interest* is a rate applied to the face or par value of a security that is then paid to the investor in cash. Treasury bills and bonds pay interest. Money market accounts pay dividends, although amounts are calculated like interest and often referred to as interest on bank statements.

Dividends   *Dividends* are per share payments to shareholders. There are two types: cash and stock.

- **Cash dividends** pay a certain cash amount per share to each stockholder. For example, a $1 per share cash dividend pays each stockholder $1 for each share held. Cash dividends are normally paid by large companies; smaller companies need cash to grow.
- **Stock dividends** pay a certain number of stock shares per share to each stockholder. A stock split is a type of stock dividend. For example, a 2-for-1 stock split doubles the number of shares each stockholder owns. Although this cuts the per share value in half, the value is expected to rise again over time.

Capital Gains   A stock's price indicates what another investor is willing to pay for it. When the stock's price is higher than what you paid, you have a gain on your investment. When the stock's price is lower than what you paid, you have a loss on your investment. A capital gain (or loss) can be realized or unrealized:

- **Realized gains (or losses)** are the gains or losses you can record when you sell an investment. If an investment is taxable, the realized gain or loss must be reported on your tax return.
- **Unrealized gains (or losses)** are the gains or losses based on your purchase price and the current market value for investments you have not yet sold. Because the investment has not been sold, the gain is not realized and does not have to be reported on your tax return.

Risk

Risk is your chance of making or losing money on an investment. Although all investments have some element of risk involved, some investments are more conservative (less risky) than others.

There is a direct relationship between risk and return. The higher the potential return, the higher the risk. The lower the risk, the lower the potential return. For example, money market accounts and one-year T-bills are considered relatively conservative investments. On June 26, 2000, they earned an average of 3.73 percent and 6.17 percent, respectively. Stocks, on the other hand are considered more risky. On June 26, 2000, the rates of return for a one-year investment in Intuit, Apple, and Amazon.com were 32 percent, 152 percent, and –38 percent, respectively. As these examples show, you can make more money in the stock market, but you can also lose some.

Caution   *These examples are for illustrative purposes only. Exact accuracy is not guaranteed. I am neither recommending nor advising against an investment in any of these securities.*

Goal

Goal refers to your goal as an investor. You should choose an investment based on its ability to meet your goals. There are two main goals: income and growth.

- **Income investments** generate income for investors in the form of dividends and interest. Investors get regular cash payments. Income investments are popular with investors who are retired and living on fixed incomes. Income investments include money market accounts, T-bills, bonds, stocks of larger ("blue chip") companies, and some mutual funds.

- **Growth investments** grow in market value. Growth investments are popular with younger people who want to build a "nest egg" for their later years. Growth investments include stocks of smaller companies and some mutual funds.

Taxability

The *taxability* of an investment refers to how it is taxed. This matters most to individuals in high tax brackets. Generally speaking, investments fall into three categories: taxable, nontaxable, and tax-deferred:

- **Taxable investments** are fully taxed by the federal and local government. You must report and pay taxes on interest and dividend income, as well as capital gains. Capital losses can be deducted from income (within certain limitations) to reduce your tax bill. Visit the Taxes channel on Quicken.com or talk to your tax advisor for more information.

- **Nontaxable investments** are not taxed by the federal government. They may, however, be taxed by local governments such as your state government. Examples of nontaxable investments include municipal bonds.

- **Tax-deferred investments** are investments for which income is not taxed until it is withdrawn. An example is an investment set up as a tax-deferred annuity. In this case, you invest as much as you like. Income, when earned, is automatically reinvested into the account but is not taxed at that time. The value of the account continues to grow. When you're 59 1/2 years old, you can begin withdrawing money from the account. Income on the investment is taxed then, when you're likely to be in a lower tax bracket.

Getting Started

If you've never invested money before, the following sections outline some things you might want to consider doing to get started on the right track.

Doing Your Research

Would you go grocery shopping blindfolded? Groping around on the shelves for beef stew, only to wind up with dog food? Poking meat packages for porterhouse steak, only to wind up with bacon ends?

Investing without research is like shopping blindfolded. You spend money but don't know what you've purchased until it's paid for. Even then, you may not know—until it's too late and you've lost money.

The Investment Research feature available in Quicken Deluxe and the Investing channel on Quicken.com offer literally hundreds of resources you can tap into to get almost any information you can imagine about a company. Even if you don't know where to start, these features can help you search for stocks and mutual funds that meet criteria you specify. You can get news, price histories, and ratings. You can get financial results. You can even participate in message boards to see what other investors think is hot. I explain how to take advantage of these features later in this chapter.

If you're not sure *what* you should be looking for, the Investment Research feature and the Investing channel can help, too. They offer links to basic information that goes far beyond the basics I provide at the beginning of this chapter. Spend a few hours learning about the types of investments that interest you. Then check out the individual investments themselves. Gather information before you make a decision.

Remember, it's your money. Put it where it'll work hardest for you.

Finding a Broker

If you decide to invest in stocks and bonds, you need a broker. (It's a lot cheaper than buying a seat on the stock exchange.) A stockbroker or brokerage firm can handle the purchases and sales of securities. Nowadays, there are three kinds of brokers:

- **Full service brokers** can buy and sell securities for you, based on your instructions. But these people also research investments for you and tell you about the ones they think are hot. They also keep an eye on the securities you own and tell you when they think one of them may lose value. Based on their recommendations, you can buy or sell. Fees for full service brokers are higher than any other—a typical stock purchase or sale could cost well over $100 in commissions. But you're getting more service for your money—you're paying someone to do investment research for you. If you decide to use a full service broker, track his or her performance carefully; if your broker is not meeting your expectations, you might want to find another broker.

- **Discount brokers** can buy and sell securities for you, too. They usually don't offer any advice, though. They're much cheaper than full-service brokers—a typical stock purchase or sale could be $25 to $60.

- **Deep discount brokers** can also buy and sell securities for you. They don't offer advice either. They're dirt cheap—I've seen fees as low as $8 per trade.

You have two main ways to contact your broker to buy or sell stock:

- **Telephone trading** enables you to give buy or sell instructions by phone, either by speaking to someone at the brokerage firm or by entering information using your telephone keypad.

- **Online trading** enables you to enter buy or sell instructions using your computer and Internet connection. This is fast, convenient, and cheap. In fact, companies that offer both telephone and online trading usually offer online trading for less money.

Tip   *I've been using online trading for over three years now, and I'm very happy with it. I can do more trades for less money. My brokerage firm can process orders within 60 seconds of receiving them. They even allow me to trade on margin—that's the brokerage term for credit—and they pay interest on any cash balance in my account!*

If you're interested in telephone trading, you can find a broker the same way you'd find a bank: ask your friends or check your local phone book. Or ask your bank—some banks offer brokerage services or are connected with brokerage firms. You can also find broker information on Quicken.com; just click the Find a Broker link on the Investing channel's home page.

If you're interested in online trading, your first stop should be Quicken.com. It provides information and links to a number of online brokerage firms. See what each one has to offer and select the one with the best deal for you.

 GET SMARTER   When shopping for a broker, use the Broker Comparison Worksheet at the end of this chapter to take notes about and compare different services and fees.

Getting Advice from a Pro

If you don't want a full service broker but you do want investment advice, find a financial advisor. Many banks have financial advisors on staff, and they can usually provide good, objective advice about investing. They often even handle investment transactions for you (which really makes them a full service broker).

The trick (I think) is finding an advisor who is objective. Most of the ones I've spoken to deal only with certain types of investments or certain fund families. While these might be great investments, the fact that the advisor doesn't even deal with others makes me wonder how objective he or she can be.

The other problem I've found with financial advisors is something I call "tunnel vision." They ask you a few questions about your risk tolerance, look at your financial statements (generated by Quicken, of course), and come up with a plan. But your life might not be that simple. You may, for example, be interested in minimizing taxes or saving up for a large expenditure you plan to make within the next five years. Your investment strategy should consider your financial objectives, your current status, and your future plans. If your financial advisor can't consider all of these things when developing a plan, you'd better find another advisor.

Quicken.com also offers information and links for finding a financial advisor. If you can't get a good recommendation from a knowledgeable friend, be sure to tap into Quicken.com's online resources to see what's out there.

Remember to Diversify!

I'm not a financial planner and, in this lawsuit-crazy era we live in, I don't like to give advice. But here's a one-word piece of advice I must share, one that can help minimize your investment risks: *diversify*.

I can explain with my version of an old story. Farmer Joe has chickens. Every day, he takes a wicker basket to the hen house and collects the eggs. One day, on his way back from the hen house, the basket breaks, dropping the eggs all over the farmyard. As you can imagine, almost every egg breaks. That day, Farmer Joe learned the hard way that he should never put all of his eggs in one basket.

The eggs and basket story applies to your finances, too. If all your investment dollars are in one security and that security fails, you're liable to lose a lot of money. Now take that a step further. If all your investment dollars are in the stock market and the stock market takes a turn for the worse, you're also liable to lose money.

I'm not saying that you shouldn't have "favorite" investments or that you shouldn't invest in the stock market. I'm saying that you should spread your investment dollars among multiple securities and types of investments. If you don't put your eggs in one basket, you can't lose them all.

Tip   *Quicken's Asset Allocation feature makes it easy to see how your investments are allocated among different types of asset classes. I tell you more about this feature a little later in this chapter.*

Learn More with Quicken and Quicken.com

The Activities area of Quicken's Investing Center window offers a number of links you can click to learn more about investing and the investing features within Quicken. If you're brand new to investing or Quicken (or both), I highly recommend that you check out each of these links before you begin to invest.

Investing Basics

The Investing Basics link connects you to the Internet and opens the Quicken.com Investing Basics page. Figure 8-1 shows what this page looked like on June 26, 2000; it changes regularly so it won't look exactly the same when you check in.

Like most pages on Quicken.com, the Investing Basics page contains dozens of links you can click to learn more about specific topics. In this case, most of the links point to articles with basic information and advice about investing.

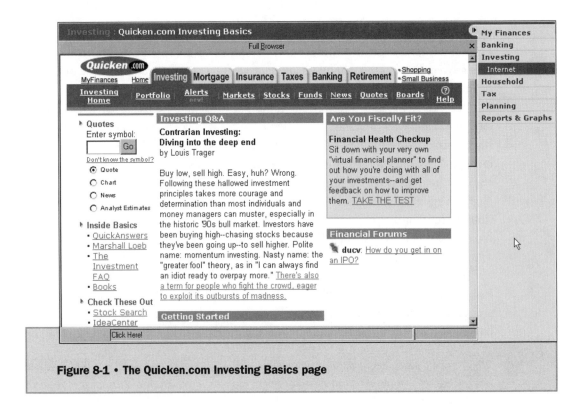

Figure 8-1 • The Quicken.com Investing Basics page

Tip *You may find the Financial Health Checkup link especially helpful to get objective insight about your financial "fitness." This interactive feature takes 20 minutes to work through and is very complete.*

Learn About Quicken's Investing Features

The Learn About Quicken's Investing Features link displays an onscreen help window with more information about Quicken's investing features, including all of the ones covered in this book. You may find this helpful to get a complete overview of the investing features available to you.

Where Should I Invest My Money?

The Where Should I Invest My Money? link displays a screen within Quicken that summarizes the steps you should follow for creating a sound investment strategy. Each step includes a link you can click to use Quicken or Quicken.com features to perform related tasks.

Using Quicken and Quicken.com Investing Resources

Now that we've covered the basics, let's take an in-depth look at some specific Quicken and Quicken.com features that can help you invest wisely and maximize your investment returns.

Investment Research

The Investment Research feature within Quicken offers quick access to information about stocks and mutual funds on Quicken.com.

To start, choose Investing | Investment Research or click the Investment Research link in the Activities area of the Investing Center window. The Evaluate tab of the Investment Research window appears (see Figure 8-2). Here's a rundown of the research features available from this window.

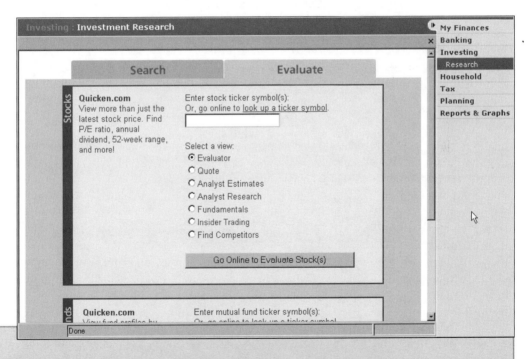

Figure 8-2 • Use the Evaluate tab of the Investment Research window to zero in on information about a specific stock or mutual fund

Evaluating Investments

The Evaluate tab (see Figure 8-2) enables you to access information about specific stocks or mutual funds.

Stocks Stocks offers quotes and other market information for any stock. Enter the stock's ticker symbol in the box, select a view option, and click the Go Online To Evaluate Stock(s) button. Quicken connects to the Internet and displays a page with quote information for the stock. Figure 8-3 shows the Evaluator view for Intuit June 26, 2000.

Tip *You can use links on the left side of the window to switch to other views for the company without going back to the Evaluate tab of the Investment Research window.*

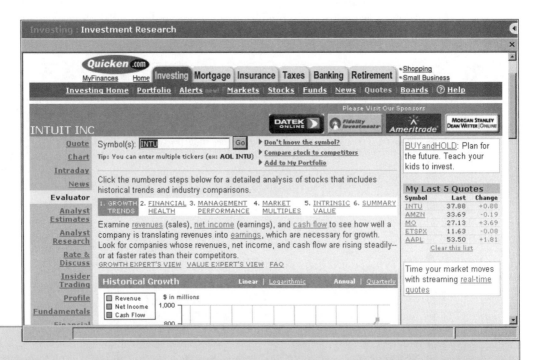

Figure 8-3 • The Evaluator page for a stock provides a wealth of information you can use to judge the value of a company

Mutual Funds   You can use the Mutual Funds area of the Evaluate tab to get the Morningstar profile, performance data, or other information for a mutual fund. (Morningstar is a mutual fund rating service.) Simply enter the fund's ticker symbol in the text box, select an option, and click the Go Online To Evaluate Fund(s) button. Quicken connects to the Internet and displays a page with the requested information.

 GET SMARTER   When evaluating mutual funds, use the Mutual Funds Comparison Worksheet at the end of this chapter to take notes about and compare different ratings, returns, and expenses.

Searching for Investments

If you're looking for companies or mutual funds to invest in, start with the Search tab of the Investment Research window (see Figure 8-4). It offers a number of links you can click to search for stocks, mutual funds, or bonds in which to invest.

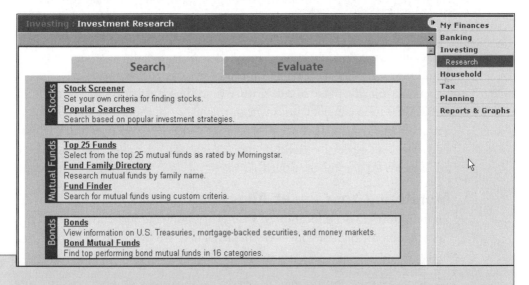

Figure 8-4 • Use the Search tab of the Investment Research window to find companies that meet your investment criteria

Stocks   The Stocks links enable you to search for stocks based on criteria you specify or predefined search criteria.

Mutual Funds   The Mutual Funds links enable you to search for mutual funds by Morningstar rating, fund family, or criteria you specify.

Bonds   The Bonds links take you to Quicken.com pages where you can learn more about bonds and bond mutual funds.

Asset Allocation

Many investment gurus say that an investor's goals should determine his or her asset allocation. If you're not sure what your asset allocation should be, Quicken can help. It includes a wealth of information about asset allocation, including sample portfolios with their corresponding allocations. You can use this feature to learn what your target asset allocation should be to meet your investing goals. Then you monitor your asset allocation and, if necessary, rebalance your portfolio to keep it in line with what it should be.

Determining Your Ideal Asset Allocation

To get started, take a moment to learn more about what asset allocation is and why it's important. Choose Investing | Asset Allocation Guide or click the Asset Allocation Guide link in the Activities area of the Investing Center window. The Asset Allocation window appears (see Figure 8-5). It explains what asset allocation is and how Quicken can help you monitor your asset allocation.

To take full advantage of this feature, read the information on the right side of the window. You can click links within the text or in the left column to learn more about a specific topic. If you're new to asset allocation, you may find the See Model Portfolios link especially useful. It shows suggested asset allocations based on risk and returns for a number of portfolios.

Monitoring Your Asset Allocation

To monitor the asset allocation of your portfolio, you must enter asset class information for each of your investments. There are two ways to do this:

- Manually enter asset class information. Although this isn't difficult for stocks, it can be time consuming for investments that have an asset class mixture, such as mutual funds.

- Download asset class information. If you have a connection to the Internet, this is the best way to enter this information. With a few clicks, Quicken does all of the work in seconds. The information is complete and accurate.

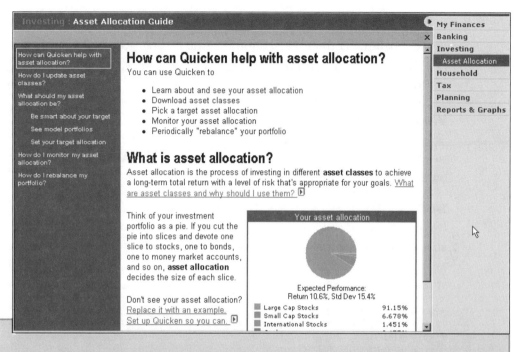

Figure 8-5 • The Asset Allocation Guide explains what asset allocation is and how it can help you meet your investment goals

No matter which way you decide to enter asset allocation information, you start with the Edit Security dialog box. Choose Investing | Security List or press CTRL-Y to open the Security List window. Select the security for which you want to enter asset class information and click the Edit button on the button bar to display the Edit Security dialog box. Check or change the options in the Asset Class area:

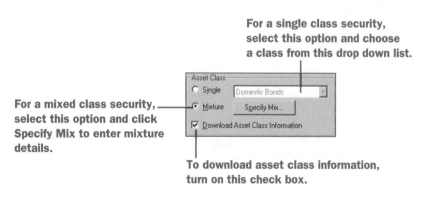

For a single class security, select this option and choose a class from this drop down list.

For a mixed class security, select this option and click Specify Mix to enter mixture details.

To download asset class information, turn on this check box.

You have two options:

- Manually enter the asset class information as discussed in Chapter 6.
- Turn on the Download Asset Class Information check box and download the asset class information as discussed in Chapter 7.

Viewing Your Asset Allocation

To see a pie chart of the asset allocation for your investments, switch to the Investing Center window and click the Current link in the Asset Allocation area on the right side of the window. Figure 8-6 shows what it might look like.

Setting Your Target Asset Allocation

If you know what you want your asset allocation to be, you can set up a target asset allocation. Quicken can then display your target in the pie chart beside the current asset allocation chart on the Investing Center page so you can monitor how close you are to your target.

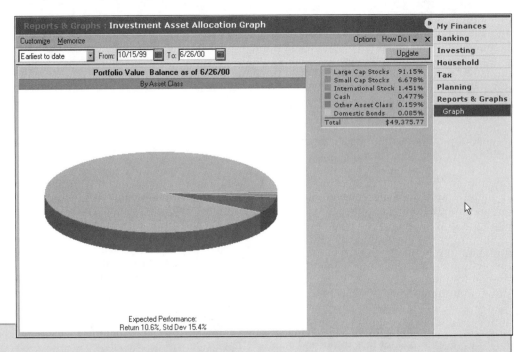

Figure 8-6 • The Investment Asset Allocation Graph shows how your portfolio is allocated among various asset classes

Right-click on the Target pie chart in the Asset Allocation area of the Investing Center window to display a shortcut menu. Choose Customize Target Allocation. The Set Target Asset Allocation dialog box appears. This illustration shows what it looks like with a sample allocation already entered:

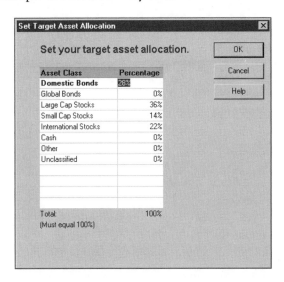

Enter the desired percentages for each class of asset. When the total of all percentages equals 100, click OK to save your settings. The Target chart in the Asset Allocation area of the Investing Center window changes accordingly:

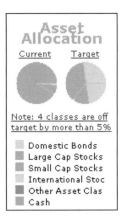

Rebalancing Your Portfolio

If your current asset allocation deviates from your target asset allocation, you may want to rebalance your portfolio. This means buying and selling investments to bring you closer to your target asset allocation.

Note *Brokerage fees and capital gains impacts often are related to buying and selling securities. For this reason, you should carefully evaluate your investment situation to determine how you can minimize costs and capital gains while rebalancing your portfolio. If small adjustments are necessary to bring you to your target asset allocation, you may not find it worth the cost to make the changes. Use this information as a guideline only!*

Quicken can tell you exactly how you must change your current asset allocation to meet your target asset allocation. Choose Investing | Portfolio Rebalancer or click the Portfolio Rebalancer link in the Activities area of the Investing Center window. The Portfolio Rebalancer window shown in Figure 8-7 appears. It provides instructions and shows you how much you must adjust each asset class to meet your targeted goals.

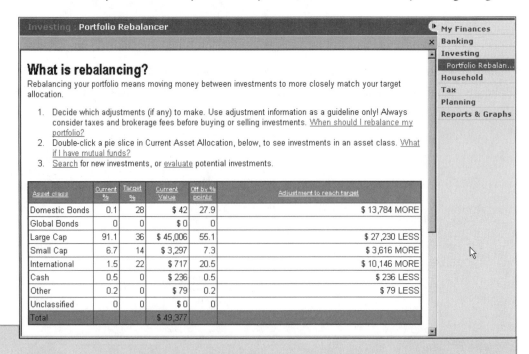

Figure 8-7 • The Portfolio Rebalancer window tells you what adjustments you need to make to bring your asset allocation closer to target

Here's an example. Figure 8-7 indicates that I need $13,764 more invested in domestic bonds and $27,230 less invested in large cap stock. If I wanted to meet my target asset allocation, I could sell $13,000 worth of my large cap stock investments and reinvest the funds in domestic bonds. This would change my asset allocation, bringing it closer to target, without changing the total value of my portfolio.

 Tip *You can quickly identify securities in an asset class by clicking the class's pie slice in the Current Asset Allocation chart at the bottom of the window. (You'll have to scroll down to see it.)*

Capital Gains Estimator

Quicken's Capital Gains Estimator enables you to estimate capital gains or losses and their related tax implications *before* you sell a security. The information it provides can help you make an informed decision about which security to sell.

Getting Started

Choose Investing | Capital Gains Estimator or click the Capital Gains Estimator link in the Activities area of the Investing Center window. The Capital Gains Estimator window appears (see Figure 8-8). This feature has been completely updated for Quicken 2001 so it's more intuitive and easier to use.

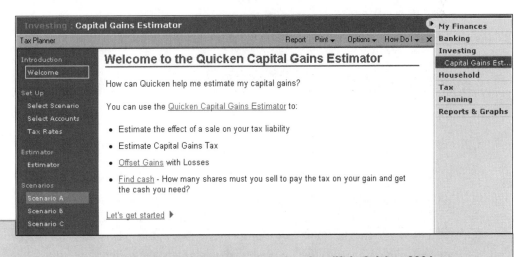

Figure 8-8 • The Capital Gains Estimator got a complete face-lift in Quicken 2001

Start by reading the information in the right side of the window. It explains what the Capital Gains Estimator does and offers links for learning more about specific terms and topics. Then click each of the links in the left side of the window, in turn, to step through the process of setting up the Capital Gains Estimator for your situation. You'll be prompted to name and choose a scenario, select taxable investment accounts to include, and set your tax rate.

Tip *When setting up your tax rate, you can get more accurate rate information by completing the Tax Planner. I explain how in Chapter 14.*

Adding Proposed Sales

In the Estimator screen (see Figure 8-9), you indicate proposed sales. The Step 1 area shows all the securities you hold in the accounts you selected during the setup process. There are two ways to add a proposed sale:

- Double-click the icon to the left of the security that you want to sell. Then enter the number of shares and sales price in the Add to Scenario dialog box that appears (shown next) and click OK. If you have multiple purchase lots for the security, this automatically sells the oldest lots first.

- If necessary, click once on the folder icon to the left of the security that you want to sell to display the purchase lots. Then click on the lot you want to sell. This enables you to specify exactly which lots are to be sold.

No matter which method you use, the sale is added to the Step 2 area of the window, which lists all of the proposed sales (see Figure 8-9).

To adjust the number of shares to be sold, click in the shares field for the proposed sale (in the Step 2 area) and enter a new value. The value you enter must be less than or equal to the number of shares purchased in that lot.

You can repeat this procedure for as many proposed sales as you like. For simplicity's sake, Figure 8-9 shows four examples, each with the same number of

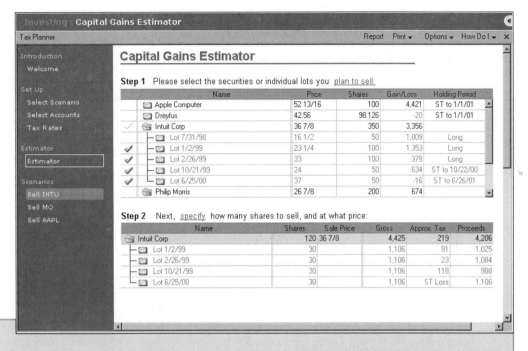

Figure 8-9 • Use the Estimator screen of the Capital Gains Estimator to indicate proposed sales

shares for the same security, but for different purchase lots. You can mix and match any sales you like. For example, say you own 10 different securities and want to sell off something to raise a certain amount of cash. You can create proposed sales for each security, each of which would result in the amount of cash you need.

Reading the Results

When proposed sales and tax rates have been entered, you can see the true power of the Capital Gains Estimator. Take a good look at Figure 8-9. Of all the proposed sales, the last one, which results in a short-term loss, is the only one that would not be taxed. Taxes on the other sales vary based on the difference between the purchase and sales price (your gain) and the length of time the security was held. Since short-term capital gains are taxed at a higher rate than long-term capital gains, you can pay less taxes on the sale of securities that you hold for more than a year. You can see this in the Lot 1/2/99 and Lot 10/21/99 sales—although the purchase prices were very close, you could save $37 in taxes by selling the Lot 1/2/98 shares. That means you get to keep more of the proceeds.

Figure 8-9 shows the Capital Gains Estimator's Proceeds View. You can change to the Gains View by choosing Options | View Sales by Gains on the button bar. Here's what it looks like for the same four proposed sales:

Name	Shares	Sale Price	Gain/Loss	Approx. Tax	Net Gain
Intuit Corp	120	36 7/8	890	219	671
Lot 1/2/99	30		406	81	325
Lot 2/26/99	30		113	23	91
Lot 10/21/99	30		380	118	262
Lot 6/25/00	30		-10	ST Loss	-10

If you scroll down in the Estimator screen, you'll find more information about the proposed sale and its tax implications in the Step 3 area, including the gross profit and net proceeds from all proposed sales. You can click links to view the results of additional calculations, such as the tax situation before and after executing the proposed sales and gain or loss on the proposed sales.

Using Scenarios

You can repeat this process for each of the three scenarios supported by the Capital Gains Estimator. Then, to compare the scenarios, simply click the scenario name on the left side of the Capital Gains Estimator window while the Estimator screen is displayed. The proposed sales and results for each scenario appear within the window.

Investment Performance

In addition to the Portfolio View window, which I discuss in Chapter 6, Quicken offers a other tools for monitoring and evaluating an investment's performance. The two I find most useful are Multiple Security Charting and the How Are My Investments Doing? window. Here's a look at each of these features so you can see how they can help you.

Multiple Security Charting

Quicken displays a chart of a security's prices right in the Security Detail View window. This is a great way to see trends in a single security's values. But what if you want to compare that security to another one? Or to a popular index? That's where Multiple Security Charting comes in.

To begin, choose Investing | Multiple Security Charting or click the Multiple Security Charting link in the Activities area of the Investment Center window. The Multiple Security Charting window appears (see Figure 8-10). Use it to set options and select securities for the chart you want to create. To select more than one security, hold down CTRL while clicking each security name. When you click the Go Online To Chart button, Quicken connects you to the Internet and displays a Quicken.com page with the chart you requested (see Figure 8-11).

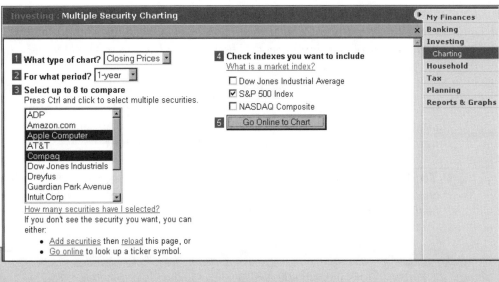

Figure 8-10 • Options set in the Multiple Security Charting window

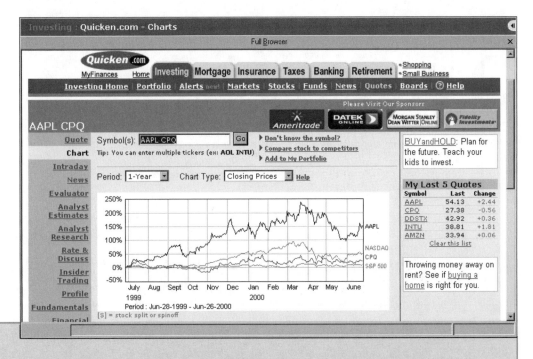

Figure 8-11 • The chart created on Quicken.com using options shown in Figure 8-10

How Are My Investments Doing?

Quicken offers a number of reports and graphs you can use to check on the performance of your investments. The How Are My Investments Doing? window offers a quick way to access many of them.

In the Activities area of the Investing Center window, click the How Are My Investments Doing? link. The How Are My Investments Doing? window appears (see Figure 8-12). It displays two graphs at the top of the window with links to a number of investment reports, graphs, and features below them.

Tip *You can customize or see a full-screen view of a graph by right-clicking it and choosing the appropriate command from the menu that appears. I tell you more about customizing reports and graphs in Chapter 13.*

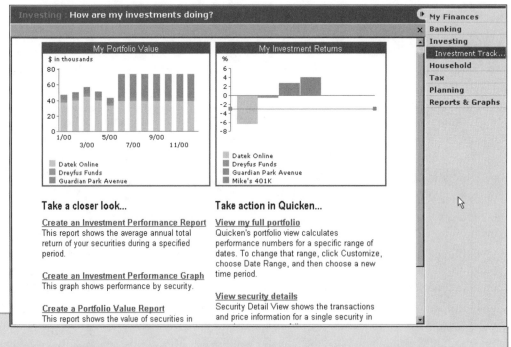

Figure 8-12 • The How Are My Investments Doing? window offers options for viewing investment performance

Here's a quick rundown of the reports you can access from this window:

- **Investment Performance Report** provides the internal rate of return of investments during a specific period. The report includes dates, actions, transaction descriptions, investments, returns, and average annual return on investment. This report offers a good way to compare the performance of one security to another.

- **Investment Performance Graph** shows your monthly portfolio value and the average annual rate of return for each of your securities.

- **Portfolio Value Report** provides the value of your investment portfolio on a specific date. The report includes the security name, number of shares, current price, cost basis, unrealized gain or loss, and balance for each security in your portfolio.

- **Investment Income Report** displays the income and expenses from investments during a specific period.

You can also access these reports from the Investing submenu under the Reports menu. The following additional reports and graphs are available from this menu:

- **Capital Gains Report** reports capital gains (and losses) from the sale of investment securities for a specific period. The report includes the security name, number of shares, purchase and sale dates, selling price, basis, and gain or loss.

- **Investment Asset Allocation Graph** displays the asset allocation of your investments. It's a full-screen view of the asset allocation graph in the Investing Center window.

- **Investment Transactions Report** provides a summary of all investment-related transactions for a specific period. The report includes the date, account, action, security name, category, price, number of shares, commission, cash amount, investment value, and net transaction value for each transaction.

- **Portfolio Value and Cost Basis Graph** displays a line graph of the cost of your investments and your portfolio's current value.

Worksheets

Use the following two worksheets to help you compare and evaluate brokerage firms and mutual funds.

Broker Comparison Worksheet (page 1)

Basic Information

Instructions: Enter information for each brokerage firm, one per column.

Company Name			
Agent Name			
Phone Number			
Type of Brokerage Firm (circle one)	Full/Discount	Full/Discount	Full/Discount
Comments			

Trading Fees

Instructions: Enter fees for each of the services listed. If fees vary based on the number of shares in the transaction, base the fee on 1,000 shares. If a service is not available, enter N/A. If a service is free, enter $0. Enter additional trading fees at the end of each section if necessary.

Broker-assisted telephone trading			
Market Orders			
Limit Orders			
Options (per trade)			
Options (per contract)			
Bonds			
Treasury Bills			
Mutual Funds			
Touch-tone telephone trading			
Market Orders			
Limit Orders			
Options (per trade)			
Options (per contract)			
Bonds			
Treasury Bills			
Mutual Funds			

Broker Comparison Worksheet (page2)			
Online Trading			
Market Orders			
Limit Orders			
Options (per trade)			
Options (per contract)			
Bonds			
Treasury Bills			
Mutual Funds			

Other Fees

Instructions: Enter fees for each of the services listed. Enter additional fees at the end of this section if necessary.

Real-time Quotes			
Return Check Fee			
Wire Transfer Fee			
Stock Certificate Issuance Fee			
Check Writing Fee			
Stock Transfer Fee			
Cash Transfer Fee			

Interest Rates

Instructions: Enter the interest rate charged or paid for the following items.

Margin Rates (for <$50,000)			
Account Cash Balance Rates			

Mutual Funds Comparison Worksheet			
Basic Information			
Instructions: Enter information for each fund, one per column.			
Family Name			
Phone Number			
Fund Name			
Ticker Symbol			
Manager Name			
Manager Tenure			
Category			
Goal			
Minimum Initial Purchase			
Comments			
Ratings			
Instructions: Enter ratings information from the fund's Morningstar profile.			
Stars			
Return			
Risk			
Returns			
Instructions: Enter the current average returns for each period listed. You can get this information from the fund's profile.			
3 Months			
Year to Date			
1 Year			
3 Years			
5 Years			
10 Years			
Fees			
Instructions: Enter values for the expense ratio and each of the fees charged by the fund.			
Expense Ratio			
Front Load			
Deferred Sales Charge			
Redemption Fee			
12b-1 Fee			

Managing Your Household Finances

This part of the book explains how you can use Quicken to keep track of your general household finances. It starts with coverage of assets, such as a car and home, and the loans that you may have used to finance them. Then it moves on to some Quicken tools that can help you organize and keep track of important household information. Finally, it provides some useful information about how you can use Quicken and Quicken.com to save money on home, car, and insurance expenses.

This part of the book has two chapters:

Chapter 9: Monitoring Assets and Loans

Chapter 10: Minimizing Home, Car, and Insurance Expenses

Monitoring Assets and Loans

In This Chapter:

- *Quicken Household Overview*

- *Setting Up Asset and Loan Accounts*

- *Tracking a Loan*

- *Adjusting Asset Values*

- *Using Quicken Home Inventory*

- *Using the Emergency Records Organizer*

Assets and loans (or liabilities) make up your net worth. Bank and investment accounts, which I cover in Chapters 4 and 6, are examples of assets. Credit card accounts, which I cover in Chapter 4, are examples of liabilities. But there are other assets and liabilities you may want to track with Quicken, including a home, car, recreational vehicle, and related loans. By including these items in your Quicken data file, you can quickly and accurately calculate your net worth and financial fitness.

In this chapter, I explain how to set up asset and liability accounts to track your possessions and any outstanding loans you used to purchase them. I also tell you how you can use Quicken Home Inventory and the Emergency Records Organizer to create detailed records of your belongings and other important information.

The Basics

Before you begin, it's a good idea to have a clear understanding of what assets, liabilities, and loans are and how they work together in your Quicken data file.

Assets and Liabilities

An *asset* is something you own. Common examples might be your house, car, camper, computer, television set, and patio furniture. Most assets have value—you can sell them for cash or trade them for another asset.

Although you can use Quicken to track every single asset you own in its own asset account, doing so would be very cumbersome. Instead, you'll normally account for high-value assets in individual accounts and lower-value assets in a Home Inventory asset account. For example, you may create separate asset accounts for your home and your car, but group personal possessions such as your computer, television, and stamp collection in a single Home Inventory asset account. This makes it easy to track all your assets, so you have accurate records for insurance and other purposes.

A *liability* is something you owe—often to buy one of your assets! For example, if you buy a house, chances are you'll use a mortgage to fund it. The mortgage, which is a loan that is secured by your home, is a liability. You can use Quicken to track all of your liabilities, so you know exactly how much you owe at any given time.

Loans

A *loan* is a promise to pay money. Loans are commonly used to buy assets, although some folks often turn to debt consolidation loans to pay off other liabilities—I tell you more about that in Chapter 16.

Here's how it works: The lender gives the borrower money in exchange for the borrower's promise to pay it back. (The promise is usually in writing, with lots of signatures and initials.) The borrower normally pays back the loan with periodic payments to the lender that include interest on the loan balance or *principal*. In this way, the amount of the loan is reduced after each payment. The borrower also incurs interest expense while the lender earns interest income.

While most people think of a loan as something you owe (a liability), a loan can also be something you own (an asset). For example, say you borrow money from your brother to buy a car. In your Quicken data file, the loan is related to a liability—money that you owe your brother. In your brother's Quicken data file, the loan is related to an asset—money that is due to him from you.

Note   *I tell you more about loans in Chapter 10, including how you can use Quicken.com to help you find the best loan deals.*

Quicken Household Overview

Quicken groups all of its asset- and liability-related commands and features in two separate places: the Household menu and the Household Center window. Here's a quick look at each.

The Household Menu

Quicken's Household menu, which is shown next, includes a variety of commands you can use to work with assets, liabilities, and other household finance issues, including many online features. I cover most of these features in this chapter and the next.

There are two commands that you might find especially useful as you work with Quicken's household-related features:

- **Household Accounts** displays a submenu that lists all of your asset and liability accounts. This offers a quick and easy way to open the register for a specific account; simply choose its name from the menu.
- **Household Services** displays a submenu of household-related services available from Quicken, Quicken.com, and other providers. This is where you'll find commands for getting a free credit report, obtaining telephone and Internet rates, and saving on energy bills.

The Household Center Window

The Household Center window (see Figure 9-1) is full of information about your asset and liability accounts, as well as links to household-related Quicken and Quicken.com features and services. To open the Household Center window, click its QuickTab on the right side of the screen.

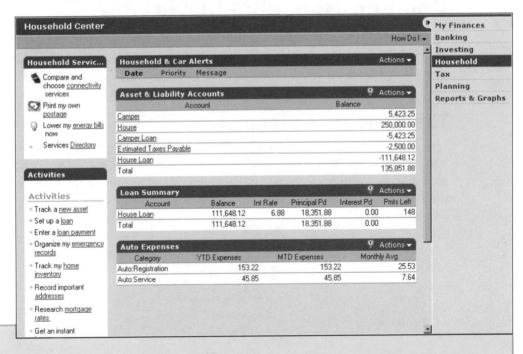

Figure 9-1 • The Household Center window is a great place to access information about your assets and liabilities, as well as Quicken's household-related features

The Household Center window is separated into three main parts: Household Services, Activities, and household snapshots.

Household Services The Household Services area lists a few of the most commonly used services available for Quicken users. Click an underlined link to access that service. For a complete list of services, click the Directory link in the Household Services area.

Activities The Activities area offers clickable links to Quicken features. These are separated into Activities and Questions:

- **Activities** includes links you can click to access Quicken and Quicken.com features. Most of these features can also be accessed via the Household menu.

- **Questions** includes links you can click to answer specific questions, such as "Can I afford to buy a home?" or "How do I estimate the value of my car?"

Household Snapshots Household snapshots fill most of the Household Center window. They include information about your asset and liability accounts and related expenses. The Actions menu for each snapshot offers commands that apply to the snapshot or information it contains. The following snapshots appear in this window:

- **Household & Car Alerts** displays alerts related to your asset and liability accounts, including your home and car accounts. I tell you about alerts in Chapter 11.

- **Asset & Liability Accounts** displays a list of your asset and liability accounts, complete with balances. You can click an account name to open the register window for that account.

- **Loan Summary** lists all of your loans, along with the balance, interest rate, amount of principal and interest paid, and number of payments left.

- **Auto Expenses** lists all of the expenses related to your automobile—those expenses you recorded by entering transactions with the Auto category or one of its subcategories.

Setting Up Accounts

To track an asset or liability with Quicken, you must set up an appropriate account. All transactions related to the asset or liability will be recorded in the account's register.

In this section, I tell you about the types of accounts you can use to track your assets and liabilities and explain how to set up each type of account.

Choosing the Right Account

Quicken offers four household account types for tracking assets and liabilities.

House (with or without Mortgage)   A house account is for recording the value of a house, condominium, or other real estate. When you create a house account, Quicken asks whether there is a mortgage on the property. If there is, you can have Quicken create a related liability account for you or associate the house account with an existing liability account. This makes it possible to set up both your house asset account and mortgage liability account at the same time.

Vehicle (with or without Loan)   A vehicle account is similar to a house account, but it's designed for vehicles, including cars, trucks, and recreational vehicles. Quicken asks if there is a loan on the vehicle; if there is, it can create a related liability account or link to an existing liability account.

Asset   An asset account is for recording the value of other assets, such as personal property. For example, my Quicken data file includes asset accounts for my horses, my computer equipment, and my personal possessions.

Tip   *When you use Quicken Home Inventory to record the value of your personal possessions, Quicken automatically creates an asset account with the total value. I explain how to use Quicken Home Inventory later in this chapter.*

Liability   A liability account is for recording money you owe to others. As mentioned earlier, when you create a house or vehicle account, Quicken can automatically create a corresponding liability account for you. You can create a liability account to record other debts that are not related to the purchase of a specific asset.

Creating Asset and Liability Accounts

Chapter 2 explains how to use the Asset Account Setup dialog box to create new Quicken accounts. In this section, I provide information about the kinds of data you'll need to enter to create asset and liability accounts. All of this information appears in the Summary tab of the Account Setup dialog box that appears at the end of the account creation process. Here's what the dialog box looks like for a house; it looks similar for a vehicle:

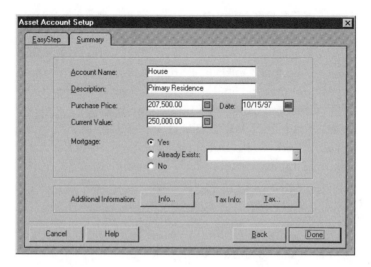

And here's what the dialog box looks like for a liability:

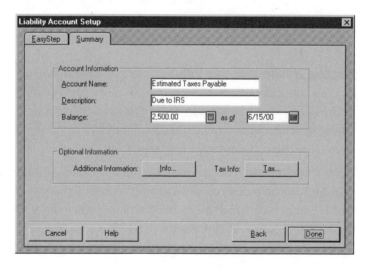

Account Name   Give the account a name that clearly identifies the asset or liability. For example, if you have two cars and plan to track them in separate asset accounts, consider naming the account with the make and model of the car. *Jeep Wrangler* and *Toyota MR-2* do a better job identifying the cars than *Auto 1* and

Auto 2. When creating a liability account, you may want to include the word *mortgage* or *loan* in the account name so you don't confuse it with a related asset.

Starting Point Information   For house and vehicle accounts, Quicken prompts you to enter information about the asset's purchase, including the acquisition date and purchase price. You can find this information on your original purchase receipts. Quicken also asks for an estimate of the current value. This is the amount that will appear as the asset account balance.

For assets and liabilities, Quicken prompts you for a starting date and value (asset) or amount owed (liability). If you don't know how much to enter now, you can leave it set to zero and enter a value when you know what to enter. I explain how to adjust asset values later in this chapter.

Related Mortgage or Loan   When creating a house or vehicle account, Quicken asks whether there is a related mortgage or loan. You have three options:

- **Yes, Create A Liability Account For Me** tells Quicken that there is a loan and that it should create a liability account.
- **There Is A Mortgage/Loan And I'm Already Tracking It In Quicken** enables you to select an existing liability account to link to the loan.
- **The House/Vehicle Is Paid For, So I Don't Need A Liability Account** tells Quicken that there is no loan so no liability account is necessary.

Getting House and Car Values   When you create a house or car asset account, Quicken offers to connect to the Internet to download current value information. If you have an Internet connection, just follow the prompts that appear onscreen to download the data. I tell you more about obtaining current asset values from the Internet in Chapter 10.

Loan Information   If you indicated that Quicken should create a liability account for a house or vehicle, it automatically displays the Edit Loan dialog box, which you can use to enter information about the loan. If you set up a liability account, Quicken asks if you want to set up an amortized loan to be associated with the liability. I explain how to set up a loan later in this chapter.

Tracking a Loan

Quicken makes it easy to track the principal, interest, and payments for a loan. Once you set up a loan and corresponding liability or asset accounts, you can make payments with Quicken using QuickFill (see Chapter 11), scheduled transactions (see Chapter 11), or online payments (see Chapter 5). The Loan feature keeps track of all the details so you don't have to.

> **Note** *I cover QuickFill and scheduled transactions in Chapter 11 and online payments in Chapter 5.*

Setting Up a Loan

There are two ways to set up a loan:

- Create a house, vehicle, or liability account with a related mortgage or loan as discussed earlier in this chapter. Quicken automatically prompts you for loan information.
- Choose Household | Loans or press CTRL-H to display the View Loans window (see Figure 9-2 later in this chapter). Then click New in the window's button bar to create a new loan.

The method you use determines what dialog boxes and prompts appear. For example, if you create a loan when you create a house account, Quicken displays the Edit Loan dialog box that summarizes all loan information in two screens. If you create a loan by clicking the New button in the View Loans window, Quicken displays the Loan Setup dialog box with EasyStep tab screens to walk you through the loan creation process. It doesn't matter which method you use; the information you need to enter is basically the same. Here's what you can expect.

Type of Loan   The Loan Setup dialog box starts by prompting you for a loan type. You have two options:

- **Borrow Money** is for loans for which you're borrowing money from a lender, such as a car loan, mortgage, or personal loan. Quicken uses a liability account to record the loan.
- **Lend Money** is for loans for which you're the lender. Quicken uses an asset account to record the money owed from the borrower.

Loan Account   The Loan Setup dialog box prompts you to enter the account for the loan. Again, you have two options:

- **New Account** enables you to set up a brand-new account for the loan.
- **Existing Account** enables you to select one of your existing accounts for the loan. This option is only available if you have already created the appropriate type of account for the loan.

Loan Dates and Amounts   No matter how you create the loan, you'll be prompted for information about the loan creation, amount, and payments. It's important to be accurate; get the numbers directly from a loan statement or agreement if possible. Quicken can calculate some of the values—such as the loan balance and monthly payments—for you.

When you've finished entering loan information, a series of Summary tab windows display entered and calculated values. The following illustrations show the Edit Loan dialog box screens for a $130,000, 15-year mortgage started on October 15, 1997; these windows are virtually identical to the last two screens that appear in the Loan Setup dialog box when you create a loan from the View Loans window:

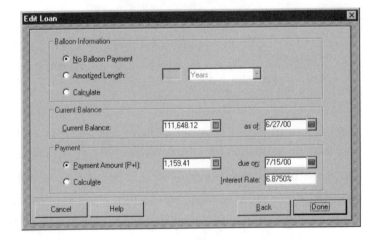

Setting Up Payments

When you set up a loan, Quicken automatically prompts you to set up payment information by displaying the Edit Loan Payment (or Set Up Loan Payment) dialog box:

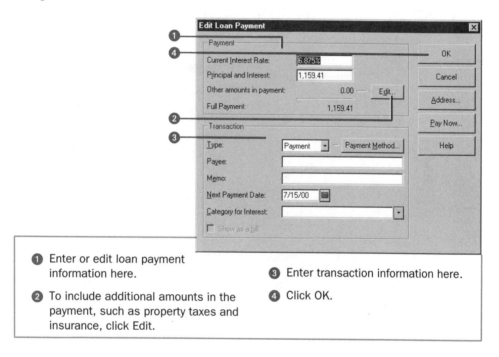

① Enter or edit loan payment information here.

② To include additional amounts in the payment, such as property taxes and insurance, click Edit.

③ Enter transaction information here.

④ Click OK.

Enter information in this dialog box to set up the payment. If the total payment should include additional amounts for property taxes, insurance, or other escrow items, click the Edit button. This displays the Split Transaction window, which you can use to enter categories, memos, and amounts to be added to the payment.

In the Transaction area of the dialog box, you can specify the type and method for the transaction. For type, there are three options on the drop-down list:

- **Payment** is a transaction recorded in your account register only. You must manually write and mail a check for payment. This is covered in Chapter 4.

- **Print Check** is a transaction recorded in the Write Checks dialog box and account register. You can use the Print Check command to print the check, and then you can mail it for payment. This is also covered in Chapter 4.

- **Online Pmt** creates a payment instruction to be processed by your financial institution for use with online payment. This is covered in Chapter 5. This option only appears if at least one of your bank accounts is enabled for Quicken's online payment feature.

For payment method, click the Payment Method button. The Select Payment Method dialog box appears:

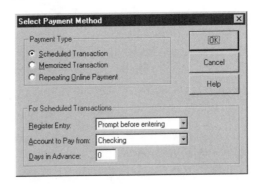

This dialog box offers three Payment Type options:

- **Scheduled Transaction** is a transaction scheduled for the future. If you select this option, you must also choose options and enter values to specify how Quicken should enter the transaction, which account should be used to pay, and how many days in advance it should be entered and paid. All this is covered in Chapter 11.
- **Memorized Transaction** is a transaction memorized for use with QuickFill or the Quicken Financial Calendar. This is also covered in Chapter 11.
- **Repeating Online Payment** is a recurring online payment instruction processed by your financial institution. This option is only available if you selected Online Pmt in the Edit Loan Payment or Set Up Loan Payment dialog box. If you select this option, you must also select a repeating online payment transaction from a drop-down list. (If you have not already created a transaction to link to this loan payment, select one of the other options and return to this dialog box after you have created the required transaction. Consult Chapter 5 for more details.)

Creating an Associated Asset Account

At the conclusion of the payment setup process, Quicken may display a dialog box asking if you want to create an asset to go with the loan. This enables you to set up an asset account for the full purchase price of your new home or car. Click Yes to create a new account; click No if you have already created one. I discuss creating an asset account earlier in this chapter.

Reviewing Loan Information

The View Loans window displays information about your loans, as shown in Figure 9-2. You can open this window by choosing Household | Loans or by pressing CTRL-H.

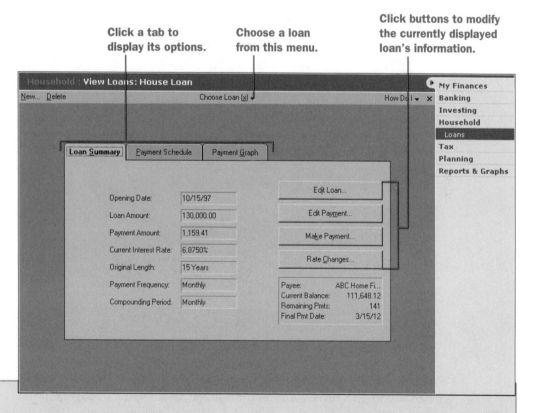

Figure 9-2 • The View Loans window displays information about your loans

Button Bar Options

The View Loans window's button bar offers options for working with loans:

- **New** enables you to create a new loan. I explain how this option works earlier in this chapter.
- **Delete** removes the currently displayed loan. This option does not remove any transactions related to the loan. It simply removes the loan information.
- **Choose Loan** displays a menu of your current loans. Use it to choose the loan you want to display in the window.
- **How Do I** provides instructions for working with the View Loans window.

Window Tabs

The tabs along the top of the window's information area enable you to view various pieces of information about a loan.

Loan Summary   Loan Summary (see Figure 9-2) summarizes the loan information.

Payment Schedule   Payment Schedule displays a schedule of past and future payments. You can turn on the Show Running Totals check box to display cumulative totals, rather than individual payment information.

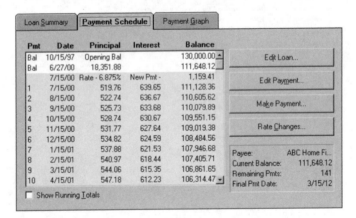

Payment Graph   The Payment Graph displays a graph of the loan payments. Where the two lines meet indicates the point at which you start paying more toward the loan principal than for interest. You can point to a position on a graph line to display its value.

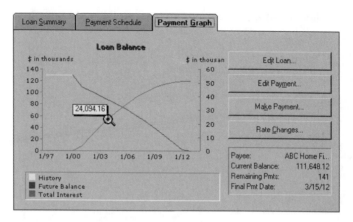

Modifying Loan Information

Once you've created a loan, you can modify it as necessary to record corrections, changes in the interest rate, or changes in payment methods. You can do all these things with buttons in the View Loans window (see Figure 9-2).

Changing Loan Information

If you discover a discrepancy between the loan information in the View Loans window and information on statements or loan agreement papers, you can change the loan information in Quicken.

If necessary, choose the loan account's name from the Choose Loan menu in the button bar to display the information for the loan that you want to modify. Then click the Edit Loan button. A series of Edit Loan windows enables you to change just about any information for the loan. Modify values and select different options as desired. Click Done in the last window to save your changes.

Changing the Interest Rate

If you have an adjustable rate mortgage, you'll periodically have to adjust the rate for the loan within Quicken to match the rate charged by the lender.

If necessary, choose the loan account's name from the Choose Loan menu in the button bar to display the information for the loan whose rate you want to change.

Then click the Rate Changes button. The Loan Rate Changes window appears. It lists all the loan rates throughout the history of the loan:

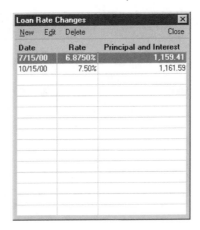

To insert a rate change, click the New button in the window's button bar. The Insert an Interest Rate Change dialog box appears:

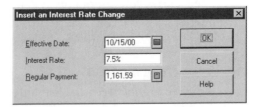

Enter the effective date and new rate in the appropriate text boxes. Quicken automatically calculates the new loan payment. When you click OK, the rate appears in the Loan Rate Changes window. Click the Close button to dismiss the window. Quicken recalculates the loan payment schedule for you.

Recording Other Asset Transactions

Part of tracking assets is keeping track of their current values and modifying account balances when necessary. Like a bank or investment account, which I discuss in Chapters 4 and 6, activity for an asset account appears in its account register.

To open an asset account's register, choose its name from the Household Accounts submenu under the Household menu or click its name in the Household Center window. The Account Register window, which is shown in Figure 9-3, appears.

Adjustment for market value

Opening balance

Adjustment for improvement

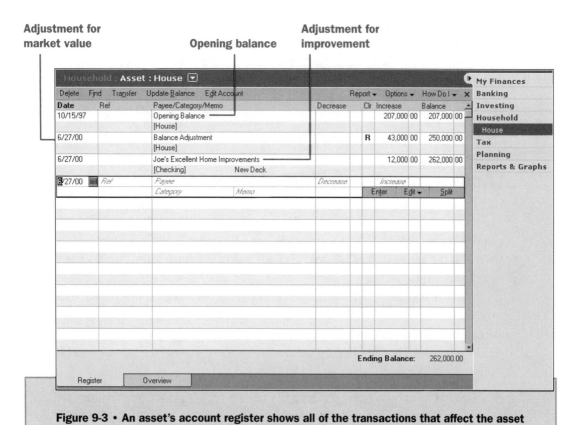

Figure 9-3 • An asset's account register shows all of the transactions that affect the asset

- **Delete** removes the currently selected transaction.
- **Find** enables you to search for transactions in the window. I discuss searching for transactions in Chapter 4.
- **Transfer** enables you to create a transfer transaction. I cover transfers in Chapter 4, too.
- **Update Balance** enables you to create a transaction to update the value of the asset. I discuss this option later in this section.
- **Edit Account** enables you to modify account information.
- **Report** is a menu that offers a variety of reporting options for account information.

- **Options** is a menu that offers a variety of options for changing the view of the window.
- **How Do I** provides instructions for completing tasks with the Account Register window.

In this section, I explain how you can record changes in asset values due to acquisitions and disposals, improvements, market values, and depreciation.

Adding and Disposing of Assets

The most obvious change in an asset's value occurs when you add or remove part of the asset. For example, I have a single asset account in which I record the value of my horses and related equipment. When I buy a new saddle, it increases the value of the account. Similarly, when I sell one of my horses, it decreases the value of the account.

In many instances, when you add or dispose of an asset, money is exchanged. In that case, recording the transaction is easy: Simply use the appropriate bank account register to record the purchase or sale and use the asset account as a transfer account in the category field. Here's what the purchase of a new saddle might look like in my credit card account:

4/1/00		Triple D Western World		958	45				1,104	65
		[Horses & Tack]	New Saddle							

And here's the same transaction in my Horses and Tack asset account:

4/1/00		Triple D Western World				958	45	7,458	45
		[WF MasterCard]	New Saddle						

If the asset was acquired without an exchange of cash, you can enter the transaction directly into the asset account, using the Gift Received category (or a similar category of your choice) to categorize the income. Similarly, if the asset was disposed of without an exchange of cash, you can enter the transaction into the asset account register using the Gifts Given or Charity (or other appropriate category) to categorize the write-off.

Updating Asset Values

A variety of situations can change the value of a single asset. The type of situation will determine how the value is adjusted. Here are three common examples.

Recording Improvements

Certain home-related expenditures can be considered improvements that increase the value of your home. It's important to keep track of improvements because they raise the property's tax basis, thus reducing the amount of capital gains you have to record (and pay tax on) when you sell the house.

Tip   *Your tax advisor can help you determine which expenditures can be capitalized as home improvements.*

Since most home improvements involve an expenditure, use the appropriate banking account register to record the transaction. Be sure to enter the appropriate asset account (House, Condo, Land, and so on) as a transfer account in the Category field. You can see an example of a home improvement entry in the asset account register shown in Figure 9-3.

Adjusting for Market Value

Real estate, vehicles, and other large-ticket item assets are also affected by market values. Generally speaking, real estate values go up, vehicle values go down, and other item values can vary either way depending on what they are.

To adjust for market value, click the Update Balance button in the button bar of the account register for the asset you want to adjust. The Update Account Balance dialog box appears:

```
Update Account Balance: Jeep Wrangler                    X

  1.  Enter the current balance for this account.
      Update Balance to:         18,000.00          ▣
      Adjustment Date:           6/27/00          ▦

  2.  Choose a category for the balance adjustment.
      Category for Adjustment:   Auto              ▾
          OK              Cancel              Help
```

Use this dialog box to enter the date and market value for the asset. Then select a category or transfer account to record the gain or loss of value. When you click OK, the entry is added to the account register:

6/27/00		Balance Adjustment	6,125 84	R		18,000 00
		Auto				

Tip *If you don't want the adjustment to affect any category or account other than the asset, choose the same asset account as a transfer account. When you click OK, a dialog box will warn you that you are trying to record a transfer into the same account. Click OK again. You can see an example of an adjustment like this in Figure 9-3.*

 GET SMARTER You can use Quicken to periodically download information about the market value of your home or car, which you can then use to update asset values in your Quicken data file. I tell you how to download market value information in Chapter 10.

Recording Depreciation

Depreciation is a calculated reduction in the value of an asset. Depreciation expense can be calculated using a variety of acceptable methods, including straight line, sum of the year's digits, and declining balance—consult your accountant or tax advisor for details. Normally, it reduces the asset's value regularly, with monthly, quarterly, or annual adjustments. Depreciation is commonly applied to property used for business purposes since depreciation expense on those assets may be tax deductible.

Tip *If you think depreciation on an asset you own may be tax deductible, use Quicken to track the depreciation expense. Otherwise, depreciation probably isn't worth the extra effort it requires to track.*

To record depreciation, create an entry in the asset account that reduces the value by the amount of the depreciation. Use a Depreciation Expense category to record the expense. The transaction might look something like this:

6/27/00	Record Depreciation		200 00		17,800 00
	Auto:Depreciation Jeep Depreciation				

Shortcut *You can set up monthly, quarterly, or annual depreciation transactions as scheduled transactions so Quicken will automatically record them when they are due. I tell you about scheduled transactions in Chapter 11.*

Quicken Home Inventory

Quicken Home Inventory is a separate program that comes with Quicken Deluxe. You can open it from within Quicken, enter or edit information about the things in your home, and then update your Quicken data file with item valuations.

Quicken Home Inventory is excellent for providing detailed information about your possessions. This information is extremely valuable in the event of a burglary, fire, or other loss when you need to provide details to the police and/or insurance company. Enter this information and print reports to keep in a safe place. Then, once a year or so, update the entries and prepare a fresh report so your printed files are up to date.

Entering and Updating Information

To start, choose Household | Quicken Home Inventory or click the Home Inventory link in the Activities area of the Household Center window. The Quicken Home Inventory program starts and appears onscreen, over your Quicken program window (see Figure 9-4). You can use this List View window to add or modify summary information about each inventory item.

Tip *Although you can use Quicken Home Inventory to track every possession in every room, from the ceiling lamp to the carpeting, entering that kind of detail isn't really necessary. Instead, enter the most valuable items, the ones that would be most difficult or costly to replace. This will save you time while enabling you to record your most important belongings.*

To add an item to the home inventory, begin by choosing a home location from the drop-down list near the top of the window. Click the New button at the bottom of the window to start a new line. Then enter basic information about the item on the line and press ENTER.

Shortcut *A quick way to enter a standard item is to choose the item category and then double-click one of the suggested items in the list on the right side of the window. Modify the values if desired and press ENTER.*

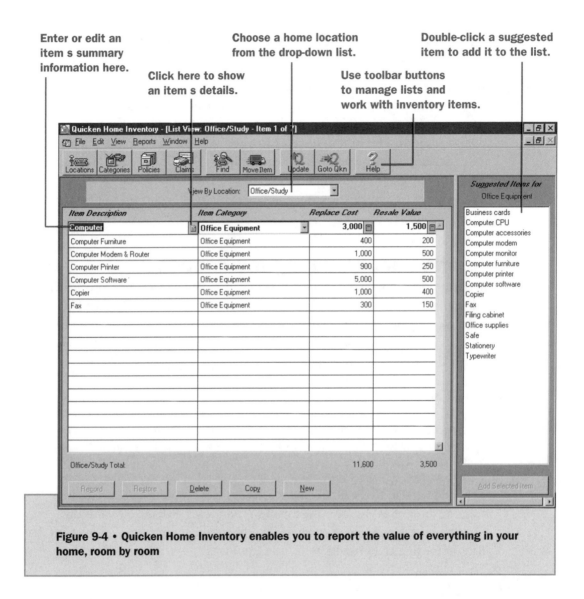

Enter or edit an
item s summary
information here.

Choose a home location
from the drop-down list.

Double-click a suggested
item to add it to the list.

Click here to show
an item s details.

Use toolbar buttons
to manage lists and
work with inventory items.

Figure 9-4 • Quicken Home Inventory enables you to report the value of everything in your home, room by room

To add details about an item, select it and click the icon beside its description. Use the Detail View window, which is shown next, to enter more information about the item, such as its make and model, its serial number, and its purchase date. You can also click buttons in this window to enter information about the receipts and other records you have on hand for the item and changes in its resale value.

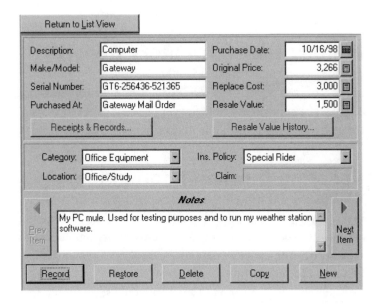

Customizing Options

You can customize the drop-down and scrolling lists that appear in Quicken Home Inventory by clicking buttons on the toolbar at the top of the window (see Figure 9-4).

- **Locations** enables you to add, modify, or remove names for rooms in your home. It also displays a list of entered items by location.
- **Categories** enables you to add, modify, or remove item categories. It also displays a list of entered items by category.
- **Policies** enables you to add, modify, or remove insurance policy names. It also displays a list of entered items by insurance policy.
- **Claims** enables you to add, modify, or remove insurance claims. It also displays a list of entered items by claim.

> **Caution**   *Don't confuse "categories" in Quicken Home Inventory with "categories" in Quicken. The two terms are used differently. Quicken Home Inventory categories have nothing to do with Quicken categories.*

Printing Home Inventory Reports

The Reports menu in the Quicken Home Inventory program window offers a number of basic reports you can use to print inventory information. This is extremely useful when applying for homeowner or home office insurance, when the insurance company requires detailed information about certain types of belongings.

Updating Quicken Information

When you've finished entering or modifying information in Quicken Home Inventory, click the Update button on its toolbar. A small dialog box appears, asking you whether you want to send inventory data to the Home Inventory account in your Quicken data file. Click Yes. Then choose File | Exit to close Quicken Home Inventory.

When you switch back to Quicken, you'll see a Home Inventory account—even if you didn't create one—with a balance corresponding to the resale value of home inventory items. When you open the account from the Account List window, Quicken Home Inventory automatically launches, enabling you to add or update information.

Emergency Records Organizer

The Emergency Records Organizer (ERO) enables you to track personal, financial, and legal information that may come in handy in the event of an emergency. It consists of a number of forms you can fill in with information. You can enter as much or as little information as you like. You can go into great detail on subjects that are important to you and completely ignore others. You can update and print the information at any time. It's this flexibility—and the fact that all information can be stored in one place—which makes the ERO a useful tool.

To open the ERO, choose Household | Emergency Records Organizer or click the Emergency Record link in the Activities area of the Household Center window.

Its main window, which provides an introduction to its features, appears. Read what's in the window or click the Getting Started link to learn more.

Creating and Updating Records

To create or modify ERO records, click the ERO's Create/Update Records tab to display the entry window, as shown in Figure 9-5. The window has three parts: the area drop-down list, the topic list, and the entry form.

To enter the information you want to organize, follow the steps as they appear in the window and click Save. You can then click New Record to add another record for the same area and topic, or repeat the steps to add records for other areas or topics.

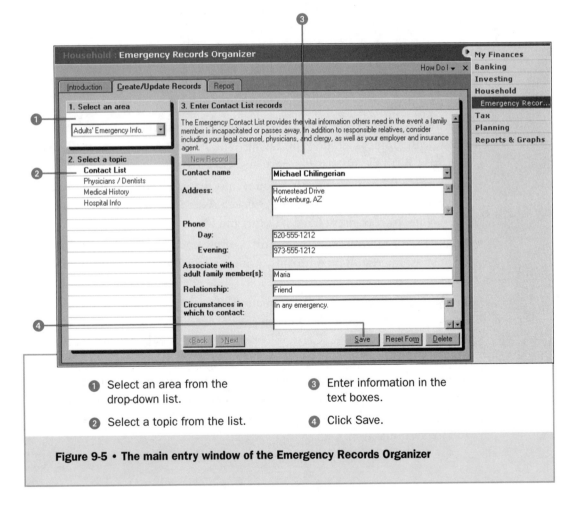

1 Select an area from the drop-down list.

2 Select a topic from the list.

3 Enter information in the text boxes.

4 Click Save.

Figure 9-5 • The main entry window of the Emergency Records Organizer

Areas and Topics

The ERO offers 11 different areas of information, each with its own set of topics:

- **Adults' Emergency Info** is information you may need in the event of an adult's health-related emergency. Topics include Contact List (refer to Figure 9-5), Physicians/Dentists, Medical History, and Hospital Information.

- **Children's Emergency Info** is information you may need in the event of a child's health-related emergency. Topics include Contact List, Physicians/ Dentists, Medical History, and Hospital Information.

- **Adults' Important Info** is important information about the adults in your home or family. Topics include Summary (for birth date, social security number, driver's license number, and so on), Residence, Employment/Business, Business Partners, Education, Marriage Info, and Military Record.

- **Children's Important Info** is important information about the children in your home or family. Topics include Child's Summary (for birth date, school, grade, and social security number), School, Caretaker, Schedules, and Guardian.

- **Personal & Legal Docs** is for information about important personal and legal documents. Topics include Will, Living Will, Funeral Arrangements, Powers of Attorney, Birth Certificate, Passport, and Tax Records.

- **Accounts** is for bank and other account information. Topics include Quicken Bank Acct., Quicken Credit Acct., Quicken Asset Acct., Quicken Liability Acct., Checking, Savings, Credit/Debit, and Other Accounts.

- **Income** is for information about sources of income. Topics include Salary, Dividends, Interest, Rental Income, Annuity, Trust Fund, Alimony, Child Support, and Other.

- **Invest and Retirement** is for information about regular and retirement investments. Topics include Quicken Invest. Acct., IRA Account, 401(k) Account, Money Market, Cert. of Deposit, Stocks, Bonds, Mutual Funds, Keogh/SEP Plan, Pension, and Social Security.

- **Auto/Home/Property** is for general information about your property and vehicles. Topics include Property, Prev Residence, Safe Deposit Box, Post Office Box, Safe, Alarm Information, Storage, Pets, Automobile, Motorcycle, and Recreational.

- **Insurance** is for insurance information. Topics include Life Insurance, Medical Insurance, Dental Insurance, Auto Insurance, Property Insurance, Disability Insurance, and Other Insurance.
- **Mortgage/Loans** is for information about loans. Topics include Mortgage, Personal Loans, Auto Loans, and School Loans.

Tip   *At this point, you might be wondering about the wisdom of keeping all kinds of important—and often private—information in one place. After all, the burglar who took your stamp collection and fax machine could also take your computer. Fortunately, you can back up and password-protect your Quicken data file. I show you how in Appendix A.*

Entry Form

The entry form that appears when you choose an area and select a topic (see Figure 9-5) varies with the area and topic. Each form offers labeled text boxes for entering appropriate information. You can enter as much information as you like and skip over as many fields as you like. You won't get an error message for entering "wrong" information.

When you've finished filling in a form for a topic, click the Save button in the entry form part of the window. Then, to create a new record in the same area, click the New Record button and fill in a fresh form. You can view and edit other records at any time by clicking the Prev or Next button.

Printing Reports

The ERO includes its own reporting feature, which makes it easy to generate reports for a variety of purposes based on the information you entered. You can give printed reports to people who may need them and lock others up in a secure place for when you need them.

Click the Report tab on the ERO window to display the report options (see Figure 9-6). You can select a report from the drop-down list at the top of the window and preview it in the area below. Then click Print to print the currently selected report. It's as simple as that.

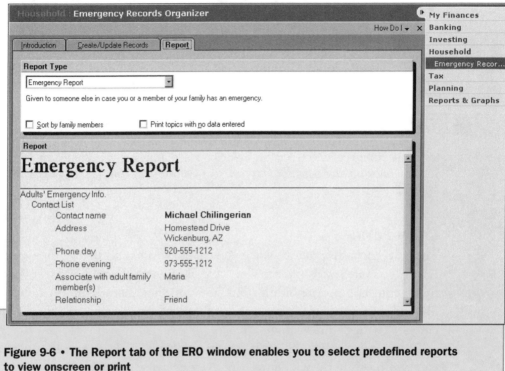

Figure 9-6 • The Report tab of the ERO window enables you to select predefined reports to view onscreen or print

Here's a quick list of the reports so you know what's available:

- **Emergency Report** (shown in Figure 9-6) is to give to someone in case of a family emergency.
- **Caretaker Report** is for someone taking care of your home or pet while you are away.
- **Survivor's Report** is for your lawyer or heirs in the event of your death.
- **Summary of Records Entered Report** lists the areas, topics, and record names you've entered in the ERO. It does not provide any detailed information.
- **Detail Report** lists everything you've entered into the ERO. As the name implies, it provides detail and can be used as a kind of master list.

Minimizing Home, Car, and Insurance Expenses

Chapter 10

In This Chapter:

- Mortgage and Loan Basics

- Preparing for a Major Purchase

- Insurance Basics

- Mortgage Research

- Home and Car Value Downloads

- Shopping for Insurance Online

- Loan and Insurance Worksheets

Possibly the biggest purchase you'll ever make is the purchase of a new home or car. These aren't the kinds of things you buy on a whim. They require research and planning. Not only is it important to find the right living space or vehicle, it's important to get the right financing. You want the best deal on a loan, with a low interest rate and monthly payments that won't stretch your budget.

As your assets, family, and responsibilities grow, so does your need for insurance. Insurance can protect you from financial hardship in the event of loss, theft, or damage to your assets. It can help you cover medical costs and make ends meet if illness or injury requires extensive medical care or prevents you from working. It can provide for your family if something happens to you.

In this chapter, I tell you about the tools within Quicken and on Quicken.com that you can use to learn more about financing a home or car and obtaining the insurance you need to protect your possessions and family. Along the way, I provide useful information about loans and insurance to give you a good idea of what's available. As you'll see in this chapter, Quicken can help you get the information you need to make informed decisions that can save you money.

Mortgage and Loan Basics

Before you start shopping for a loan—or for a home or car, for that matter—it's a good idea to have an understanding of loan basics. What kinds of loans are there? What are their benefits and drawbacks? Which is the right one for your purchase? What things are important when comparing one loan to another? In this section, I answer all of these questions and more.

Types of Loans

There are several types of loans, some of which are designed for specific purposes. Here's a quick summary of what's available, along with their pros and cons.

Mortgage

A *mortgage* is a long-term loan secured by real estate. Most mortgages require a 10 percent or higher down payment on the property. Monthly payments are based on the term of the loan and the interest rate applied to the principal. The interest you pay on a mortgage for a first or second home is tax deductible. If you fail to make mortgage payments, your house could be sold to pay back the mortgage.

A *balloon* mortgage is a special type of short-term mortgage. Rather than make monthly payments over the full typical mortgage term, at the end of the fifth, seventh, or tenth year, you pay the balance of the mortgage in one big "balloon" payment. Some balloon mortgages offer the option of refinancing when the balloon payment is due.

Home Equity Loans or Lines of Credit

A *home equity loan* or *second mortgage* is a line of credit secured by the equity in your home—the difference between its market value and the amount of outstanding debt. Your equity rises when you make mortgage payments or property values increase. It declines when you borrow against your equity or property values decrease. A home equity loan lets you borrow against this equity.

There are two benefits to a home equity loan: Interest rates are usually lower than other credit, and interest may be tax deductible. For these reasons, many people use home equity loans to pay off credit card debt, renovate their homes, or buy cars, boats, or other recreational vehicles. (I used a home equity line of credit last year to buy a new Jeep. Not only did I get a low rate, but the interest I paid on the loan is tax deductible.) But, like a mortgage, if you fail to pay a home equity reserve, your house could be sold to satisfy the debt.

Reverse Equity Loans

A *reverse equity loan* provides homeowners who own their homes in full with a regular monthly income. Instead of you paying the lender, the lender pays you. This type of loan is attractive to retirees who live on a fixed income. The loan is paid back when the home is sold—often after the death of the homeowner. (You can imagine how the next of kin feel about that.)

Car Loans

A *car loan* is a loan secured by a vehicle such as a car, truck, or motor home. Normally, you make a down payment and use the loan to pay the balance of the car's purchase price. Monthly payments are based on the term of the loan and the interest rate applied to the principal. Interest on car loans is not tax deductible.

Personal Loans

A *personal loan* is an unsecured loan—a loan that requires no collateral. Monthly payments are based on the term of the loan and the interest rate applied to the principal. You can use a personal loan for just about anything. Some people use them to pay off multiple smaller debts so they have only one monthly payment. Interest on personal loans is not tax deductible.

Loan Considerations

When applying for a loan, a number of variables have a direct impact on what the loan costs you now and in the future. Be sure to ask about all these things *before* applying for any loan.

GET SMARTER   The Loan Comparison Worksheet and Mortgage Comparison Worksheet at the end of this chapter enable you to take notes about the loans and mortgages you research. Use them to compare options before you make a decision.

Interest Rate

The *interest rate* is the annual percentage applied to the loan principal. Several factors affect the interest rate you may be offered:

- **The type of loan** affects the interest rate offered because, generally speaking, personal loans have the highest interest rates, whereas mortgages have the lowest. From highest to lowest between these two types are a used car loan, a new car loan, and a home equity reserve or line of credit.
- **The loan term** affects the interest rate offered because the length of a loan can vary the interest within a specific loan type. For example, for car loans, the longer the term, the lower the rate.
- **The amount of the down payment** has an effect on the interest rate offered because the more money you put down on the purchase, the lower the rate may be.
- **Your location** affects the interest rate offered because rates vary from one area of the country to another.
- **The lender** affects the interest rates because rates also vary from one lender to another. Certain types of lenders have lower rates than others.

SAVE MONEY   When we purchased our current home, we used a mortgage company, rather than a bank, and got a considerably lower rate than what the local banks were offering.

Two kinds of interest rates can apply to a loan: fixed and variable.

- **Fixed rate** applies the same rate to the principal throughout the loan term.
- **Variable rate** applies a different rate to the loan throughout the loan term. For example, the loan may start with one rate and, each year, switch to a different rate. The rate is usually established by adding a certain number of percentage points to a national index, such as treasury bill rates. A cap limits the amount the rate can change. Mortgages with this type of rate are referred to as *adjustable rate mortgages,* or *ARMs*.

 SAVE MONEY   When we purchased our first home in the mid-1980s when interest rates were high, we selected an ARM. When interest rates dropped, so did the rate on our mortgage. If we'd selected a fixed-rate mortgage when we bought that home, we would have had to refinance to get the same savings. But because rates were much lower when we bought our current home, we selected a fixed rate to protect us from possible rate increases in the future.

Term

A loan's *term* is the period of time between the loan date and the date payment is due in full. Loan terms vary depending on the type of loan.

- Mortgage loan and home equity reserve loan terms are typically 10, 15, 20, or 30 years.
- Balloon mortgage loan terms are typically 5, 7, or 10 years.
- Car loan terms are typically 3, 4, or 5 years.

Down Payment

A *down payment* is an up-front payment toward the purchase of a home or car. Most mortgages require at least 10 percent down; 20 percent down is preferred.

 SAVE MONEY   If you make only a 10 percent down payment on a home, you may be required to pay for the cost of private mortgage insurance. This protects the lender from loss if you fail to pay your mortgage, but increases your monthly mortgage payments.

Application Fees

Most lenders require you to pay an application fee to process your loan application. This usually includes the cost of obtaining a property appraisal and credit report. These fees are usually not refundable—even if you are turned down.

Mortgage Closing Costs

In addition to the application fee and down payment, many other costs are involved in securing a mortgage and purchasing a home. These are known as *closing costs*. Here's a brief list of the types of costs you may encounter. Because they vary from lender to lender, they could be a deciding factor when shopping for a mortgage. Note that most of these fees are not negotiable.

- **Origination fee** covers the administrative costs of processing a loan.
- **Discount or "points"** is a fee based on a percentage rate applied to the loan amount. For example, 1 point on a $150,000 mortgage is $1,500.
- **Appraisal fee** covers the cost of a market-value appraisal of the property by a licensed, certified appraiser.
- **Credit report fee** covers the cost of obtaining a credit history of the prospective borrower(s) to determine credit worthiness.
- **Underwriting fee** covers the cost of underwriting the loan. This is the process of determining loan risks and establishing terms and conditions.
- **Document preparation fee** covers the cost of preparing legal and other documents required to process the loan.
- **Title insurance fee** covers the cost of title insurance, which protects the lender and buyer against loss due to disputes over ownership and possession of the property.
- **Recording fee** covers the cost of entering the sale of a property into public records.
- **Prepaid items** are taxes, insurance, and assessments paid in advance of their due dates. These expenses are not paid to the lender but are due at the closing date.

GET SMARTER   The Real Estate Settlement Procedures Act of 1974 requires that your lender provide a Good Faith Estimate of closing costs. This document summarizes all of the costs of closing on a home based on the mortgage the lender is offering. If you're not sure what a fee is for, check the Mortgage Glossary available in Quicken.com's Mortgage channel.

Preparing for a Major Purchase

Whether you're buying a home, car, or recreational vehicle, you'll need to do some planning before you make your purchase. In this section, I tell you what information a lender wants to know about you, as well as how you can determine what a loan will cost you.

Gathering Financial Fitness Information

Before anyone lends you money (except maybe Big Louie, who works out of the back room of a bar on the bad side of town), you'll need to provide some assurance that you can pay it back, with interest, within the allotted time. Before a potential lender starts examining your financial fitness, you should. Then you'll know in advance what the lender will discover, and if there are problems, you can fix them.

Your Net Worth

Start by taking a look at your net worth. If you've been faithfully recording all your financial information in Quicken, this is easy. Choose Reports | Own & Owe | Net Worth Report. Quicken creates a Net Worth Report, which shows all of your assets and liabilities. The difference between these two is your net worth. The bigger this number is, the better off you are.

> **Tip**   *You can customize the Net Worth report to include only the accounts you specify. I tell you more about creating reports in Chapter 13.*

Not all of the numbers on your Net Worth report will interest a lender. They're interested primarily in cash, cars, real estate, investments, credit card balances, and other debt. If your home inventory values your T-shirt collection at $5,000, so what? T-shirts aren't easily exchanged for cash to make mortgage payments.

Debt Reduction

If all of your assets and liabilities have been recorded in Quicken and your net worth is a negative number, stop right here! No one (except maybe Big Louie) will loan you money, because too many others already have. Turn to Chapter 16, where I cover saving money and reducing debt. You'll need to follow the advice and instructions there before you can even think about applying for a loan. You might also find the budgeting and forecasting information in that chapter helpful to get your spending under control.

Credit Report

A lender is also going to be very interested in your credit history. Credit reports are created and maintained by third-party credit monitoring organizations such as Experian, Equifax, and Trans Union. They know everything about your finances—sometimes even things that aren't true. Before you apply for a loan, you may want to see what a credit report says about you. If there are errors, you can get them fixed before someone uses them to form a bad opinion of you.

Quicken Deluxe users can obtain a free credit report as part of a trial offer from CreditCheck. Choose Household | Credit Research to display the CreditCheck main window, which provides basic information about reports available to you and how you can obtain them. If you have Internet access, you can click one of the Order Now buttons to connect to the Internet and order your credit report. If you don't have Internet access, you can click a link to get a toll-free number to call for the report.

Getting Current Interest Rates

Before you can estimate the monthly payments on a loan, you need a good idea of what the current interest rates are. You have three ways to research this information: check the newspaper, call banks, or look it up on Quicken.com.

Caution *Interest rates change often, sometimes on a daily basis. Although short-term variations are usually small, rates over a few weeks or months old usually aren't very accurate.*

Checking a Recent Newspaper

Many banks and other lenders advertise their rates in the financial pages of the newspaper. Some newspapers summarize this information for you. For example, the big paper in my area, the *Arizona Republic*, has a weekly listing of organizations offering mortgages, complete with rates and phone numbers.

Checking with Local Banks

Get out the phone book and call a few banks in your area. Ask them what their rates are. Most banks will provide this information over the phone.

Looking Up Rates on Quicken.com

Quicken.com offers up-to-date rates on all kinds of loans. All you need is an Internet connection to check them for yourself. Choose Finance | Quicken on the Web | Quicken.com. Your computer connects to the Internet and displays the Quicken.com home page. Click the Banking tab near the top of the window to display the Banking channel's home page. You can find average rates for home equity, car, and personal loans in the Today's Rates area of that page. Click the link for a specific type of rate to get more information about that rate:

Calculating the Cost of a Loan

Once you have an idea of what the interest rate for a loan will be, you can use one of two different planning tools within Quicken to determine how much the loan will cost you.

Loan Calculator

Quicken's Loan Calculator can quickly calculate the principal or periodic payment for a loan. Choose Planning | Financial Calculators | Loan. The Loan Calculator dialog box appears:

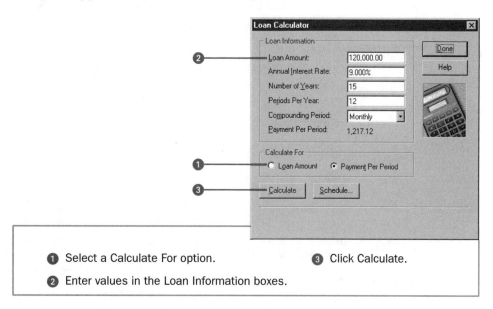

① Select a Calculate For option.   ③ Click Calculate.

② Enter values in the Loan Information boxes.

Begin by selecting one of the two calculation options:

- To calculate the amount of loan you can afford, select the Loan Amount option. Then you can enter an affordable monthly payment in the Payment Per Period box.
- To calculate the periodic payment, select the Payment Per Period option. Then you can enter the amount of the loan in the Loan Amount box.

Enter values in the Loan Information area boxes. When you've finished, click Calculate. The calculated value appears. You can try different values to play "what if" until you have a good idea of how the loan could work for you. With the information this provides, you should be able to tell whether you can afford the home or car you have your eye on; or, if you haven't started looking yet, it can tell you how much you can afford to spend.

Tip   *Click the Schedule button in the Loan Calculator dialog box to see an amortization table that shows the amount of principal and interest paid for each loan period throughout the life of the loan.*

Refinance Calculator

If you already own a home and are thinking about refinancing, you can try the Refinance Calculator. Choose Planning | Financial Calculators | Refinance. The Refinance Calculator dialog box appears:

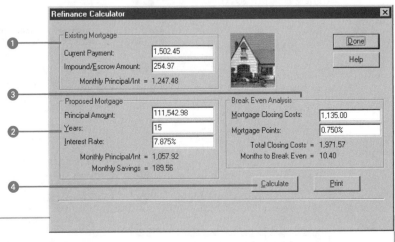

1 Enter values from your current mortgage in the Existing Mortgage boxes.

2 Enter values from the proposed mortgage in the Proposed Mortgage boxes.

3 Enter closing costs and points for the proposed mortgage in the Break Even Analysis boxes.

4 Click Calculate.

Enter values for your current mortgage and proposed mortgage in the text boxes to calculate your monthly savings with the new mortgage. If you enter closing costs and points for the proposed mortgage, you can even calculate how many months it will take to break even after paying these fees.

Insurance Basics

Buying insurance can be baffling. Not only do you need to know what kinds of insurance are available, but you need to know which type you need, how much coverage you should have, and where you can get it.

In this section, I provide some basic information about insurance types and some of the terminology you need to know to understand what a policy covers.

Tip   *If you have access to the Internet, you can learn everything you need to know about insurance at the Insurance Basics pages of the Quicken Insurance Web site. Use your Web browser to visit **http://www.insuremarket.com/tools/basics/**.*

GET SMARTER   Before you start shopping for insurance—whether you shop online via Quicken and Quicken.com or by phone with a phone book—be sure you know the basic information about the type of insurance you want to buy. Understanding insurance options is the only way to be sure that you are purchasing all the insurance coverage you need without being sold extra coverage for the benefit of an insurance company or commissioned salesperson.

Types of Insurance

If you think insurance is limited to home, life, and auto, think again. Here's a quick rundown of the different types of insurance available today.

Auto Insurance

Auto insurance covers specific auto-related losses you may incur during the term of the insurance policy. Auto insurance can be broken down into several parts:

- **Liability insurance**, which is required by law in most states, covers injuries or damage to others or their property. Many insurance advisors recommend that you carry enough liability insurance to protect all of your assets in the event of a lawsuit. This is usually much more than the minimum required by law.

- **Collision insurance** covers damage to your car when the damage results from colliding with another car or object or overturning your car. Although this coverage is not required by law, it is usually required by a lender if the car is purchased with an auto loan.
- **Comprehensive insurance** covers damage to your car when the damage results from causes other than a collision—for example, theft, hail, fire, flood, or vandalism. Although this coverage is not required by law, it is usually required by a lender if the car is purchased with an auto loan.
- **Uninsured and underinsured motorist insurance** covers injury or damage to you, your passengers, and your car in the event that your car is hit by someone who either doesn't have any insurance or doesn't have enough insurance to cover the cost of the accident.
- **Medical payments insurance** covers you and your passengers for reasonable medical (and funeral) expenses incurred as a result of an accident.

Auto insurance rates are affected by where you live, drive, and park your car; the make and model of your car; your age; and your driving record. Many insurance companies offer discounts for good drivers and multiple policies within the same household.

Home Insurance

Home insurance covers financial losses caused by theft, storms, fires, and other similar occurrences that could cause loss or damage to your home and property. It also covers damages resulting from injuries to other people for which you are held legally responsible.

There are different types of home insurance:

- **Homeowners insurance** covers a house and the homeowner's property including the house itself, other structures on the property, personal property within the house or on the property, and liability lawsuits brought against the homeowner for injuries sustained on the property.
- **Renters insurance** covers the personal property of someone renting a home or apartment.
- **Condo or co-op insurance** covers the homeowner's personal property and liability lawsuits brought against the homeowner for injuries sustained within the condo or co-op.

Home insurance rates are affected by the value of your home, the location of your home, the year your home was built, and the proximity of your home to a fire hydrant or fire station.

Life Insurance

Life insurance is money that an insurance company pays to your named beneficiary when you die. There are several types of life insurance:

- **Term life** pays a specific lump-sum amount to your beneficiary when you die. A term life policy is designed specifically to protect your family by providing money to replace your salary and cover the cost of your funeral.
- **Cash value policies**, such as whole life, variable life, universal life, and universal variable life, pay a specific lump-sum amount to your beneficiary when you die. But they also build a cash value account that you can use for noninsurance purposes while you're alive.

Annuities

An *annuity* is a contract between you and an insurance company in which you pay a premium and, in return, the insurance company promises to make benefit payments to you or to another named beneficiary. This is usually done through the use of investments managed by the insurance company.

Annuities can be classified by the timing of the benefit payments and how the annuity earnings accumulate.

Immediate Versus Deferred Annuities   An *immediate* annuity begins paying you benefits within one month to one year of its purchase. A *deferred* annuity accumulates earnings over a period of time and then begins paying you benefits after a specific date—typically a retirement date.

Fixed Versus Variable Annuities   A *fixed* annuity guarantees a fixed rate of return for a specific time period. A *variable* annuity pays a return that varies based on the performance of the investments you select.

Business Continuation Insurance

Business continuation insurance protects your company from financial loss caused by the death or the long-term disability of a key employee. There are three types:

- **Business overhead expense (BOE) insurance** pays business overhead expenses, such as rent, salaries, and utilities, while a business owner is disabled.
- **Key person disability insurance** protects your company while a key employee is disabled.
- **Key person life insurance** covers the cost of losses due to the death of a key employee.

Disability Income Insurance

Disability income insurance covers a percentage of your lost income if you cannot work or perform the duties required by your occupation because you are disabled. The coverage and rates for disability income insurance vary depending on the broadness of the coverage and the amount of benefits to be paid.

Long-Term Care Insurance

Long-term care insurance covers the cost of long-term care, which includes custodial care, to help with the activities of daily life, whether at home or in a nursing home.

Medical Insurance

Medical or health insurance covers the cost of medical care. There are three different types:

- **Employer-provided medical insurance** is usually subsidized by your employer, making it more cost effective than individual medical insurance. Medical plans vary from one provider and company to another.
- **Individual medical insurance** is available directly from insurance companies for individuals. This is often the only option for nonworking or self-employed individuals and their families.
- **Medicare** Part A coverage provides mandatory basic hospitalization for all U.S. citizens over the age of 65. An additional voluntary program (Part B) provides coverage for doctor bills at a monthly cost. Medicare usually covers only 50 percent of the average senior citizen's health care bills and can be supplemented with Medigap insurance.

Umbrella Liability Insurance

Umbrella liability insurance may indeed cover you for injuring someone with your umbrella, but that's not its only purpose. It covers injuries to other people or damage to their property for which you are legally responsible. It's an expansion of the basic liability coverage of your auto and home insurance.

Insurance Terminology

Part of what makes buying insurance so tough sometimes is the terminology used to describe policy terms. Here are a few of the terms you should know when researching insurance policies.

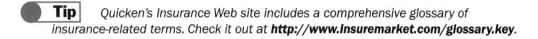

Tip   *Quicken's Insurance Web site includes a comprehensive glossary of insurance-related terms. Check it out at* ***http://www.insuremarket.com/glossary.key****.*

Premium   A premium is the amount paid for an insurance policy. Premiums may be paid annually, semiannually, quarterly, or on some other payment plan.

Binder   A binder is a temporary insurance policy issued while the paperwork on the permanent policy is being processed.

Renewal   A renewal is either a new policy or a document from the insurance company stating that the terms and conditions of your old policy remain in effect for a specific period of time.

Claim   A claim is your request for reimbursement at the loss of insured property. You file a claim with your insurance company after a loss has occurred.

Floater   A floater is a type of insurance policy that covers moveable property, such as jewelry.

Endorsement   An endorsement is an amendment to an insurance policy that changes its terms.

Named Perils   Named perils are specific dangers that a policy insures you against. These dangers are named in the insurance policy. For example, a homeowner's policy might include the following named perils: fire, hail, and wind.

Exclusion   An exclusion is an insurance policy provision that denies coverage for a certain type of loss. For example, flood damage is often excluded from homeowners' insurance policies. (If you live in an area prone to flooding, you can get flood insurance through the U.S. government.)

Limit   A limit is the maximum amount a policy will pay on a covered loss. For example, if you have a $3,000 limit and the loss is $5,000, your insurance company will pay only $3,000.

Deductible   A deductible is the amount of out-of-pocket expenses you have to pay before an insurance company begins paying on a covered loss. For example, if your car has $1,500's worth of covered damages and your deductible is $500, you pay $500, and the insurance company pays $1,000. If you have only $300's worth of covered damages, you pay the whole thing. In most cases, raising your deductible will lower your insurance premium.

Appraisal   An appraisal is an evaluation of the value of the property you want to insure when you buy insurance, or the amount of loss when you file a claim for covered property.

Depreciation   Depreciation is the amount of money deducted from the value of an item to account for age and use. For example, if you paid $15,000 for your car four years ago, it may be worth only $9,000 today. The $6,000 difference is depreciation.

Replacement Value   Replacement value is the amount it would cost to replace or rebuild a covered item based on current market prices. For example, the replacement cost of a three-year-old stereo system would be the amount it would cost to buy a comparable stereo system today.

Actual Cash Value   Actual cash value is the amount you originally paid for an item minus the item's depreciation.

No-Fault Insurance   No-fault insurance covers the cost of repairs and medical expenses for minor accidents, regardless of who caused the accident. No-fault insurance helps speed up the insurance process and lowers insurance costs, but may limit the right to sue for damages.

Using Quicken and Quicken.com Household Resources

Now that we've covered the basics of loans and insurance, let's take a closer look at some specific Quicken and Quicken.com features that can help you minimize your home, car, and insurance expenses.

Researching Mortgages

The Quicken Loans window is a great place to learn all about mortgages and find a mortgage that's right for you. You can even apply for a mortgage online.

Choose Household | Mortgage Research Online to open the Quicken Loans window (see Figure 10-1). This window is full of links to the Quicken Loans Web site, where you can learn more about mortgages, refinancing, and buying a home. To get information about available mortgages in your area use the Find Loans NOW! form. Select a state and enter the property value and loan amount and click the QuickenLoans! button. Quicken connects to the Internet and displays a Quicken Loans page like the one shown in Figure 10-2.

Use this form to find
mortgages in your area.

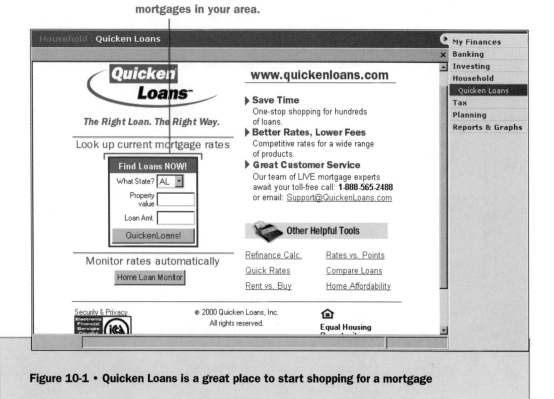

Figure 10-1 • Quicken Loans is a great place to start shopping for a mortgage

Downloading Home and Car Values

Ever wonder what your home is worth? Or your car? Stop wondering! If you have
an Internet connection, you can use commands within Quicken to look up home
and car values and store them in your Quicken data file.

Note   *This feature works with home and car account types only. If you track a
home or car as a regular asset, you'll have to convert it to a home or car account before
you can download values. To do this, choose Household | Home Values Download or
Household | Car Values Download and follow the instructions in step 2 in the window
that appears.*

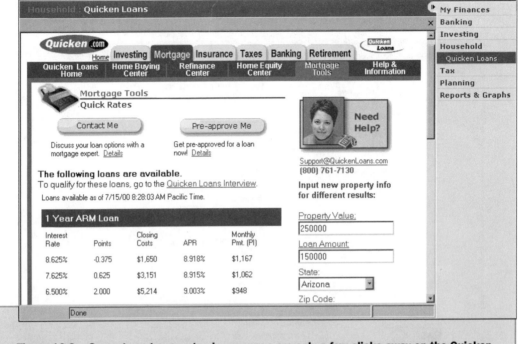

Figure 10-2 • Current mortgage rates in your area are only a few clicks away on the Quicken Loans Web site

Downloading Estimated Home Values

Quicken enables you to download the estimated value of your home based on home sales in your area. This information is stored in the Overview tab of the account register for your home and can be used, if desired, to update the value of your home in your house account.

You can learn more about how the home values download feature works by choosing Household | Home Values Download. Quicken displays the Estimate the Value of Your Home window, which provides step-by-step instructions for downloading home values.

If you have already created a home asset account, you can skip right to the download process. Open the register for your home account and click the Overview tab at the bottom of the window. In the Home Value Downloads area, choose Download Recent Home Sales from the Action pop-up menu. A dialog box appears; use it to enter the address and size of your home:

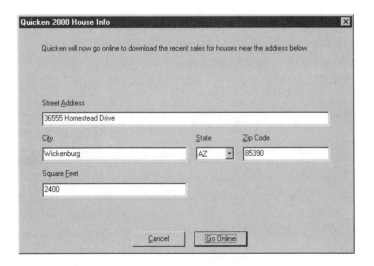

When you click Go Online, Quicken connects to the Internet, displaying a Download Status dialog box while it works. When it has finished, it displays a dialog box that tells you about the home sales that were downloaded. Click OK. When you return to the Overview tab of the house account register, you'll see the results of the download:

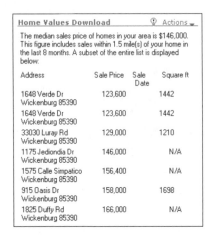

Caution   *Although the home sales information downloaded by Quicken is accurate, it may not include all home sales or sales of homes similar to yours. If the values Quicken comes up with seem extraordinarily high or low, you may want to consult a local Realtor for a more accurate market valuation.*

Getting the Estimated Value of Your Car

You can also go online to get the estimated value of your car. You can then use this information to update the balance of your car account so it reflects current market values.

Note *This feature works with automobile model years 1989 through 2000, so don't expect it to come up with a value for that 1957 Chevy in your garage.*

You can learn more about how the car values download feature works by choosing Household | Car Values Download. Quicken displays the Estimate the Value of Your Car window, which provides step-by-step instructions for downloading car values.

If you have already created an auto asset account, you can skip right to the download process. Open the Overview tab of the account register window for your car. Make sure the Account Attributes area includes the make, model, year, and odometer reading for your car; if it does not, enter these pieces of information in the appropriate fields. Here's what it might look like:

Enter information about the car here.

Account Attributes	☿ Actions ▾
Account Name	Jeep Wrangler
Description	1999 Jeep Wrangler
Make	Jeep
Model	Wrangler
Year	1999
Odometer Reading	10245
Download value monthly?	Not Enabled
Vehicle Loan Account	(none)

How you proceed depends on whether this is the first time you're downloading car value information or you are repeating the download process to update information you already have.

First Time Download Click the question mark (?) beside Estimated Market Value in the Account Status area:

Click this link to download car value information.

Account Status	☿ Actions ▾
Estimated Market Value	?
Current Balance	18,000.00
Last Transaction	6/29/00

A dialog box appears, telling you that Quicken will go online. Click OK. Quicken connects to the Internet, displaying a Download Status dialog box as it works. When it's finished, it displays a dialog box telling you that the download from Edmunds was successful. (Edmunds is a company that provides value information for automobiles and other vehicles; you can visit the Edmunds Web site at **http://www.edmunds.com/**.) Click OK. Quicken displays the downloaded price range in the Account Status area of the Overview tab for the car account:

Downloaded values
appear here.

Account Status		Actions
Estimated Market Value	14,910.00 to 19,975.00	
Current Balance	18,000.00	
Last Transaction	6/29/00	

Subsequent Downloads   Once you've downloaded value information for your car, you can use new links in the Account Status area to get a more exact figure for your car's value at any time. Just click the link beside Estimated Market Value (as shown in the previous illustration) and follow the instructions that appear on screen to connect to Edmunds and download the information.

Tip   *You can instruct Quicken to automatically download car values on a monthly basis. Click the link beside Download Value Monthly? in the Account Attributes area to toggle the setting for the link. When it says Enabled, Quicken will automatically download the updated information during an Internet connection each month.*

Getting Insurance Quotes

You can use Quicken InsureMarket to learn about the insurance you may need and to shop for insurance online. To get started, choose Household | Insurance Research Online or click the Insurance Quote link in the Activities area of the Household Center. Quicken displays the InsureMarket window (see Figure 10-3).

You can access a number of features from this page:

- To get a life insurance or auto insurance quote, enter your ZIP code in the appropriate box and click the Go button. Then follow the instructions that appear on screen to enter information for your quote.
- To learn about specific types of insurance, click the link for the type of insurance that interests you.
- To use planning tools for evaluating your insurance needs, click the link in the Insurance Tools and Information area.
- To get information about major insurance companies participating on Quicken InsureMarket, click the link in the Companies Offering Insurance On Quicken InsureMarket area.

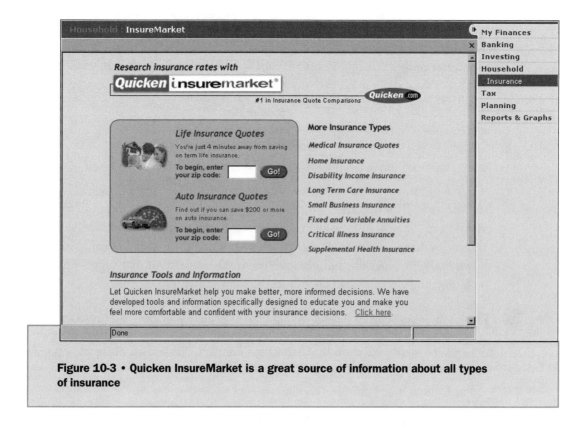

Figure 10-3 • Quicken InsureMarket is a great source of information about all types of insurance

Worksheets

Use the following worksheets to compare and evaluate different loans, mortgages, and insurance policies.

Loan Comparison Worksheet			
Basic Information			
Instructions: Enter information for each loan, one per column.			
Lender Name			
Contact Name			
Phone Number			
Comments			
Amount of Loan			
Rates and Fees			
Instructions: Enter rate and fee values for each loan.			
Application Fee			
Other Fees			
Term (in months)			
Annual Interest Rate			
Payment Calculations			
Instructions: Calculate the monthly payments. Use the Loan Calculator within Quicken for accuracy (choose Planning | Financial Calculators | Loan). Then calculate the total of all payments and fees.			
Monthly Payment			
Total Payments (monthly payment × number of months)			
Total Payments Plus Fees			

Mortgage Comparison Worksheet (page 1)					

Basic Information

Instructions: Enter information for each mortgage, one per column. Note: You can get most of this information from the Good Faith Estimate the lender should provide.

Lender Name			
Contact Name			
Phone Number			
Comments			

Purchase Price and Down Payment Information

Instructions: Enter the purchase price, down payment, and loan amount for each mortgage. For the best comparison, these should be the same.

Purchase Price									
Down Payment		%	$		%	$		%	$

Basic Loan Information

Instructions: Enter values for each mortgage. Then calculate monthly payments. Use the Loan Calculator within Quicken for accuracy (choose Planning | Financial Calculators | Loan). Total the monthly payments for the life of the mortgage.

Annual Interest Rate						
Term (in years)						
Fixed or Variable						
If Variable, Adjustment Period and Cap	Period	Cap	Period	Cap	Period	Cap
Monthly Payments						
Total Monthly Payments (Term × 12 × Monthly Payments)						

Mortgage Comparison Worksheet (page 2)						

Closing Costs

Instructions: Enter expected closing costs for each loan. Do not include prepaid amounts that are due at closing. Not all of these fees may apply; use space at the bottom of this section to enter other fees not listed here.

Origination Fee	%	$		%	$		%	$
Discount Fee (Points)	%	$		%	$		%	$
Credit Report Fee						
Lenders Inspection Fee						
Tax Service Fee						
Application Fee						
Underwriting Fee						
Courier Fee						
Settlement Fee						
Document Preparation Fee						
Notary Fee						
Administration Fee						
Title Insurance Fee						
Recording Fee						
City/County Tax Stamps						
State Tax Stamps						
Recordation Tax						

Mortgage Comparison Worksheet (page 3)			
Loan Program Fee			
Pest Inspection Fee			
Final Inspection Fee			
Total Closing Costs	$	$	$

Total Mortgage Costs

Instructions: Add the Total Monthly Payments to the Total Closing Costs to arrive at the total cost of each mortgage.

Total Mortgage Costs	$	$	$

Term Life Insurance Worksheet			

Basic Information

Instructions: Enter information and values for each policy, one per column.

Company Name			
Agent Name			
Phone Number			
Policy Name			
Coverage Amount			
Annual Premium			
Comments			

Features and Options

Instructions: Check off the features and options included with each policy. If a feature or option is not included, leave the space blank. If it is available as an option for which you must pay more, enter an O (for option) or the additional amount you must pay. You can enter additional features and options at the bottom of the form.

Guaranteed Level Premium			
Guaranteed Renewable			
Guaranteed Convertible			
Accelerated Death Benefit			
Disability Waiver Option			
Accidental Death Option			
Child Rider			
Other Insured Option			

Auto Insurance Worksheet (page 1)		

Basic Information

Instructions: Enter information for each policy, one per column.

Company Name			
Agent Name			
Phone Number			
Comments			

Coverage and Cost

Instructions: Enter the limits and/or deductibles for each category of coverage in one column and the corresponding premium cost in the other. You can enter additional coverage options at the bottom of the section. Be sure to subtotal the Premiums column.

Standard Coverage	Limits or Deductibles	Premiums	Limits or Deductibles	Premiums	Limits or Deductibles	Premiums
Bodily Injury Liability		$		$		$
Property Damage Liability						
Medical Payments						
Personal Injury Protection						
Uninsured/ Underinsured Motorist: • Bodily Injury • Property Damage						
Comprehensive						
Collision						

Auto Insurance Worksheet (page 2)						
Additional Coverage Options	Limits or Deductibles	Premiums	Limits or Deductibles	Premiums	Limits or Deductibles	Premiums
Rental Reimbursement		$		$		$
Towing/ Labor						
Emergency Road Service						
Electronic Equipment Protection						
Sound Reproducing/ Tapes and Compact Disks						
Auto Loan/ Lease Gap						
Premium Total	$		$		$	

Auto Insurance Worksheet (page 3)			

Discounts

Instructions: Enter discounts offered by each insurance company. You can enter additional discounts at the bottom of the section. Be sure to total the discounts.

Multipolicy	$	$	$
Multicar Coverage			
Safety Equipment			
Good Driver			
Antilock Brakes			
Antitheft System			
Driver Training			
Discount Total	$	$	

Policy Cost

Instructions: Subtract the discount total from the premium total to arrive at the total cost of the policy with the options you selected.

Policy Cost	$	$	$

Working with Quicken Data

This part of the book tells you about some of the other things you can do with the information you enter in your Quicken data file. It begins by telling you about time-saving Quicken features for automating data entry, then goes on to explain how to reconcile bank and credit card accounts and create reports and graphs.

The three chapters in this part of the book are:

Chapter 11: Automating Your Quicken Transactions

Chapter 12: Reconciling Accounts

Chapter 13: Creating Reports and Graphs

Automating Your Quicken Transactions

Chapter 11

In This Chapter:

- *QuickFill and Memorized Transactions*

- *Financial Calendar*

- *Scheduled Transactions*

- *Paycheck Setup*

- *Quicken Alerts*

- *Address Book*

- *One Step Update and the PIN Vault*

Quicken includes a number of features to automate the entry of transactions. You got a glimpse of one of them, QuickFill, in Chapter 4. In this chapter, I tell you about QuickFill and the other features you can use to automate transaction entries or remind yourself when a transaction is due. I also explain how you can use Quicken's One Step Update feature to handle all of your online tasks at once. I'm sure you'll agree that these features can make data entry quicker and easier.

Tip   *Before you read this chapter, make sure you have a good understanding of the data entry techniques covered in Chapter 4.*

QuickFill and Memorized Transactions

As you enter transactions, Quicken is quietly working in the background, memorizing information about each transaction. It creates a database of memorized transactions, organized by payee name. It then uses the memorized transactions for its QuickFill feature.

Tip   *By default, the QuickFill feature is set up to work as discussed here. If it does not, check the QuickFill options to make sure they are properly set. I tell you how at the end of this section.*

How It Works

QuickFill works in two ways:

- When you enter the first few characters of a payee name in the Write Checks or account register window, Quicken immediately fills in the rest of the name. When you advance to the next text box or field of the entry form, Quicken fills in the rest of the transaction information based on the last transaction for that payee.
- You can select a memorized transaction from the drop-down list in the payee field of the Write Checks or account register window. Quicken then fills in the rest of the transaction information based on the last transaction for that payee.

QuickFill entries include amounts, categories, and memos. They can also include splits and classes. For example, you might pay the cable or satellite company for television service every month. The bill is usually the same amount each month. The second time you create an entry with the company's name, the rest of the transaction is filled in automatically. You can make adjustments to the amount or other information as desired and save the transaction. It may have taken a minute or so to enter the transaction the first time, but it'll take only seconds to enter it every time after that.

Working with the Memorized Transaction List

If desired, you can view a list of memorized transactions, as shown in Figure 11-1. Just choose Banking | Memorized Transaction List, or press CTRL-T.

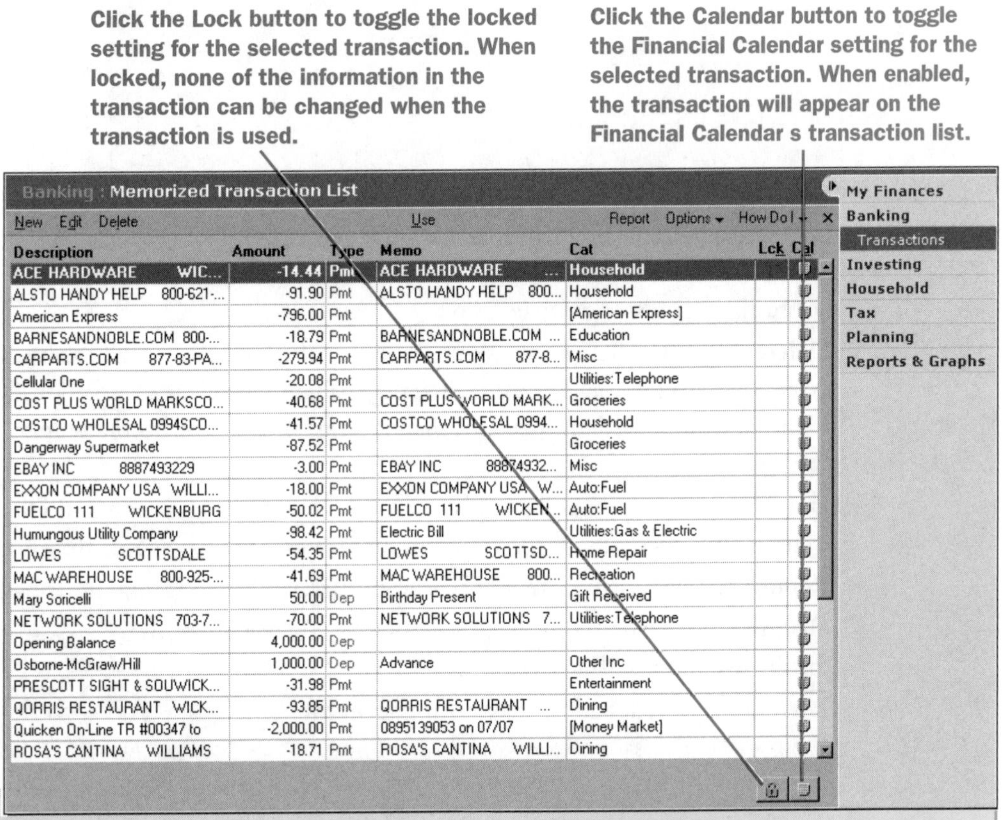
Click the Lock button to toggle the locked setting for the selected transaction. When locked, none of the information in the transaction can be changed when the transaction is used.
Click the Calendar button to toggle the Financial Calendar setting for the selected transaction. When enabled, the transaction will appear on the Financial Calendar s transaction list.
Banking : Memorized Transaction List

Figure 11-1 • Each line in the Memorized Transaction List represents the last transaction recorded for a payee

You can use buttons on the button bar to add, modify, delete, or use memorized transactions:

- **New** displays the Create Memorized Transaction dialog box, which you can use to create brand-new transactions without actually entering them into any register of your Quicken data file. Just use the dialog box's form (shown next) to enter transaction information and click OK. The new transaction appears in the Memorized transaction List window.

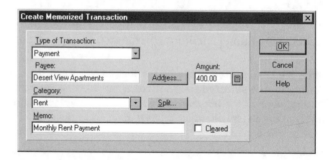

- **Edit** displays the Edit Memorized Transaction dialog box for the currently selected transaction. This dialog box looks and works like the Create Memorized Transaction dialog box.

- **Delete** displays a dialog box asking you to confirm that you really do want to delete the selected memorized transaction. If you delete the transaction, it is removed from the Memorized Transaction List only—not from any register in the Quicken data file.

- **Use** displays the appropriate register for entering the transaction and fills in the transaction's information for you. You must click Enter to accept the entry.

- **Report** displays a Payee Report for the currently selected transaction's payee.

- **Options** offers commands for changing the sort order and other view options for the Memorized Transaction List.

- **How Do I** provides additional information for completing tasks with the Memorized Transaction List window.

Tip *Quicken can remember the first 2,000 transactions you enter—that's 2,000 payees! After that, it stops memorizing transactions. You can use the Delete button in the Memorized Transaction List window to delete old transactions to make room for new ones. You can also use options in the General tab of the General Options dialog box to have Quicken automatically delete unused memorized transactions after the number of months you specify. I tell you how in Chapter 1.*

Setting QuickFill Options

You can customize the way QuickFill works by setting options in the Register Options and Write Checks Options dialog boxes. These settings affect the way the QuickFill feature works in account register and Write Checks windows.

To set QuickFill options for account register windows, choose Edit | Options | Register. Click the QuickFill tab to see the dialog box shown in the following illustration. To set QuickFill options for the Write Checks window, choose Edit | Options | Write Checks. In the dialog box that appears, click the QuickFill tab:

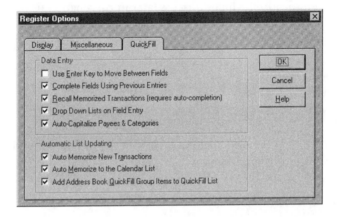

- **Use Enter Key To Move Between Fields** enables you to use both the ENTER and TAB keys to move from field to field when entering data.
- **Complete Fields Using Previous Entries** enters transaction information using the information from previous entries. This option is turned on by default.
- **Recall Memorized Transactions** uses memorized transactions to fill in QuickFill entries. This option, which is not available if the Complete Fields Using Previous Entries option is disabled, is turned on by default.
- **Drop Down Lists On Field Entry** automatically displays the drop-down list when you advance to a field with a list. This option is turned on by default.
- **Auto-Capitalize Payees & Categories** automatically makes the first letter of each word in a payee name or category uppercase. (It's like having a persistent copy editor built right in to Quicken!) This option, which is only available in the Register Options dialog box, is turned on by default.

- **Auto Memorize New Transactions** tells Quicken to automatically enter all transactions for a new payee to the Memorized Transaction List. This option is turned on by default.
- **Auto Memorize To the Calendar List** tells Quicken to automatically add memorized transactions to the Transaction List in the Financial Calendar window. This option is turned on by default. You'll learn more about the Financial Calendar window in the next section.
- **Add Address Book QuickFill Group Items To QuickFill List** tells Quicken to add entries from the Financial Address Book to QuickFill drop-down lists. This feature, which I discuss later in this chapter, is only available in Quicken Deluxe.

Financial Calendar and Scheduled Transactions

Quicken's Financial Calendar feature keeps track of all your transactions by date. It also enables you to schedule one-time or recurring transactions for the future.

Opening the Financial Calendar

To open the financial calendar, choose Finance | Calendar or press CTRL-K. The Financial Calendar window, which is shown in Figure 11-2, appears.

You can use button bar options to work with the window's contents:

- **Note** enables you to enter a note for the selected date. The note you enter appears on the calendar (as shown in Figure 11-2) and in the Quicken Alerts window (see Figure 11-4 later in this chapter).
- **<Prev Month** and **Next Month>** enable you to move from one month to another.
- **Go To Date** enables you to go to a specific calendar date.
- **Options** offers additional commands for viewing and working with the Financial Calendar window.
- **How Do I** provides additional information for completing tasks with the Financial Calendar window.

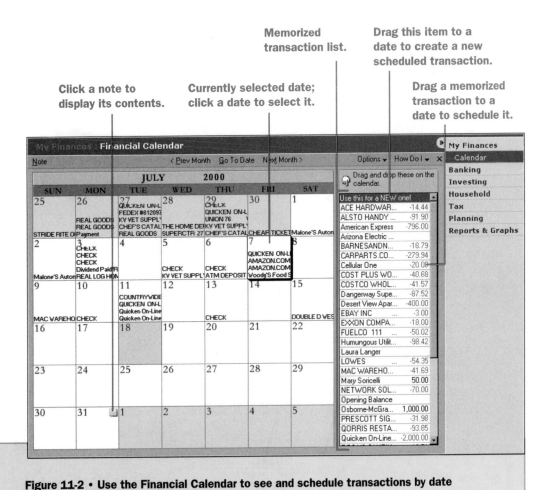

Figure 11-2 • Use the Financial Calendar to see and schedule transactions by date

When you double-click a calendar date (or single-click a selected date), a window listing all the transactions for that date appears, as shown next. You can use buttons at the bottom of the window to work with transactions:

- **New** enables you to create a new scheduled transaction.
- **Edit** enables you to modify the currently selected transaction.

- **Delete** removes the selected transaction.
- **Register** opens the account register for the selected transaction.
- **Pay Now** processes or records the selected transaction immediately. This option is only available for transactions scheduled for future dates.

Creating a Scheduled Transaction

You can create a scheduled transaction right from within the Financial Calendar window (see Figure 11-2).

- To schedule a transaction based on a memorized transaction, drag a transaction from the transaction list on the right side of the window to the date on which you want the transaction to occur.
- To schedule a transaction that is not based on a memorized transaction, drag the Use This For A NEW One! item from the transaction list on the right side of the window to the date on which you want the transaction to occur.

The New Transaction dialog box appears, as shown next. It's a lot like the Create Memorized Transaction dialog box, but it has additional options for scheduling transactions. Use it to enter information about the transaction:

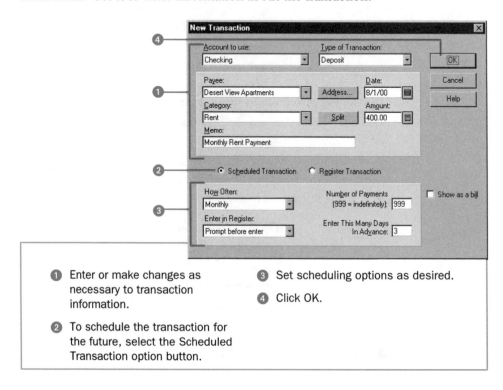

① Enter or make changes as necessary to transaction information.

② To schedule the transaction for the future, select the Scheduled Transaction option button.

③ Set scheduling options as desired.

④ Click OK.

When the Scheduled Transaction option button is selected, four scheduling options appear at the bottom of the dialog box:

- **How Often** enables you to specify how often the transaction should be recorded. Your options are Only Once (the default option), Weekly, Every Two Weeks, Twice A Month, Every Four Weeks, Monthly, Every Two Months, Quarterly, Twice A Year, and Yearly.

- **Number Of Payments** is available if you choose any How Often option except Only Once. Enter the number of payments you want to schedule. For example, if you are scheduling a transaction for monthly payments on a four-year car loan and four payments have already been made, you'd choose Monthly from the How Often drop-down list and enter 44 in the Number Of Payments text box. Entering 999 in this box tells Quicken to continue making payments indefinitely.

- **Record In Register** enables you to specify how you want the transaction recorded. Your options are Automatically Enter and Prompt Before Enter (the default option). If you choose Prompt Before Enter, Quicken reminds you that a transaction must be recorded by displaying a message in the My Finances window shortly before payment is due.

- **Record This Many Days In Advance** enables you to specify how many days before the transaction date the transaction should be entered. For example, you might want transactions for checks and other payments to be entered a week in advance so your account balance reflects these items before they're actually paid. This can prevent you from spending money that will be needed for future transactions.

Caution *Scheduling a transaction is not the same as recording it. You must record a transaction in order to have it appear in the appropriate register or print a check for it. Choosing the Automatically Enter option from the Record in Register drop-down list is a good way to ensure that a scheduled transaction is properly recorded.*

Working with the Scheduled Transaction List

The Scheduled Transaction List (see Figure 11-3) displays a list of all future transactions. To view and work with the list, choose Banking | Scheduled Transaction List, or press CTRL-J.

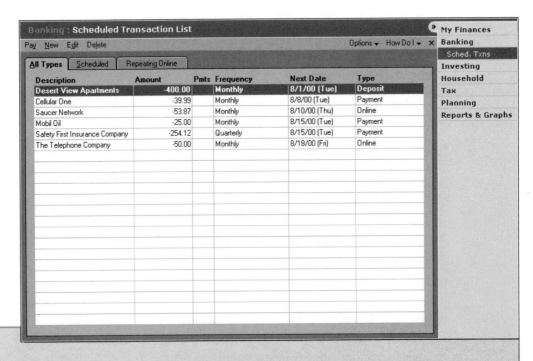

Figure 11-3 • You can use the Scheduled Transaction List to view and work with scheduled transactions

You can use button bar options to create, modify, delete, or enter scheduled transactions:

- **Pay** immediately enters the selected transaction into the appropriate register.
- **New** enables you to create a new scheduled transaction.
- **Edit** enables you to modify the selected transaction.
- **Delete** removes the scheduled transaction. It does not remove any transactions that have already been entered in a register.
- **Options** offers commands for changing the way the Scheduled Transaction List window is sorted.
- **How Do I** provides instructions for completing tasks with the Scheduled Transaction List window.

Tip *You can also use the Scheduled Transaction List window to view and work with repeating online payments, which I discuss in Chapter 5.*

Using Paycheck Setup

The Paycheck Setup feature (also known as the Paycheck wizard) offers yet another way to automate transactions. You use it to enter information about your regular payroll check and its deductions. Then, when payday comes along, Quicken automatically enters the payroll deposit information based on the Paycheck Setup transaction.

Tip *Although you can use Paycheck Setup to record payroll checks with varying amounts and deductions—such as a check with varying hourly wages or overtime pay—it can be a real time-saver if your paycheck is the same (or almost the same) every payday. If your paycheck does vary, be sure to include all possible deductions, even if their values are often zero. Then it'll be easy to just plug in different values when you need to.*

Start by choosing Banking | Banking Activities | Set Up My Paycheck As A Register Transaction. The Paycheck Setup dialog box appears. The first screen provides general information about Paycheck Setup and how it works. Click Next to begin.

Tip *If you have already set up a paycheck, following these instructions displays the Manage Paychecks window.*

The Paycheck Setup window uses the EasyStep approach to prompt you for information about your paycheck. When you're finished entering information, a summary of the paycheck information appears in a Summary tab like this one:

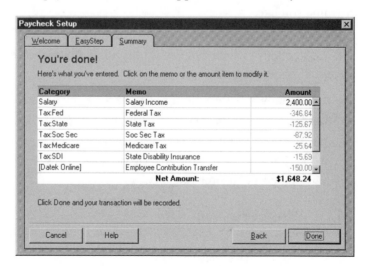

Here's a quick discussion of the kinds of information you'll be prompted to enter.

Parts of Paycheck to Track   You start by telling Quicken which parts of your paycheck you want to track. Turn on check boxes to indicate the kinds of information included on your paycheck. Later, you'll be prompted for information about each option you selected. Your options are:

- **401(k) Or Other Retirement Plan Contributions** are deductions from your gross pay for retirement plans.
- **Employee Stock Purchase Plan (ESPP)** is a deduction from your gross pay for a company stock purchase plan.
- **Deposits To Other Bank Accounts** occur when your paycheck's net amount is deposited to more than one bank account.
- **Payment To Loan From Employer** are payments deducted from your paycheck to pay back money borrowed from your employer, including advances on your pay.
- **Payment To Loan From 401(k)** is a deduction from your gross pay to pay back a loan on your 401(k) plan.
- **Flexible Spending Account** is a deduction from your gross pay for contributions to a Health Care Flexible Spending Account or Dependent Care Flexible Spending Account.

Paycheck Name and Frequency   Enter a name for the paycheck and specify how often you're paid. The paycheck name is simply an identifier—you can call it anything you like.

Recent Paycheck Information   Enter the date of your most recent paycheck and the account to which you usually deposit it. You'll then be prompted for three pieces of information:

- **Gross Amount** is the amount of pay before any deductions.
- **Net Amount** is the amount you actually deposit.
- **Category** is the Quicken category in which you want to record the source of paycheck funds. By default, the Salary category is selected, but you can choose any appropriate income category.

Other Sources of Income   Quicken prompts you to enter categories for any additional sources of income with corresponding amounts. This could include commissions, bonuses, tips, and advances.

Deductions   Enter the standard tax deductions taken from your gross pay. Quicken suggests common categories; enter amounts beside each category. Try not to get depressed when entering this information. When you advance to the next EasyStep window, you'll get a chance to enter even more tax deductions and their corresponding categories. Then you'll be prompted to enter information about other deductions you selected in the very first step of Paycheck Setup. The options that appear vary depending on the options you selected. Choose accounts and enter amounts as necessary. One final deduction screen gives you one more chance to enter deductions. (If you enter deductions everywhere Quicken offers to accept them, you probably won't be taking much home!)

Reminder Options   Quicken offers to remind you to enter paycheck information:

- Click Yes to have Quicken create a scheduled transaction with a split that includes all the deductions and other information you entered. This transaction appears in the Quicken Reminders window (see Figure 11-4 in the following section). Quicken reminds you to record this information on the date it is expected.

- Click No to enter the transaction just once. You might want to use this option if your paycheck varies greatly from one pay period to the next and you want to go through the Paycheck Setup process again each payday.

Alerts

Quicken's Alert feature monitors your Quicken data file and displays alerts based on the options you set. The alerts work with many different accounts and categories and can really help keep your financial situation under control.

The Quicken Alerts Window

The Quicken Alerts window (see Figure 11-4) lists all your alerts, as well as upcoming bills and scheduled transactions. To display this window, choose Finance | Alerts.

My Finances : Quicken Alerts					My Finances
			How Do I ▾ X		Alerts
					Banking
Alerts			Actions ▾		Investing
Date	Priority	Area	Message		Household
6/23/00	Medium	Investment	AMZN: Analyst: Thomas Weisel initiated coverage at Buy.		Tax
6/28/00	Medium	Investment	AMZN: Analyst: ABN AMRO initiated coverage at Buy.		Planning
7/13/00	Medium	Investment	WFC: Analyst: Lehman Brothers initiated coverage at Buy.		Reports & Graphs
7/17/00	Medium	Investment	ELNK: Price rose 9%.		
7/17/00	Medium	Investment	Investments: Export your portfolio to Quicken.com, so you can track it while you're away fr...		
7/17/00	Low	Investment	Online: Datek Online now offers online services		
7/17/00	Medium	Investment	PVSW: Price dropped -8%.		
7/18/00	Medium	Tax, General	Withholding: You may be under withholding your federal income tax.		

Bills and Scheduled Transactions					Actions ▾
Name	Status	Due Date	Amount	Account	Action
Bills					
Cellular One		8/8/00	-39.99	Business Checking	Enter Skip
Saucer Network		8/10/00	-53.87	Checking	(Auto) Skip
Mobil Oil		8/15/00	-25.00	Checking	Enter Skip
Deposits and Other Scheduled Transactions					
Desert View Apartments		8/1/00	-400.00	Checking	Enter Skip
ABC Company		8/1/00	1,648.24	Checking	Enter Skip
Safety First Insurance Company		8/15/00	-254.12	Checking	Enter Skip
The Telephone Company		8/18/00	-50.00	Checking	Enter Skip

Figure 11-4 • The Quicken Alerts window lists alerts and upcoming transactions

Tip   *What's great about Quicken alerts is that many of the alerts work automatically in the background, based on downloaded information. You can see an example in Figure 11-4, which includes investment information downloaded with the Quotes and Info feature I discuss in Chapter 7.*

Setting Alerts

To set up alerts, choose Finance | Setup Alerts. The Set Up Alerts dialog box appears. It includes five tabs for setting up alerts throughout Quicken. Here's what the Account Max Balances options on the Banking tab look like:

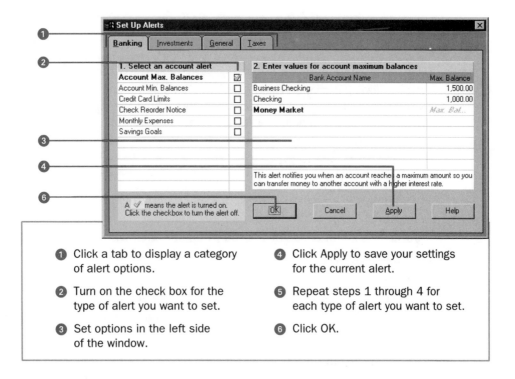

① Click a tab to display a category of alert options.

② Turn on the check box for the type of alert you want to set.

③ Set options in the left side of the window.

④ Click Apply to save your settings for the current alert.

⑤ Repeat steps 1 through 4 for each type of alert you want to set.

⑥ Click OK.

To set an alert, turn on its check box and enter options on the left side of the window. Click Apply to apply each alert after you set it; then click OK when you have finished setting alerts to save them.

Alert Options

The Set Up Alerts dialog box separates alerts into four major categories, each with its own collection of alerts. Here's an overview so you can explore them on your own.

Banking   The alerts in the Banking tab notify you about account balances, check reorder notices, monthly expenses, and savings goals. Use these alerts to keep account balances and spending under control and to prevent yourself from running out of checks.

SAVE MONEY If an account that does not earn interest has a higher balance than necessary, you can move that money into an interest-bearing account to earn money on it. Use the Account Max Balances alert so you know when it's time to move your money. Likewise, many banks waive a monthly fee if your account balance remains above a certain amount throughout the month. Use the Account Min Balances alert to help keep your balances above the minimum, thus avoiding or minimizing bank fees.

Investments   The alerts in the Investment tab can remind you to download quotes and export portfolio information. They can also provide additional alert information about the securities you own and watch when you download data from Quicken.com as discussed in Chapter 7.

General   The alerts in the General tab remind you to regularly download online transactions, check the status of insurance policies due to expire or be renewed, and make changes due to mortgages or loans for which interest rates will change.

Taxes   Alerts in the Taxes tab can keep track of your earnings and spending and alert you to situations that may impact your taxes. I tell you more about Quicken's tax options in Chapter 14.

Address Book

Quicken's Address Book feature automatically stores the address information you enter when using the Write Checks window. You can also use this feature to modify or delete existing information or add new entries.

Quicken's address book can handle most contact management needs—even those that have nothing to do with your personal finances. You can even use it to keep track of friends and family members and build holiday card lists.

Tip   *Keeping track of addresses with the Address Book makes it easy to insert addresses when writing checks and to look up contact information when you need to follow up on transactions.*

Displaying the Address Book Window

Choose Finance | Address Book to display the Address Book window (see Figure 11-5). It lists all the entries in the address book and offers button bar options to work with its contents:

- **New** enables you to create a new Address Book entry.
- **Edit** enables you to edit the selected entry.
- **Delete** removes the address book entry. It does not affect transactions in which the entry was used.
- **Modify** offers several commands for modifying the selected entry or selecting multiple entries.
- **Sort** enables you to change the order of entries in the window.
- **Print** offers commands for printing Address Book entry information.
- **How Do I** provides instructions for working with the Address Book window.

Use the Group drop-down list to view entries by group.

Use the Column Sets drop-down list to determine which columns appear in the window.

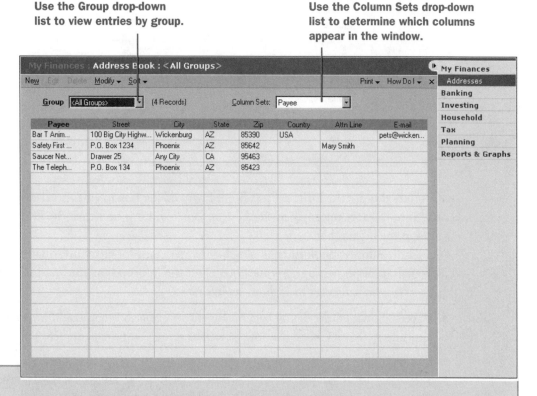

Figure 11-5 • Use the Address Book to keep track of the organizations and individuals you do business with

Adding or Modifying Address Book Entries

To add a new Address Book entry, click the New button on the button bar of the Address Book window (see Figure 11-5). The Edit Address Book Entry dialog box appears:

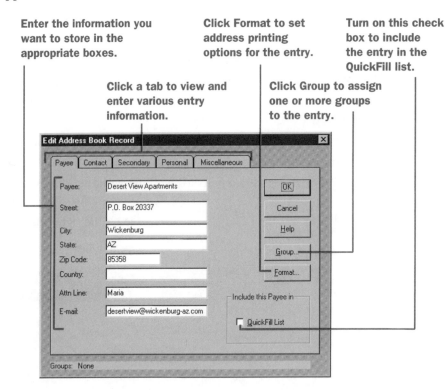

Enter the information you want to store in the appropriate boxes.

Click Format to set address printing options for the entry.

Turn on this check box to include the entry in the QuickFill list.

Click a tab to view and enter various entry information.

Click Group to assign one or more groups to the entry.

You can also use the Edit Address Book Entry dialog box to edit an existing entry. Simply select the entry in the Address Book window and click the Edit button in the button bar.

The Edit Address Book Entry dialog box has five tabs for entry information. Click a tab to display its options and then enter the information you want to store. Here's what you can enter in each of the five tabs:

- **Payee** (shown on the facing page) is for the information that would normally appear in a Write Check window, as well as some additional contact information.

- **Contact** is for the name, title, phone numbers, and Web site of a specific person.

- **Secondary** is for a secondary mailing address and e-mail address.

- **Personal** is for personal information, such as spouse and children's names, birthday and anniversary, and still more phone numbers.
- **Miscellaneous** is for additional information, such as user-defined fields and notes.

Printing Entry Information

You can print the information in the list in two formats: list and label. List prints information in list format; label prints mailing labels.

Start by clicking an entry to select it or using the Group drop-down list at the top of the window to display the entries that you want to print. Then choose one of the options on the Print menu on the button bar.

List Choosing List displays a Print dialog box just like the one that appears when printing Quicken reports. Use it to enter printing options and then click OK to print the list. Consult Chapter 13 for more information about printing lists and reports.

Label Choosing Label displays the Print Labels dialog box. It includes a list of commonly used Avery label products; be sure to select the right one before you click the Print button to print.

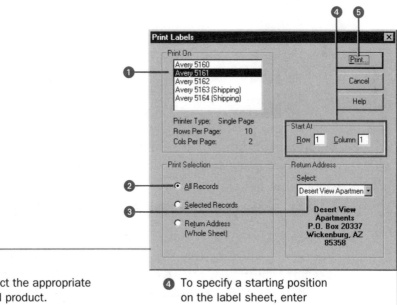

1. Select the appropriate label product.

2. Select a Print option.

3. If you select Return Address, choose an address.

4. To specify a starting position on the label sheet, enter values here.

5. Click Print.

Tip   *You can print a sheet of return address labels. Simply choose an address from the drop-down list in the Return Address area and select the Return Address (Whole Sheet) option in the Print Selection area. Then click Print.*

Envelope   Choosing Envelope displays the Print Envelope dialog box, which is shown next. Use it to print #10 envelopes for address book records. Just set options in the dialog box, put envelope stock into your printer, and click the Print button.

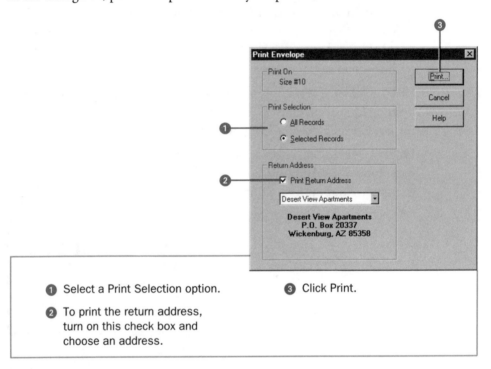

❶ Select a Print Selection option.

❷ To print the return address, turn on this check box and choose an address.

❸ Click Print.

One Step Update and the PIN Vault

As discussed in Chapters 5 and 7, the bank account sync, portfolio export, and WebEntry features use One Step Update to update information on the Web and download transactions entered on the Web. But that's not all One Step Update can do. This Quicken Deluxe feature makes it possible to handle many of your connection chores at once. When used in conjunction with the PIN Vault feature, you can click a few buttons, enter a single password, and take a break while Quicken updates portfolio and account information for you.

Using One Step Update

The idea behind One Step Update is to use one command to handle multiple online activities. This eliminates the need to use update commands in a variety of locations throughout Quicken. One command and dialog box does it all.

Setting Up the Update

Choose Finance | One Step Update or click the Online button in the toolbar. The One Step Update Download Selection dialog box (shown next) appears. It lists all the items that can be updated. Red check marks appear to the left of each item that will be updated when you connect. You can click in that first column to toggle the check marks there:

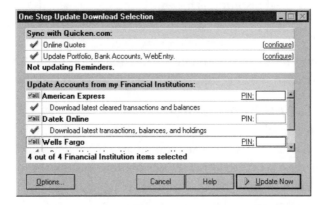

The dialog box is split into two areas:

Sync with Quicken.com   This section lists activities for synchronizing your Quicken data with Quicken.com, including:

- **Online Quotes** downloads security prices and news headlines from Quicken.com and stores them in your Quicken data file. This option, which I discuss in Chapter 7, can be customized by clicking the Options button and then setting options in the Quotes tab of the Customize Quicken Download dialog box that appears.
- **Update Portfolio Export**, which I discuss in Chapter 7, copies information from the portfolio in your Quicken data file to the Web so you can view it on Quicken.com. This option can be customized by clicking the Options button and then setting options in the Investment Accounts tab of the Customize Quicken Download dialog box.

- **WebEntry**, which I discuss in Chapter 5, downloads transactions you enter on Quicken.com to your Quicken data file. This option can be customized by clicking the Options button and then setting options in the Misc tab of the Customize Quicken Downloads dialog box.

- **Reminders** copies the upcoming transactions in the Quicken Alerts window (discussed earlier in this chapter) to the Web so you can view them on Quicken.com. This option can also be customized by clicking the Options button and then setting options in the Misc tab of the Customize Quicken Downloads dialog box.

Update Accounts from my Financial Institutions   This section lists each of the financial institutions for which you have enabled online account access, online payment, or online investment tracking. I discuss these features in Chapters 5 and 7. Because a PIN is required to access each of your financial institutions, a PIN box appears for each one. You must enter the appropriate PIN in each box to download transactions and update account balances in this area.

Updating Information

Make sure check marks appear beside the items you want to update in the One Step Update Download Selection dialog box. If necessary, enter PINs in the text boxes beside financial institutions for which you want to update data. Then click Update Now.

Quicken establishes a connection to the Internet and begins transferring data. A Quicken Download Status dialog box appears as it works:

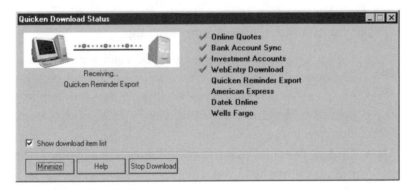

When the update is complete, the Quicken Download Summary dialog box appears. It summarizes the activity for the update:

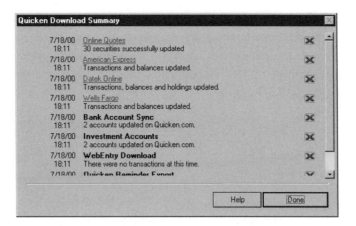

Tip   *You can display the Quicken Download Summary dialog box for the last update by choosing Finance | Download Summary.*

The PIN Vault

You might find it a nuisance to have to type in each PIN when you use the One Step Update feature. This is when the PIN Vault can help.

Quicken's PIN Vault feature enables you to store all your Quicken PINs in one central location. The PINs are then protected with a single password. When you use One Step Update, you enter just one password to access all financial institutions.

Tip   *You must have Online Account Access or Online Payment set up with two or more institutions to use the PIN Vault feature.*

Setting Up the PIN Vault

Choose File | PIN Vault | Setup. The PIN Vault Setup window appears. It provides some introductory information. Click next to display the first window of the EasyStep tab.

Follow the instructions in each EasyStep tab to choose financial institutions and enter corresponding PINs. You'll enter each PIN twice because the characters you type do not appear onscreen; this is a secure way of making sure you enter the same thing both times. You can do this for any combination of financial institutions for which you have set up online access.

When you've finished, select the No option when asked whether you want to enter additional PINs. A dialog box appears; use it to enter a master password to protect the PIN vault:

When you click Next, the Summary tab of the PIN Vault Setup window appears. It displays a list of your financial institutions and indicates whether a PIN has been stored for each one:

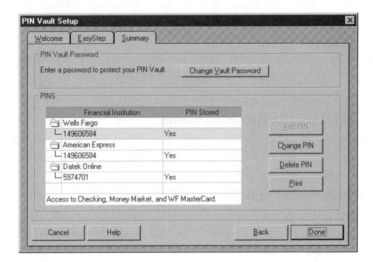

You can use buttons in this dialog box to change or delete a selected PIN, print all PINs, or change the Vault password. When you've finished working with the window's contents, click Done. Quicken creates the PIN Vault.

Using the PIN Vault

Using the PIN Vault is easy. Simply choose Finance | One Step Update or click the Online button in the toolbar. The PIN Vault Password dialog box, which is shown next, appears. Enter your password and click OK. Then continue using One Step Update in the usual way with one difference: You don't have to enter PINs for any of the financial institutions for which a PIN has been entered in the PIN Vault.

Tip   *You can also use the PIN Vault in conjunction with the Update/Send button in the Online Center window. Open that window and then click the PIN Vault button on the button bar. The PIN Vault Password dialog box appears for any financial institution you want to update.*

Editing the PIN Vault

Once you've created a PIN Vault, you can modify it to change PINs or add PINs for other financial institutions. Choose File | PIN Vault | Edit. In the PIN Vault Password dialog box that appears, enter the password that protects the PIN Vault and click OK.

The Modify PIN Vault dialog box appears. It looks and works much like the Summary tab of the PIN Vault Setup dialog box. Use it to make changes to the PIN Vault as desired. When you've finished, click Done.

Deleting the PIN Vault

You can delete the PIN Vault if you decide you no longer want to use the PIN Vault feature. Choose File | PIN Vault | Delete. Then click Yes in the confirmation dialog box that appears. Quicken deletes the PIN Vault. From then on, you'll have to enter PINs for each financial institution when you use One Step Update.

Reconciling Accounts

In This Chapter:

Chapter 12

One of the least pleasant tasks of manually maintaining a bank account is balancing or reconciling it monthly. If you're good about it, you faithfully turn over your bank statement each month and use the form your bank provides to balance the account. There's a lot of adding when it comes to totaling the outstanding checks and deposits, and the longer you wait to do the job, the more adding there is. And for some reason, it hardly ever comes out right the first time you try. Maybe you've even failed so many times that you've given up. I know someone who opens a new checking account once a year just so she can start fresh after 12 months of not being able to balance her account. That's *not* something I recommend.

In this chapter, I explain why you should reconcile your bank statements and how you can do it—quickly and easily—with Quicken.

The Importance of Reconciling Accounts

Reconciling your checking account is very important. It enables you to locate differences between what you think you have in the account and what the bank says you have. It can help you track down bank errors (which do happen once in a while) or personal errors (which, unfortunately, seem to happen more frequently). Completely balancing your checking account and making adjustments as necessary can prevent you from accidentally bouncing checks when you think you have more money than you really do. That can save you the cost of bank fees and a lot of embarrassment.

If you keep track of all bank account activity with Quicken, reconciling your bank accounts is easy. You don't need to use the form on the back of the bank statement. You don't even need a calculator. Just use Quicken's reconciliation feature to enter beginning and ending bank balances, check off cleared transactions, and enter the transactions you missed. You'll find you're successful a lot more often with Quicken helping you out.

Tip   *You can use Quicken's reconciliation feature to balance any Quicken banking account—including credit card accounts. Although this chapter concentrates on checking accounts, I provide additional information for reconciling credit card accounts, too.*

Reconciliation Basics

Reconciling an account refers to the process of comparing transactions in your account register to transactions on the account statement sent to you by your bank. Transactions that match are simply checked off. Transactions that appear only in one place—your account register or the bank's account statement—need to be accounted for.

In this section, I cover the basics of reconciling an account with Quicken: comparing transactions, making adjustments, and finishing up.

Getting Started

To reconcile a bank account, you must have the statement for the account. Bank statements usually come monthly, so you won't have to wait long.

With statement in hand, open the account register for the account you want to reconcile. Then click the Reconcile button on the button bar. What happens next depends on whether the account is enabled for online access.

Accounts without Online Account Access

If the account is not enabled for online access, the Reconcile Bank Statement dialog box appears. It gathers basic statement information prior to reconciling the account. Enter balance, service charge, and interest earned information in the appropriate boxes and click OK to continue:

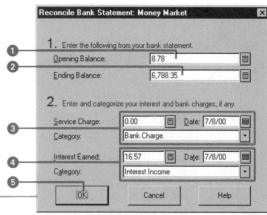

❶ Check the opening balance to make sure it matches the opening balance on your statement. If it doesn't, make changes as necessary.

❷ Enter the ending balance from your statement.

❸ If the bank charges a fee, enter the amount, date, and category for the charge.

❹ If the account earned interest, enter the amount, date, and category for the interest.

❺ Click OK.

Accounts with Online Account Access

If the account is enabled for online account access, Quicken may begin by displaying a dialog box that reminds you to download recent transactions or compare downloaded transactions to transactions in your register. If so, be sure to do this; it's the only way you can be sure that all transactions recorded by the bank are included in your account register.

 Quicken displays the Reconcile Online Account dialog box, which is new in Quicken 2001:

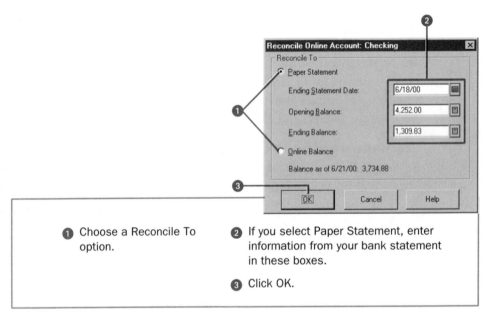

1. Choose a Reconcile To option.

2. If you select Paper Statement, enter information from your bank statement in these boxes.

3. Click OK.

As you can see, this dialog box offers two options for reconciling the account:

- **Paper Statement** enables you to reconcile the information in your Quicken account register to your bank statement. It is a traditional account reconciliation, and it works just like the account reconciliation you perform for an account without online account access. If you select this option, you must enter the bank statement ending date and ending balance in the appropriate boxes before clicking OK to continue.

- **Online Balance** enables you to reconcile the account to the balance that was last downloaded for the account. If you select this option, you don't have to enter anything in the boxes. Just click OK to continue.

Tip *I recommend reconciling to your paper bank statement whenever possible. This prevents errors or confusion that could occur in the unlikely event of an error or omission in the downloaded data.*

Comparing Transactions

The next step in reconciling the account is to compare transactions that have cleared on the statement with transactions in your account register. For this, Quicken displays the Reconcile Bank Statement window (shown in Figure 12-1), which displays all payments, checks, and deposits.

Click to place a check mark in the Clr column beside each item that appears on your bank statement.

Click Finished to complete the reconciliation, or click Finish Later to save your changes without completing the reconciliation.

When the difference is 0.00, you have successfully balanced your account.

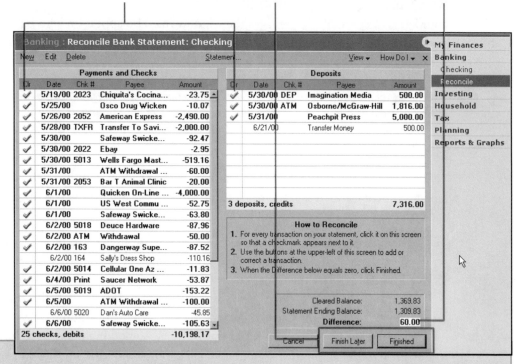

Figure 12-1 • Use the Reconcile Bank Statement window to compare your register transactions to your bank statement transactions

You can use button bar buttons within this window to work with its contents:

- **New** switches you to the account register window for the account you are reconciling so you can enter a new transaction.
- **Edit** switches you to the selected transaction in its account register window so you can modify it.
- **Delete** removes the selected transaction from the account register.
- **Statement** displays the Reconcile Bank Statement dialog box shown earlier or the Reconcile Paper Statement dialog box (which is similar to the top half of the Reconcile Online Account dialog box shown earlier) so you can check or change entries there.
- **View** offers options to change the sort order of the window's contents.
- **How Do I** provides instructions for completing specific tasks with the window.

Reconciling to a Bank Statement

Your job is to check off the items in the window that also appear on your bank statement. While you're checking off items, be sure to check off the same items with a pen or pencil on your bank statement.

Tip *If the account is enabled for online account access and you have been downloading and comparing transactions regularly to accept them into your account register, many of the transactions in the Reconcile Bank Statement window may already be checked off.*

While you're checking off transactions in Quicken and on your bank statement, look for differences between them. Here are some of the differences you might encounter:

- An item that appears on the bank statement but not in your account register is an item that you did not enter. There are a number of reasons why you may have omitted the transaction. Perhaps it was a bank adjustment that you were not informed about. Or maybe you simply forgot. In Figure 12-1, the $60 difference between the Cleared Balance and the Statement Ending Balance is due to the failure to enter an ATM transaction—something many of us forget to do! To enter an omitted transaction, click the New button on the button bar to switch to the register window. Enter the transaction in the register, shown next, and click the Return to Reconcile button to continue the reconciliation. Then click to place a check mark in the Clr column beside the item to mark it cleared.

- An item that appears on both your account register and bank statement but has a different amount or date could be due to an error—yours or the bank's. If the error is yours, you can edit the transaction by double-clicking it in the Reconcile Bank Statement window. This displays the account register window with the transaction selected. Edit the transaction and click ENTER. Then click the Return To Reconcile button to continue the reconciliation.

- Items that appear in your account register but not on the bank statement are items that have not cleared the bank yet. These are usually transactions prepared just before the bank's closing date, but they can be older. Do not check them off. Chances are, you'll check them off the next time you complete a reconciliation.

Tip   *If, during a bank reconciliation, you discover any uncleared items that are older than two or three months, you should investigate why they have not cleared the bank. You may discover that a check (or worse yet, a deposit) was lost in transit.*

Reconciling to an Online Balance

If you've recently downloaded and accepted transactions for the account, reconciling to an online balance shouldn't take much effort. Items you've already reviewed and accepted will be checked off. Some more recent transactions may not be checked off because they haven't cleared your bank yet. Your job is to look for older transactions that appear in your Quicken account register that aren't checked off. These could represent stale payments that may have been lost in transit to the payee or errors (or duplications) you made when manually entering information into your Quicken account register. Follow up on all transactions over 60 days old to see why they haven't been included with your downloaded transactions.

Finishing Up

When you reconcile a bank account with Quicken, your goal is to make the difference between the Cleared Balance and the Statement Ending Balance zero. You can monitor this progress at the bottom of the Reconcile Bank Statement window, as shown in Figure 12-1.

When the Difference Is Zero...

If you correctly checked off all bank statement items and the difference is zero, you've successfully reconciled the account. Congratulations. Click the Finish button.

If You Can't Get the Difference to Zero...

Sometimes, try as you might, you just can't get the difference to zero. Here are a few last things to check before you give up:

- Make sure all the amounts you checked off in your account register are the same as the amounts on the bank statement.
- Make sure you included any bank charges or earned interest.
- Make sure the beginning and ending balances you entered are the same as those on the bank statement.

If you checked and rechecked all these things and still can't get the difference to zero, click Finished. Quicken displays a dialog box that indicates the amount of the difference and offers to make an adjustment to your account register for the amount. Click Adjust to accept the adjustment. The amount of the adjustment will be recorded without a category:

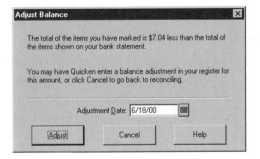

But next month, don't give up!

Other Reconciliation Tasks and Features

Quicken offers a number of other reconciliation features that you might find useful. Here's a quick look at them.

Reconciling Credit Card Accounts

You can reconcile a credit card account the same way you reconcile a bank account. If you try to enter all credit card transactions as you make them throughout the month, it's a good idea to use the reconciliation feature to compare your entries to the credit card statement, just to make sure you didn't miss any. If you simply enter all credit card transactions when you get your statement, reconciling to the statement really isn't necessary.

When you begin the reconciliation process, Quicken displays either the Credit Card Statement Information dialog box or the Reconcile Online Account dialog box, depending on whether the credit card account has online account access features enabled. Both of these dialog boxes are shown next; they're very similar to the ones that appear when you reconcile a bank account.

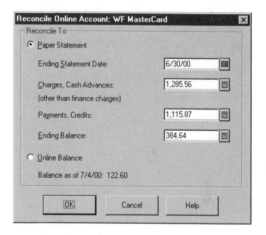

Enter information in the appropriate text boxes and click OK to move on to the Reconcile Credit Statement, which looks and works almost exactly like the Reconcile Bank Statement window that is shown in Figure 12-1.

At the conclusion of a credit card reconciliation, Quicken may display the Make Credit Card Payment dialog box (shown next), offering to prepare a credit card payment for you. This is particularly handy if you like to pay your credit card bill after reconciling your statement to your entries. Select an account and payment method and click OK. Quicken prepares the transaction for you.

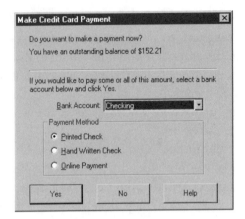

Printing a Reconciliation Report

At the end of a reconciliation, Quicken displays a dialog box that offers to create a reconciliation report. If you click Yes, the Reconciliation Report Setup dialog box appears; set report options in the dialog box and click Print to print the report:

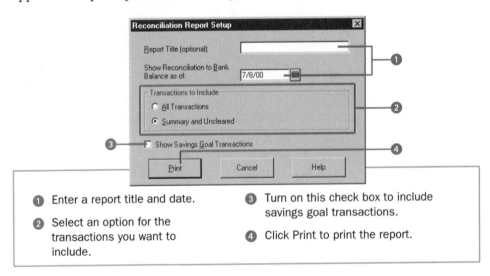

❶ Enter a report title and date.

❷ Select an option for the transactions you want to include.

❸ Turn on this check box to include savings goal transactions.

❹ Click Print to print the report.

Tip *I don't usually create one of these reports. I have enough paper filed away! But if your reconciliation required an adjusting entry, it might be a good idea to document it by printing a reconciliation report. You can then file the report with your bank statement and canceled checks.*

Identifying Reconciled Items

As shown in the next illustration, Quicken uses the Clr column in an account register to identify items that either have cleared the bank or have been reconciled:

- **c** indicates that the item has cleared the bank. You'll see a **c** in the Clr column beside items that you have checked off during a reconciliation if you have not completed the reconciliation. You'll also see a **c** beside items downloaded and accepted using Quicken's online banking feature, which I discuss in Chapter 5.
- **R** indicates that the item has been reconciled.

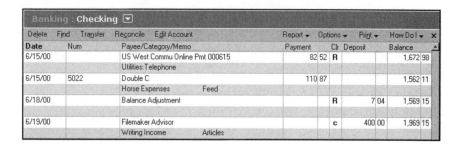

Caution   *To prevent errors in your account registers, do not edit transactions that have been reconciled.*

Creating Reports and Graphs

In This Chapter:

- *Types of Reports and Graphs*

- *Creating Reports and Graphs*

- *Customizing and Memorizing Reports and Graphs*

- *Printing Reports and Graphs*

At this point, you'll probably agree that entering financial information into Quicken is a great way to organize it. But sometimes organizing information isn't enough. Sometimes you need to see concise summaries of the information you entered, in the form of balances, activity reports, and graphs.

Quicken's highly customizable reports and graphs enable you to view and analyze your financial information. As you'll see in this chapter, they quickly and easily provide the information you need about your accounts and categories.

Quicken Reporting Overview

Quicken offers a variety of reports and graphs, each of which can be customized to meet your needs. I like to think of reports and graphs as the "fruits of my labor." I spend time entering data into Quicken so Quicken can crunch the numbers and generate the reports and graphs that I can use to analyze my spending habits, find ways to save money, and submit to financial institutions when I apply for loans.

Here's a real-life example. Last year, I applied by phone for a home equity line of credit. The bank representative asked a lot of questions about my finances, including balances on my accounts and the market value of my investments. Because I track all my finances in Quicken, all the information I needed was right in front of me, in Quicken windows and reports that I could generate within seconds. The application process took less than 15 minutes, and I got preliminary approval right away.

In this section, I tell you about the types of reports and graphs Quicken offers. Then I explain how you can use a variety of techniques to quickly create reports and graphs based on the information in your Quicken data file.

Types of Reports and Graphs

Within Quicken are essentially three kinds of reports and graphs: Easy Answer, predefined, and customized. Here's an overview of each one.

Easy Answer

Easy Answer reports and graphs answer specific, predefined questions such as:

- Where did I spend my money during the period…?
- How much did I spend on…?
- How much did I pay to…?
- Am I saving more or less?

You select a question and then provide optional information such as a date range, payee, or account. Quicken gathers the information and generates the report or graph.

Predefined

Quicken includes a number of predefined reports and graphs that are organized by topic. Each topic provides reports or graphs that answer a specific question:

- **Own & Owe** tells you what you own and owe.
- **Spending** tells you how you are spending your money.
- **Investing** tells you how your investments are doing.
- **Taxes** provides information on your tax situation.
- **Business** shows you how your business is doing.

For example, the Own & Owe topic includes the Net Worth Report, Net Worth Graph, and Account Balances Report. These reports and graphs clearly show what you own and what you owe.

Custom

You can create custom reports and graphs by customizing the predefined reports and graphs. This multiplies your reporting capabilities, enabling you to create reports or graphs that show exactly what you need to show. You can even use the memorize feature to store information about a custom report or graph so you can produce it again with just a few clicks of your mouse.

Creating Reports and Graphs

With Quicken, creating a report or graph is as simple as clicking a few buttons. There are several techniques: choosing a report or graph from the Reports menu, setting options in the Reports and Graphs Center window, using the Report button or menu on button bars, and choosing commands from contextual menus. In this section, I explain how to use all of these techniques.

The Reports Menu

Quicken's Reports menu includes a number of submenus, each of which corresponds to a report category. To create a report or graph with the Reports menu, click a category submenu, then click the name of the report or graph you want to create:

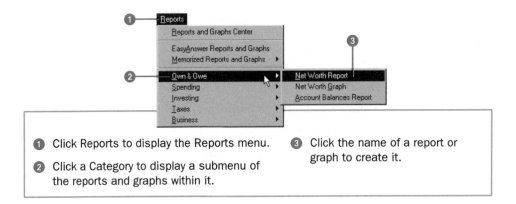

1. Click Reports to display the Reports menu.

2. Click a Category to display a submenu of the reports and graphs within it.

3. Click the name of a report or graph to create it.

Reports and Graphs Center Window

The Reports and Graphs Center window (see Figure 13-1) offers another way to create reports and graphs. Click one of the Report & Graph Topics on the left side of the window to display a list of the available reports.

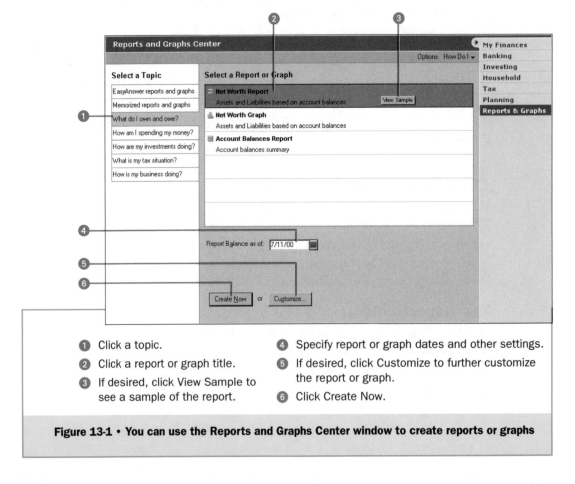

1. Click a topic.

2. Click a report or graph title.

3. If desired, click View Sample to see a sample of the report.

4. Specify report or graph dates and other settings.

5. If desired, click Customize to further customize the report or graph.

6. Click Create Now.

Figure 13-1 • You can use the Reports and Graphs Center window to create reports or graphs

To create a report or graph, click its name and then enter options in the settings area at the bottom of the window. Click Create Now to display the report or graph. Figures 13-2 and 13-3 show examples.

Tip　*Double-clicking on a number in some reports produces a QuickZoom report showing the detail for that number.*

Report Button

You can also create a report by using the Report button or menu on the button bar in some windows. This normally creates a report based on information selected within the window.

In a window that includes a Report button on the button bar, select one of the items in the window. Then click the Report button. A report appears in its own window. For example, you could create a Category Report by selecting a category in the Category & Transfer List window and then clicking the Report button.

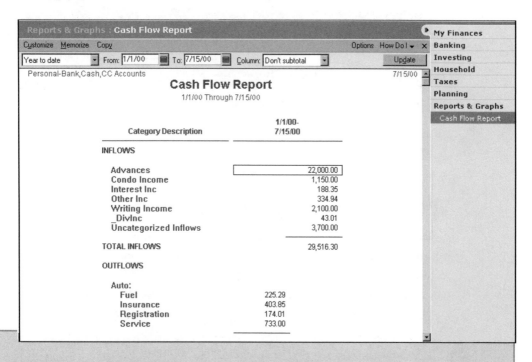

Figure 13-2 • A Cash Flow Report for year-to-date activity

Contextual Menus

The contextual menu that appears when you click the right mouse button while pointing to an item sometimes includes a command that will create a report for the item. For example, right-clicking the name of a payee in the account register window displays a menu that includes the Payments Made To command. Choosing this command creates a report that lists all payments made to that payee:

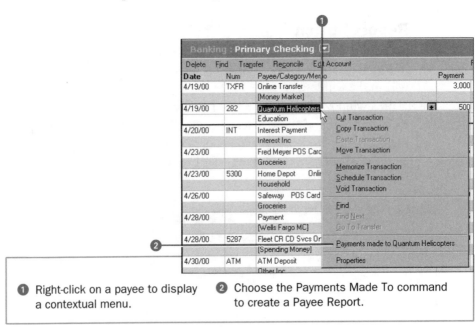

  ❶ Right-click on a payee to display   ❷ Choose the Payments Made To command
      a contextual menu.   to create a Payee Report.

Working with Reports and Graphs

Although Quicken's predefined reports and graphs can often provide just the information you need onscreen, you may want to do more with them. In this section, I explain how you can customize reports and graphs, memorize the reports and graphs you create so they're easy to recreate, and print reports and graphs so you have hard copies for your files or other purposes.

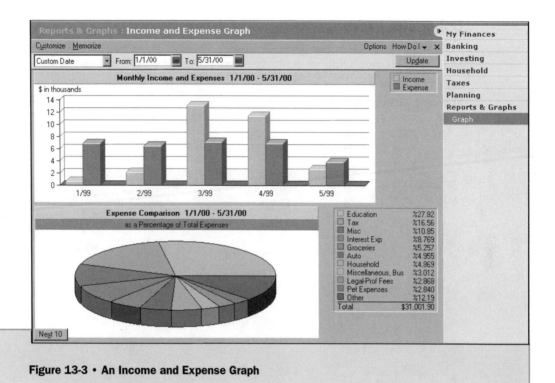

Figure 13-3 • An Income and Expense Graph

Customizing Reports and Graphs

You can customize just about any report or graph you create so it shows only the information you want to display. When you can customize it, however, depends on how you create it:

- When you create a report or graph using the Reports and Graphs Center window, you can customize it before or after you create it.

- When you create a report using commands under the Reports menu, the Report button in the button bar, or a command on a contextual menu, you can only customize it after you create it.

Customization options vary from one type of report or graph to another. It's impossible to cover all variables in this chapter. I will, however, tell you about the most common options so you know what to expect. I'm sure you'll agree that Quicken's reporting feature is very flexible when you go beyond the basics.

Using the Customize Report Dialog Box

To customize a report, click the Customize button at the bottom of the Reports and Graphs Center window or the Customize button on the button bar in the report window. The Customize Report dialog box appears. Here's what it looks like for a Cash Flow report:

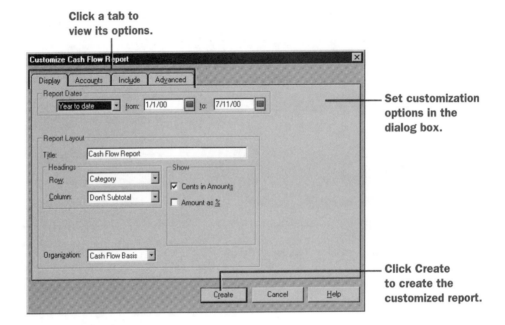

Click a tab to view its options.

Set customization options in the dialog box.

Click Create to create the customized report.

The Customize Report dialog box normally includes four tabs of options that you can set to customize the report:

- **Display** (shown in the previous illustration) enables you to set display options for the report, such as the title, row and column headings, organization, number formatting, and columns.
- **Accounts** enables you to select the accounts that should be included in the report.
- **Include** enables you to select the categories, classes, or category groups to include in the report. If desired, you can use this tab to include only transactions for which the payee, category, class, or memo contains certain text. If you use Quicken's Class feature, this tab makes it possible to generate reports by class.
- **Advanced** enables you to set additional criteria for transactions to be included in the report, such as amount, status, and transaction type.

On each tab, you also have access to the Report Dates area, which you can use to specify a date or range of dates for the report.

Once you have set options as desired, click the Create button. Quicken creates the report to your specifications. If it isn't exactly what you want, that's okay. Just click the Customize button in the button bar again and change settings in the dialog box to fine-tune the report. You can repeat this process until the report is exactly the way you want it.

Using the Customize Graph Dialog Box

To customize a graph, click the Customize button in the Create Graph dialog box. The Customize Graph dialog box appears. Here's what it looks like for an Income and Expense Graph:

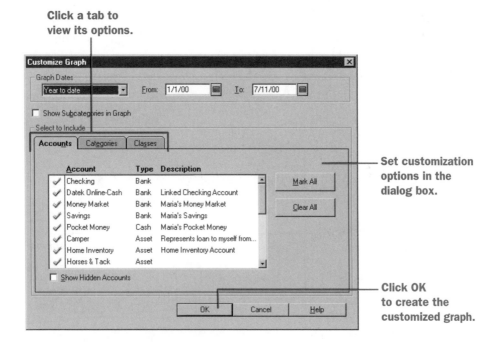

Set the date in the Graph Dates area at the top of the dialog box. Then set options in each of the dialog box's three tabs:

- **Accounts** (shown in the previous illustration) enables you to select the accounts that should be included in the graph.
- **Categories** enables you to select the categories that should be included in the graph.
- **Classes** enables you to select the classes that should be included in the graph.

When you've finished setting options, click the OK button. Quicken creates the graph to your specifications. If it isn't exactly what you want, click the Customize button in the graph window and change settings in the dialog box to fine-tune the graph. You can repeat this process until the graph is the way you want it.

Using the Customize Bar

The Customize bar beneath the button bar in a report window (see Figure 13-2) or graph window (see Figure 13-3) offers another way to customize a report or graph. Use it to change date ranges or modify subtotal settings for the report. When you make a change in the Customize bar, be sure to click the Update button to update the report or graph to reflect your change.

Dragging Column Borders

You can change the width of columns on some reports by dragging the column markers. Column markers, when available, look like gray diamonds with vertical lines above and below them. Move the mouse pointer onto a column marker and a vertical line with two arrows appears, shown next. Press the mouse button and drag to the right or left. When you release the mouse button, the column's width changes:

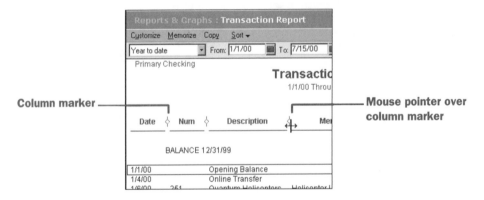

Column marker

Mouse pointer over column marker

Setting Report and Graph Options

The Options button on the button bar of a report or graph window displays the Report and Graph Options dialog box, which enables you to set default options for creating reports and graphs:

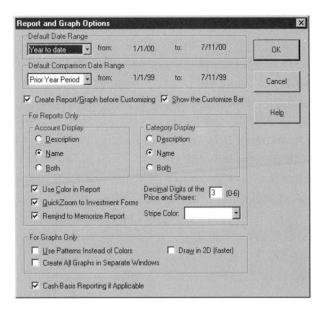

- **Default Report Date Range** and **Default Comparison Date Range** enable you to specify a default range for regular and comparison reports. Choose an option from the drop-down list. If you choose Custom, you can enter exact dates.

- **Create Report/Graph Before Customizing** tells Quicken to create the report or graph immediately when you choose its name from a submenu under the Reports menu. This skips the Reports and Graphs Center window.

- **Show The Customize Bar** tells Quicken to display the Customize bar in the report or graph window, right beneath the button bar.

- **Account Display** and **Category Display** enable you to set what you want to display for each account or category listed in the report: description, name, or both.

- **Use Color In Report** tells Quicken to use color when displaying report titles and negative numbers.

- **QuickZoom To Investment Forms** tells Quicken to display the investment form for a specific investment when you double-click it in an investment report. With this check box turned off, Quicken displays the investment register transaction entry instead.

- **Remind To Memorize Report** tells Quicken to ask if you want to memorize a customized report when you close the report window. I tell you about memorizing reports and graphs a little later in this chapter.
- **Decimal Digits Of The Price And Shares** enables you to specify the number of decimal places to display for per share security prices and number of shares in investment reports.
- **Use Patterns Instead Of Colors** tells Quicken to fill graph bars or pie slices with patterns rather than colors. You might find this feature useful if you have a black-and-white printer.
- **Create All Graphs In Separate Windows** tells Quicken to create each part of a graph in a separate window. For example, the graph in Figure 13-3 is really two graphs; with this check box turned on, each graph appears in a separate window.
- **Draw In 2D (Faster)** tells Quicken to draw two-dimensional graphs rather than three-dimensional graphs. This can speed up the creation of graphs, especially on slower computers.

- **Cash-Basis Reporting If Applicable** tells Quicken to create reports based on actual cash payments rather than accrued income and expenses.

Set options as desired and click OK. Your settings are saved for use with all the reports you create.

Memorizing Reports and Graphs

You'll often create a predefined report and customize it to create a report you want to be able to see again and again. Rather than creating and customizing the report from scratch each time you want to see it, you can memorize its settings. Then, when you want to view the report again, just select it from a list, and it appears. You can do the same for graphs.

Memorizing a Report

To memorize a report, start by creating and customizing a report. When it looks just the way you want it, click the Memorize button on the button bar. The Memorize Report dialog box shown next appears. Enter a name for the report in the Title text box. Then select one of the three Report Dates options and click OK.

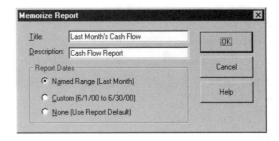

- **Named Range** applies the named range currently in use in the report. Named date ranges, such as Year to Date, Last Quarter, or Last Year, use dates relative to the current date. When you use this option, the dates change as necessary each time you create the report.
- **Custom** applies the exact dates currently in use in the report. When you use this option, the dates are always exactly the same when you display the report.
- **None** instructs Quicken to use the Default Report Date setting in the Report Options dialog box, which I tell you about earlier in this chapter.

Memorizing a Graph

Memorizing a graph works almost the same way as memorizing a report. There are just less options to set. Create and customize a graph. When it looks just the way you want it to, click the Memorize button in the button bar. The Memorize Graph dialog box appears, which is shown next, appears. Enter a name for the graph in the Graph Name text box and click OK.

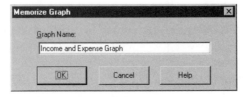

Viewing a Memorized Report or Graph

When you memorize a report or graph, it appears in the Memorized Reports and Graphs topic in the Reports and Graphs Center window (see Figure 13-4). Click the name of the report or graph to display it.

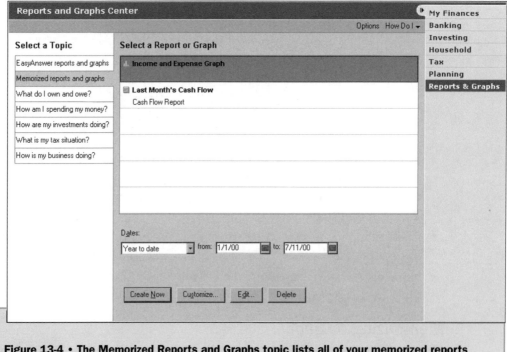

Figure 13-4 • The Memorized Reports and Graphs topic lists all of your memorized reports and graphs

Printing Reports and Graphs

You can print reports and graphs. This enables you to create hard copies for your paper files or for use when applying for loans or completing your tax returns.

Tip   *When I applied for my mortgage, I was able to create and print all kinds of useful reports to include with my mortgage application forms. I don't know if it helped me get the mortgage, but it saved the time I would have spent manually duplicating needed information.*

Printing a Report

To print a report, choose File | Print Report, or press CTRL-P. The Print dialog box appears:

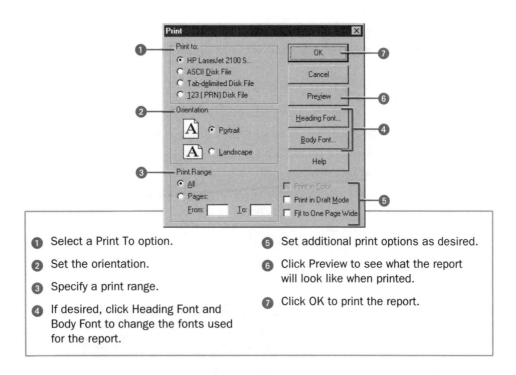

1. Select a Print To option.

2. Set the orientation.

3. Specify a print range.

4. If desired, click Heading Font and Body Font to change the fonts used for the report.

5. Set additional print options as desired.

6. Click Preview to see what the report will look like when printed.

7. Click OK to print the report.

Begin by selecting a Print To option. You have four choices:

- **[Your Printer]** (the first option) prints to your printer. The wording of this option varies depending on the name of your default printer. This is the option you'll probably select most often.
- **ASCII Disk File** enables you to create a text file that includes all the information in the report. You can import the resulting file into a word processing program.
- **Tab-Delimited Disk File** enables you to create a tab-delimited text file that includes all the information in the report. In a tab-delimited text file, each column is separated by a tab character, making it easier to import the file into spreadsheet or database programs.
- **123 (.PRN) Disk File** enables you to create a comma-delimited text file that is easily recognized by Lotus 1-2-3 and other spreadsheet programs.

Next, select an orientation: Portrait or Landscape. These are standard options offered by all programs. The icon beside each orientation illustrates the position of the paper.

Set a print range: All or Pages. All prints all the pages of the report; this is the default setting. Pages enables you to enter the first and last page number you want to print.

Set additional print options as desired:

- **Print In Color** enables you to print in color—if you have a color printer.
- **Print In Draft Mode** substitutes a printer font for the fonts you may have selected for the report. This can speed printing. With this option turned on, the Print In Color and Fit To One Page Wide options are not available.
- **Fit To One Page Wide** scales the report so that it fits widthwise on the page. This sometimes involves changing the font size.

You can change the fonts used for the report by clicking the Heading Font and Body Font buttons. Each one displays a dialog box that you can use to specify a font, font style, and font size:

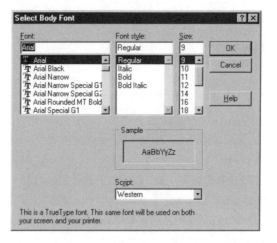

You can click the Preview button in the Print dialog box to see what the report will look like when printed. This gives you one last chance to check the appearance of the report before committing it to paper. Figure 13-5 shows what one of my memorized reports looks like in the Print Preview window.

When you've finished setting options in the Print dialog box, click the OK button to print the report.

Use buttons along the top of the window to print, navigate, or close the preview.

Click on the report to magnify it.

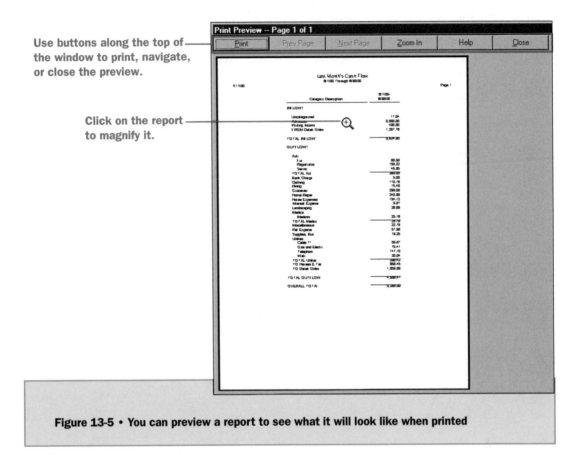

Figure 13-5 • You can preview a report to see what it will look like when printed

Printing a Graph

Printing a graph is easy. Just choose File | Print Graph, or press CTRL-P. Quicken doesn't ask any questions with a dialog box. It simply sends the graph to the printer and prints it.

Saving Money and Achieving Your Goals

This part of the book tells you about the Quicken and Quicken.com features you can use to save money on your income tax and make tax preparation quicker and easier. It also shows you the Quicken planning features you can use to save money and make your dreams come true. Its three chapters are:

Chapter 14: Minimizing Your Taxes with Quicken

Chapter 15: Using Quicken to Plan for the Future

Chapter 16: Saving Money with Quicken

Minimizing Your Taxes with Quicken

Chapter 14

In This Chapter:

- *Tax Planning Basics*

- *Including Tax Information in Categories*

- *Quicken Taxes Overview*

- *Tax Planner*

- *Deduction Finder*

- *Tax Reports*

Tax time is no fun. It can force you to spend hours sifting through financial records and filling out complex forms. When you're done with the hard part, you may be rewarded with the knowledge that you can expect a refund. But it is more likely that your reward will be the privilege of writing a check to the federal, state, or local government—or worse yet, all three.

Fortunately, Quicken can help. Its reporting features can save you time. Its planning features can save you money and help you make smarter financial decisions. By using the tax tools that are part of Quicken or available on Quicken.com, the next tax season may be a little less depressing. In this chapter, I show you how.

The Importance of Tax Planning

Don't underestimate the importance of tax planning. Doing so can cost you time and money. In this section, I explain why tax planning is important and give you some tips on what you can do to plan for tax time.

Why Plan for Tax Time?

Use the following scenarios to get yourself thinking about how a little planning now can save you time and money later.

Mary's Interest Expense Lesson

Mary is a homeowner who has been using her credit cards a little more than she should. She decides to cut up most of the cards and is now reducing her debt by paying a little more than the minimum monthly payment on each credit card account. Mary never considered the tax benefit of using a home equity loan, with tax-deductible interest, to pay off her credit card debt. Silly Mary doesn't even realize that the home equity reserve's interest rate might even be half the rate she pays the credit card companies.

John's Capital Gains Lesson

John invests in the stock market. He's been holding shares in Company A for five years, in Company B for a year and a half, and in Company C for a few months. All three investments have been doing well. Now John wants to buy a new car. He needs to liquidate some of his investments for the down payment. Because selling all shares of Company C would give him just the right amount of money, he sells them. What John didn't consider is that the gain on the sale of Company C is recognized as a short-term capital gain. If he'd sold some shares of Company A or B, he could have recorded a long-term capital gain, which is taxed at a lower rate.

Jean's Record-Keeping Lesson

Jean's young daughter has a serious medical problem that requires frequent trips to a big city hospital 50 miles away and other trips to doctors all over the state. Jean drives her in the family car, or if her teenage son needs the car for work, she takes a cab. Her daughter's condition has improved greatly, and the prognosis is good. But Jean's family health insurance doesn't cover all the transportation costs for the hospital and doctor visits. She was just told by a friend that she can deduct the cost of medical transportation from her income taxes. She's spent hours trying to compile a list of the dates of all those long drives and she wishes she'd asked for cab ride receipts.

Pete's Estimated Tax Lesson

Pete is a freelance writer who is having a very good year. By the end of June, he estimated that he'd already earned twice as much as he did the previous year. To celebrate, he bought a new car and took a two-week vacation in Peru. He also invested heavily in a mutual fund with good returns and a high front-end load. He feels great to have finally made the big time. But the estimated tax payments Pete has been making this year aren't nearly enough to cover his April 15 tax bill. He never considered increasing the payments to reduce his year-end tax bill, investing in a tax-deferred annuity or tax-free municipal bond to reduce his taxable income, or even saving some of his cash for April 15.

Learn from Their Mistakes, Not Yours

Mary, John, Jean, and Pete may as well be real people—I'm sure plenty of people find themselves in their situations every year. These examples illustrate the same basic point: Understanding the tax rules and planning ahead for tax time can save you time and money.

What You Can Do

Unless you're a tax accountant, you probably don't know all the tax laws. Fortunately, you don't need to know all the laws, just the ones that can affect you. Then, with the knowledge of what you can include on your tax returns, you can take steps to make smart decisions and keep track of items you can deduct.

Learning About Tax Rules

At tax time, people fall into two categories: those who do their own taxes and those who find (and probably pay) someone else to do their taxes for them.

If you do your own taxes, you can learn a lot about tax laws by reading the tax forms and publications for your return. If you pay a tax preparer, you can really get your money's worth by asking him or her about how you could save money. Any good tax preparer should be able to tell you.

Either way, you can also learn tax rules and get tips and advice by consulting the Tax Center within Quicken Deluxe or the Taxes Channel on Quicken.com (see Figure 14-1). You will learn about these resources throughout this chapter.

Saving Receipts and Recording Transactions

When you know that items are deductible, make a special effort to save receipts and record them in the proper Quicken categories. The receipts provide documentation for the expenditures, especially the date and amount. Recording them in the right account makes it possible to quickly generate reports of tax-deductible expenditures when it's time to fill out your tax return. It also enables you to display up-to-date deduction information in the Tax Center window.

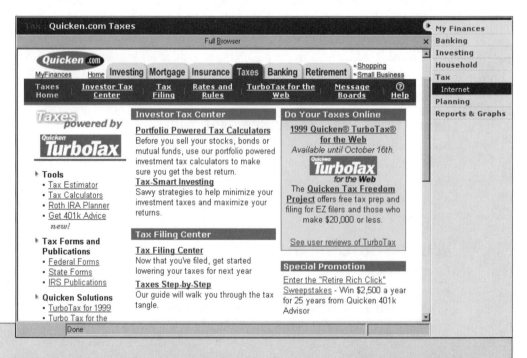

Figure 14-1 • The Taxes Channel on Quicken.com is chock-full of tax-related information and features

Analyzing All Options Before Making a Decision

Many people make decisions based on limited information—or worse yet, no information at all. As a Quicken user, you have access to all kinds of information and decision-making tools. Use Quicken.com to learn about finance-related opportunities. Go the extra step to research how an opportunity could affect your tax bill. Finally, use Quicken's built-in tools—such as the Tax Planner, Deduction Finder, and Capital Gains Estimator—to help you make an informed decision.

Quicken Taxes Overview

Quicken groups all of its tax commands and features in two separate places: the Taxes menu and the Tax Center window. Here's a quick look at each.

Tip   *As you may have already realized, Quicken offers numerous ways to access each of its features and commands. Rather than include them all in the book, I'll concentrate on the quickest and easiest ways.*

The Taxes Menu

Quicken's Taxes menu includes a variety of commands you can use to access Quicken's tax features:

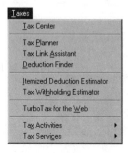

You might find a few commands especially useful as you work with Quicken's tax features:

- **TurboTax for the Web** enables you to use Intuit's online tax preparation feature to file your taxes via the Web, without any special software. Although I don't discuss this feature in detail in this book, I highly recommend that you check it out if you're looking for an easy, cost-effective way to prepare and file your taxes.

- **Tax Activities** displays a submenu of tax-related tasks that aren't used as often as those on the main Taxes menu. These include tasks such as setting up your paycheck, comparing taxable or text exempt yields, and estimating your capital gains. I cover these tasks in this chapter and elsewhere in this book.
- **Tax Services** displays a submenu of tax-related services available from Quicken, Quicken.com, and other providers.

The Tax Center Window

The Tax Center window (see Figure 14-2) is full of information about your tax situation, as well as links to tax-related Quicken and Quicken.com features and services. To open the Tax Center window, click its QuickTab on the right side of the screen.

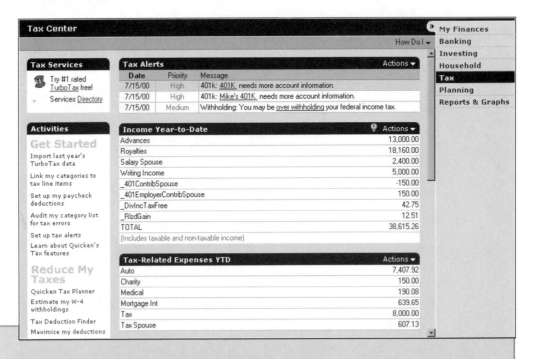

Figure 14-2 • The Tax Center window is a great place to access information about your tax situation, as well as Quicken's tax features

The Tax Center window is separated into three main parts: Tax Services, Activities, and tax snapshots.

Tax Services   The Tax Services area lists the most commonly used services available for Quicken users. Click an underlined link to access that service. For a complete list of services, click the Directory link in the Tax Services area.

Activities   The Activities area offers clickable links to Quicken features. This is where you'll find commands to set up Quicken with your tax information, plan for tax time, and generate tax reports.

Tax Snapshots   The Tax Center snapshots fill most of the Tax Center window. They include information about your income and tax-related expenses. The Actions menu for each snapshot offers commands that apply to the snapshot or information it contains. The following snapshots appear in this window:

- **Tax Alerts** displays alerts related to your taxes. I tell you about alerts in Chapter 11.
- **Income Year-to-Date** displays all income categories with balances greater than zero, along with the year-to-date amounts and total.
- **Tax-Related Expenses YTD** lists all tax-related expense categories with balances greater than zero, along with the year-to-date amounts and totals. These amounts will be your tax deductions.
- **Tax Calendar** displays upcoming dates important to taxpayers, including return and estimated tax filing dates and deadlines.
- **Projected Tax** displays an estimate of your year-end tax bill based on year-to-date amounts. This snapshot shows results based on information you enter in your Tax Profile and the Tax Planner, both of which are covered in this chapter.

Tax Information in Accounts and Categories

As discussed briefly in Chapter 2, Quicken accounts and categories can include information that will help you at tax time. In this section, I tell you more about this feature, including why you should use it and how you can set it up.

Why Enter Tax Information?

By including tax information in Quicken accounts and categories, you make it possible for Quicken to do several things:

- **Prepare tax reports** that summarize information by tax category or schedule.
- **Display tax information in the Tax Center window**, which shows an up-to-date summary of your tax situation.
- **Save time using the Tax Planner**, a feature of Quicken Deluxe that can import information from your Quicken data file based on tax information you enter.
- **Distinguish between taxable and nontaxable investments**, which enables you to create accurate reports on capital gains, interest, and dividends.
- **Use TurboTax to prepare your tax return,** enabling you to import Quicken information into TurboTax based on tax form and line items, thus eliminating the need to manually prepare tax returns or manually enter data into TurboTax.

SAVE TIME   By spending a few minutes setting up tax information for your accounts and categories, you can save hours compiling information for your returns.

Including Tax Information in Accounts

You enter an account's tax information in the Tax Schedule Information dialog box for the account. Open the register for the account for which you want to enter tax information and click the Overview tab at the bottom of the window. Then choose Set Tax Attributes from the Actions pop-up menu in the Account Attributes area:

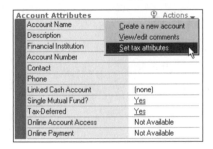

The Tax Schedule Information dialog box appears:

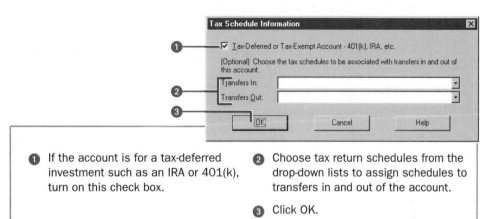

❶ If the account is for a tax-deferred investment such as an IRA or 401(k), turn on this check box.

❷ Choose tax return schedules from the drop-down lists to assign schedules to transfers in and out of the account.

❸ Click OK.

Set tax-related options in this dialog box as desired. The Transfers In and Transfers Out drop-down lists enable you to map account activity to specific lines on a wide variety of tax return forms and schedules. When you're finished, click OK. Repeat this process for all accounts for which you want to enter tax information.

Tip   *For a 401(k) account, set the Transfers In schedule to W-2 Salary. This ensures accurate reporting of 401(k) transactions throughout Quicken.*

Including Tax Information in Categories

There are two ways to enter tax information for Quicken categories:

- Enter tax form and schedule information for a single category in the Edit Category dialog box.
- Match multiple categories to tax forms and schedules with the Tax Link Assistant.

Using the Edit Category Dialog Box

The Edit Category dialog box is handy when you need to set tax information for just one or two categories. Open the Category & Transfer List window and select the category for which you want to enter tax information. Then click the Edit button on the button bar to display the Edit Category dialog box:

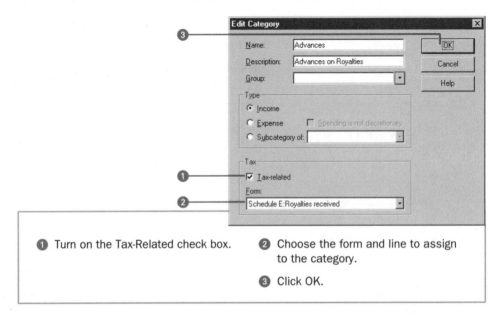

● Turn on the Tax-Related check box.   ● Choose the form and line to assign to the category.

                                         ● Click OK.

> **Shortcut**   *Quicken automatically sets tax information for many of the categories it creates. You can see which categories are tax related and which tax form lines have been assigned to them right in the Category & Transfer List window. Concentrate on the categories without tax assignments; some of these may require tax information, depending on your situation.*

If the category's transactions should be included on your tax return as either income or a deductible expense, turn on the Tax-Related check box. Then use the Form drop-down list to select the form or schedule and line for the item. When you've finished, click OK. Repeat this process for all categories that should be included on your tax return.

> **Tip**   *You can also enter tax information when you first create a category. The Set Up Category dialog box looks and works very much like the Edit Category dialog box. I tell you more about the Set Up Category dialog box in Chapter 2.*

Using the Tax Link Assistant

The Tax Link Assistant offers a quick and easy way to set tax information for multiple categories, all in one place. Choose Taxes | Tax Link Assistant to display the Tax Link Assistant dialog box; use this dialog box to match your Quicken categories to tax form or schedule line items:

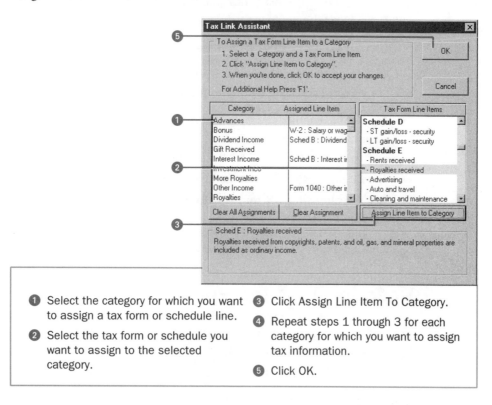

① Select the category for which you want to assign a tax form or schedule line.

② Select the tax form or schedule you want to assign to the selected category.

③ Click Assign Line Item To Category.

④ Repeat steps 1 through 3 for each category for which you want to assign tax information.

⑤ Click OK.

It is not necessary to match all categories—just the ones that should appear on your tax return. When you've finished, click OK to save your settings. The information is recorded for each category.

Planning to Avoid Surprises

One of the best reasons to think about taxes before tax time is to avoid surprises on April 15. Knowing what you'll owe before you owe it can help ensure that you pay just the right amount of taxes up front—through proper deductions or estimated tax payments—so you don't get hit with a big tax bill or tax refund.

SAVE MONEY   You may think of a big tax refund as a gift from Uncle Sam. Well, it isn't. It's your money that Uncle Sam has been using, interest free, for months. When you overpay your taxes, you're giving up money that you could be using to reduce interest-bearing debt or earn interest or investment income. Make sure you don't overpay taxes throughout the year so you can keep your money where it'll do you the most good.

Quicken offers a number of built-in tax planning tools that you can use to keep track of your tax situation throughout the year:

- **Tax Profile** enables you to record information that Quicken needs to accurately calculate the Projected Tax in the Tax Center window. This information also forms the basis of calculations used in the Tax Planner.
- **Tax Planner** helps you estimate your federal income tax bill for 2000 and 2001.
- **Tax Withholding Estimator** helps you determine whether your withholding taxes are correctly calculated.

Here's a closer look at these features.

Updating Your Tax Profile

Quicken uses information in your Tax Profile to project estimated taxes in the Tax Center window and form the basis of entries in the Tax Planner. It's a good idea to periodically check your Tax Profile for completeness and accuracy so Quicken has the most up-to-date information available when making calculations.

Shortcut   *If you're a TurboTax user, you can import Tax Profile information from TurboTax directly into Quicken. Choose Taxes | Tax Activities | Import TurboTax Data File. Then use the dialog box that appears to locate and import your TurboTax data.*

Choose Review My Tax Profile from the Actions pop-up menu in the Projected Tax area of the Tax Center window:

The Review Your Tax Profile dialog box appears:

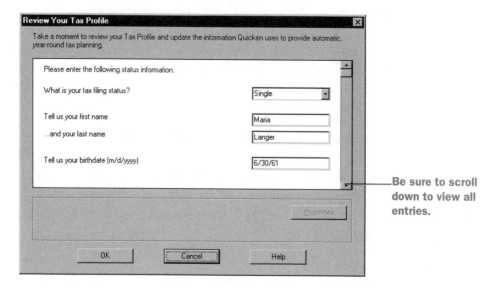

Be sure to scroll
down to view all
entries.

There are two ways you can use this dialog box:

- Enter only the information that is not automatically entered by Quicken, including your name, date of birth, filing status, and amounts not recorded in Quicken. Then let Quicken automatically enter the other information based on transactions entered for tax-related categories. This is the quickest and most accurate way to use Quicken's tax planning features.

- Manually enter all requested information that applies to your tax situation. The amounts you enter will override any amounts automatically entered by Quicken. This is the best way to use Quicken's tax-planning features if your income and tax-related expenses are seasonal or otherwise irregularly timed.

Caution   *Quicken can only accurately enter amounts if you properly set up tax information for all tax-related categories as instructed earlier in this chapter.*

When you're finished, click OK. The information in the Projected Tax area of the Tax Center window is updated automatically.

Using the Tax Planner

Quicken Tax Planner includes features from Intuit's TurboTax product to help you estimate your federal income tax bill for 2000 and 2001. While this can help you avoid surprises, it can also help you see how various changes to income and expenses can affect your estimated tax bill. Although the Tax Planner feature is not new in Quicken 2001, it did get a complete facelift and now looks and works more like Quicken's other planners.

Working with the Quicken Tax Planner Window

To open Quicken Tax Planner, choose Taxes | Tax Planner. The Tax Planner window's first screen, which explains how Quicken can help with tax planning, appears. Read the information there and click the Let's Get Started link at the bottom of the window. The Tax Planner Summary screen for the Projected scenario (see Figure 14-3) appears.

Click a link to view a specific type of income or expense.

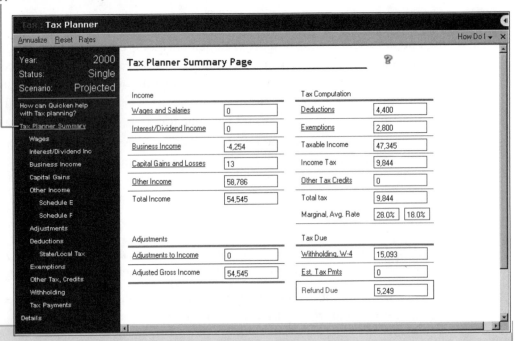

Figure 14-3 • The Tax Planner Summary screen displays a summary of all information stored in the Tax Planner

Entering Tax Planner Data

Data can be entered into the Tax Planner from three different sources:

- **TurboTax** data can be imported into Quicken. Choose Taxes | Tax Activities | Import TurboTax Data File. Then use the dialog box that appears to locate and import your TurboTax data. This information can be used to project current year amounts in the Tax Planner.

- **Quicken** data can be automatically entered into the Tax Planner. This works only if you have properly set up your tax-related Quicken categories with appropriate tax return line items as discussed earlier in this chapter.

- **User Entered** data can override any automatic entries. Use this to enter data that isn't entered any other way or has not yet been entered into Quicken—such as expected year-end bonuses or tax-deductible expenses.

Here's how it works. Click a link in the navigation bar on the left side of the Tax Planner window to view a specific type of income or expense. Then click a link within the window for a specific item. Details for the item appear in the bottom of the window, as shown next. If desired, change the source option and, if necessary, enter an amount. The options you can choose from vary depending on whether TurboTax data is available or the item has transactions recorded in Quicken. For example, in the following illustration, TurboTax data is not available, but transactions have been entered in Quicken. You can always manually override any automatic source entries.

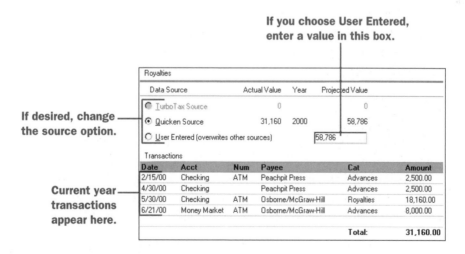

You can repeat this process for any Tax Planner items you want to check or change.

> **Tip** *To reset values to automatically entered Quicken amounts, click the Reset button on the Tax Planner window's button bar, click Reset To Quicken Actual Values on the menu that appears, and then click the Yes button in the dialog box that appears.*

Annualizing Amounts

Amounts are automatically annualized. That means Quicken automatically calculates an annual amount based on year-to-date amounts. You can specify whether some of the items should be annualized by clicking the Annualize button in the Tax Planner window's button bar. This displays the Annualize Quicken Tax Data dialog box:

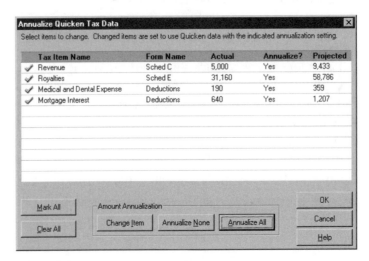

Select an item you want to change and click the Change Item button to toggle its annualize setting. Repeat this process for each item you want to change. Then click OK to save your settings.

Using Scenarios

The scenarios feature of the Tax Planner enables you to enter data for multiple scenarios—a "what-if" capability that you can use to see tax impacts based on various changes in entry data. For example, suppose you're planning to get married and want to see the impact of the additional income and deductions related to your new spouse. You can use a scenario to see the tax impact without changing your Projected scenario.

To use this feature, click the word Scenario in the navigation bar on the left side of the Tax Planner window. The Tax Planner Options screen shown next appears.

Choose a different scenario from the Scenarios drop-down list. Set other options in the window as desired. Then use the Tax Planner to set values for the new scenario and view the tax impact in the Tax Planner Summary screen.

```
┌─────────────────────────────────────────────────────────┐
│ Tax Planner Options                                     │
│                                                         │
│                                                         │
│  Select the Tax Year, Filing Status and Scenario you'd like to use: │
│                                                         │
│  ─────────────────────────────────────────────────────  │
│                                                         │
│                   Tax Year:        │ 2000 ▾ │          │
│                Filing Status:      │ Single       ▾ │   │
│                   Scenarios:       │ Projected ▾ │      │
│  ═════════════════════════════════════════════════════  │
└─────────────────────────────────────────────────────────┘
```

Finishing Up

When you've finished using the Quicken Tax Planner, click the Close button on the button bar or switch to another window. This saves the information you entered and updates the Projected Tax calculations in the Tax Center window.

Tax Withholding Estimator

Quicken's Tax Withholding Estimator feature helps you determine whether your W-4 form has been correctly completed. It does this by comparing your estimated tax bill, as displayed in the Projected Tax area of the Tax Center window, to the amount of withholding tax deducted from your paychecks.

Using the Tax Withholding Estimator Feature

To get started, choose Taxes | Tax Withholding Estimator. The Am I Under Or Over Withholding? window appears, as shown in Figure 14-4.

Read the information and follow the instructions in the middle column of the window. You'll be prompted to enter information related to withholding taxes. The instructions are very clear and easy to follow, so I won't repeat them here. Each time you enter data and click the Adjust Tax Projection button, the Projected Refund Due or Projected Tax Due amount in the lower-right corner of the window changes. Your goal is to get the amount as close to zero as possible, which you can do by adjusting the number of W-4 allowances and additional withholding per pay period.

● **Note** ⏐   *None of the entries you make in the Tax Withholding Estimator feature will affect your Quicken data or any other tax planning feature within Quicken.*

Click a link in this column to move to a specific area of the Tax Withholding Estimator.

Read instructions and enter information in this column.

See the results of your entries in this column.

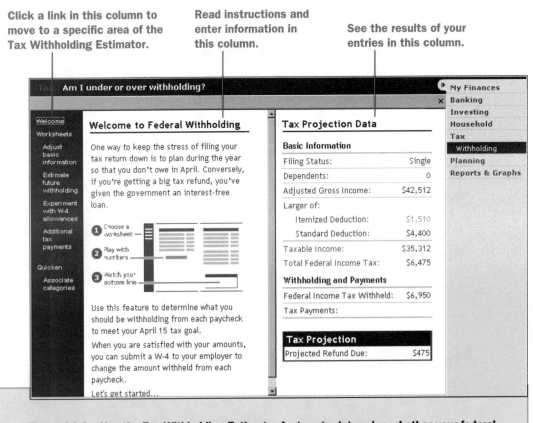

Figure 14-4 • Use the Tax Withholding Estimator feature to determine whether your federal withholding taxes are correct

Acting on the Results of Tax Withholding Estimator Calculations

What do you do with this information once you have it? Well, suppose your work with the Tax Withholding Estimator feature tells you that you should change your W-4 allowances from two to three to avoid overpaying federal withholding taxes. You can act on this information by completing a new W-4 form at work. This will decrease the amount of withholding tax in each paycheck. The result is that you reduce your tax overpayment and potential refund.

Tip   *It's a good idea to use the Tax Withholding Estimator feature periodically to make sure actual amounts are in line with projections throughout the year. (I recommend using it once every three months or so.) Whenever possible, use actual values rather than estimates in your calculations. And be sure to act on the results of the calculations by filing a new W-4 form, especially if the amount of your Projected Refund Due or Projected Tax Due is greater than a few hundred dollars.*

Minimizing Taxes by Maximizing Deductions

One way to minimize taxes is to maximize your deductions. While Quicken can't help you spend money on tax-deductible items—that's up to you—it can help you identify expenses that may be tax deductible, so you don't forget to include them on your tax returns.

Quicken offers two features to help maximize your deductions:

- **Deduction Finder** asks you questions about expenditures to determine whether they may be tax deductible.
- **Itemized Deduction Estimator** helps make sure you don't forget about commonly overlooked itemized deductions.

Deduction Finder

The Deduction Finder uses another TurboTax feature to help you learn which expenses are deductible. Its question-and-answer interface gathers information from you and then provides information about the deductibility of items based on your answers.

Working with the Deduction Finder Window

To open the Deduction Finder, choose Taxes | Deduction Finder. An Introduction dialog box may appear. Read its contents to learn more about Deduction Finder and then click OK. Figure 14-5 shows what the Deductions tab of the Deduction Finder window says about the Godiva chocolates I sent my clients for the holidays last year.

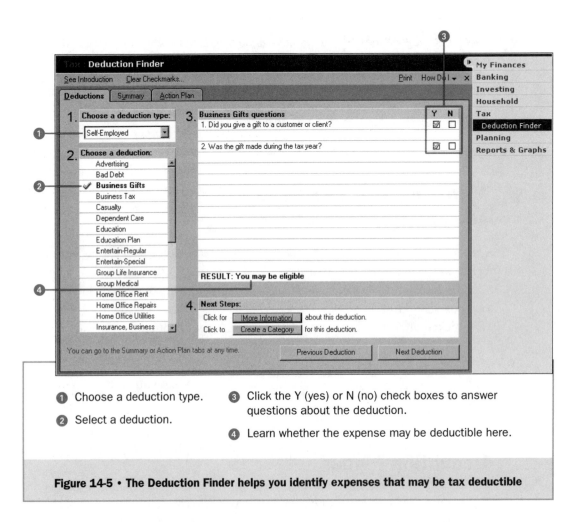

● Choose a deduction type.
● Select a deduction.

❸ Click the Y (yes) or N (no) check boxes to answer questions about the deduction.

❹ Learn whether the expense may be deductible here.

Figure 14-5 • The Deduction Finder helps you identify expenses that may be tax deductible

You can use button bar options to work with the Deduction Finder window:

- **See Introduction** displays the Introduction window, so you can learn more about how Deduction Finder works.

- **Clear Checkmarks** removes the check marks from items for which you have already answered questions.

- **Print** prints a summary of deduction information about all the deductions for which you have answered questions.

- **How Do I** provides instructions for completing tasks within the Deduction Finder window.

Finding Deductions

As you can see in Figure 14-5, the Deductions tab of the Deduction Finder window uses clearly numbered steps to walk you through the process of selecting deduction types and deductions and then answering questions. It's easy to use. You don't have to answer questions about all the deductions—only the deductions you think may apply to you. When you've finished answering questions about a deduction, the result appears near the bottom of the window. You can then move on to another deduction.

The Summary tab of the window summarizes the number of deductions available in each category, the number for which you answered questions, and the number for which you may be eligible to take deductions based on your answers to the questions:

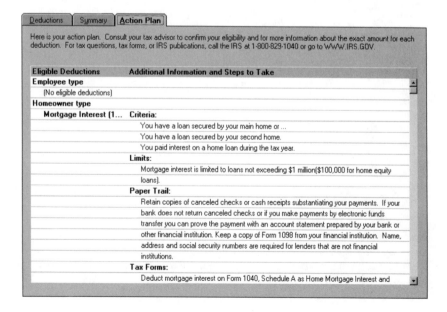

Deductions	Summary	Action Plan

Deduction types	# Available	# Answered	# Eligible
Employee type	28	0	0
Homeowner type	5	2	2
Individual type	24	6	5
Investor type	7	3	3
Medical type	11	0	0
Self-Employed type	33	4	4

When you've finished answering questions, you can click the Action Plan tab to get more information about the deductions and the things you need to do to claim them. Here's what the Action Plan tab looks like:

Deductions	Summary	Action Plan

Here is your action plan. Consult your tax advisor to confirm your eligibility and for more information about the exact amount for each deduction. For tax questions, tax forms, or IRS publications, call the IRS at 1-800-829-1040 or go to WWW.IRS.GOV.

Eligible Deductions	Additional Information and Steps to Take
Employee type	
(No eligible deductions)	
Homeowner type	
Mortgage Interest (1...	**Criteria:**
	You have a loan secured by your main home or ...
	You have a loan secured by your second home.
	You paid interest on a home loan during the tax year.
	Limits:
	Mortgage interest is limited to loans not exceeding $1 million($100,000 for home equity loans).
	Paper Trail:
	Retain copies of canceled checks or cash receipts substantiating your payments. If your bank does not return canceled checks or if you make payments by electronic funds transfer you can prove the payment with an account statement prepared by your bank or other financial institution. Keep a copy of Form 1098 from your financial institution. Name, address and social security numbers are required for lenders that are not financial institutions.
	Tax Forms:
	Deduct mortgage interest on Form 1040, Schedule A as Home Mortgage Interest and

Although you can read this Action Plan information onscreen, if you answered many questions, you may want to use the Print button on the button bar to print the information for reference.

Itemized Deduction Estimator

The Itemized Deduction Estimator feature helps make sure that you don't overlook any itemized deductions—the deductions on Schedule A of your tax return—that you might qualify for. It does this by guiding you through a review of deduction ideas and providing the information you need to know whether you may qualify.

To get started, choose Taxes | Itemized Deduction Estimator. The How Can I Maximize My Deductions? window appears, as shown in Figure 14-6.

Click a link in this column to move to a specific area of the Itemized Deduction Estimator.

Read instructions and enter information in this column.

See the results of your entries in this column.

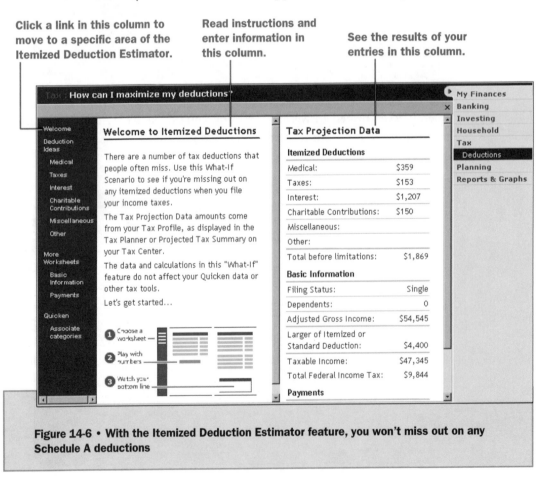

Figure 14-6 • With the Itemized Deduction Estimator feature, you won't miss out on any Schedule A deductions

Read the information and follow the instructions in the middle column of the window. You'll be prompted to enter information related to itemized deductions for medical expenses, taxes paid, interest paid, charitable contributions, and other items. The instructions are clear and easy to follow. Each time you enter information and click the Calculate Total button, the Projected Refund Due or Projected Tax Due amount in the lower-right corner of the window changes. Your goal is to get a Projected Refund Due amount as high as possible or a Projected Tax Due amount as low as possible.

Note   *None of the entries you make in the Itemized Deduction Estimator feature will affect your Quicken data or any other tax planning feature within Quicken.*

Making Smart Decisions

Your taxes can also be affected by certain taxable transactions, such as the sale of securities, or the income you earn on your investments. Quicken offers two tools to show you the tax impact of these events:

Capital Gains Estimator   The Capital Gains Estimator helps you determine which investment to sell based on capital gains tax rules. You enter information about a security sale, and Quicken calculates the tax impact. Using this feature can minimize your capital gains taxes. I explain how to use the Capital Gains Estimator in Chapter 8.

Tax-Exempt Versus Taxable Yield   The Tax-Exempt vs. Taxable Yield feature shows you the post-tax earnings of tax-exempt and taxable investments. To access this feature, choose Taxes | Tax Activities | Compare Taxable Or Tax Exempt Yields. The Tax-Exempt Investment Equivalent Yield dialog box, shown next, appears. To use it, find the yield of a tax-exempt investment in the leftmost column. Then move across the row to the column for your tax bracket. The rate there is the equivalent rate for a taxable investment—the rate a taxable investment must beat to earn more than the tax-exempt investment. For example, if I have a tax-exempt investment earning 5.0 percent and I'm in the 28 percent tax bracket, a taxable investment must earn more than 6.94 percent to be better than the tax-exempt investment.

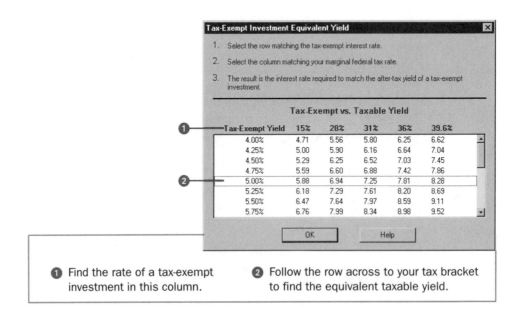

1. Find the rate of a tax-exempt investment in this column.

2. Follow the row across to your tax bracket to find the equivalent taxable yield.

Tax Reports

Quicken offers several different tax reports that can make tax time easier by providing the information you need to prepare your taxes. All of these reports are based on the tax information settings for the accounts and categories in your Quicken file.

Note   *You can learn more about Quicken's reporting feature in Chapter 13.*

To create a report, select Reports | Taxes and choose the name of the report from the submenu:

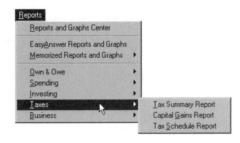

You have three tax reports to choose from:

- **Tax Summary Report** summarizes tax-related transactions, organized by category and date.
- **Capital Gains Report** summarizes gains and losses on the sales of investments, organized by the term of the investment (short or long) and the investment account.
- **Tax Schedule Report** summarizes tax-related transactions, organized by tax form or schedule and line item.

SAVE MONEY   If you pay a tax preparation specialist, be sure to furnish him or her with an accurate Tax Schedule Report from Quicken. Doing so may save the preparer time and reduce your tax preparation bill.

Using Quicken to Plan for the Future

In This Chapter:

- *Planning for Retirement*

- *Quicken Planning Overview*

- *Financial Calculators*

- *Life Event Planners*

To many people, the future is an unknown, a mystery. After all, who can say what will happen tomorrow, next year, or 10 years from now? But if you think about your future, you can usually come up with a few events that you can plan for: your marriage, the purchase of a new home, the birth of your children (and their education years later), and your retirement. (These are just examples—everyone's life runs a slightly different course.) These events, as well as many unforeseen events, all have one thing in common: They affect your finances.

In this chapter, I tell you about planning for future events and how tools within Quicken and on Quicken.com can help. I also provide plenty of information about various retirement accounts so you can learn about your options.

Planning for Retirement

Throughout your life, you work and earn money to pay your bills, buy the things you and your family need or want, and help your kids get started with their own lives. But there comes a day when it's time to retire. Those regular paychecks stop coming and you find yourself relying on the money you put away for retirement.

Retirement planning is one of the most important financial planning jobs facing individuals and couples. In this section, I tell you about the importance of planning and offer some planning steps and a word of advice based on personal experience.

The Importance of Planning

Retired people live on fixed incomes. That's not a problem—*if* the income is fixed high enough to support a comfortable lifestyle. You can help ensure that there's enough money to finance your retirement years by planning and saving now.

Poor retirement planning can lead to catastrophic results—imagine running out of money when you turn 75. Or having to make a lifestyle change when you're 65 just to accommodate a much lower income.

Planning is even more important these days as longevity increases. People are living longer than ever. Your retirement dollars may need to support you for 20 years or more, at a time when the cost of living will likely be much higher than it is today.

With proper planning, it's possible to finance your retirement years without putting a strain on your working years. By closely monitoring the status of your retirement funds, periodically adjusting your plan, and acting accordingly, your retirement years can be the golden years they're supposed to be.

Planning Steps

Retirement planning is much more than deciding to put $2,000 in an IRA every year. It requires careful consideration of what you have, what you'll need, and how you can make those two numbers the same.

Tip   *Quicken's Retirement Calculator and Retirement Planner, which I discuss later in this chapter, can help you perform many of the calculations you need to come up with a good retirement plan.*

Assess What You Have

Take a good look at your current financial situation. What tax-deferred retirement savings do you already have? A pension? An IRA? Something else? What regular savings do you have? What taxable investments do you have? The numbers you come up with will form the basis of your final retirement funds—like a seed you'll grow.

Be sure to consider property that can be liquidated to contribute to retirement savings. For example, if you currently live in a large home to accommodate your family, you may eventually want to live in a smaller home. The proceeds from the sale of your current home may exceed the cost of your retirement home. Also consider any income-generating property that may continue to generate income in your retirement years or can be liquidated to contribute to retirement savings.

Tip   *Your savings, investments, and other assets are part of your net worth. If you use Quicken to track all of your assets, you can use its reporting feature to generate a Net Worth Report. Choose Reports | Own & Owe | Net Worth Report.*

Determine What You'll Need

What you'll need depends on many things. One simple calculation suggests you'll need 80 percent of your current gross income to maintain your current lifestyle in your retirement years. You may find a calculation like this handy if retirement is still many years in the future and you don't really know what things will cost.

Time is an important factor in calculating the total amount you should have saved by retirement day. Ask yourself two questions:

- **How long do you have to save?** Take your current age and subtract it from the age at which you plan to retire. That's the number of years you have left to save.

- **How long will you be in retirement?** Take the age at which you plan to retire and subtract it from the current life expectancy for someone of your age and gender. That's the number of years you have to save for.

When I did this math, I learned that I have only 21 years left to save for a 28-year retirement. I'm glad I've been saving!

Develop an Action Plan

Once you know how much you need, it's time to think seriously about how you can save it. This requires putting money away in one or more savings or investment accounts. I tell you about your options a little later in this chapter.

Stick to the Plan!

The most important part of any plan is sticking to it. For example, if you plan to save $5,000 a year, don't think you can just save $2,000 this year and make up the $3,000 next year. There are two reasons: First, you can't "make up" the interest lost on the $3,000 you didn't save this year. Second, you're only kidding yourself if you think you'll manage to put away $8,000 next year.

If you consider deviating from your plan, just think about the alternative: making ends meet with a burger-flipping job in the local fast food joint when you're 68 years old.

Don't Wait! Act Now!

I remember when I first began thinking about retirement. I was 30 or 31 and had been self-employed for about three years. I didn't have a pension or 401(k) plan with my former employer. I didn't have much saved. I only had $2,000 in an IRA. Up until that point, I never worried about retirement, but one day, something just clicked, and retirement became something to think about.

I've done a lot of retirement planning and saving since then. While I admit that I don't have a perfect plan (yet), I've certainly come a long way in eight years. But when I consider how much more I could have saved if I'd begun five years earlier, I could kick myself for waiting.

See for yourself. Table 15-1 shows how $1,000-, $2,000-, and $5,000-per-year contributions to a tax-deferred retirement account earning 8 percent a year can grow. (These calculations do not take into consideration tax benefits or inflation.)

Savings at Age 62				
Start Age	**Years of Saving**	**$1,000/year**	**$2,000/year**	**$5,000/year**
60	2	$2,080	$4,160	$10,400
50	12	$18,977	$37,954	$94,886
40	22	$55, 457	$110,914	$277,284
30	32	$134,214	$268,427	$671,068
20	42	$304,244	$608,487	$1,521,218

Table 15-1: • Saving Regularly Is the Best Way to Save Money

Funding Your Retirement

There are many different kinds of retirement funds. In this section, I tell you about the most common: social security, pension plans, tax-deferred savings and investments, and other savings and investments.

Social Security

Social security is the government's way of helping us fund our retirement. If you work, you make mandatory contributions to the social security system. When you reach age 62, you can begin to collect benefits in the form of a monthly check. You don't have to collect social security until you reach the age of $70\frac{1}{2}$; the longer you wait, the more your monthly benefit will be. One thing is relatively certain, however: Your monthly benefit will probably not be enough to fund your retirement.

Tip   *You can find out how much you'll get from social security when you retire by obtaining a Personal Earnings and Benefit Estimate Statement (PEBES) from the Social Security Administration. Call 800-772-1213 to request your free copy.*

Pension Plans

Pension plans are among the most common—and most traditional—methods of retirement funding. They reward loyal employees by guaranteeing benefits upon retirement. There are several types of pension plans, including company pension plans and 401(k) and 403(b) plans.

Company Pension Plan

In a company pension plan, you and your employer contribute regularly to a pension fund. This is commonly referred to as a *defined benefit plan* because the final benefit can always be calculated using a formula that usually includes your years of service, final salary, and a fixed percentage rate. Benefits are usually paid monthly from your retirement date, for the rest of your life.

Most pension funds are insured by the Pension Benefit Guaranty Corporation (PBGC), a government agency that protects employer-sponsored defined benefit plans. That means the money will be there when you retire.

Company pension plans cannot be transferred from one employer to another. If you leave a job where you had a pension plan, your benefits stay with the plan until you turn 65, when you can start collecting benefits.

401(k) and 403(b) Plans

A 401(k) plan is a tax-deferred investment and savings plan that works like a personal pension fund for employees. It allows a company's employees to save and invest for their own retirement. The employee authorizes a pretax payroll deduction that is invested in one of the investment options offered by the plan. Some companies may match the employee's contribution by paying 25 percent to 100 percent into the plan.

There are two tax benefits to a 401(k) plan:

- **Reduction in taxable income**, which reduces the amount of taxable income, thus reducing the employee's income tax, because the contribution comes from pretax earnings.
- **Taxes are deferred until money is withdrawn**, which means that the contributions and earnings grow tax-deferred until withdrawal, when they are taxed as ordinary income. Because funds are normally withdrawn at retirement when the employee is in a lower tax bracket, the tax hit is reduced.

One of the benefits of a 401(k) plan over a company pension plan is portability. If you leave your job, you can take your 401(k) plan's funds to your new employer's plan or roll it over into an IRA.

A 403(b) plan is basically the same as a 401(k) plan, but it is designed for the employees of certain types of tax-exempt organizations.

Tax-Deferred Savings and Investments

You can take advantage of a number of tax-deferred savings and investments if you don't have a pension or you want to supplement one. These plans all have one thing in common: They enable you to save money for retirement without paying taxes on interest or investment earnings until they are withdrawn.

IRAs

The most well-known type of tax-deferred savings is an Individual Retirement Account (IRA). An IRA is a tax-deferred investment and savings account that acts as a personal retirement fund for people with employment income. You hear a lot about these accounts around tax time because the government allows you to deduct contributions for many types of IRAs from your taxable income, thus reducing your taxes. Here's a summary of the different types of IRAs currently available:

- **IRA** contributions (up to $2,000) can be deductible or nondeductible; earnings are tax-deferred until withdrawn after the age of $59\frac{1}{2}$, when they are taxed as ordinary income. There are two types of IRAs: regular and spousal. A regular IRA is designed for an individual, whereas a spousal IRA is designed for married couples in which only one person has employment income.

- **Roth IRA** contributions (up to $2,000) are not tax deductible. The contributions and earnings, however, can be withdrawn *tax-free* after the age of $59\frac{1}{2}$. The idea is to provide an alternative for people who expect to be in a high tax bracket when they retire. You can contribute to a Roth IRA for as long as you like.

- **SEP IRA, or Simplified Employee Pension IRA**, is provided by sole proprietors of small businesses to employees (including themselves). The employer can contribute up to 15 percent of the employee's compensation, up to $24,000. The SEP IRA is subject to the same other rules as an IRA. Employees with SEP IRAs can also contribute to regular IRAs.

- **SARSEP IRA, or Salary Reduction SEP IRA**, is provided by sole proprietors of businesses with less than 25 employees. Contributions, which can be made by both employer and employee, are tax deductible. The SARSEP IRA is subject to the same other rules as an IRA. New SARSEP IRA accounts can no longer be started; this type of savings and investment plan has been replaced by the SIMPLE IRA.

- **SIMPLE IRA or Savings Incentive Match Plan for Employees IRA**, replaced the SARSEP IRA in 1997. It's basically the same as the SARSEP IRA but can be used by companies with up to 100 employees, and allows maximum contributions of $6,000 for the employee plus the employer share. The SIMPLE IRA is subject to the same rules as an IRA. Employees with SIMPLE IRAs can also contribute to regular IRAs.

Keoghs

A Keogh plan is a tax-deferred retirement plan for self-employed individuals, including sole proprietors who report income on Schedule C and partners who report income on Schedule E. Contributions and earnings are tax deferred until withdrawn after the age of $59^{1}/_{2}$. There are two kinds of Keogh plans:

- **Profit-Sharing Keogh** plans allow contributions of up to 13.04 percent of your self-employment income, with a maximum of $30,000. The contribution percentage can be adjusted annually.
- **Money-Purchase Keogh** plans allow contributions of up to 20 percent of your self-employment income, with a maximum of $30,000. The contribution percentage you select must be the same from year to year.

Tax-Deferred Annuities

A tax-deferred annuity enables you to make contributions (that are not tax deductible) toward an investment for which the earnings are tax deferred until withdrawal, after the age of $59^{1}/_{2}$. Annuities are sponsored by insurance companies and other financial institutions and are commonly available through agents, banks, stockbrokers, and financial planners. There are two types of annuities:

- **Fixed annuities** have a guaranteed rate of return.
- **Variable annuities** have a rate of return that varies based on the performance of the securities in which annuity funds are invested.

Other Savings and Investments

Any type of savings or investment can be used to fund your retirement: stocks, bonds, mutual funds, savings accounts, certificates of deposit, money market accounts, and so on. I tell you about these things in Chapters 8 and 16.

Unlike the tax-deferred savings and investments discussed in this chapter, taxable savings and investments can be liquidated or withdrawn and spent at any time. This is a two-edged sword. Although the money will always be available in the event of an emergency, you may find it a tough source of funds to resist when a new car or boat is on your mind. To me, the main benefit of retirement funds is that they're almost untouchable. In my mind, my retirement funds don't even belong to me right now—I'm not tempted to spend them.

You shouldn't overlook the tax benefits of tax-deferred retirement funds, either. Your money will grow more quickly when earnings aren't taxed.

Quicken Planning Overview

Quicken groups all of its planning-related commands and features in two separate places: the Planning menu and the Planning Center window. Here's a quick look at each.

Tip   *As you should know by now, Quicken offers numerous ways to access each of its features and commands. Rather than include them all in the book, I'll concentrate on the quickest and easiest ways.*

The Planning Menu

Quicken's Planning menu, shown next, includes a variety of commands you can use to access Quicken's planning features, including its individual Life Event Planners and financial calculators. I cover most of these features in this chapter and in Chapters 9 and 16.

You might find a few commands especially useful as you work with Quicken's planning features:

- **Assumptions** enables you to review and edit assumptions that are shared by all Life Event Planners. You'll access assumptions often as you fine-tune and modify the plans you make with Quicken.
- **Financial Calculators** displays a submenu of specialized calculators that you can use to plan for college, retirement, and other large expenditures. Although

not nearly as detailed as Quicken's Life Event Planners, they help you perform complex calculations quickly. I cover two of these calculators—the Loan Calculator and the Refinance Calculator—in Chapter 9; I discuss the others in this chapter and in Chapter 16.

- **Planning Services** displays a submenu of planning-related services available from Quicken, Quicken.com, and other providers. This is where you'll find commands to consolidate your debt and maximize your 401(k).

The Planning Center Window

The Planning Center window is full of information about your financial plans, as well as links to Quicken's Life Event Planners. The appearance of this window varies depending on whether you have provided assumptions and other plan details; if you have, this information will appear in the window as shown in Figure 15-1. To open the Planning Center window, click its QuickTab on the right side of the screen.

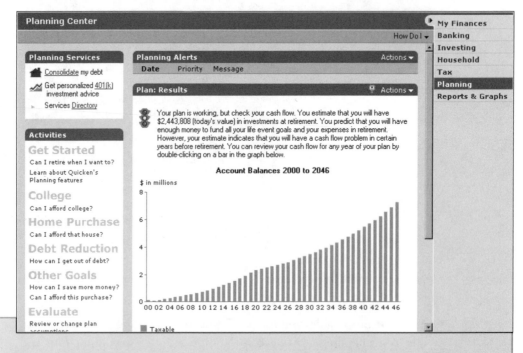

Figure 15-1 • The Planning Center window provides information about the financial plans you have set up in Quicken

The Planning Center window is separated into three main parts: Planning Services, Activities, and planning snapshots.

Planning Services   The Planning Services area lists a few of the most commonly used services available for Quicken users. Click an underlined link to access that service. For a complete list of services, click the Directory link in the Planning Services area.

Activities   The Activities area offers clickable links to Quicken features. These are separated into Life Event Activities and Other Activities:

- **Life Event Activities** offer access to each of Quicken's Life Event Planners.
- **Other Activities** include links to access other commands under Quicken's Planning menu, including commands for budgeting, forecasting, and savings goals.

Planning Snapshots   The Planning Center snapshots fill most of the Planning Center window. They include the assumptions and results for your financial plans. The Actions menu for each snapshot offers commands that apply to the snapshot or information it contains. The following snapshots appear in this window:

- **Planning Alerts** displays alerts related to your bank and credit card accounts. I tell you about alerts in Chapter 11.
- **Plan Results** displays the results of your financial plans—if you have provided assumptions and other plan details. Otherwise, it provides instructions for setting up plans.
- **Plan Assumptions** displays some of the basic assumptions for your financial plans—if you have entered them. Otherwise, it provides instructions for entering assumptions.
- **Event Status** provides information about any upcoming events you have planned.
- **Monthly Savings Targets** provides information about savings goals you have set up. I cover saving money and the Save More Planner in Chapter 16.

Using Financial Calculators

Quicken includes two financial calculators that you can use to plan for future events in your life: College Calculator and Retirement Calculator. These calculators are very similar in appearance and functionality, but each is designed for a specific purpose.

College Calculator

The College Calculator enables you to calculate savings for the cost of a college education. Choose Planning | Financial Calculators | College. The College Calculator appears:

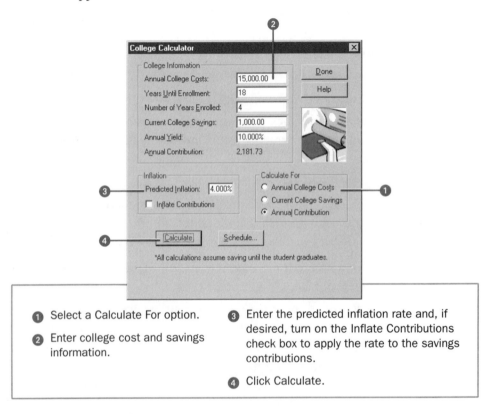

① Select a Calculate For option.

② Enter college cost and savings information.

③ Enter the predicted inflation rate and, if desired, turn on the Inflate Contributions check box to apply the rate to the savings contributions.

④ Click Calculate.

Select a Calculate For option, and then enter or select values and options throughout the dialog box. Most options are pretty straightforward and easy to understand. The Calculate For option affects which value is calculated by Quicken:

- **Annual College Costs** calculates the annual tuition you'll be able to afford based on the values you enter.
- **Current College Savings** calculates the amount of money you should currently have saved based on the values you enter.
- **Annual Contribution** calculates the minimum amount you should contribute to college savings based on the values you enter.

When you click Calculate, Quicken displays the results. You can click the Schedule button to see a printable list of deposits and tuition expenses, with a running balance total.

Retirement Calculator

The Retirement Calculator can help you calculate some of the numbers you need to plan for your retirement. To open it, choose Planning | Financial Calculators | Retirement. The Retirement Calculator appears:

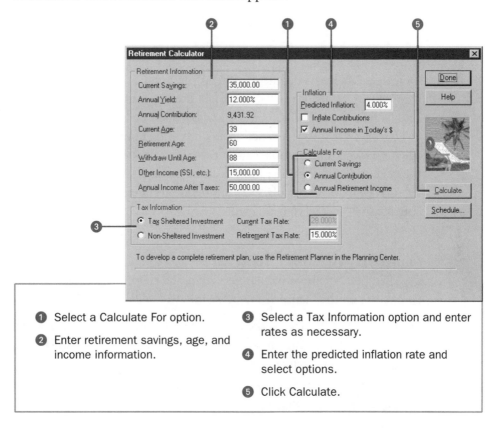

① Select a Calculate For option.

② Enter retirement savings, age, and income information.

③ Select a Tax Information option and enter rates as necessary.

④ Enter the predicted inflation rate and select options.

⑤ Click Calculate.

Select a Calculate For option, and then enter or select values and options throughout the dialog box. Most options are pretty straightforward and easy to understand. The Calculate For option affects which value is calculated by Quicken:

- **Current Savings** calculates the amount of money you should currently have saved based on the values you enter.

- **Annual Contribution** calculates the minimum amount you should contribute to a retirement account based on the values you enter.
- **Annual Retirement Income** calculates the annual amount of retirement income you'll have based on the values you enter.

Tax and inflation options make complex calculations to account for the effect of taxes and inflation on your savings dollars. When you click Calculate, Quicken displays the results. You can click the Schedule button to see a printable list of deposits and income, with a running balance total.

Using Life Event Planners

Quicken's Life Event Planners can help you build a complete financial plan for many major events of your life. You can use this feature to plan for all financial activity from now until retirement and beyond.

Here's how it works: You set up assumptions about yourself and your financial situation. Some of this information can be automatically extracted from your Quicken data; other information must be manually entered. These assumptions are used by many of the planners to provide accurate planning results based on the "big picture"—all of your finances.

A Look at the Planners

Quicken 2001 includes six planners, all of which can be accessed through commands on the Planning menu or links in the Planning Center window:

- **Retirement Planner** is the most comprehensive planner. It looks at all your current financial information, as well as the results of other planners, to help you plan for retirement.
- **College Planner** helps you plan for your children's college educations.
- **Home Purchase Planner** helps you plan for the purchase of a new home.
- **Debt Reduction Planner** helps you save money while getting out of debt as quickly as possible.
- **Save More Planner** helps you find ways to save more money.
- **Special Purchase Planner** helps you plan for special purchases, such as vacations, vehicles, and other large expenditures.

Note | *This chapter covers the Retirement, College, Home Purchase, and Special Purchase Planners. The Debt Reduction and Save More Planners are covered in Chapter 16.*

All of these planners work pretty much the same way. You enter information about your current financial situation or let Quicken enter the information for you based on account balances and category transactions. Then you tell the planner a little about the event you're planning for. For example, the College Planner needs to know how old your children are now and when you expect them to go to college. It also needs to know how much you expect the education to cost. When you enter all this information into Quicken, it performs calculations and shows you results. Planning information is saved within your Quicken data file so you can view or update it at any time.

Setting Assumptions

The best way to start using the planners is to enter assumptions. You do this with the Planning Assumptions window and various Edit Assumptions dialog boxes.

Choose Planning | Assumptions. The Planning Assumptions window, which is shown in Figure 15-2, appears.

To enter or edit information in an assumption category, click the Edit link in the topic name area. A dialog box for that topic appears. Here's the one for the About You topic:

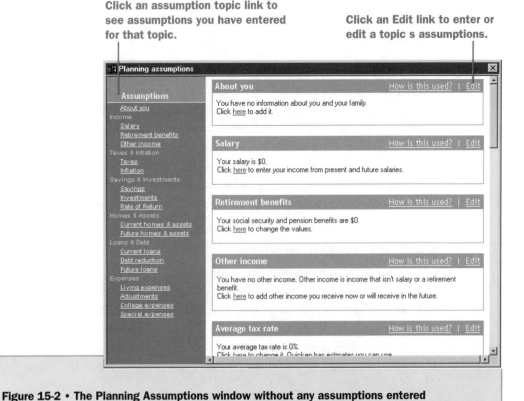

Click an assumption topic link to see assumptions you have entered for that topic.

Click an Edit link to enter or edit a topic s assumptions.

Figure 15-2 • The Planning Assumptions window without any assumptions entered

Tip   You can click the How Is This Used? link for any topic to learn how Quicken uses the information for its calculations.

Using these dialog boxes is fairly self-explanatory so I won't go into detail on every single one. Simply enter information where appropriate and click the Done or OK button to continue. The information automatically appears in the Planning Assumptions window. Here's the information I entered about me:

About you	How is this used?	Edit
		Maria
Age		39 years old
Life Expectancy		85
Retirement Age		60
Retirement Date		6/2021
Years Until Retirement		21
Years In Retirement		25

Do this for all applicable assumption topics. Be sure to read all of the information in each dialog box to fully understand what information is requested. (You can click the Help button in a dialog box for even more information.) Although you don't have to enter all requested information, the more you enter, the more accurate the plan results will be.

Caution   *If you include Debt Reduction Plan information in your assumptions, do not include the same loans in the Current Loan topic assumptions. Doing so will duplicate those loans.*

Checking Plan Results

When you've finished entering assumptions, the Plan Results area of the Planning Center window displays a summary of your plan, with a graph to show account balances. Here's what it might look like:

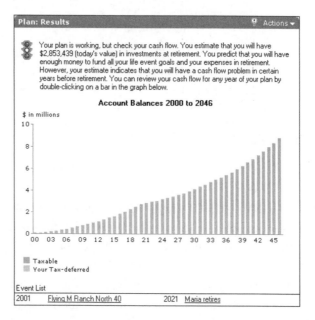

You can see a full-window version of the results in the Plan Results window. Choose Planning | Plan Results to display the window.

Note   *Be sure to read the information above the chart. Although the chart might look great—you might be a millionaire one day!—the description may warn you about problems with the plan, such as cash flow.*

To see detail for a specific year of the plan, double-click the bar for that year. A window like the one shown next appears. It provides income, expense, and tax information based on the assumptions you have entered.

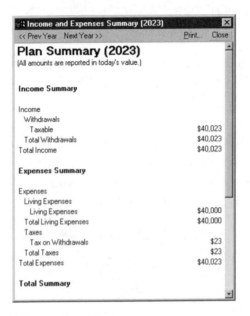

Plan results change automatically based on a variety of changes within your Quicken data file:

- When the account balances referred to in the plan change, the plan changes accordingly.
- When you change plan assumptions, the plan changes accordingly.
- When you use Life Events planners to plan for major purchases, college, retirement, and other events that affect your finances, the plan changes to include these events.
- When you play "what if" with assumptions and save the changes as your plan, the plan changes accordingly. I tell you about playing "what if" later in this chapter.

Adding Plan Details with Life Event Planners

You can add details to the assumptions of your financial plan by using Life Event Planners to add specific events to the plan. The information you enter into these plans becomes part of your overall financial plan, thus changing the Plan Results.

Here's a look at four of the Life Event Planners; the other two are covered in Chapter 16.

Tip   *When you use any of these planners to create plans, each individual plan appears in the Planning Center window and on submenus that appear on the Planning menu. This makes it easy to view and change plans.*

Retirement Planner

The Retirement Planner enables you to plan for your retirement. It is, by far, the most exhaustive planner, primarily because it requires all the information entered as plan assumptions. In fact, if you have already entered plan assumptions, you can go through the Retirement Planner very quickly; if not, it'll take you about 30 minutes to enter all the information it requires. (That information will be saved for use by other planners.)

Start by choosing Planning | Retirement Planner to display the My Retirement Plan window (see Figure 15-3). Read the information in the window, then click the Next link to begin entering information. Follow the prompts that appear to open dialog boxes and enter data for a number of topics, many of which may already include information from plan assumptions or other planners. The items you complete are checked off in the navigation bar on the left side of the window; you can also click links for items there to complete them in any order you like.

When you have finished entering information, the Your Plan screen shows your financial plan. Subsequent windows enable you to check your plan for problems, play "what if" with your plan (as I discuss later in this chapter), and view a summary of your plan.

College Planner

The College Planner enables you to plan for your child's college education. It uses information already entered as plan assumptions, as well as new information you enter about your child's college plans.

Choose Planning | College Planner to display the College Planner window. Read the information in the introduction screen and click the Next link to get started. Then follow the prompts to add or edit information about a dependent's college education. Quicken is very thorough and can even look up college cost information for you for hundreds of public, private, and specialized schools in the United States. For example, Figure 15-4 shows the College Cost screen, with information about what it would cost to send a fictitious child (my dog, Spot) to a nearby aeronautical school. (Good thing Spot doesn't have such high aspirations.)

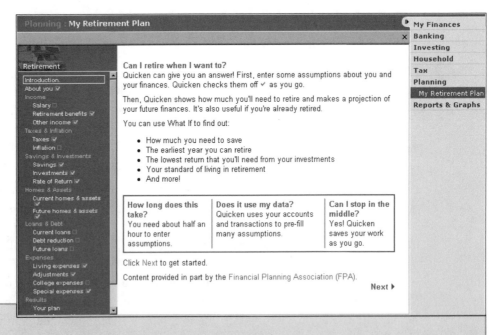

Figure 15-3 • The Retirement Planner can help you determine whether you can retire when you want to

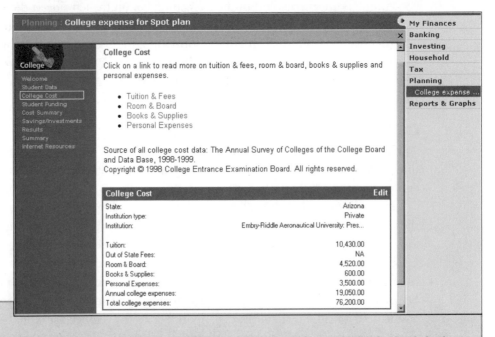

Figure 15-4 • The College Planner can estimate college costs for hundreds of schools in the United States

When you have finished entering information in the planner windows, the Results screen shows your financial plan with your child's college education included. Subsequent screens offer you a chance to play "what if" with your financial plan, summarize cost and funding information, and allow you to connect to the Internet for other resources, including college and financial aid information.

Home Purchase Planner

The Home Purchase Planner enables you to plan for the purchase of a home—either a primary residence or vacation home. Like the other planners, it prompts you for information about a specific event, but it also has built-in calculators to help you determine affordability so you can understand how a home would fit into your budget.

To get started, choose Planning | Home Purchase Planner to display the Can I Afford That House? window. Read the information on the introduction screen and click the Next link. Then follow prompts to enter information about your finances and the proposed purchase. In some cases, you can get information from your Quicken data file and from the Internet by clicking links within the window. When you're finished entering information, the planner displays its results. Subsequent screens summarize the information (see Figure 15-5) and display a glossary of terms you should know when purchasing a home.

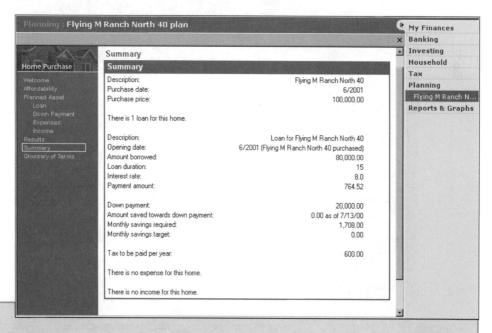

Figure 15-5 • The Summary screen for the Home Purchase Planner summarizes all information entered about the planned home purchase

Special Purchase Planner

The Special Purchase Planner enables you to plan for a major purchase, such as a new car or recreational vehicle or a costly vacation. It uses information already entered as plan assumptions, as well as new information you enter about the special purchase.

Choose Planning | Special Purchase Planner to display the Special Purchase Planner window (see Figure 15-6). Read the information in the window and follow the prompts that appear to enter all information about the purchase. When you are finished, the results window shows your financial plan with the planned purchase included. The Resources window provides links to other resources within Quicken and on Quicken.com to learn more about purchasing big-ticket items.

Playing "What If"

Once you've entered assumptions, created plans for specific events, and viewed your plan results, you might wonder how a change in one or more assumptions would affect the plan. You can use the What If Event Scenarios feature to see how the changes would affect the plan without changing the plan itself.

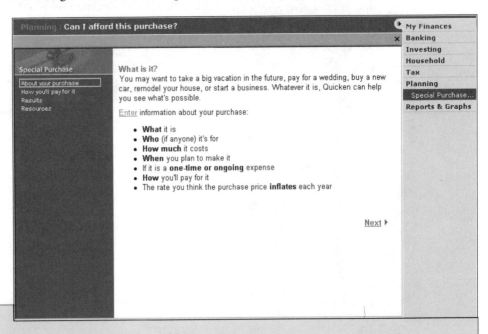

Figure 15-6 • The Special Purchase Planner helps you determine whether you can afford to buy high-ticket items

Here's an example. Say you've been offered a job in another state. The job pays about the same salary, but you can move to a town where your living expenses would be greatly reduced. You can see how the job change would affect your financial plans for the future by playing "what if" to modify existing assumptions, and then see the old and new plan results side by side.

Setting "What If" Options

Choose Planning | "What If" Event Scenarios. The What If window, which is shown in Figure 15-7, appears. The first time you use it, it displays the account balances shown in your Plan Results.

Click appropriate links on the left side of the window to open dialog boxes to change assumptions. In our example, you might use the following links:

- Click **Current Homes & Assets** to add proposed sale information about your current home.
- Click **Current Loans** to record the proposed payoff of your mortgage when you sell your current home.

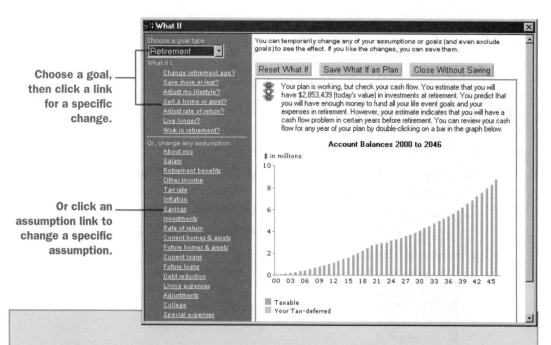

Figure 15-7 • The What If window enables you to play "what-if" with your financial plan

- Click **Future Homes & Assets** to add proposed purchase information about your new home and its associated mortgage.
- Click **Adjustments** to add a proposed adjustment for the reduced living expenses when you move to your new home.

Get the idea? Each time you make a change, the Plan Comparison chart changes. Here's what it might look like for our example:

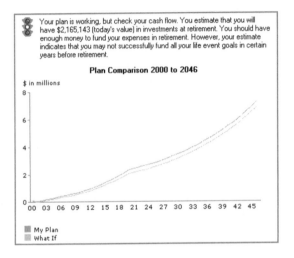

Using "What If" Results

When you've finished changing assumptions and viewing results, you can click one of the three buttons at the top of the What If window:

- **Reset What If** clears all the assumptions you changed while playing "what if." This enables you to start over.
- **Save What If As Plan** saves the assumptions you changed while playing "what if" as your actual financial plan. When the window closes, you'll see the results in the Planning Center window change accordingly.
- **Close Without Saving** simply closes the window so you can continue working with Quicken. Your settings are not saved.

Saving Money with Quicken

In This Chapter:

- *Saving Basics*

- *Reducing Debt*

- *Budgeting and Forecasting*

- *Saving Planners*

- *Investment Savings Calculator*

- *Setting Up Savings Goals*

The best way to prepare for life events is to build up your savings. Saving money is an important part of financial management. Savings enable you to take vacations and make major purchases without increasing debt, help your kids through college, handle emergencies, and have a comfortable retirement.

In this chapter, I tell you about saving money and how tools within Quicken can help. I provide plenty of information about various savings accounts so you can learn about your savings options. If you're in debt and can't even think about saving until you dig your way out, this chapter can help you, too. It also covers Quicken tools for reducing your debt.

> **Tip**   *If you don't mind risk and want to earn higher income on your savings, consult Chapter 8. It discusses investments, including stocks, bonds, and mutual funds.*

Saving Basics

Remember when you got your first "piggy bank"? It may not have looked like a pig, but it had a slot for slipping in coins and, if you were lucky, a removable rubber plug on the bottom that made it easy to get the coins out when you needed them. Whoever gave you the bank was trying to teach you your first financial management lesson: save money.

As an adult, things are a little more complex. In this section, I explain why you should save, provide some saving strategies, and tell you about the types of savings accounts that make your old piggy bank obsolete.

Why Save?

Most people save money so there's money to spend when they need it. Others save for a particular purpose. Still others save because they have so much they can't spend it all. Here's a closer look at why saving makes sense.

Saving for "Rainy Days"

When people say they are saving for a rainy day, they probably aren't talking about the weather. They're talking about bad times or emergencies—situations when they need extra cash.

For example, suppose the family car needs a new transmission. Or your beloved dog needs eye surgery. Or your daughter manages to break her violin three days before the big recital. In the "rainy day" scheme of things, these might be light drizzles. But your savings can help keep you dry.

Here are a few other examples. Suppose your employer goes bankrupt and closes up shop. Or after a three-martini lunch with a customer, you get back to the office, tell your boss what you really think of him, and quit on the spot. Or after being poked one too many times in the butt by a bull, you find it impossible to continue your career as a rodeo clown. If your paychecks stop coming, do you have enough savings to support yourself or your family until you can get another source of income? On the "rainy day" scale, this could be a torrential downpour. Your savings can be a good umbrella.

Saving for a Goal

Planning for your future often includes planning for events that affect your life— and your wallet. Saving money for specific events can help make these events memorable for what they are, rather than what they cost.

For example, take a recently engaged couple, Sally and Joe. They plan to marry within a year and buy a house right away. Within five years, they plan to have their first child. That's when Sally will leave her job to start the more demanding job of mother and homemaker. Someday, they hope their children will go to college, and they want to help cover the expenses. They also want to be able to help pay for their children's weddings. Eventually, they'll retire. And throughout their lives, they want to be able to take annual family vacations, buy a new car every six years or so, and get season tickets for the Arizona Diamondbacks.

All of these things are major events in Sally and Joe's lives. Saving in advance for each of these events will make them possible—without going into debt.

Saving for Peace of Mind

Some people save money because events in their lives showed them the importance of having savings. Children who lived through the Depression or bad financial times for their families grew up to be adults who understand the value of money and try hard to keep some available. They don't want to repeat the hard times they went through. Having healthy savings accounts gives them peace of mind.

Saving Strategies

There are two main ways to save: when you can or regularly.

Saving When You Can   When money is tight, saving can be difficult. People who are serious about saving, however, will force themselves to save as much as possible when they can. Saving when you can is better than not saving at all.

Saving Regularly   A better way to save money is to save a set amount periodically. For example, save $25 every week or $200 every month. Timing this with your paycheck makes sense; you can make a split deposit for the check. A savings like this is called an *annuity*, and you'd be surprised at how quickly the money can accumulate. Table 16-1 shows some examples based on a 4.5 percent annual interest rate.

Month	Weekly Contributions				Monthly Contributions				
	$25	$50	$75	$100	$50	$100	$200	$300	$400
1	$100	$200	$300	$401	$50	$100	$200	$300	$400
2	$226	$452	$677	$903	$100	$200	$401	$601	$801
3	$327	$653	$980	$1,307	$151	$301	$602	$903	$1,205
4	$428	$856	$1,284	$1,712	$201	$402	$805	$1,207	$1,609
5	$555	$1,110	$1,665	$2,220	$252	$504	$1,008	$1,511	$2,015
6	$657	$1,314	$1,971	$2,628	$303	$606	$1,211	$1,817	$2,423
7	$759	$1,519	$2,278	$3,038	$354	$708	$1,416	$2,124	$2,832
8	$888	$1,776	$2,664	$3,552	$405	$811	$1,621	$2,432	$3,242
9	$991	$1,982	$2,974	$3,965	$457	$914	$1,827	$2,741	$3,654
10	$1,095	$2,190	$3,284	$4,379	$509	$1,017	$2,034	$3,051	$4,068
11	$1,225	$2,449	$3,674	$4,899	$560	$1,121	$2,242	$3,363	$4,483
12	$1,329	$2,658	$3,987	$5,316	$613	$1,225	$2,450	$3,675	$4,900

Table 16-1: • Your Savings Can Grow Over Time

Types of Savings Accounts

There are different types of savings accounts, each with its own benefits and drawbacks.

Tip   *All the accounts discussed in this chapter (except where noted) should be insured by the FDIC (Federal Deposit Insurance Corporation). This organization covers savings deposits up to $100,000 per entity (person or company) per bank, thus protecting you from loss in the event of a bank failure.*

Standard Savings Accounts   All banks offer savings accounts, and most accommodate any balance. Savings accounts pay interest on your balance and allow you to deposit or withdraw funds at any time.

Holiday Clubs   A holiday club account is a savings account into which you make regular, equal deposits, usually on a weekly basis. Many banks offer these accounts, along with an option to automatically withdraw the deposit funds from your regular savings or checking account. The money stays in the account, earning interest until the club ends in October or November. The idea behind these accounts is to provide you with cash for the holidays, but there are variations on this theme, such as vacation club accounts that end in May or June.

Credit Union Payroll Savings   A bank isn't the only place where you can open a savings account. If your company has a credit union, it also offers a number of accounts. These accounts often offer the option of payroll savings deductions. This is a great feature for people who have trouble saving money, because the money comes out of their paychecks before they see (and can spend) it. It's as if the money never existed, when in reality it's accumulating in an interest-bearing account. In case you're wondering, the withdrawn funds are included in your taxable income.

Tip   *I had a payroll savings account with the credit union of my last employer. Every time I got a raise, I increased the amount of the savings withdrawal so my take-home pay was almost the same. Before I left that job, I was saving $100 a week, and I didn't miss a penny of it. Not bad!*

Certificates of Deposit   A certificate of deposit, or CD, is an account, normally with a bank, that requires you to keep the money on deposit for a specific length of time. As a reward for your patience, your earnings are based on a higher, fixed interest rate than what is available for a regular savings account. The longer the term of the deposit and the more money deposited, the higher the rate. At the CD's maturity date, you can "roll over" the deposit to a new account that may have a different interest rate, or you can take back the cash. If you withdraw the money before the CD's maturity date, you pay a penalty, which can sometimes exceed the amount of the interest earned.

Money Market Accounts   A money market account is actually a form of investment, but it should be included here because it is offered by many banks. It has a higher rate of return than a regular savings account but is not insured by the FDIC. It is considered a conservative investment and can be treated just like a savings account for depositing and withdrawing money.

Interest-Bearing Checking Accounts   Many banks offer interest-bearing checking accounts. They usually have minimum balance requirements, however, forcing you to keep a certain amount of money in the account at all times. Although it's nice to earn money on checking account funds, the interest rate is usually so low that it's better to have a regular checking account and keep your savings in a savings account or money market account.

Reducing Your Debt

It's not easy to save money if most of your income is spent paying credit card bills and loan payments. If you're heavily in debt, you might even be having trouble keeping up with all your payments. If that's the case, stop thinking about saving for a moment and start thinking about reducing your debt.

Consumer credit is a huge industry. It's easy to get credit cards—sometimes too easy. And it's a lot easier to pay for something with a piece of plastic than with cold, hard cash. The "buy now, pay later" attitude has become an acceptable way of life. It's no wonder that many Americans are deeply in debt.

Those credit card bills can add up, however. And paying just the minimum payment on each one only helps the credit card company keep you in debt—and paying interest—as long as possible. I've been there, so I know. Unfortunately, it took two experiences to set me straight. I hope you can learn your lesson the first time.

Don't despair. There is hope. Here are a few things you can do to dig yourself out of debt.

GET SMARTER   Use Quicken's Debt Reduction Planner to develop a complete plan for reducing your debt. I tell you about it later in this chapter.

Breaking the Pattern

Your first step to reducing debt must be to break the pattern of spending that got you where you are. For most people, that means cutting up credit cards. After all, it's tough to use a credit card if you can't hand it to a cashier at the checkout counter.

Before you take out the scissors, however, read this: You don't have to cut up *all* of your credit cards. Leave yourself one or two major credit cards for emergencies like car trouble or unexpected visits to the doctor. The cards that should go are the store and gas credit cards. They can increase your debt, but they can only be used in a few places.

Here's the logic behind this strategy. If you have 15 credit cards, each with a credit limit of $2,000, you can get yourself into $30,000 of debt. The minimum monthly payment for each card may be $50. That's $750 a month in minimum credit card payments. If you have only two credit cards, each with a credit limit of $2,000, you can only get yourself into $4,000 of debt. Your monthly minimum payment may be only $100. This reduces your monthly obligation, enabling you to pay more than the minimum so you can further reduce your debt.

Shopping for Cards with Better Interest Rates

Yes, it's nice to have a credit card with your picture on it. Or one that's gold, platinum, or titanium. Or one with your college, team, club, or association name on it. A friend of mine who breeds horses showed off a new Visa card with a picture of a horse on it. She told me it was her favorite. I asked her what the interest rate was, and she didn't know.

The purpose of a credit card is to purchase things on credit. When you maintain a balance on the account, you pay interest on it. The balance and interest rate determine how much it costs you to have that special picture or name on a plastic card in your wallet. Is it worth 19.8 percent a year? Or 21 percent? Not to me!

Tip *Here's a reality-check exercise: Gather together all of your credit card bills for the most recent month. Now add up all the monthly finance fees and interest charges. Multiply that number by 12. The result is an approximation of what you pay in interest each year. Now imagine how nice it would be to have that money in your hands the next time you went on vacation or needed a down payment on a new car or home.*

Low-interest credit cards are widely available. Sometimes you don't even have to look for them—offers arrive in the mail all the time. They promise low rates—usually under 10 percent a year. But you must read these offers carefully before you apply for one of these cards. Most offer the low rates for a short, introductory period—usually no longer than six months. (I got one once that offered 0 percent for the first 25 days. Big deal.) Some offer the low rate only on new purchases, while others offer the low rate only on balance transfers or cash advances. Be sure to find out what the rate is after the introductory period.

Here are two strategies for using a low-interest card:

- Consolidate your debt by transferring the balances of other credit cards to the new card. For this strategy, select a card that offers a low rate on balance transfers. When you transfer the balances, be sure to cut up the old cards so you don't use them to add more to your debt.
- Make purchases with the low-interest card. Make the new card your emergency credit card. Be sure to cut up your old emergency card so you don't wind up using both of them.

Tip   *If you really like that special picture or name on the card in your wallet, call the credit card company and ask if they can give you a better interest rate. In many instances, they can—especially when you tell them you want to close your account.*

Consolidating Your Debt

Consolidating your debt is one of the best ways to dig yourself out. By combining balances into one debt, whether through balance transfers to a single credit card or a debt consolidation loan, you're better able to pay off the balances without causing financial hardship. This is sometimes the only option when things have gotten completely out of control and you can't meet your debt obligations.

Tip   *If you own a home, consider a home equity loan to consolidate your debt. The interest rate is usually lower than any credit card or debt consolidation loan, and the interest may be tax deductible. I tell you more about home equity loans in Chapter 9.*

Using Charge Cards, Not Credit Cards

There's a difference between a credit card and a charge card:

- **Credit cards** enable you to buy things on credit. If each month you pay less than what you owe, you are charged interest on your account balance. Most major "credit cards" are true credit cards. MasterCard, Visa, and Discover are three examples. Most store "charge cards" are also credit cards.

- **Charge cards** enable you to buy things on credit, too. But when the bill comes, you're expected to pay the entire balance. You don't have to pay any interest, but if you don't pay the entire balance on time, you may have to pay late fees and finance charges. American Express is an example of a charge card.

The benefit of charge cards is that they make it impossible to get into debt. How can you owe the charge card company money if you must pay the balance in full every month? Using these cards prevents you from overspending. Every time you use the card to make a purchase, a little accountant in the back of your head should be adding the charge to a running total. You should stop spending when that total reaches the limit of your ability to pay.

Tip   *Chapters 4 and 5 explain how you can use Quicken to track credit card balances manually or online. This includes charge cards. If you use Quicken to keep track of expenditures, you won't need that little accountant in the back of your head.*

If you don't want an American Express card (for whatever reason), use another major credit card as a charge card. Just pay the entire balance each time you get a bill. If you don't carry a balance, you won't be charged interest.

If You Can't Stop Spending, Get Help

Many people who are deeply in debt may have a spending problem. They can't resist buying that fifth pair of running shoes or that trendy new outdoor furniture. They don't need the things they buy, but they buy them anyway. There's nothing wrong with that if your income can support your spending habits, but if your net worth is less than $0, it's a real problem—one that might require counseling to resolve.

The next time you make a purchase, stop for a moment and think about what you're buying. Is it something you need? Something you can use? Something you can justify spending the money on? If you can't answer yes to any of these questions, don't buy it. If you have to buy it anyway, it's time to seek professional help.

Living Debt-Free

It is possible to live debt-free—and you don't have to be rich to do it. Just learn to stop relying on credit cards to make your purchases and to spend only what you can afford to.

With the exception of my mortgage, I've been debt-free for the past four years. I do have major credit and charge cards, but I pay their balances in full every month, along with the bills I get for utilities and other living expenses. My trick: I only spend what I can afford to. I'm able to save whatever money I don't spend, and I don't pay a penny of nondeductible interest. Compared to the feeling I had (twice) when I was drowning in debt, being debt-free feels great! Try it sometime and see for yourself.

Budgeting and Forecasting

When money is tight or you're interested in meeting financial goals, it's time to create a budget and monitor your spending. But if you're serious about managing your money, you might want to create a budget before you need one. While Quicken's categories give you a clear understanding of where money comes from and where it goes, budgets enable you to set up predefined amounts for each category, thus helping you to control spending.

Budgets also make it easier to create forecasts of your future financial position. This makes it possible to see how much cash will be available at a future date—before the holidays, for summer vacation, or for the day you plan to put down a deposit on a new car.

In this part of the chapter, I tell you how to create a budget and use it to monitor your spending habits. I also explain how to create a forecast so you can glimpse your financial future.

Budgeting

The idea behind a budget is to determine expected income amounts and specify maximum amounts for expenditures. This helps prevent you from spending more than you earn. It also enables you to control your spending in certain categories. For example, say you realize that you go out for dinner a lot more often than you should. You can set a budget for the Dining category and track your spending to make sure you don't exceed the budget. You'll eat at home more often and save money.

In this section, I explain how to set up a budget and use it to keep track of your spending. I think you'll agree that budgeting is a great way to keep spending under control.

Organizing Categories into Groups

Budgets are based on transactions recorded for categories and subcategories. (That's why it's important to categorize all your transactions—and not to a Miscellaneous category!) Quicken also enables you to organize categories by category groups. Grouping similar categories together can simplify your budget.

You can see the group to which each category is assigned in the Category & Transfer List window (see Figure 16-1). Choose Finance | Category & Transfer List to display it.

Tip   You don't have to use the Groups feature when creating your budget. It's entirely optional.

The Default Groups   By default, Quicken includes several category groups that it assigns to the categories it creates when you first set up your Quicken data file:

- **Income** is for earned income, such as your salary, and miscellaneous income items, such as interest, dividends, and gifts received.

- **Mandatory Expenses** are expenses you can't avoid, such as fuel for your car, groceries, rent, and insurance.

Click Edit to change the group assignment for the selected category.

Group assignments appear in this column. If an entry is blank, a group has not yet been assigned.

Category	Type	Description	Group	Tax	Tax Item
Advances	Income				
Bonus	Income	Bonus Income	Income	T	W-2:Salary or wages, self
Condo Income	Income				
Consulting	Income	Consulting Income	Business Income	T	Schedule C:Gross receipts or …
Div Income	Income	Dividend Income	Income	T	Schedule B:Dividend income
Finance Charge	Income	Finance Charge Income	Business Income	T	Schedule C:Gross receipts or …
Gift Received	Income	Gift Received	Income		
Gr Sales	Income	Gross Sales	Business Income	T	Schedule C:Gross receipts or …
Interest Inc	Income	Interest Income	Income	T	Schedule B:Interest income
Invest Inc	Income	Investment Income	Income	T	
Other Inc	Income	Other Income	Income	T	Form 1040:Other income, misc.
Other Inc, Bus	Income	Other Business Income	Business Income	T	Schedule C:Other business in…
Royalties	Income				
Salary	Income	Salary Income	Income	T	W-2:Salary or wages, self
Services	Income	Service Income	Business Income	T	Schedule C:Gross receipts or …

My Finances : Category & Transfer List

New   Edit   Delete

Report   Options ▾   How Do I ▾   ✕

My Finances
Categories
Banking
Investing
Household
Tax
Planning
Reports & Graphs

Figure 16-1 • The Category & Transfer List window displays all categories and the names of the groups to which they are assigned

- **Discretionary** is for expenses you can avoid (or at least minimize), such as entertainment, subscriptions, and vacation.
- **Business Income** is for income from your business.
- **Business Expenses** is for expenses for running your business.

Tip *The Business Income and Business Expenses groups are only included if you indicated that you use Quicken to track the activity of a small business when you first set up your Quicken data file.*

Assigning Categories to Groups   You can assign a category to a group when you create or edit the category. In the Category & Transfer List window (see Figure 16-1), either click the New button or select an existing category and click the Edit button. The Set Up Category or Edit Category dialog box appears. Click the arrow next to the Group box to display the Group drop-down list, which looks like this:

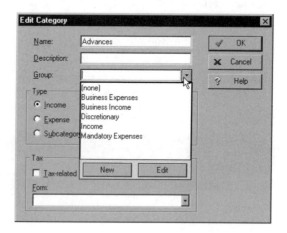

You have three options:

- Click the name of an existing group to assign it to a category.
- Click the New button to display a dialog box for creating a new group. When you enter a group name and click the OK button in the dialog box to save it, the new group is assigned to the category and appears in all group lists.
- Click the Edit button to display the Manage Category Groups dialog box, which you can use to create, edit, or delete groups.

When you have assigned a group to the category, click OK to save it with the category. It appears in the Category & Transfer List window.

Creating a Budget

Quicken can automatically generate a budget for you based on past transactions. You can edit the budget it creates to meet your needs. Or you can create a budget from scratch.

Creating a Budget Automatically

The quickest and easiest way to create a budget is to let Quicken do it for you based on your income and expenditures. For Quicken to create an accurate budget, however, you must have several months of transactions in your Quicken data file. Otherwise, the budget may not reflect all regular income and expenses.

Choose Planning | Budgeting to display the Budget window. Then choose the Autocreate command on the button bar's Edit menu to display the Automatically Create Budget dialog box; use this dialog box to set options for the budget.

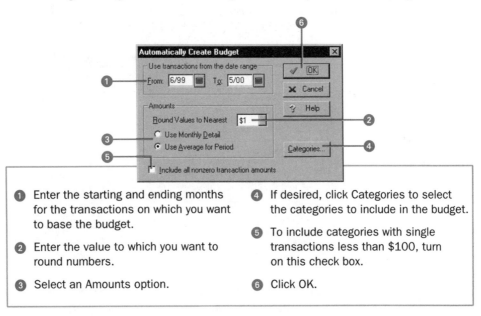

① Enter the starting and ending months for the transactions on which you want to base the budget.

② Enter the value to which you want to round numbers.

③ Select an Amounts option.

④ If desired, click Categories to select the categories to include in the budget.

⑤ To include categories with single transactions less than $100, turn on this check box.

⑥ Click OK.

Tip   *If you have never created a budget, Quicken may display a dialog box offering to create a budget for you based on the past year's information. You can click OK to generate the budget and display it in the Budget window.*

The Amounts option you select will affect the budget as follows:

- **Use Monthly Detail** copies the values for each month to the corresponding month in the budget.
- **Use Average For Period** enters monthly averages based on the period in the date range.

Tip *Select Use Monthly Detail if you have a full year's worth of transactions (or close to it) and you have seasonal income (such as a teaching job) or expenses (such as a vacation home). Select Use Average For Period if you have less than six months of transactions or don't have seasonal income or expenses.*

The Categories button displays the Select Categories To Include dialog box, shown next. You can use this dialog box to select specific categories to budget. You may find this useful if you only want to budget certain categories, such as dining, clothing, and entertainment. Click to toggle the check boxes beside each category name. The categories with check marks will be included in the budget when you click OK.

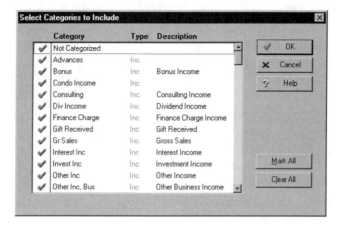

When you click OK in the Automatically Create Budget dialog box, Quicken creates a budget and displays it in the Budget window (see Figure 16-2).

You can use options on the button bar to work with the budget:

- **Categories** displays a dialog box you can use to specify categories to be included in the budget.
- **Edit** offers commands for modifying the budget. I discuss these options in the section "Modifying a Budget" later in this chapter.

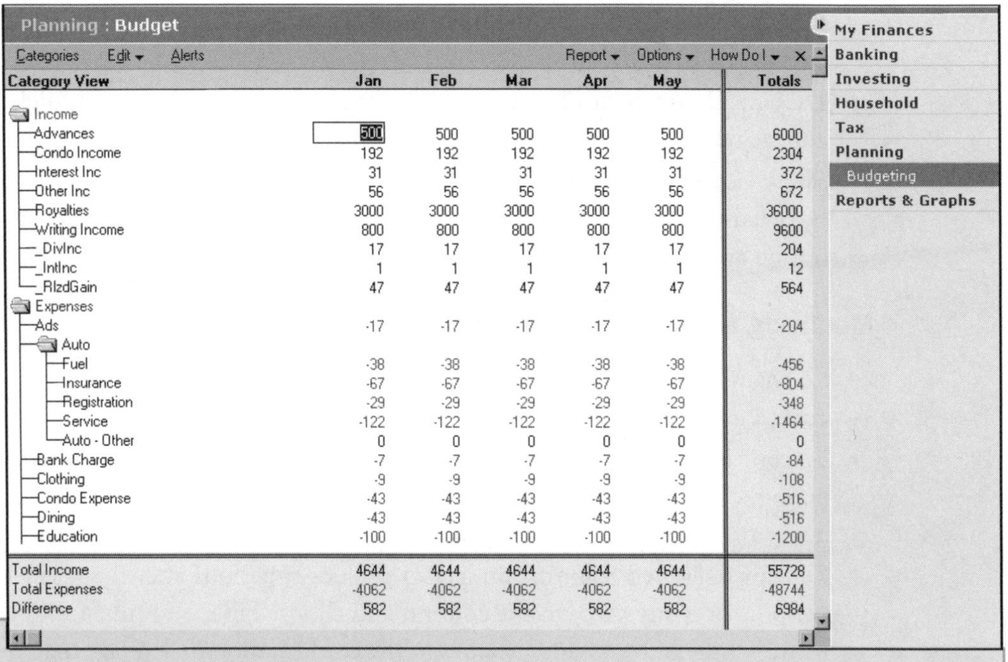

Figure 16-2 • The Budget window displays your budget

- **Alerts** displays the Monthly Expenses alert in the Set Up Alerts dialog box, which I discuss in Chapter 12. You can use this dialog box to set up spending alerts corresponding to budget amounts.

- **Report** offers a number of budget reporting options.

- **Options** offers commands for changing the view of the budget. I discuss these options in the next section of this chapter.

- **How Do I** provides instructions for completing specific tasks with the Budget window.

Changing the View of a Budget   You can modify your view of the budget with commands under the Options menu on the button bar:

- **Display Current Month** displays the budget for just the current month.

- **Display Current Quarter** displays the budget for just the current quarter. Quicken automatically adds monthly values to display a quarterly budget.

- **Display Current Year** displays the budget for just the current year. Quicken automatically adds monthly values to display an annual budget.

- **Display Months** displays the budget for all months in the year. This option is selected by default.
- **Display Quarters** displays the budget for all quarters in the year. Quicken automatically adds monthly values to display a quarterly budget.
- **Show Category Groups** organizes categories by groups. This option is selected by default. If you do not want to organize categories by groups, select this option again to turn it off.

Modifying a Budget   You can modify a budget in a number of ways:

- To change a specific budget value, click the value you want to change and enter a new value.
- To copy a selected category value to all budget periods after the selected value's period, choose Fill Row Right from the Edit menu on the button bar. Click Yes in the confirmation dialog box that appears.
- To copy a selected column's budget to all budget periods after the selected period, select any value in the column and choose Fill Columns from the Edit menu on the button bar. Click Yes in the confirmation dialog box that appears.
- To accurately enter biweekly budget amounts (such as a biweekly paycheck), click a value for the category and choose Two-Week from the Edit menu on the button bar. This displays the Set Up Two-Week Budget dialog box, which you can use to enter an expected budget value and exact starting date:

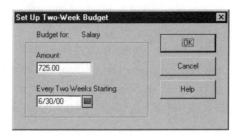

- To clear all entries for a category, select any entry in the category and choose Clear Row from the Edit menu on the button bar. Click Yes in the confirmation dialog box that appears.
- To clear all entries for a budget, choose Clear All from the Edit menu on the button bar. Click Yes in the confirmation dialog box that appears.

Whenever you make a budget change, Quicken automatically recalculates the totals for you.

Creating a Budget from Scratch   If you prefer, you can create a budget from scratch. This is more time consuming, but it forces you to look at each category carefully to estimate future expenses. The previous sections provide most of the information you need to create a budget from scratch. Here are the steps to follow; not all steps may be necessary, depending on your situation:

1. Choose Planning | Budgets to open the Budget window (refer to Figure 16-2).
2. Choose Clear All from the Edit menu on the button bar to clear all values out of an existing budget.
3. If desired, change the budget view by selecting a command from the Options menu on the button bar.
4. Click the Categories button on the button bar to choose budget categories with the Select Categories To Include dialog box.
5. Enter values for categories. You don't have to enter a minus sign for expenditures; Quicken enters it automatically for you.
6. Use commands under the Edit menu on the button bar to copy category or column values.

Managing Multiple Budgets

Quicken enables you to have more than one budget. Simply save one budget and create another.

Saving a Budget   Quicken automatically saves budget information, but if you have more than one budget, you must save each one separately. To save a budget, choose Save Budget from the Options menu on the button bar. The budget is saved as *Budget*.

Creating a New Budget   To create additional budgets, first choose Other Budgets from the Options menu on the button bar. The Manage Budgets dialog box appears:

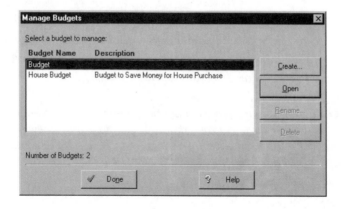

Then click the Create button to display the Create Budget dialog box, which you can use to set options for a budget, including the name, description, and how it should be created:

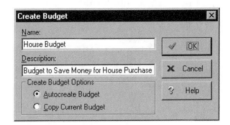

If you select the Autocreate Budget option in the Create Budget dialog box and you click OK, the Automatically Create Budget dialog box appears. Use it to set options as explained earlier in this chapter. When you've finished adjusting these settings, the new budget will appear in the Budget window (refer to Figure 16-2).

Managing Budgets   As you've probably guessed, you use the Manage Budgets dialog box, shown earlier, to work with budgets when you have more than one. Select a budget and click one of the buttons to work with it:

- **Open** opens the selected budget.
- **Rename** displays a dialog box you can use to change the name and description of the selected budget.
- **Delete** deletes the selected budget.

Tip   *Neither the Rename nor Delete button in the Manage Budgets dialog box is available if the selected budget is currently open.*

Comparing a Budget to Actual Transactions

Once you have created a budget you can live with, it's a good idea to periodically compare your actual income and expenditures to budgeted amounts. Quicken lets you do this a number of different ways.

Tip   *Make sure you compare budgeted amounts to actual results for the period for which you have recorded data. For example, don't view a year-to-date Budget Report if you began entering data into Quicken in March. Instead, customize the report to show actual transactions beginning in March.*

Budget Reports   The Reports menu on the button bar in the Budget window offers two different reports for comparing budgeted amounts to actual results:

- **Budget Report** (see Figure 16-3) displays the year-to-date actual and budgeted transactions.
- **Monthly Budget Report** displays the actual and budgeted transactions by month.

In both reports, favorable differences appear as black, positive numbers; unfavorable differences appear as red, negative numbers.

Tip   *I tell you about creating reports, including how to customize them, in Chapter 13.*

Budget Variance Graph   Choosing Budget Variance Graph on the Reports menu on the Budget window's button bar creates two charts in the Budget Variance Graph window (see Figure 16-4):

- **Actual Versus Budgeted Net Income** shows the favorable and unfavorable differences between actual and budgeted income amounts.
- **Actual Versus Budgeted Category Groups** shows the budgeted, actual, and over-budget values for each of the category groups.

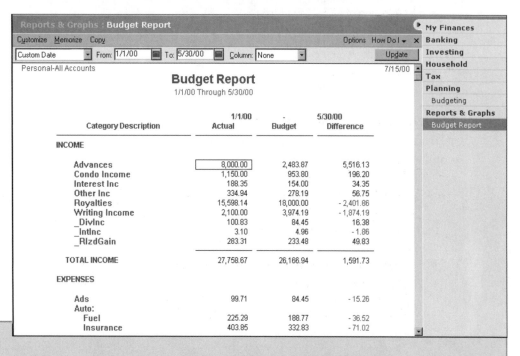

Figure 16-3 • A Budget Report compares actual to budgeted amounts

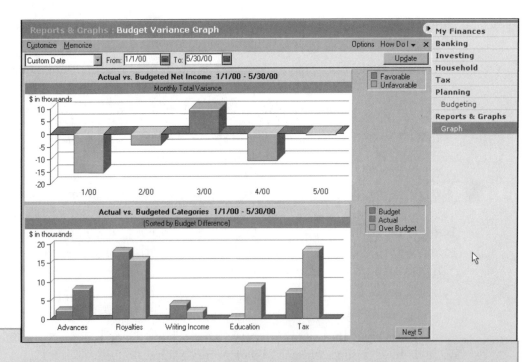

Figure 16-4 • **The Budget Variance Graph window displays variances between budgeted and actual amounts**

Tip   *I explain how to create graphs, including how to customize them, in Chapter 13.*

Budget Comparison Graphs   You can display budget graphs in the My Finances window. This feature enables you to keep an eye on the budget categories and groups that interest you most.

To use this feature, switch to the My Finances window and customize it as instructed in Chapter 1. The items or snapshots that provide budget information are:

- **Budget Goal Progress** tracks spending for a single category's budget. This helps you monitor spending for a specific category that's important to you.
- **Budgeted Categories** compares actual category amounts with your budget.
- **Budgeted Net Income** displays a chart that compares your budgeted to actual net income.

- **Budgets** displays a chart that compares your actual to budgeted income and expenses.
- **Category Group Budget** tracks progress against your budget by category group.

Tip   *You can customize any of these graphs by right-clicking it and choosing the Customize This Chart or Customize This Graph command from the contextual menu that appears.*

Using Alerts

If you're not interested in fancy reports and charts but want to be alerted when you spend too much, you can automatically save budgeted amounts as alerts.

In the Budget window (see Figure 16-2), choose Save As Alerts from the Options menu on the button bar. The Save Budget Alerts Options dialog box appears; use it to set options for saving budgeted amounts as Quicken alerts:

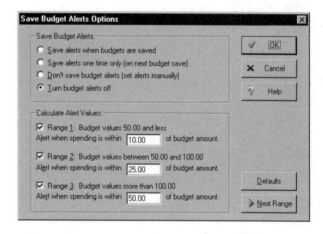

The dialog box offers four options for using alerts with budgeted amounts:

- **Save Alerts When Budgets Are Saved** automatically updates alerts with budgeted amounts every time you change and save your budget.
- **Save Alerts One Time Only** updates alerts with budgeted amounts only once—the next time you save your budget.
- **Don't Save Budget Alerts** lets you manually set alerts for budgeted spending. I explain how to set up alerts in Chapter 11.
- **Turn Budget Alerts Off** disables the budget alerts feature.

You can also set up ranges for alerting you about actual spending that approaches budgeted amounts. For example, say a category's budget is $90. Quicken can alert you that you're approaching the budgeted amount when you spend $65 or more. Default values for this feature are set in the bottom of the dialog box; you can click the Next Range button to continue modifying ranges if desired. To disable this feature, simply turn off the check boxes for each range.

Once set up, Quicken monitors spending in the background. When you enter a transaction that causes a category to exceed (or approach) its spending limit, a dialog box appears to scold you.

Forecasting

Forecasting uses known and estimated transactions to provide a general overview of your future financial situation. This "crystal ball" can help you spot potential cash flow problems (or surpluses) so you can prepare for them.

Opening the Cash Flow Forecast Window

Your financial forecast appears in the Cash Flow Forecast window, which also offers commands and options to modify the forecast. To open this window, choose Planning | Cash Flow Forecast. Before you enter forecasting data, the forecast will probably look like a straight line. You can see a completed forecast (which is much more interesting) in Figure 16-5.

Creating a Forecast

A forecast without data is like a crystal ball that's full of fog—it doesn't show you much. To get a clear picture, you need to enter data about future transactions. Quicken lets you do this in two ways:

- Automatically create a forecast based on existing scheduled transactions and register transactions or based on a budget.
- Manually enter known and estimated income and expense items for the forecast period.

Tip   *In my opinion, the best way to create a forecast is to let Quicken automatically create it for you and then fine-tune it by entering additional items that do not appear in your budget or register.*

Automatically Creating a Forecast   On the Cash Flow Forecast window's button bar, select Update Forecast from the Options menu to display the Automatically Create Forecast dialog box:

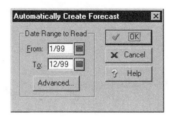

> **Tip**   *The Automatically Create Forecast dialog box may appear automatically the first time you open the Cash Flow Forecast window.*

How you proceed depends on the kind of data you use—budget data or register data.

- To create a forecast with budget data, enter beginning and ending dates for which you have a budget. This will normally be the current year. Click the Advanced button to display the Advanced AutoCreate dialog box, shown next. Select Create Both in the top part of the dialog box and From Budget Data in the bottom part of the dialog box. Click Done to save your settings and then click OK in the Automatically Create Forecast dialog box to create the forecast. Figure 16-5 illustrates a forecast based on a budget.

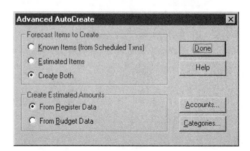

- To create a forecast based on register data, enter beginning and ending dates for which you have register data. The time span should cover at least six months, and for best results, it should cover a full year. Click the Advanced button to display the Advanced AutoCreate dialog box. Select Create Both in the top part of the dialog box and From Register Data in the bottom part of the dialog box. Click Done to save your settings and then click OK in the Automatically Create Forecast dialog box to create the forecast.

A red line (not illustrated) indicates a forecasted deficit.

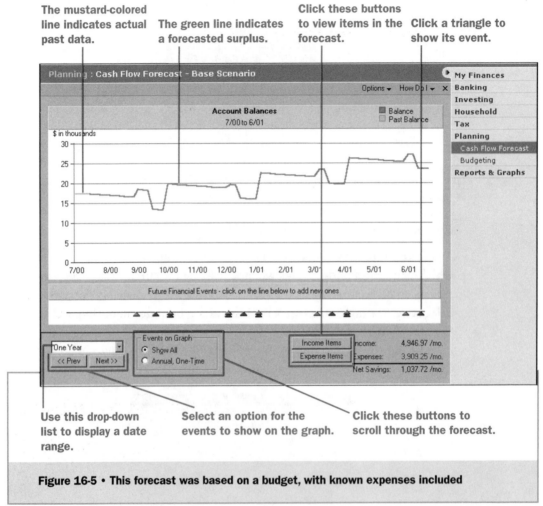

The mustard-colored line indicates actual past data.

The green line indicates a forecasted surplus.

Click these buttons to view items in the forecast.

Click a triangle to show its event.

Use this drop-down list to display a date range.

Select an option for the events to show on the graph.

Click these buttons to scroll through the forecast.

Figure 16-5 • This forecast was based on a budget, with known expenses included

Entering Income and Expense Items

Once you've created a forecast, you can fine-tune it by entering or modifying known or estimated events. Click the Income Items or Expense Items button in the Cash Flow Forecast window (see Figure 16-5). The Forecast Income Items or Forecast Expense Items window appears; use this window to add, modify, or delete items:

**To edit an item, click it to
select it and enter a new value.**

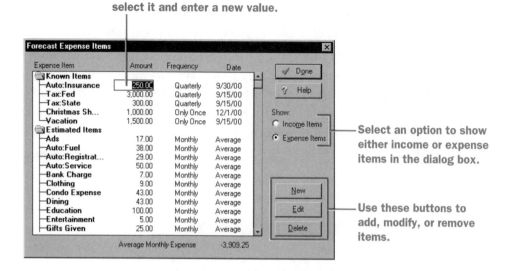

Select an option to show
either income or expense
items in the dialog box.

Use these buttons to
add, modify, or remove
items.

When you click the New or Edit button, the Create New Income/Expense Item
or Edit Income/Expense Item dialog box appears (see the following illustration).
Use this dialog box to enter or edit information for a forecast item. The exact
name of the dialog box varies, depending on how you're using it, but the options
are the same.

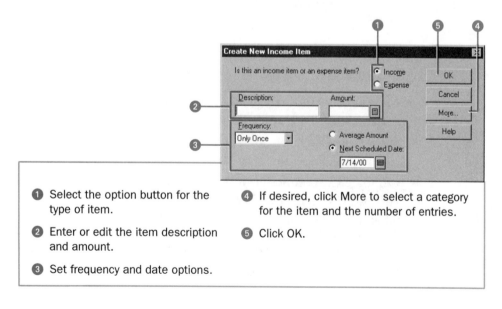

❶ Select the option button for the
type of item.

❷ Enter or edit the item description
and amount.

❸ Set frequency and date options.

❹ If desired, click More to select a category
for the item and the number of entries.

❺ Click OK.

Working with Scenarios

When you create a single forecast, you create a forecast for the *base scenario*. Just as you can have multiple budgets, you can also have multiple forecast scenarios.

Creating a New Scenario   To create a new scenario, choose Manage Scenarios from the Options menu on the Cash Flow Forecast window's button bar. The Manage Forecast Scenarios dialog box, which is shown next, appears. Click the New button to display a dialog box in which you can enter a scenario name and choose to copy the existing scenario. When you click OK, the new scenario's name appears as the selected scenario on the Scenario Data drop-down list.

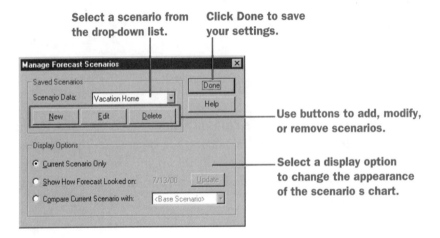

Select a scenario from the drop-down list.

Click Done to save your settings.

Use buttons to add, modify, or remove scenarios.

Select a display option to change the appearance of the scenario s chart.

Changing a Scenario's Display   The Display Options in the Manage Forecast Scenarios dialog box let you change the display of a selected scenario:

- **Current Scenario Only**, which is the default option, displays only one scenario in the Forecasting window.
- **Show How Forecast Looked On** enables you to update the scenario for the current date. Select this option and then click the Update button.
- **Compare Current Scenario With** enables you to include two scenarios in the Forecasting window (see Figure 16-6). This makes it easy to see how one differs from the other.

Select the option you want and click Done to apply it.

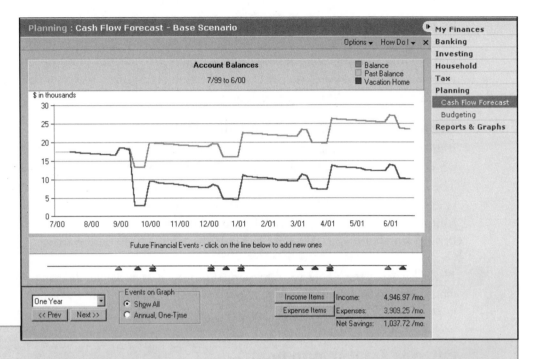

Figure 16-6 • You can include two scenarios in the Cash Flow Forecast window. This makes it easy to see how they compare

Quicken Savings Tools

Quicken offers a number of features you can use to help you save money, including financial planners, savings goals, and the Investment Savings Calculator.

Debt Reduction Planner

The Debt Reduction Planner is a tool for helping you reduce your debt. You enter information about your financial situation, and Quicken develops a debt reduction plan for you.

 SAVE MONEY   In my opinion, the Debt Reduction Planner is one of the best planning features of Quicken. Not only is it thorough and easy to use, but it is an excellent tool for teaching people how they can get out of debt as quickly as possible, saving hundreds (if not thousands) of dollars in interest charges.

To get started, choose Planning | Debt Reduction Planner. If you have explored this feature before, the Debt Reduction window appears with a chart showing the information you previously entered (refer to Figure 16-7 later in this chapter). If you have never used it before, the Debt Reduction dialog box appears, enabling you to create a new debt reduction plan.

Creating a New Debt Reduction Plan

If necessary, click the New Plan button on the button bar of the Debt Reduction window. If a dialog box warns that you will overwrite your current plan, click Yes. The Debt Reduction dialog box appears, displaying its Welcome screen. Insert your Quicken Deluxe CD in your CD-ROM drive and click the Next button to continue. An introductory movie plays to tell you what the Debt Reduction Planner can do for you. When it has finished, click the Next button to begin.

Note   *If you don't have your Quicken Deluxe CD-ROM available, you can skip the movie. But I do recommend viewing it the first time you use the Debt Reduction Planner.*

Entering Debt Information

When you click the Next button after viewing the movie, the Debts tab of the window appears. It should look something like this:

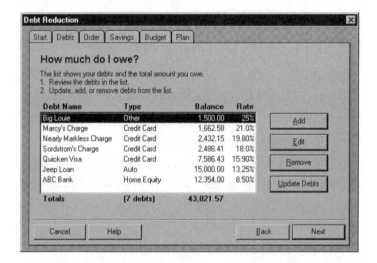

This tab lists all your current debts. Use the buttons to the right of the list to modify it:

- If the debt list is not complete, click the Update Debts button to import current debt information from your Quicken data file.
- To add a debt that you do not track in Quicken, click the Add button. The Edit Debt Reduction dialog box appears; use it to enter information about the debt and click OK to add it to the list:

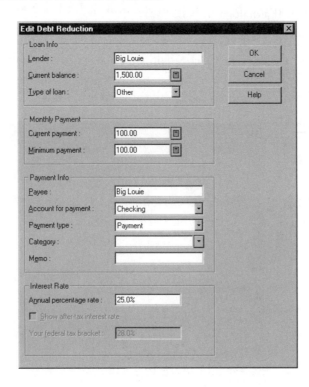

- To modify information about a debt, select it and click the Edit button to display the Edit Debt Reduction dialog box. Make changes as desired and click OK to save the changes.
- To remove a debt from the list, select it and click the Remove button. In the confirmation dialog box that appears, click Yes. This removes the debt from the Debt Reduction Planner but does not remove it from your Quicken data file. You may want to use this feature to remove a long-term debt such as a mortgage so you can concentrate on higher interest, short-term debt.

When the debt list shows all of your debts, click the Next button to continue.

Tip *If required information is missing from one or more debts, Quicken will tell you and then display the Edit Debt Reduction dialog box for each debt so you can update the information. You must complete this process before you can continue.*

Next, Quicken tells you about your current debt situation, including your total debt, your total monthly payments, and a projection of when you will be debt-free based on the debt information you provided. Click Next to continue.

Setting the Order of Debts

The Order tab of the Debt Reduction dialog box puts your debts in the order of cost, with the highest at the top. Read the instructions that appear onscreen and click Next when prompted to view the ordered list. It might look something like this:

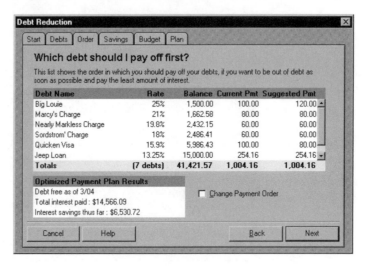

This tab sets the debt payoff order so that the most expensive debt is paid off first, thus saving you interest charges. The Suggested Pmt column offers a suggested payment amount; following the suggestion makes it possible to pay off the debts faster without increasing your total monthly payments. If desired, you can turn on the Change Payment Order check box to change the order in which debts are paid off—this, however, will cost you more and increase the payoff time. Click Next to continue.

If you turn on the Change Payment Order check box and click the Next button, the dialog box changes to enable you to change the order of debts. Click a debt to select it and then click the Move Up or Move Down button to change its location in the list. When you've finished, click Next.

Using Savings to Pay Off Debt

The Savings tab begins by playing a movie that tells you why you might want to use savings and investments to pay off your debt. Listen carefully—the movie is full of good information! When the movie is finished, click Next.

Quicken summarizes your current savings and investments and enables you to specify how much of your savings should be applied to your debt:

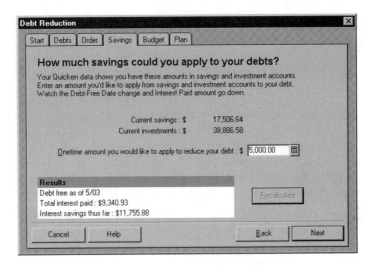

Enter a value in the text box and click the Recalculate button. The Results area shows the effect of your change. Click Next to continue.

Adjusting Your Budget

The Budget tab offers options for helping you reduce your spending, which can, in return, help you reduce your debt. It begins by displaying a movie with tips and instructions. When the movie is finished, click Next to continue.

Quicken displays a list of your top four expenses, with text boxes for entering the amount by which you can cut back on each one each month:

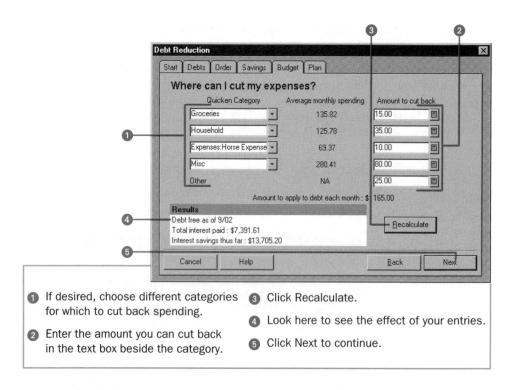

① If desired, choose different categories for which to cut back spending.

② Enter the amount you can cut back in the text box beside the category.

③ Click Recalculate.

④ Look here to see the effect of your entries.

⑤ Click Next to continue.

Enter the amounts by which you can cut back for the categories that appear or for different categories you select from the drop-down lists. Quicken automatically suggests that you apply the savings to the debt, thus adjusting the Results area for your entries. Click Next to continue.

Reviewing the Plan

The Plan tab displays your custom debt reduction action plan:

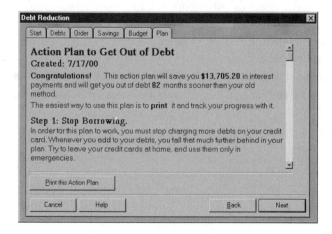

Scroll through the debt reduction plan to see what it recommends. Better yet, click the Print This Action Plan button to print a copy you can refer to throughout the coming months. Click Next to continue.

Next, Quicken offers to track your debt reduction plan for you. You can toggle the settings on two different check boxes to enable this feature:

- **Keep Track Of My Debt Reduction Plan** tells Quicken to alert you if you fall behind on debt reduction and to include your debt in budgeting in forecasting models. (I tell you about alerts in Chapter 11 and about budgeting and forecasting earlier in this chapter.)

- **Set Up Scheduled Transactions For My Monthly Payments** tells Quicken to schedule transactions for the monthly payments included in your debt reduction plan. This makes it impossible for you to forget about debt reduction payments. (I tell you about scheduling payments in Chapter 11.)

Turn on the check box for each option that you want to enable and then click Next.

Viewing the Debt Reduction Plan Graph

When you click Done in the final screen of the Debt Reduction dialog box, the Debt Reduction window appears (see Figure 16-7). It uses a graph to compare debt reduction using your current method (the blue line) and using your new debt reduction plan (the green line).

Modifying the Plan

Once you have a debt reduction plan, you can modify it in a number of ways:

- Click the Update Debt Balances button on the button bar to import the current balances of your debt into the Debt Reduction Planner.
- Enter new values in the Current Plan area at the bottom of the Debt Reduction window.
- Click the New Plan button on the button bar to create a new plan from scratch.

No matter which method you choose, Quicken will automatically revise the graph and other information to reflect your changes.

Modify values here to
change the plan summary.

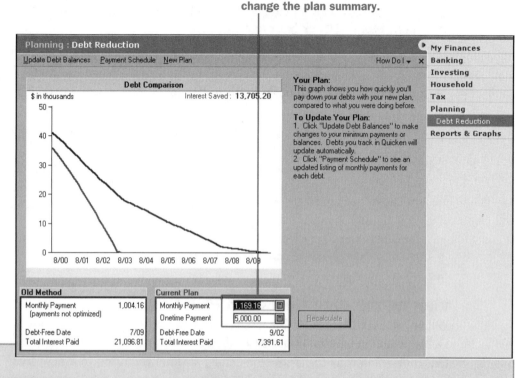

Figure 16-7 • The Debt Reduction Plan window clearly illustrates how quickly you can get out of debt and save interest costs by using Quicken's plan

Save More Planner

Quicken's Save More Planner helps you figure out how to save more money. It uses a simple equation to point out where the money comes from, where it goes, and what's left over. Then it offers valuable advice on how you can save that money and more, using Quicken to help you.

Choose Planning | Save More Planner to display the How Can I Save More? window (see Figure 16-8). Click the Next button in the introduction window and follow the prompts that appear to enter information, perform calculations, and learn more about saving money with Quicken.

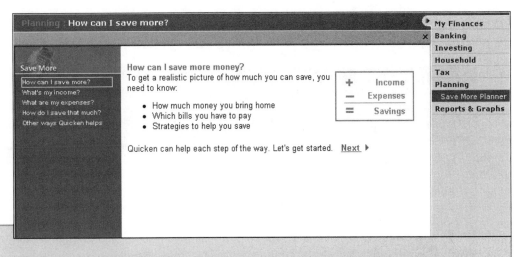

Figure 16-8 • Use the Save More Planner to learn how you can save more money

Savings Goals

Quicken's Savings Goals feature helps you save money by "hiding" funds in an account. You set up a savings goal and make contributions to it using the Savings Goals window. Although the money never leaves the source bank account, it is deducted in the account register, thus reducing the account balance in Quicken. If you can't see the money in your account, you're less likely to spend it.

Tip *This really works. I used this technique with a paper check register years ago. Not only did it help me save money, but it prevented me from bouncing checks in the days when I kept a dangerously low checking account balance.*

Open the Savings Goals window by choosing Planning | Savings Goals. Figure 16-9 shows what the window looks like with one savings goal already created.

The top half of the Savings Goals window lists the savings goals you have created with Quicken. The bottom half shows the progress for the selected goal. You can use button bar options to work with window contents:

- **New** enables you to create a savings goal.
- **Edit** enables you to modify the selected savings goal.
- **Delete** removes the selected savings goal.

Progress and information for
the selected goal appears here.

Savings goals are
listed here.

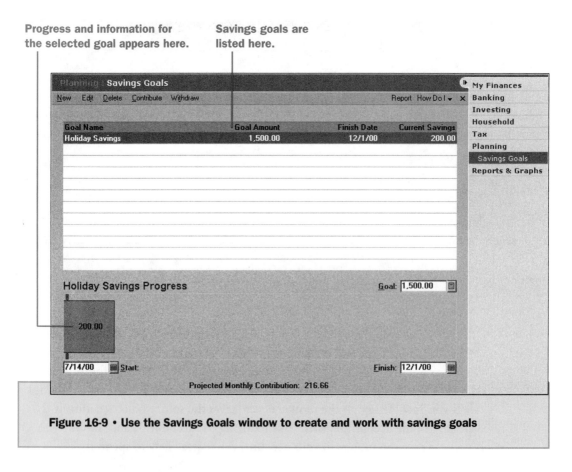

Figure 16-9 • Use the Savings Goals window to create and work with savings goals

- **Contribute** enables you to contribute funds from a Quicken account to the selected savings goal.
- **Withdraw** enables you to remove funds from a savings goal and return them to a Quicken account.
- **Report** creates a report of the activity for savings goals.
- **How Do I** provides instructions for performing specific tasks with the Savings Goals window.

Creating a Savings Goal

To create a savings goal, click the New button on the button bar in the Savings Goals window. The Create New Savings Goal dialog box appears:

Enter the information for your savings goal in the text boxes. The name of the savings goal cannot be the same as any Quicken category or account. For the Finish Date, enter the date by which you want to have the money saved. For example, if you're using savings goals to plan for a vacation, the Finish Date should be shortly before the date you want to start the vacation. When you've finished, click OK to add the savings goal to the list in the Savings Goals window.

Contributing Funds to a Savings Goal

To contribute funds to a savings goal, select the savings goal in the Savings Goals window and click the Contribute button on the button bar. The Contribute To Goal dialog box appears:

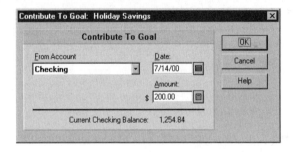

Select the account from which you want to transfer the money from the drop-down list. The balance of the account appears in the bottom of the dialog box. Then enter the amount of the transfer in the Amount box. By default, Quicken suggests the projected monthly contribution amount, but you can enter any amount you like. When you've finished, click OK.

As shown in the next illustration, Quicken creates an entry in the account register of the account from which the money was contributed. It also updates the progress bar and information in the Savings Goals dialog box.

7/14/00		Contribution towards goal	200	00			1,054	84
		[Holiday Savings]						

> **Tip** *When you create a savings goal, Quicken creates an asset account to record the goal's transactions and balance. To automate contributions to the goal, you can create a scheduled transaction to periodically transfer money from one of your bank accounts to the savings goal asset account. I tell you about scheduled transactions in Chapter 11.*

Meeting Your Goal

Once you have met your savings goal, you can either withdraw the funds from the savings goal so they appear in a Quicken account or delete the savings goal to put the money back where it came from.

Withdrawing Money In the Savings Goals window, select the savings goal from which you want to withdraw money. Click the Withdraw button on the button bar. The Withdraw From Goal dialog box (shown next), which works very much like the Contribute To Goal dialog box, appears. Use it to remove funds from the savings goal and put them back into the account from which they were contributed:

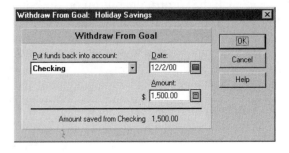

Deleting a Savings Goal In the Savings Goals window, select the savings goal you want to delete and click the Delete button on the button bar. A dialog box appears, asking if you want to keep the savings goal account for your records:

- Click Yes to transfer the funds back to the original account(s) and keep the savings goal account.
- Click No to transfer funds back to the original account(s) and delete the savings goal account.

Financial Calculators

Quicken includes three financial calculators that you can use to help yourself save money: the Investment Savings Calculator, College Calculator, and Retirement Calculator. These calculators are very similar in appearance and functionality, but each is designed for a specific purpose.

Investment Savings Calculator

The Investment Savings Calculator, which is one of Quicken's financial calculators, enables you to calculate savings annuities. Choose Planning | Financial Calculators | Savings. The Investment Savings Calculator appears:

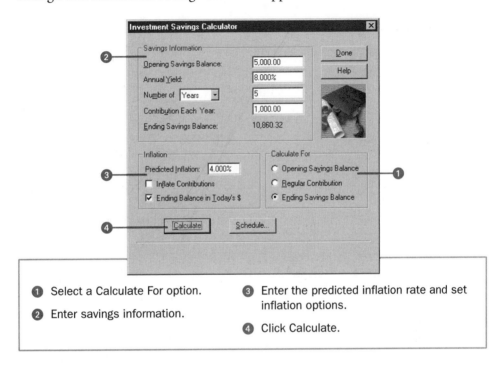

① Select a Calculate For option.

② Enter savings information.

③ Enter the predicted inflation rate and set inflation options.

④ Click Calculate.

Select a Calculate For option and then enter or select values and options throughout the dialog box. Most options are pretty straightforward and easy to understand. The Calculate For option affects which value is calculated by Quicken:

- **Opening Savings Balance** calculates the amount of money you should currently have saved based on the values you enter.
- **Regular Contribution** calculates the minimum amount you should regularly contribute to savings based on the values you enter.
- **Ending Savings Balance** calculates the total amount saved at the end of the savings period based on the values you enter.

The Inflation options enable you to enter a predicted inflation rate and then apply that rate to the contributions and to the calculation of the present value of the final balance. When you click Calculate, Quicken displays the results. You can click the Schedule button to see a printable list of deposits with a running balance total.

Managing Quicken Files

In This Appendix:

- *Backing Up and Restoring Data Files*

- *Importing and Exporting Data*

- *Performing Other File Management Tasks*

- *Password-Protecting Quicken Data*

Appendix

All the data you enter in Quicken is stored in a Quicken data file. This file includes all account and category setup information, transactions, and other data you have entered into Quicken.

Commands under Quicken's File menu enable you to perform a number of file management tasks, including backing up, restoring, importing, exporting, renaming, and deleting data files. In this appendix, I cover all of these tasks.

Caution   *Technically speaking, your Quicken data file really consists of a number of files with the same name and different extensions. Manipulating these files without using Quicken's file management tools can cause errors.*

Backing Up Your Quicken Data File

Imagine this: You set up Quicken to track all of your finances, and you record transactions regularly so the Quicken data file is always up to date. Then one evening, when you start your computer to surf the Net, you find that your hard drive has died. Not only have your plans for the evening been ruined, but your Quicken data file is also a casualty of your hard drive's untimely death.

If you back up your Quicken data as regularly as you update its information, the loss of your Quicken data file would be a minor inconvenience, rather than a catastrophe. In this section, I explain how to back up your Quicken data file and how to restore it if the original file is lost or damaged.

Tip   *May 1, 1993, and March 12, 2000, are the two days I lost hard drives. I learned a valuable lesson about backing up data the first time, and it really saved my skin the second time. Heed my warning: Back up your document files! Don't learn the hard way about the importance of backing up data.*

Backing Up

Quicken makes it very difficult to forget backing up. Every third time you exit the Quicken program, it displays the Automatic Backup dialog box, which prompts you to back up your data file:

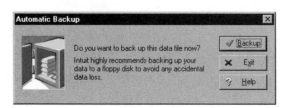

Tip   *You can also begin the backup process by choosing File | Backup or pressing CTRL-B at any time while using Quicken.*

When this dialog box appears, click the Backup button. Another dialog box may appear, telling you that you need to have a formatted floppy disk and label available. It also recommends that you alternate between two disks for backup purposes. This means you'll always have two versions backed up in case one version is bad. Click the Yes button to continue.

The Select Backup Drive dialog box appears next:

Tip   *You don't have to back up to a floppy disk. You can back up to any disk, including a Zip disk or other removable media. Do not back up to your hard drive. Doing so defeats the purpose of backing up!*

Insert your disk in the disk drive and choose the drive designation letter from the Backup Drive drop-down list. Then select one of the two File to Back Up options:

- **Current File** backs up just the currently open Quicken data file. This is the option you'll probably select most often.
- **Select From List** enables you to select the Quicken data file you want to back up from a list of data files. This option is only useful if you have more than one Quicken data file.

After making your selection, click the OK button.

If you're backing up to media other than a floppy disk (such as a Zip disk), a Backup Directory dialog box appears. Use it to select the disk directory in which the backup files should be saved. Then click OK to continue.

Quicken backs up the data to the disk. It displays a status window as it works. The Quicken data file may disappear from the screen momentarily. When the backup is complete, a dialog box tells you that the file has been backed up successfully. Click the OK button.

Tip   *If your Quicken data file is too large to fit on one disk, Quicken will prompt you to insert additional formatted disks until the backup is complete. Follow the instructions that appear onscreen to complete the backup.*

Restoring

In the event of loss or damage to your data file, you can restore from backup. Start Quicken and then choose File | Restore Backup File. The Select Restore Drive dialog box appears:

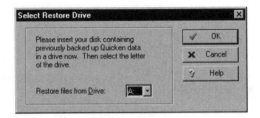

Choose the drive designation letter for the drive containing the backup files from the Restore Files From Drive drop-down list. Click OK to continue. The Restore Quicken File dialog box appears next:

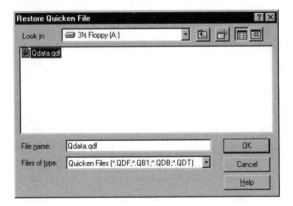

Use this dialog box to locate and select the data file that you want to restore. Then click OK. One of two things may happen:

- If the file has the same name as the Quicken data file currently in use, a dialog box appears asking if you want to overwrite the file in use. To replace the current file with the backup copy, click OK.

- If the file has the same name as another Quicken data file in the QUICKENW directory on your hard disk, a dialog box appears warning you that you will overwrite the existing file. If you're sure you want to restore the backup and overwrite the existing file with the same name, click OK.

Quicken restores the file from the backup copy. It places a copy of the restored file in the QUICKENW directory on your hard disk, displaying a status window as it works. When it has finished, it displays a dialog box telling you that the file has been restored successfully. Click OK.

Importing and Exporting Data

Quicken supports its QIF format for importing data from other versions of Quicken to Quicken 2001, or exporting Quicken 2001 for Windows data for use with other versions of Quicken.

Importing Quicken Data

You can import data saved in Quicken QIF format into Quicken 2000 for Windows. You might find this useful when converting Quicken for Macintosh or QuickBooks files to Quicken format. Simply use the program's Export command to create the QIF format file. Then import the data into Quicken.

Tip   *Quicken 2001 can automatically open files created with most versions of Quicken for Windows (.QDF extension), Quicken for DOS (.QDF extension), or Microsoft Money (.MNY extension). In most cases, you don't need to use the Import command for these files; use the Open command instead. Additional converters are available on the Quicken technical support Web site (**http://www.intuit.com/support/quicken/**). That's also where you can find details about converting Quicken for Macintosh data files.*

Before you import a QIF format file into your Quicken data file, back up the data file. Remember, Quicken automatically saves all changes to a data file. If something goes wrong with the import, your original data file could be damaged or could contain some incorrect transactions. I explain how to back up a data file earlier in this appendix.

To import a QIF format file, choose File | Import | QIF File. The QIF Import dialog box appears. Click the Browse button to display the Import From QIF File dialog box:

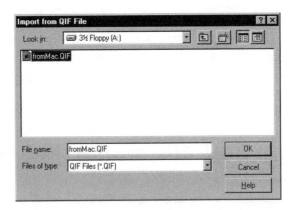

After you locate and select the QIF format file that you want to import, click OK to go back to the QIF Import dialog box, which looks like this:

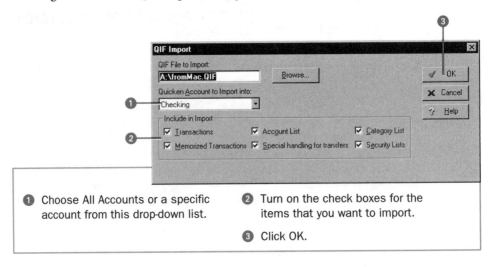

❶ Choose All Accounts or a specific account from this drop-down list.

❷ Turn on the check boxes for the items that you want to import.

❸ Click OK.

Set options as desired in the QIF Import dialog box. If you are importing into a brand-new Quicken file that does not include any accounts or categories, be sure to turn on the Account List, Category List, and Security List check boxes. When you have finished, click OK to begin the import.

If you are importing data for which a category or class does not exist in the current data file, a dialog box appears asking if you want to create new categories or classes for imported items. Click Yes to have Quicken create categories and classes as necessary. Quicken displays a status dialog box as it imports the transactions. Another dialog box tells you when the import is finished. Click OK. You can then begin working with the revised data file.

Note *The Import submenu under the File menu also offers options for importing TurboTax files and WebConnect files. I tell you about TurboTax in Chapter 14 and about WebConnect in Chapter 5.*

Exporting Quicken Data

You can also export Quicken data to QIF format. Choose File | Export | QIF File to display the QIF Export dialog box:

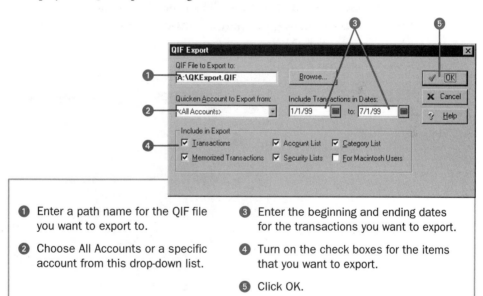

❶ Enter a path name for the QIF file you want to export to.

❷ Choose All Accounts or a specific account from this drop-down list.

❸ Enter the beginning and ending dates for the transactions you want to export.

❹ Turn on the check boxes for the items that you want to export.

❺ Click OK.

Set options in the dialog box as desired. Each option changes the amount of data exported. When you have the options set the way you want them, click OK. Quicken exports the data, creating a file with the name you specified.

> **Tip** *You can also use options in the Print dialog box to save report data as a file on disk. The file can then be imported into other applications such as word processors, spreadsheets, or databases. I explain how to use the Print command to save data to a file in Chapter 13.*

Other File Management Tasks

The File Operations submenu under Quicken's File menu enables you to perform several other tasks with Quicken data files. Here's a quick summary of each command, with tips for when you may find them useful.

Copying the Current Data File

The Copy command enables you to copy the current data file to a different disk or save a copy with a different name. When you choose File | File Operations | Copy, the Copy File dialog box, shown next, appears. Use it to set transactions for the copy and then click OK to save the copy on disk.

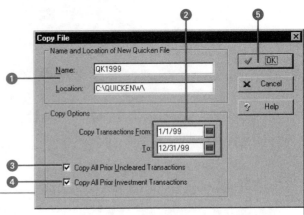

① Enter a name and directory path for the data file copy.

② Enter the beginning and ending dates for the transactions you want to include in the copy.

③ To copy all uncleared transactions prior to the date range, turn on this check box.

④ To copy all investment transactions prior to the date range, turn on this check box.

⑤ Click OK.

When the copy is finished, a dialog box asks if you want to continue working with the original data file or the new copy. Select the appropriate options and click OK to continue working with Quicken.

Deleting a Data File

The Delete command enables you to delete a data file. When you choose File | File Operations | Delete, the Delete Quicken File dialog box appears. Use it to locate and select the data file you want to delete:

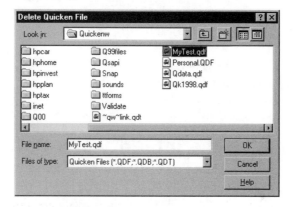

When you click OK, another dialog box appears asking you to confirm that you want to delete the file. You must type in **Yes** to delete the file.

● **Caution** *Deleting a Quicken data file permanently deletes all of its data, so use this command with care!*

Renaming a Data File

The Rename command enables you to rename a data file. When you choose File | File Operations | Rename, the Rename Quicken File dialog box, shown next, appears. Use it to select the file you want to rename and enter a new name. When you click OK, Quicken changes the name of the main data file you selected and all of its support files.

Tip   *This is the best way to rename a data file. Renaming files in Windows Explorer could cause information to be lost.*

Checking the Integrity of a Data File

The Validate command enables you to check the integrity of a Quicken data file. This command is particularly useful if you believe that a file has been damaged. When you choose File | File Operations | Validate, the Validate Quicken File dialog box appears. It looks very much like the Delete Quicken File dialog box, illustrated earlier in this chapter. Use it to locate and select the file you want to validate. When you click OK, Quicken checks its integrity and reports back to you with one of the following dialog boxes:

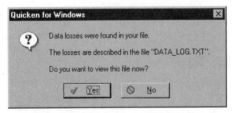

This dialog box appears when the file may have suffered data loss.

This dialog box appears when the file has no problems.

Making a Year-End Copy of a Data File

The Year-End Copy command enables you to create two different types of file copies suitable for year-end data storage: Archive and Start New Year. When you choose File | File Operations | Year-End Copy, the Year-End Copy dialog box appears. Select a Year-End Action and click OK.

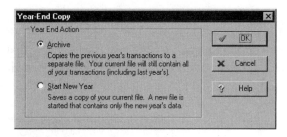

Creating an Archive

An *archive* is a copy of the previous year's transactions saved in a separate file. All transactions remain in the current file. Use this if you want a separate record of a year's transactions but you want to continue working with the data in your current data file.

When you choose this option, the Archive File dialog box appears:

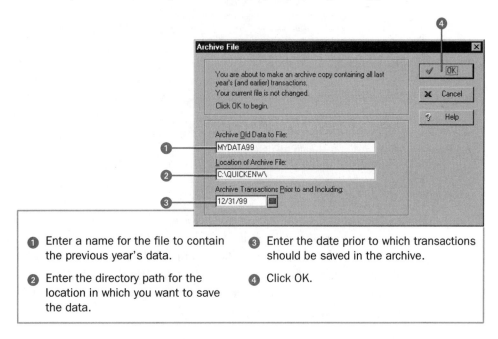

① Enter a name for the file to contain the previous year's data.

② Enter the directory path for the location in which you want to save the data.

③ Enter the date prior to which transactions should be saved in the archive.

④ Click OK.

Set options in the dialog box and click OK. Quicken creates the archive file as specified. When it has finished, it displays a dialog box that enables you to select the file you want to work with: the Current file or the Archive file. Select the appropriate option and click OK to continue working with Quicken.

Creating a New Year File

The Start New Year option in the Year-End File dialog box saves a copy of the current file, and then creates a new file with just the transactions from the current year. Use this if you want to keep your current file small.

When you choose this option, the Start New Year dialog box appears:

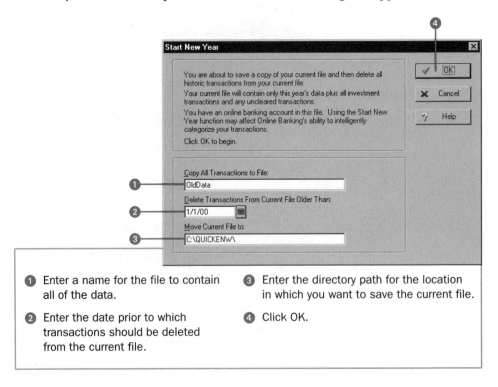

1 Enter a name for the file to contain all of the data.

2 Enter the date prior to which transactions should be deleted from the current file.

3 Enter the directory path for the location in which you want to save the current file.

4 Click OK.

Set options in the dialog box and click OK. Quicken copies the current file and saves it with the name you specified. It then deletes all prior year transactions and saves the file as the current file. When it's finished, it displays a dialog box that enables you to select the file you want to work with: the Old file or the File for the New Year. Select the Option button for the file you want and click OK to continue working with Quicken.

Password-Protecting Quicken Data

Quicken offers two types of password protection for your data: file passwords and transaction passwords. In this section, I tell you how these options work.

Protecting a Data File

When you password-protect a data file, the file cannot be opened without the password. This is the ultimate in protection—it prevents unauthorized users from even seeing your data.

Setting Up the Password

Choose File | Passwords | File to display the Set Up Password dialog box. Enter the same password in each text box and then click OK.

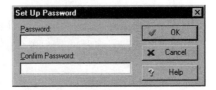

Opening a Password-Protected Data File

When you open a data file that is password protected, the Quicken Password dialog box appears:

You must correctly enter your password and then click OK to open the file.

Protecting Existing Transactions

When you password-protect existing transactions, the transactions cannot be modified unless the password is properly entered. This prevents unauthorized or accidental alterations to data.

Setting Up the Password

Choose File | Passwords | Transaction to display the Password To Modify Existing Transactions dialog box, shown next. Enter the same password in the top two text boxes. Then enter a date before which the transactions cannot be modified and click OK.

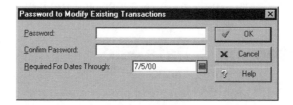

Modifying a Password-Protected Transaction

When you attempt to modify a transaction that is protected with a password, the Quicken Password dialog box appears. You must correctly enter your password and then click OK to modify the transaction.

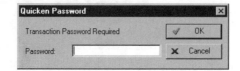

Password Tips

Here are a few things to keep in mind when working with passwords:

- Passwords can be up to 16 characters in length and can contain any character, including a space.
- Quicken does not distinguish between uppercase and lowercase characters.
- If you forget your password, you will not be able to access the data file. Write your password down and keep it in a safe place—but not on a sticky note attached to your computer monitor.
- To change or remove a password, choose File | Passwords | File, or choose File | Passwords | Transactions. The Change Password dialog box or the Change Transaction Password dialog box appears. To change the password, enter the old password in the first text box and the new password in the second and third text boxes. To remove the password, enter the existing password in the first text box and leave the next two text boxes empty. When you click OK, the password is removed or changed.

Remember, your data file is only as secure as you make it. Quicken's password protection can certainly help prevent unauthorized access to your Quicken data files.

Index

E